WHAT JOHN KNOWS

RESOURCES FOR BIBLICAL STUDY

Editor
Davina C. Lopez, New Testament

Number 109

WHAT JOHN KNOWS

Storytelling in the Fourth Gospel

Edited by
Douglas Estes

 PRESS

Atlanta

Copyright © 2025 by SBL Press

All rights reserved. No part of this work may be reproduced or transmitted in any form or by any means, electronic or mechanical, including photocopying and recording, or by means of any information storage or retrieval system, except as may be expressly permitted by the 1976 Copyright Act or in writing from the publisher. Requests for permission should be addressed in writing to the Rights and Permissions Office, SBL Press, 825 Houston Mill Road, Atlanta, GA 30329 USA.

The Library of Congress Control Number is on file with the Library of Congress.

Contents

Abbreviations vii

Introduction
    Douglas Estes 1

1. Eyewitness
    Richard Bauckham 9

2. Spirit
    Tyler Smith 25

3. Imagination
    Douglas Estes 41

4. Tradition
    Edward H. Gerber 59

5. Philosophy
    George L. Parsenios 77

6. Rhetoric
    Jo-Ann A. Brant 93

7. Scripture
    Catrin H. Williams 109

8. Gospel
    Wendy E. S. North 129

9. Testimony
    Paul N. Anderson 143

10. Memory
   Christopher A. Porter 165

11. Community
    Stan Harstine 185

12. Identity
    Andrew J. Byers 201

Bibliography 219
Contributors 247
Ancient Sources Index 251
Modern Authors Index 267
Subject Index 272

Abbreviations

Primary Sources

B.J.	Josephus, *Bellum judaicum*
BMIN	Richard of Saint Victor, *Benjamin Minor* (*De duodecim patriarchis*)
CD	Damascus Document
Cels.	Origen, *Contra Celsus*
Conf.	Augustine, *Confessionum libri XIII*
De an.	Aristotle, *De anima*
Descr.	Pausanias, *Graeciae descriptio*
Eth. eud.	Aristotle, *Ethica eudemia*
Eth. Nic.	Aristotle, *Ethica Nicomachea*
Hypoth.	Philo, *Hypothetica*
Inst.	Quintilian, *Institutio oratoria*
Inv.	Cicero, *De inventione rhetorica*
Leg.	Philo, *Legum allegoriae*
Mem. rem.	Aristotle, *De memoria et reminiscentia*
Phaedr.	Plato, *Phaedrus*
Praem.	Philo, *De praemiis et poenis*
Praep. ev.	Eusebius, *Praeparatio evangelica*
Prog.	Aelius Theon, *Progymnasmata*
Resp.	Plato, *Respublica*
Rhet.	Aristotle, *Rhetorica*
Rhet. Her.	Rhetorica ad Herennium
Soph.	Plato, *Sophista*
Subl.	Longinus, *De sublimitate*
Theaet.	Plato, *Theaetetus*
Virt.	Philo, *De virtutibus*
Vit. Apoll.	Philostratus, *Vita Apollonii*

Secondary Resources

AB	Anchor Bible
ABD	*Anchor Bible Dictionary*
AGJU	Arbeiten zur Geschichte des antiken Judentums und des Urchristentums
AJP	*American Journal of Philology*
AnBib	Analecta Biblica
ANTC	Abingdon New Testament Commentaries
AYBRL	Anchor Yale Bible Reference Library
BAR	*Biblical Archaeology Review*
BCAW	Blackwell Companions to the Ancient World
BETL	Bibliotheca Ephemeridum Theologicarum Lovaniensium
BEvT	Beiträge zur evangelischen Theologie
BibInt	Biblical Interpretation Series
BibThS	Biblisch-Theologische Studien
BICA	*Biologically Inspired Cognitive Architectures*
BLS	Bible and Literature Series
BNTC	Black's New Testament Commentaries
BPC	Biblical Performance Criticism
BSL	Biblical Studies Library
BZNW	Beihefte zur Zeitschrift für die neutestamentliche Wissenschaft
CBET	Contributions to Biblical Exegesis and Theology
CBQ	*Catholic Biblical Quarterly*
CDPS	*Current Directions in Psychological Science*
CE	Cambridge Elements
CPQR	Cardiff Papers in Qualitative Research
CSRP	Cambridge Studies in Religion and Platonism
CV	*Communio Viatorum*
ECC	Eerdmans Critical Commentary
ECL	Early Christianity and Its Literature
EDNT	*Exegetical Dictionary of the New Testament*
Eth. eud.	Aristotle, *Ethica eudemia*
Eth. nic.	Aristotle, *Ethica nicomachea*
ETL	*Ephemerides Theologicae Lovanienses*
EvQ	*Evangelical Quarterly*
GRLH	Garland Reference Library of the Humanities

HBT	*Horizons in Biblical Theology*
HT	*History and Theory*
HThKNT	*Herders Theologischer Kommentar zum Neuen Testament*
HTR	*Harvard Theological Review*
Thuc. id.	Dionysius of Halicarnassus, *De Thucydidis idiomatibus*
IMP	Investigating Medieval Philosophy
Inst.	Quintilian, *Institutio oratoria*
IRT	Issues in Religion and Theology
ITQ	*Irish Theological Quarterly*
JBL	*Journal of Biblical Literature*
JBT	*Jahrbuch für biblische Theologie*
JEP: LMC	*Journal of Experimental Psychology: Learning, Memory, and Cognition*
JHP	*Journal of the History of Philosophy*
JMS	Johannine Monograph Series
JPers	*Journal of Personality*
JS	Johannine Studies
JSNT	*Journal for the Study of the New Testament*
JSNTSup	Journal for the Study of the New Testament Supplement Series
JTS	*Journal of Theological Studies*
KEK	Kritisch-exegetischer Kommentar über das Neue Testament
LCL	Loeb Classical Library
LHBOTS	Library of Hebrew Bible/Old Testament Studies
LNTS	The Library of New Testament Studies
LSJ	Liddell, Scott, and Jones' A Greek-English Lexicon
LXX	Septuagint
MnemSup	Mnemosyne Supplements
NCBC	New Century Bible Commentary
Neot	*Neotestamentica*
NICNT	New International Commentary on the New Testament
NovT	*Novum Testamentum*
NovTSup	Supplements to Novum Testamentum
NPNF	Nicene and Post-Nicene Fathers
NRSV	New Revised Standard Version

NTD	Das Neue Testament Deutsch
NTL	New Testament Library
NTS	*New Testament Studies*
NTT	New Testament Theology
NTTS	New Testament Tools and Studies
OASIcs	OpenAccess Series in Informatics
P&B	Pragmatics & Beyond
PNTC	Pillar New Testament Commentaries
PPR	*Philosophy and Phenomenological Research*
Prog.	Theon, *Progymnasmata*
PRS	Psychology, Religion, and Spirituality
PT	*Philosophy Today*
P.W.	Thucydides, *History of the Peloponnesian War*
RBS	Resources for Biblical Study
Resp.	Plato, *Republic*
Rhet.	Aristotle, *Rhetoric*
SANt	Studia Aarhusiana Neotestamentica
SBFA	Studium Biblicum Franciscanum Analecta
SBLDS	Society of Biblical Literature Dissertation Series
SBLMS	Society of Biblical Literature Monograph Series
SCCB	Studies in Cultural Contexts of the Bible
SemeiaSt	Semeia Studies
SJT	*Scottish Journal of Theology*
SNTSMS	Society for New Testament Studies Monograph Series
STR	Studies in Theology and Religion
Sym.	Plato, *Symposium*
SymS	Symposium Series
TBN	Themes in Biblical Narrative
Theaet.	Plato, *Theaetetus*
THL	Theory and History of Literature
TIN	Theory and Interpretation of Narrative
TSAJ	Texte und Studien zum antiken Judentum
TTS	Theologische Texte und Studien
TynB	*Tyndale Bulletin*
UPGCL	Utrecht Publications in General and Comparative Literature
WUNT	Wissenschaftliche Untersuchungen zum Neuen Testament

ZECNT	Zondervan Exegetical Commentary on the New Testament
ZNW	*Zeitschrift für die neutestamentliche Wissenschaft und die Kunde der älteren Kirche*
ZTK	*Zeitschrift für Theologie und Kirche*

Introduction

Douglas Estes

The Gospel of John is not an encyclopedia, a legal contract, a grocery list, or a cookbook. It is a story, a narrative—one that is "so prominent that it would be difficult to overstate its impact on world culture."[1] It is also a story that purports to say something about the past (John 21:24). In order to say something about the past, the storyteller must *know* something of the past. Thus, the storyteller makes numerous epistemological claims when he purports to speak about the past. This is true whether the storyteller composes a factual or a fictional story. In a fictional story about the past, the storyteller must still know something about the people, the culture, the geography, and the language in order to tell a sensible story. The more a fictional storyteller knows about the past, the more reliable the storyteller seems to the audience, and the more factual the story feels. This is also true of factual stories—the more the storyteller knows about the past, the more reliable the storyteller seems to the audience, and the more factual the story feels. What unites the fictional and the factual is that both depend upon stories.

Stories are not the only way to provide information about the past. Annals and chronicles are not stories, but they do speak of the past. However, annals and chronicles are incapable of making sense of the past.[2] If later readers want to make sense of the past, they must do so through stories about the past. Narrative is the "obligatory form" by which we discover meaning about the past.[3] This discovery process is highly epis-

---

1. Douglas Estes, introduction to *How John Works: Storytelling in the Fourth Gospel*, ed. Douglas Estes and Ruth Sheridan, RBS 86 (SBL Press, 2016), 1.

2. Douglas Estes, *The Temporal Mechanics of the Fourth Gospel: A Theory of Hermeneutical Relativity in the Gospel of John*, BibInt 92 (Brill, 2008), 184.

3. Alun Munslow, *Deconstructing History*, 2nd ed. (Routledge, 2006), 3.

temological, as when readers read stories about the past, they learn about the past; but for those readers to learn about the past, a storyteller must first learn about the past in order to tell the story from which readers learn.[4] This brings us to the foundational questions of this book: What does the storyteller behind the Gospel of John know and learn about the past in order to create a story that purports to speak about the past? To what degree should readers of the gospel trust that the stories the storyteller tells are more factual than fictional? This second question pivots on the assertions by the gospel that it is telling a story that is true (John 19:35; 21:24).

Narrative Epistemology in the Gospel of John

Looking over the history of the reception and interpretation of the Fourth Gospel, merely asking these questions is peak Popean—rushing in where angels fear to tread. This is because "the prevalent scholarly opinion in the modern era has come to relegate the Johannine Gospel to the canons of myth and theology rather than history," meaning that the gospel's storyteller knows little about his topic and that his stories are far more fictional than factual.[5] The prevalent scholarly opinion makes a distinctly epistemological claim: The creator of the Fourth Gospel knows little about Jesus, even if he knows enough about Hellenistic Jewish life and culture to compose his story. However, this claim is not as binary as it appears; the creator of the gospel knows *something* about Jesus. What he knows is not nothing, nor is it everything. He does know something about Jesus.[6]

In the study of epistemology, most claims are propositional: a person knows *that* something is something.[7] Although the Fourth Gospel does make many propositional claims, it also makes many claims that are not purely propositional. There are other ways of knowing beyond proposi-

---

4. Leon J. Goldstein, *Historical Knowing* (University of Texas Press, 1976), xix.

5. Paul N. Anderson, "Prologue: Critical Views of John, Jesus, and History," in *Critical Appraisals of Critical Views*, vol. 1 of *John, Jesus, and History*, ed. Paul N. Anderson, Felix Just, S.J., and Tom Thatcher, SymS 44 (Society of Biblical Literature, 2007), 1. For example, see Gerd Theissen and Annette Merz, *The Historical Jesus: A Comprehensive Guide* (Fortress, 1998), 25.

6. The conclusion to this is that the Fourth Gospel is historiography; for discussion, see Richard Bauckham, *The Testimony of the Beloved Disciple: Narrative, History, and Theology in the Gospel of John* (Baker Academic, 2007).

7. Richard Fumerton, *Epistemology*, First Books in Philosophy (Blackwell, 2006), 1.

tions: knowing how things work, knowing views or opinions, believing, the nature of truth, and more that are still within the realm of epistemology.[8] These areas of knowing are much more difficult to assess because they are more complex and nuanced than propositions. When it comes to knowing, classical epistemology holds two distinct avenues for knowing: sense experience and reason.[9] These two avenues for knowing are quite broad and they each represent many different smaller but distinct aspects of knowing. For example, we can divide these broader avenues into knowing by perception, memory, introspection, intuition, induction, and testimony.[10] With the Gospel of John, we have to amend this to add a third major avenue for knowing: divine revelation. As such, knowing is more representative of a plane than a single line. Even though this is a very simple overview of epistemology, we can see that knowing about something is not simple but is indeed a complex act.

While epistemology can be quite treacherous philosophically, our interests lie in a more concrete area: What and how does an ancient person like John know in order to write a gospel? This is a subject that has been dealt with quite sparingly in modern discussions of the gospel. The reason is that the point of debate about the testimony of John has centered on the transmission of ideas through sources that the author assembled to compose the gospel more so than the complex web of knowledge the author possessed that contributed to his creation of the gospel. Put another way, whereas modern debates are largely mechanical emphasizing *atomism* (intricate theories of specific source transmission), John, as an ancient writer, would have used a more *continuous* (natural understanding built on natural relationships) approach to writing the gospel. The difficulty, though, is that *if* John's Gospel is based on testimony, as well as other streams of knowing, then these introduce a very complex algorithm into the epistemological equation. The study of epistemology teaches us that in order to know something—especially something we have witnessed at least in part ourselves—and to then retell that same something in a meaningful way is a highly intricate process that engages many different streams

---

8. Fumerton, *Epistemology*, 2.
9. Sven Bernecker, *Reading Epistemology: Selected Texts with Interactive Commentary* (Blackwell, 2006), 2.
10. Robert Audi, *Epistemology: A Contemporary Introduction to the Theory of Knowledge*, 2nd ed. (Routledge, 2003), 6.

in our river of knowledge.[11] Not just one stream of knowing—our ability to compile data, for example—but many streams of knowing—compiling, discerning, comprehending, imagining, remembering, depicting, to name just a few examples. How do these streams unite into one rushing river of story that became the Gospel of John?

This weakness is self-evident in the epistemological questions in prevalent scholarly studies of the Fourth Gospel. In the modern period, if a scholar were to ask, "What does John know?," the answer would appeal to the author's sources. No matter how robustly a scholar presents these findings, looking for sources nonetheless limits the storyteller to a compiler and turns a story into an amalgamation of chronicle entries. By virtue of telling a story, however, the Evangelist is not a compiler and his work, not an amalgamation. This behavior was not limited to just the Fourth Evangelist; this was the way ancient people understood the past they wrote about.[12]

It is by now well known that the fertilizer that fed the prevalent scholarly opinion is often a mixture of empiricism, positivism, and good old-fashioned skepticism. By no means does this revelation cast a negative mark on biblical scholarly opinion itself; after all, this was the scholarly attitude across numerous disciplines during the late modern period. In the early nineteenth century, Leopold von Ranke, a German historian and epistemologist, criticized contemporaneous scholars whom he considered to be too accepting of tradition and unwilling to track down primary sources. He argued that the past, and historical events in particular, could be retold by a historian with exact precision: *wie es eigentlich gewesen* ("as it actually happened").[13] This idea had a profound effect on the last two hundred years; it was (and still is) embraced by scholars who believe in the possibility of a completely objective, neutral

---

11. Mary Lindemann, introduction to *Ways of Knowing: Ten Interdisciplinary Essays*, ed. Mary Lindemann, Studies in Central European Histories 31 (Brill, 2004), xvii.

12. Jonas Grethlein, "Social Minds and Narrative Time: Collective Experience in Thucydides and Heliodorus," *Narrative* 23 (2015): 124. This is not to claim that ancient people did not have nonnarrative genres—they had their own versions of annals, chronicles, saying sources, cookbooks, and more.

13. Leopold von Ranke, *Geschichte der romanischen und germanischen Völker von 1494 bis 1535* (Reimer, 1824), vi. His expression soon took on a life of its own with historians outside of Germany.

history.[14] Alun Munslow aptly summarizes the situation by the end of the twentieth century:

> The modernist empiricist historical method handed down from the nineteenth century requires and assumes historical explanation will emerge in a naturalistic fashion from the archival raw data, its meaning offered as interpretation in the form of a story related explicitly, impersonally, transparently, and without resort to any of the devices used by writers of literary narratives, viz., imagery or figurative language.[15]

While von Ranke was accurate in some of his criticisms of the romanticism found in early-modern histories, his ideas were later carried to their logical conclusion: anything that is not purely objective history is not real history.[16] When we apply von Ranke's narrow approach to John, the conclusion we reach is that the gospel is profoundly untrue.[17] The flaw in this method was not the fertilizer but the soil itself—it assumes incorrectly on how one can know the past and presumes against the obligatory form for learning about the past: story. This is why it may not be an overstatement to agree with Munslow that the epistemological study of the Fourth Gospel, like history, "must be reassessed at its most basic level."[18] The recent narrative turn in biblical studies provides just this opportunity.[19] It also reflects the ancient perspective on storytelling about the past (Cicero, *Inv.* 1.19).

---

14. Hayden White, *The Content of the Form: Narrative Discourse and Historical Representation* (Johns Hopkins University Press, 1987), 71; and Martin Bunzl, "How to Change the Unchanging Past," *Clio* 25 (1996): 182.

15. Munslow, *Deconstructing History*, 12.

16. There is some question as to whether von Ranke's views were misunderstood by later generations; see Michael I. Carignan, "Fiction as History or History as Fiction? George Eliot, Hayden White, and Nineteenth-Century Historicism," *Clio* 29 (2000): 396; and Arthur C. Danto, *Narration and Knowledge* (Columbia University Press, 1985), 131.

17. "I have demonstrated what critical scholars have said quietly for years, that this Gospel is not literally true." Maurice Casey, *Is John's Gospel True?* (Routledge, 1996), 229. Professor Casey was my internal reader at Nottingham. I am grateful for our dialogues.

18. Munslow, *Deconstructing History*, 2.

19. For the Gospel of John, this began with the publication of R. Alan Culpepper's *Anatomy of the Fourth Gospel: A Study in Literary Design* (Fortress, 1983).

Knowing and Telling Stories about Jesus

When a writer creates a text, whether in the ancient world or the modern world, the process is more complicated than shuffling around sources. Or, to put it another way, there are texts that are largely shuffled sources—annals and chronicles—but these two kinds of texts are not stories, and they bear no resemblance to the Gospel of John. Instead, it was necessary for the Fourth Evangelist to know something about which he was writing. The writing of the gospel involved a significant process tapping into many different ways of knowing for the author. This is demonstrable because raw history—witnessed sensations, events, and/or sources—were transformed into a coherent, cohesive narrative.

Storytellers create meaningful stories by way of their meaningful ideas. In this book, we invite you to consider more fully what you know about what John knew and perhaps to reconsider what John knew when he created his meaningful story. Epistemological studies of the gospels are not common, largely because there is the (inaccurate) impression that one would have to get into the mind of the author. But the question of testimony in John is an epistemological one; avoiding it because it is complicated is not a viable option. We not only want to know what John claims but, just as much, how he knows what he claims. This book will not provide all the answers; we will introduce many new ideas with a broad brush, painting a rough sketch to which much more detail can be added over time. With contributions from a group of international scholars, who each know about the Gospel of John in numerous, distinct ways, the intent of this volume is get to the root of what John knows and how he knows it. Along with *How John Works*, this volume seeks to continue the narrative turn and consider twelve ways that the creator of John's Gospel knew about his story of Jesus.[20] In all likelihood, these twelve are only the beginning; there are other epistemological undercurrents in John that we did not have space to include. Similar to narratives, among these essays there is a great deal of continuity but, in some places, flare-ups of divergences; however, the essays work together to help the reader understand the raw materials—the creative knowledge and expe-

---

20. Estes and Sheridan, *How John Works*.

riences—that led to the story in the Gospel of John.²¹ This, then, is what John knows.

---

21. Many thanks and much appreciation to Ruth Sheridan and Brian D. Johnson for their uncredited but significantly meaningful contributions encouraging the creation of this volume.

1
Eyewitness

Richard Bauckham

The Gospel of John claims to be written by an eyewitness. By no means all scholars agree with that statement, and so the aim of this chapter is to substantiate it in greater detail than previous discussions have done (including my own). I shall trace the literary indications provided by the gospel that its author was an eyewitness of many of the events it narrates. It is important to stress from the outset that our concern here is with the gospel's own claim to be an eyewitness account. I shall not be assessing the historical credibility of the gospel as an account of Jesus. Important as that task is, it is a distinct task and should not be confused with the hermeneutical task of understanding what the gospel itself claims. My purpose here is to show that, in subtle but deliberate ways, the gospel portrays itself as an eyewitness account. By the end of the gospel, readers come to realize that the eyewitness-author is the anonymous character who is sometimes described as "the disciple Jesus loved,"[1] though he is also described in other ways too. The references to this character and his gradual disclosure of his identity as the author are woven into the literary design of the gospel. We shall need to attend closely to the literary strategies by which the author writes his claim to be an eyewitness into the narrative.

The Claim to Eyewitness Authorship

The author's claim to have been an eyewitness of events the gospel recounts is first made in the prologue (1:14) and then emphatically in the conclud-

---

1. The identity of this disciple is debated but will not be discussed here. I have argued my own view of the matter in Richard Bauckham, *Jesus and the Eyewitnesses: The Gospels as Eyewitness Testimony*, 2nd ed. (Eerdmans, 2017), 412–71, 550–89.

ing section of the gospel (21:24). Following the momentous words, "the Word became flesh and lived among us," the prologue claims, "we saw his glory."[2] Who are the "we" among whom the author includes himself? Probably a majority of scholars have understood it to refer to the eyewitnesses, who saw Jesus in the flesh, but others assume that "we" includes the readers, whether all Christians or specifically the members of the Johannine community. On the latter view, "we saw" refers to the perception of the divine presence in Jesus by faith. Certainly, it cannot refer to physical sight alone, for many who saw Jesus in the flesh did not perceive his glory. But the evidence of the rest of the gospel shows that what is meant is the combination of sight and insight that happened when the disciples saw Jesus's glory revealed in his "signs" (2:11; 11:40, 45) during the time when he "lived among us." The gospel makes an emphatic distinction between those who saw and believed and later believers who believe without seeing (20:8, 18, 25, 29). The latter, the readers of the gospel, need the testimony, given in the gospel, of those who did see. This limited meaning of "we" in 1:14 is confirmed by the contrasting "we all" in 1:16, where the "all" signals that all believers are now included.

First-time readers of the gospel know from the prologue that the gospel is written by an eyewitness and embodies his own testimony as well as perhaps also that of others. But not until the closing section of the gospel (21:24–25) do they learn for sure which of the disciples is the author. This closing section, along with the whole of chapter 21, has usually been seen as an appendix added later to the gospel by an editor or editors, but for the argument of this essay it is important to maintain that, on the contrary, the whole of chapter 21 belongs to the original design of the gospel. I have argued this view in detail elsewhere,[3] and an increasing number of scholars are now in agreement. In my view, the gospel has an epilogue (21:1–23) sandwiched between a two-stage conclusion (20:30–31; 21:24–25). Here I shall focus on the two stages of the conclusion.

The two stages are parallel but not repetitive. At every point where they are parallel, the second stage makes an advance on the first stage. For example, both stages speak of what is and is not written in the book. But while the first stage refers to "many other *signs*" that Jesus did that are not included, the second stage speaks more generally of "many other *things*

---

2. Here my translation. Otherwise, biblical quotations are from the NRSV unless indicated.

3. Bauckham, *Jesus and the Eyewitnesses*, 358–69.

that Jesus did." With regard to the witness on which the gospel is based, there is a carefully designed two-stage disclosure of the Beloved Disciple's role in the production of the book. The first stage does not use the word "witness" but implies it in saying that the signs were done "in the presence of his disciples." (Readers may here recall the role of all the disciples as witnesses evoked in 15:27.) The second stage of the conclusion introduces the notion of witness explicitly and narrows down the witness to that of the Beloved Disciple. This focusing on the role of the Beloved Disciple occurs also in what the two stages say about the writing of the gospel. The first stage, by using the passive "are written," avoids disclosing the authorship of the gospel, reserving this information for the second stage, where we learn that it is the Beloved Disciple who "is testifying to these things and has written them" (21:24). This does not exclude a role for other disciples as witnesses (which is implied in 20:30) but explains that, since the Beloved Disciple was the author, his witness gathers up and includes the testimony of any others whose witness has informed the gospel.

The plain sense of 21:24 is that the Beloved Disciple was the author of the gospel. The phrase "has written them" need not mean that he personally wielded the pen. He may have dictated to a scribe, as was common in the ancient world, just as Pilate is said to have written the inscription on the cross (19:21), even though he doubtless did not inscribe the words himself. But the words were his, and similarly the Beloved Disciple was, in the usual sense of the word, the author of the gospel. Many scholars have found it incredible that an eyewitness could have authored this gospel and propose instead that he was, in some rather remote sense, merely the authority behind the traditions on which the gospel depends. But no parallels to such a meaning of the words have been adduced. If the Beloved Disciple's real authorship of the gospel is thought incredible, then it would be better to conclude either that 21:24 was added by someone who mistakenly thought the Beloved Disciple was the author or that it makes a deliberately fictional claim, putting the gospel into the category of apostolic pseudepigrapha.[4]

From 21:22–23 many readers get the impression that, by the time this passage was written, the Beloved Disciple was already dead. The "rumor that this disciple would not die" does make most sense at a time when most of the other disciples of Jesus had died and the Beloved Disciple

---

4. Bauckham, *Jesus and the Eyewitnesses*, 358–63.

was a rare survivor from that generation. But it is entirely possible that he himself, completing his gospel in old age, wished to correct this mistaken interpretation of Jesus's quoted words. But his purpose in quoting them is also to introduce the disclosure of his authorship of the gospel. If verses 21–23 are read in connection with verse 24, we find a typically Johannine *double entendre* at work. While the disciple may not survive to the parousia in person, his *witness*, written in the gospel, will. Just as he can say that John the Baptist "is testifying" to Jesus (1:15),[5] because, when the gospel is read, he continues to do so, so, for as long as the gospel is read, it will be true that the Beloved Disciple "is testifying" to the whole content of his gospel (21:24).

So it is not necessary to regard 21:24–25 as a later addition by one or two redactors. The shift of grammatical person, from the third person to the first-person plural in verse 24, is necessary and natural, because the author is moving from speaking about himself as a character in the narrative to addressing his readers directly. It was common in ancient historiography, when an author appeared in his own narrative as a character, for him to refer to himself in the third person.[6] The transition from third to first person in 21:24 embodies such an author's uniquely double relationship to the narrative and its readers: as a character, alongside others, in the narrative, and also as the narrator who may step out of the narrative and address his readers directly. The question arises whether in the first person plural "we know" the author speaks merely for himself or as one of a group. I have argued in detail elsewhere that this is an example of a characteristically Johannine "we of authoritative testimony," comparable with other usages (in Greek as in many languages) in which a single person's authority is emphasized by the use of plural words (compare the "royal we" in English or the once common "authorial we").[7] In that case, the phrase "we know that his testimony is true" would be equivalent to "he knows that he tells

---

5. My translation.

6. Howard M. Jackson, "Ancient Self-Referential Conventions and Their Implications for the Authorship and Integrity of the Gospel of John," *JTS* 50 (1999): 1–34. Thus Josephus, in his *Jewish War*, frequently appears in the narrative as "Josephus."

7. Bauckham, *Jesus and the Eyewitnesses*, 369–83; cf. John 3:10–13; 1 John 1:1–5; 4:11–16; 3 John 9–12. On this view, the transition from "we" in verse 24 to "I" in verse 25 is unproblematic. It frequently occurs in ancient literature; see Andreas J. Köstenberger, "'I Suppose' (οἴμαι): The Conclusion of John's Gospel in Its Literary and Historical Context," in *The New Testament in Its First Century Setting: Essays on Context and Background in Honour of B. W. Winter on His Sixty-Fifth Birthday*, ed. P.

the truth" in another reference to the eyewitness testimony embodied in the gospel (19:35). Alternatively, it could be that in "we know" the author includes himself in a group of disciples, other eyewitnesses who endorse his witness.[8] In either case, we should recognize that this "we" forms an *inclusio* with the "we" of 1:14, meaning that in both cases a group of disciples is intended or that in both cases a "we of authoritative testimony" is used. I favor the latter possibility, both because of the relationship between 21:24 and 19:35 and because of the likelihood that few, if any, other eyewitnesses were still alive when the author completed his gospel.

References to the Eyewitness-Author within the Narrative

In order to understand the gospel's claim to eyewitness testimony, we must consider the references within the gospel narrative to the disciple who turns out, at the end of the gospel, to be also the author. They are curiously heterogeneous. A character described as "the disciple Jesus loved" appears, with that identifying description, on four occasions (13:23-26; 19:25-26; 20:2-10; 21:2, 7, 20-24). But there are also two occasions on which anonymous disciples appear who are not given this epithet (1:35-40; 18:15-16). Whether either or both of these is the same person as "the disciple Jesus loved" is disputed. Finally, there is reference to an anonymous witness who is not even explicitly designated a disciple (19:35). The identity of this figure is also disputed. In my view, all these characters are the same, but this can be recognized only retrospectively. When each appears in the narrative, the narrator describes the character in a way appropriate to their appearance at that juncture. Only as the whole narrative unfolds and especially as the gospel concludes can readers recognize that they are all the same and all identical with the author. I shall now explain how this process of retrospective identification works.

In 13:23 a character is introduced as "one of his disciples, the one Jesus loved."[9] First-time readers are likely to assume that this is his first appear-

---

J. Williams, Andrew D. Clarke, Peter M. Head, and David Instone-Brewer (Eerdmans, 2004), 72-88.

8. This interpretation probably lies behind the story of the composition of John's Gospel in the Muratorian Canon and variations of the same story elsewhere in patristic literature, where the disciples of Jesus request John to write a gospel that embodies their common testimony.

9. My translation.

ance in the narrative. There is an obvious reference back to 13:23 in 19:26: "the disciple whom he [Jesus] loved." In 20:2 the description is fuller: "the other disciple, the one Jesus loved." Within the same narrative he is called just "the other disciple" (20:3, 4, 8). In 21:7 we meet him again as "that disciple whom Jesus loved" and realize that he must be one of the two anonymous disciples already mentioned in 21:2. He reappears at the end of this narrative and for the last time, with a remarkably full description: "the disciple Jesus loved, who also leaned back on his breast at the supper and said, 'Lord, who is it who is going to betray you?'" (21:20).[10] This description alludes closely to 13:25. For the purpose of identifying this character, it would have been quite sufficient to call him just "the disciple Jesus loved." The additional description is designed to create an *inclusio* between his first and last appearances as "the disciple Jesus loved." It is noteworthy that in both cases this disciple is related in some way to Peter, as he is also in 20:2–10 and 21:7. The *inclusio* indicates that the story of these two disciples that began in 13:23–26 ends here, at the end of the gospel.

The phrase "the disciple Jesus loved" cannot be a title that was commonly used by others to refer to this disciple outside the context of the gospel itself. In that case, it would have had a fixed linguistic form, whereas, in fact, the Greek word used in the phrase is usually *ēgapa* (13:23; 19:26; 21:7, 20) but once *ephilei* (20:2). (This variation needs no explanation other than the Evangelist's habit of varying his vocabulary.) Moreover, the phrase is too cumbersome to have been used as a title (hence the variation in 20:3, 4, 8), which is why modern scholars invented the term "the Beloved Disciple" for convenience of reference. But we should not let this modern term obscure the gospel's actual usage, which is contextualized within the narrative. "The disciple Jesus loved" is an appropriate description in those passages in which it is used. It focuses on this disciple's special intimacy with Jesus, which explains his place next to Jesus at the supper (13:23) and the fact that Jesus entrusts his mother to his care (19:26–27). This intimacy is doubtless also connected with this disciple's special perceptiveness when he understands the significance of the disposition of the grave-clothes (20:8) and when he recognizes the mysterious miracle worker on the shore as Jesus (21:7). Doubtless the phrase "the disciple Jesus loved" tells us what the author thinks it is most important for us to know about this character,

---

10. My translation.

but because the description is contextual, he does not have to be called this on every occasion.

At first sight, it seems unlikely that the reference in 18:15 to "another disciple" can be to the disciple who was introduced in 13:23–26. The indefinite phrase seems completely inappropriate for a disciple who has already appeared in the narrative, and it is not surprising that many commentators have been unsure whether 18:15–16 refers to "the Beloved Disciple." The evidence that it does comes later in the gospel, when 20:2 refers to "the other disciple, the one whom Jesus loved." Earlier references to "the disciple Jesus loved" (13:23; 19:26) cannot explain how he can be called here "*the* other disciple." The phrase must refer back to 18:15. Thus 20:2 makes a retrospective identification of the disciple of 18:15–16 with the disciple of 13:23–26 and 19:26–27. Evidently, readers of 18:15–16 did not need to know, at that stage of the narrative, that this disciple was the one Jesus loved. What they needed to know was that "he was known to the high priest" (18:15), since that explains his role in the narrative. Only in a retrospective accumulation of appearances of the eyewitness-author would his special relationship to Jesus become significant. The double description in 20:2, as "the other disciple, the one Jesus loved," serves to gather him up together with "the disciple Jesus loved" into this accumulating character who finally emerges as the author in 21:24.

A similar process of retrospective identification applies to the anonymous disciple of 1:35–40, who could not, on first acquaintance with Jesus, have been called "the disciple Jesus loved." A key element in the retrospective identification of this disciple is what Jesus says to all the disciples who are with him at the last supper, "You also are to testify because you have been with me from the beginning" (15:27). This indicates that "the disciple Jesus loved" must have been with Jesus long before his appearance in 13:23. If, as the reader discovers in 21:24, he was in fact the preeminent witness to the events of the whole gospel, then it makes very good sense that he should be one of the first two disciples of Jesus, the one who is unnamed in 1:35–40. A further indication that this disciple is the Beloved Disciple is given with the literary subtlety characteristic of this gospel in 21:20–23. We have already observed that the way the disciple is described in 21:24 forms an *inclusio* with his first appearance *as* "the disciple Jesus loved" (13:23). But it also forms an *inclusio* with 1:35–40. The statement that "Peter turned and saw the disciple whom Jesus loved following them" (21:20) echoes the statement that "Jesus turned and saw them [the two disciples of John the Baptist] following him" (1:38). The parallel between the two passages continues with the statement that the two disciples "remained" with Jesus (1:39) and Jesus's words about the Beloved Disciple, "If it is my will that he remain..." (21:22). The "following" and "remaining" have a limited, literal sense in 1:35–40, but their meaning is enhanced by the echoes in 21:20–23.[11] It turns out that the Beloved Disciple is the "follower" of Jesus who, differently from Peter's way of following, will "remain" as the living witness to Jesus until he embodies his witness in the permanent form of the gospel. Thus, just as 20:2 gathers up the indefinite "other disciple" of 18:15–16 into the character of the disciple Jesus loved, so 21:20–23 gathers up the anonymous disciple of 1:35–40 into the same character.[12]

The reference to an anonymous witness in 19:35 takes a quite different form from the other references to anonymous disciples. As a parenthetical comment by the narrator, it is one of many in this gospel, but unlike others it addresses the readers in the second person plural ("that you also may believe"), which is otherwise paralleled only in the similar words of the first part of the gospel's two-part conclusion (20:31: "so that you may believe"). Moreover, only in 19:35 is an anonymous character explicitly characterized as a witness who "has testified," referring to an activity of witnessing at a time later than the gospel's narrative. Here alone, prior to the concluding verses of the gospel, are readers explicitly told that what the anonymous character "saw," within the narrative, is something to which he "testified" later, beyond the narrative. In other words, here we learn, unambiguously, something about the gospel's claim to embody eyewitness testimony. We also learn (a point that commentators rarely notice) that this eyewitness is still alive at the time of writing ("he knows that he is telling the truth").

The narrative itself leaves it unclear whether this anonymous witness is the disciple who was present at the cross a few verses earlier (19:26–27). Since no other male disciples have been mentioned, this seems a natural assumption, but it is not explicit because, as in 18:15–16, in the immediate context readers do not need to know it. The identification only becomes unambiguous in retrospect, when readers are finally told which character in the narrative was also the author of the gospel (21:24). This revelation

---

11. Note also the motif of "following" (referring to the Beloved Disciple and to Peter) in 18:15; 20:6.

12. For a fuller discussion of the identity of the anonymous disciple in 1:35–40, see Richard Bauckham, *Gospel of Glory: Major Themes in Johannine Theology* (Baker, 2015), 141–50.

of the Beloved Disciple's authorship echoes the language of 19:35 very closely. Now we learn that the witness who "has testified" to what happened immediately after Jesus's death also testifies to all the contents of the gospel narrative ("these things") and has testified to them by writing them.

In the light of 21:24, readers can make one last retrospective identification—this time of the "we" of 1:14. The "we" of 21:24 forms an *inclusio* with the "we" of 1:14. As we have already considered, this could mean either that reference is made in both cases to a group of disciples, including the author, or, more likely, in both cases simply to the author himself.

What Did He Witness?

The first step in clarifying what the gospel's eyewitness claim amounts to must be to consider what the author-eyewitness witnesses on each occasion on which he appears within the narrative. The second step will be to see what emerges when we relate these various acts of witness to each other and consider them as a series.

The anonymous disciple of 1:35-40 is identified as a disciple of John the Baptist who witnessed John's declaration that Jesus was the Lamb of God (1:36). This provides a direct link between the witness of John the Baptist to Jesus, which the prologue singles out as of singular importance (1:6-8, 15), and the witness of the Beloved Disciple, which the conclusion to the gospel treats as extending to the whole narrative (21:24). Because he witnessed John's witness, the Beloved Disciple can include it in his own witness. This passage also adumbrates the Beloved Disciple's credentials to be a witness to Jesus: he was with Jesus at "the beginning" (cf. 15:27) and had time, ahead of any of the other disciples except Andrew, to begin to get to know Jesus intimately.

In 13:23-26, the Beloved Disciple's privileged position, reclining to Jesus's right, enables him to have a private exchange with Jesus, not overheard by others, and therefore alone to understand what Jesus does when he gives the piece of bread to Judas. It shows Jesus willingly accepting the fate that his Father has ordained for him. A comparison here with Mark's account of the supper is illuminating, since in my view John knew Mark's Gospel and expected his readers to know it.[13] Although John only rarely

---

13. Richard Bauckham, "John for Readers of Mark," in *The Gospels for All Christians: Rethinking the Gospel Audiences*, ed. Richard Bauckham (Eerdmans; T&T Clark, 1997), 147-71. See also the chapter by Wendy E. S. North in the present volume.

uses Mark as a source, John 13:21-26 is quite close to Mark 14:17-20. But what the Beloved Disciple observes is a narrative plus by comparison with Mark. The Beloved Disciple is not adduced as a witness for what Mark already recorded but as a witness to what went unobserved except by the Beloved Disciple. This is an indication of the way the Beloved Disciple's witness functions in the gospel in relation to Mark's narrative: it always reveals something not known to Mark.

We can also compare John 18:15-27 with Mark 14:54-72. Initially, the disciple "known to the high priest" functions to explain something that Mark leaves unexplained: how Peter got into the courtyard of the high priest's house (18:15-16; cf. Mark 14:54a). The fact that John gives a little more detail about the fire (18:18; cf. Mark 14:54b) functions to indicate that the anonymous disciple observes the subsequent conversations around it. In the story of Peter's three denials, John's major narrative plus by comparison with Mark is the identification of the third questioner. Mark refers vaguely to "the bystanders" (Mark 14:70), but John to "one of the slaves of the high priest, a relative of the man whose ear Peter had cut off" (John 18:26). This recalls John's account of the arrest in Gethsemane, where John, alone among the evangelists, identifies Peter as the man who wielded the sword and gives the name of his victim (18:10; cf. Mark 14:47). The two passages evince the inside knowledge of a disciple who must have been a frequent visitor to the high priest's house. But their significance as a narrative plus by comparison with Mark is that they highlight the danger Peter is in, when a man who had seen Peter injure his own relative in Gethsemane claims to identify him. Peter's denial of Jesus is therefore made more understandable.

Mark narrates Peter's denials after his account of the trial of Jesus before Caiaphas (Mark 14:53-72), implying that they took place at the same time as the trial. John recounts the events thus: the first of Peter's denials (18:17-18); Jesus's trial before Annas (18:19-23); that Annas sent Jesus to Caiaphas (18:24); Peter's second and third denials (18:25-27); then that Jesus was taken from Caiaphas to Pilate (18:28). The fact that John says Jesus was taken to Caiaphas and that Peter's second and third denials took place while Jesus was with Caiaphas, but, quite remarkably, says nothing at all about what happened before Caiaphas, shows that John takes Mark's narrative as read. But he has a major plus to add to Mark's account: the trial before Annas. This, we should assume, was witnessed by the disciple who was "known to the high priest" (i.e., Annas). When we relate the "other disciple" of 18:15 to the whole passage 18:15-28 it is clear why he is described as "known to the high priest," rather than as "the disciple Jesus loved."

The view, popular among some Johannine scholars, that the Beloved Disciple is portrayed as the ideal disciple, a representative of the discipleship to which readers should aspire, plainly does not work in 13:23–26 or in 18:15–28. The anonymous disciple's role in these passages is as a unique observer of events that he witnessed. As I have argued at length elsewhere he is portrayed not as the ideal disciple but as the ideal witness, whose witness qualifies him to be the ideal author of a gospel.[14] The one passage in which "the disciple Jesus loved" can with some plausibility be understood as playing a representative role is 19:26–27. Among the many interpretations that detect symbolic overtones in this passage, the most plausible is probably the view that the cross initiates new relationships among believers and between believers and Jesus. The Beloved Disciple becomes a brother to Jesus, representing all disciples, who are subsequently called his brothers by Jesus (20:17), while disciples also now relate to each other as fictive kin (mothers and children). But this approach neglects the fact that the narrative's emphasis is on the entrusting of Jesus' mother to the disciple's caring responsibility: he takes her "into his own home." It is doubtful whether this or any of the more ambitious symbolic interpretations can do justice to this obvious feature of the literal meaning.

Sjef van Tilborg offers an attractive interpretation that connects verses 26–27 closely with the immediately following statement, in verse 28, that "Jesus knew that all was now completed" or "fulfilled" (*tetelestai*). Verse 28 connects this notion of completion with the fulfillment of scripture, which is a major theme of John's passion narrative. Van Tilborg therefore proposes that in entrusting his mother to the Beloved Disciple's care Jesus fulfils his scriptural obligation to provide for his mother's support (on the basis of Exod 20:12; Deut 5:16).[15] In that case, the disciple here witnesses one of Jesus's last acts of fulfillment of scripture (preceding the last one in 19:28). He is the ideal witness, observing something additional to Mark's narrative of the crucifixion, not the representative of disciples in general.

Accordingly, whereas Mark's eyewitnesses stand at a distance from the cross (14:40; cf. Luke 23:49), hearing only what Jesus cries in a loud voice

---

14. Richard Bauckham, "The Beloved Disciple as Ideal Author," *JSNT* 49 (1993): 21–44; see also Cornelis Bennema, *Encountering Jesus: Character Studies in the Gospel of John*, 2nd ed. (Fortress, 2014), 299–315.

15. Sjef van Tilborg, *Imaginative Love in John*, BibInt 2 (Brill, 1993), 9–12.

(Mark 15:33, 37), in John the women and the Beloved Disciple stand close to the cross (19:25), able to hear Jesus's words (19:26-27, 28, 30) and to observe the flow from his wounded side (19:34). The detail of the jar of sour wine (19:29) resembles the detail of the charcoal fire (18:18): neither adds anything of importance to Mark's account but signals to the reader who knows Mark that the Beloved Disciple was there.

As we have seen, 19:35 is distinctive in that here the anonymous character is not confined to his role within the narrative (as one who "saw" the events) but acquires a role in the world of the narrator (as one who "has testified" and "knows that he tells the truth") and even in relation to the readers (he "has testified so that you also may believe"). The emphasis on the truth of the testimony suggests that, of all the specific occasions on which appeal is made to the witness of the Beloved Disciple, this is the most significant. He saw that the soldiers refrained from breaking Jesus's bones and that a soldier pierced his side, from which blood and water flowed. The significance of these observations is, not only that they fulfill the scriptural passages quoted in verses 36-37, but also that they show Jesus to be the new Passover lamb, sacrificed for the sin of the world, as John the Baptist had declared him to be (1:29, 35). So the Beloved Disciple who, at his first appearance in the gospel, witnessed that witness of John the Baptist, here witnesses its fulfillment. In the gospel's perspective, it is these events immediately following Jesus's death, witnessed only by the Beloved Disciple, that reveal its significance as the salvific event toward which the whole gospel narrative from John the Baptist's testimony onward has pointed. Whether the Beloved Disciple understood the full significance of what he saw at the time or only later is not clear, but in either case his perceptiveness as the ideal witness who added insight to sight is implied.

This perceptiveness is more explicit in the narrative of Peter and the Beloved Disciple at the empty tomb (20:2-10), which focuses on the details of what both saw in the tomb. In this case the Beloved Disciple's perceptive insight into what he saw occurred at the time (20:8), making him the first disciple to believe that Jesus had risen. The point is that the disposition of the grave clothes disproved Mary Magdalene's supposition that the body had been stolen, and from this the Beloved Disciple drew the believing conclusion that Jesus had risen. The fact that he "saw and believed" (20:8) should be read in connection with the words of Jesus to Thomas: "Blessed are those who have not seen and yet have come to believe" (20:29). The Beloved Disciple belongs with Thomas and the other disciples to those who believed because they saw. He was ahead of those others because he believed already, on the evidence of the grave clothes, before seeing the risen Jesus. But that makes him an exceptionally perceptive witness who saw and believed, not a representative of later believers who must believe without seeing. As in all the other cases, he is an eyewitness to a historically specific circumstance.

Finally, he does see the risen Jesus in 21:7 and recognizes who he is before the other disciples, maintaining the portrayal of the Beloved Disciple as the especially perceptive witness who is therefore also the ideal witness.

When we view these seven occasions of witness as a series, what seems most striking about them is that on each occasion the eyewitness-author observes a specific narrative detail: John's designation of Jesus as the Lamb of God, Jesus's words when he gave the bread to Judas, precisely who asked Peter the third question, Jesus's commendation of his mother to this disciple's care, that Jesus's bones were not broken, that his side was pierced and blood and water came out, the disposition of the grave clothes in the tomb, and the unexpected draft of fish. In some cases he alone among the disciples witnessed this specific event (13:23–26; 19:35); in other cases only a few others did (Andrew in 1:35; the three women disciples in 19:26–27; Peter in 20:6–7; the other six disciples in 21:5–6).[16] All of them are unique to this gospel.[17] In most cases, fulfillment of scripture is involved (1:35; 13:18; 19:28, 36–37; 20:9),[18] underlining the key significance of these events. In most cases, the eyewitness-author is especially perceptive as to the theological meaning of the event, whether at the time (20:8; 21:7) or perhaps later (13:25–29?; 19:35–37?).

All these observations make it clear that the Beloved Disciple is not portrayed as a representative figure but as a unique one. As eyewitness-author, he highlights what only he (or with few others) was in a position to observe and the significance he alone perceived. Nor does he function

---

16. 18:25–27 is distinctive: the Beloved Disciple is the only disciple to witness Peter's denials, other than Peter himself.

17. 21:3–6 would be an exception if Luke 5:1–10 is considered the same event. I am inclined to think that the Beloved Disciple is able to identify Jesus in 21:7 because he remembers this earlier event.

18. In 18:25–27, the fulfillment of Jesus's prophecy is involved (13:38). In some cases, the scripture that is fulfilled is one that Jesus himself had cited (7:38 [cf. 19:34]; 13:18–19), and in a key case John the Baptist's identification of Jesus from scripture is fulfilled (1:29, 35: cf. 19:32–36).

merely to add Johannine theological commentary on the gospel events. The events he highlights as witnessed by him are unique to his gospel and, in particular, absent from parallel accounts in Mark. He offers in his gospel something distinctive, both in remembered events and in interpretative insight: the twin characteristics of testimony.

Less Explicit Eyewitness Testimony

These seven acts of witness to which the eyewitness-author has chosen to draw special attention cannot be all that his claim to "testify" (21:24) amounts to. In some way, his testimony embraces all the events of the gospel ("these things"). Two questions arise: one concerning the extent of his own personal presence at the events he narrates, the other concerning his dependence on the eyewitness testimony of others.

By highlighting his explicit presence in the narrative at 13:23; 18:15-16; 19:26-27; and 19:35, the eyewitness-author must imply his presence at much of what happens between these points—certainly at the supper and in Gethsemane and in the courtyard of Annas's house. If he was a Jerusalem resident, as the narrative gives ground for at least guessing, and "known to the high priest," this is plausible. But what is the implication of the fact that he appears at the very beginning of John's story of Jesus at 1:35 but not again until 13:23? These verses themselves, along with 15:27, must presuppose that he was present at least at some of the events of the intervening chapters. But it is relevant to consider here the well-known fact that John's story is predominantly set in Jerusalem, even though it presupposes that Jesus was well-known in Galilee and must have spent considerable time there. After chapter 1, only four stories are set in Galilee—the wedding at Cana, the healing of the royal official's son, the feeding miracle (with the walking on the water attached to it),[19] and the fishing miracle. This would be consistent with the indications that the Beloved Disciple was a Jerusalem resident. But if the gospel gives us reason to suppose that he witnessed some of the events set in Jerusalem in the first half of the gospel, it provides no ground for being more specific.

Another distinctive feature of John's Gospel is the prominence of disciples of Jesus who do not appear at all in the other gospels (Nathanael,

---

19. 6:1–21 is an unusual case where John takes over a whole narrative from Mark, while characteristically adding some distinctive detail.

Nicodemus, Lazarus) or who play no role as individuals in those gospels (Philip, Thomas, Andrew) or who feature much more prominently in John than elsewhere (Martha and Mary of Bethany). This may reflect a particular circle of disciples to which the Beloved Disciple belonged and indicate eyewitness informants on whom he was dependent for events he did not personally witness. An especially interesting case is Nathanael, who is given some prominence among the five original disciples of Jesus (1:45–51) and is also among the five named disciples in the epilogue (21:2). Only at this last appearance do we learn the apparently redundant fact that he came from "Cana of Galilee" (note this full designation, as in 2:1 and 4:46). Here Nathanael participates in one of the only four stories set in Galilee and reminds us that two of the others were set in Cana (2:1; 4:46), a place that is unmentioned in the other gospels. This seems another case of retrospective identification, whereby it is suggested that Nathanael was the eyewitness from whom the eyewitness-author learned the stories of the two miracles at Cana.

Conclusion

This chapter has explored the way in which the gospel presents itself as eyewitness testimony. It is primarily as an eyewitness that the author knows what he tells his readers about the events of the history of Jesus. This does not exclude his indebtedness to other eyewitnesses, such as Nathanael, or his use of the Gospel of Mark as a source he respects but wishes to supplement. His self-presentation of eyewitness-author belongs in the context of the importance of eyewitness testimony to Jesus in the early Christian movement. He explicitly inserts himself into that context in 15:27, with the claim that Jesus's disciples were to be his witnesses because they had been with him "from the beginning" (cf. Luke 1:2; Acts 1:21–22). His self-presentation of eyewitness-author also belongs in the context of the historiographical literature of the time, to which eyewitness testimony was considered virtually indispensable.[20] The best historiography was thought to that written by someone who had himself been an eyewitness of significant events within his narrative.

---

20. See, e.g., Craig S. Keener, *Christobiography: Memory, History, and the Reliability of the Gospels* (Eerdmans, 2019), 243–47.

Finally, for understanding this gospel's eyewitness claim, two further features of ancient historiography are worth recalling. First, the gospel author is undoubtedly a skilled storyteller. In the ancient world (and until quite recently), good historians were expected to engage their readers through good storytelling. Telling a true story required a degree of literary creativity, which was not considered inconsistent with writing good history. Second, eyewitness testimony is not incompatible with interpretation, theological or otherwise. All memory entails interpretation, but in this gospel, especially, we surely have the fruit of extended reflection on the author's and others' memories. The prejudice, found in some Johannine scholarship, that an eyewitness could not have written such an interpretative gospel as this is misjudged. Precisely because of his closeness to Jesus, this "disciple Jesus loved" may well have thought himself authorized to interpret more profoundly than others the Jesus he remembered so well.

2

Spirit

Tyler Smith

The Spirit plays a remarkable and, from a modern perspective, positively strange role in John's narrative epistemology. When you or I think about how we know what we know and about what gives us confidence in our knowledge, we tend not to imagine an ethereal and cognitive pneumatic agent playing a role. But something very much like such an agent is an operative and driving force in the narrative world of the Fourth Gospel.

The narrative of the Fourth Gospel unfolds as a series of encounters between the divine revealer Jesus and human characters who encounter the words of God through him. In dramatic dialogues, those characters routinely misunderstand what he says. Often polysemy (e.g., 3:3, 8, 13, 17; 7:8; 13:1; 15:21; 19:30) or figurative language (e.g., 2:20; 3:4; 4:11; 6:26; 8:33; 11:11–12, 24; 14:5–8) lies at the root of the misunderstanding.[1] The misunderstandings create space for Jesus to clarify or say more,[2] though it is often difficult to gauge how successful these elaborations are in leading characters to a fuller understanding. This ambiguity may be by design.

The Johannine audience, meanwhile, is cognitively primed to understand the words of Jesus on a profounder level than characters in the narrative, giving the audience an epistemological advantage over characters.[3] Alongside its ability to make sense of figurative language and

---

1. References in this chapter without a book specified can be assumed to refer to the Fourth Gospel. Unless otherwise noted, all scriptural translations follow the NRSV.

2. For discussion of the repeating schema, see, e.g., C. Milo Connick, "The Dramatic Character of the Fourth Gospel," *JBL* 67 (1948): 167.

3. In this essay, I prefer the term *audience* over *readers* as it better captures the aural and visual transmission dynamics that would have dominated in the history of the gospel's reception.

polysemy, the audience is also better equipped to appreciate Johannine irony, when unwitting characters say something apparently meant to be negative, critical, or incredulous to or about Jesus, but which, to the audience, is significant and true on a profounder level (see, e.g., 3:2; 4:12; 6:42; 7:28–29, 35; 8:22; 9:24, 40; 11:48–50; 12:19; 19:3, 14, 22).[4] That the audience is positioned to appreciate these epistemological shortcomings in Johannine characters contributes to our confidence in the present volume with its aim of describing John's narrative epistemology. Literary readings of the Fourth Gospel as narrative have discussed the cognitive mismatch between audience and characters with reference to the priming techniques that equip the audience to appreciate the profounder register of the gospel's revelatory words and images. Among these hermeneutical and cognitive aids, the prologue and the narrator's intermittent explanatory comments are especially important.[5] Built into the narrative itself, however, is a theological explanation for the audience's attainment of understanding: that explanation involves the work of the divine spirit (*pneuma*).

In short, the epistemological situation assumed by the Fourth Evangelist is one in which "the world" has been alienated from God, who nevertheless loves it (3:16). Johannine language describing this state of alienation is cognitive and metaphorical: those living in the uninspired world are spiritually darkened, dead, blind, deceived, and ignorant. To be in such a state is ipso facto to be in a posture of unbelief toward Jesus and his revelation. Jesus's inspired revelation, meanwhile, invites hearers to believe in him as God's anointed one (i.e., the Christ or Messiah). To believe in Jesus entails, inter alia, that one will desire to emulate his ethical posture, his way of interacting with those he encounters.[6] Both the revelatory witness and the response of faith redound to the glory of God.

---

4. On Johannine irony, see Paul D. Duke, *Irony in the Fourth Gospel* (John Knox, 1985); G. W. MacRae, "Theology and Irony in the Fourth Gospel," in *The Gospel of John as Literature: An Anthology of Twentieth-Century Perspectives*, ed. Mark W. G. Stibbe, NTTS 17 (Brill, 1993), 103–13.

5. On divine priming and the Fourth Gospel, see Tyler Smith, *The Fourth Gospel and the Manufacture of Minds in Ancient Historiography, Biography, Romance, and Drama*, BibInt 173 (Brill, 2019), 183–84, 238–41.

6. On ethics and imitation in the Fourth Gospel, see Richard A. Burridge, *Imitating Jesus: An Inclusive Approach to New Testament Ethics* (Eerdmans, 2007); Christopher W. Skinner and Sherri Brown, eds., *Johannine Ethics: The Moral World of the Gospel and Epistles of John* (Fortress, 2017); Smith, *Fourth Gospel and the Manufacture of Minds*, 71–75, 218–27.

Johannine metaphors for being in this better and inspired state mirror the language noted above: instead of walking in darkness, the Johannine believer walks in light; instead of death, life; instead of blindness, sight; instead of deception, truth; and instead of ignorance, knowledge. The present chapter considers what role in the Johannine epistemological paradigm is played by the pneuma in moving the believer from the one state to the other. After a brief account of what John says about pneuma, we will discuss pneuma in connection to the epistemological status of Jesus, then other characters in the Johannine drama, and finally those in the world beyond the narrative horizon of the Fourth Gospel, especially the implied author and gospel audience.

The Spirit at Work in the Fourth Gospel

As with many dimensions of this enigmatic gospel, it is difficult to provide a straightforward account of Johannine pneumatology (the study of all things spirit-related and, in biblical studies, especially the Holy Spirit).[7] Reasonable minds have disagreed about the personality and agency of the Johannine pneuma, about the stability and continuity of the spirit's identity, about the timeline of the giving of the spirit and what that gift entails, and about how the Johannine spirit is to be understood in connection or contrast to pneumatic discourses in other ancient Jewish and non-Jewish texts.[8] Whatever one makes of those questions, it is clear that pneuma plays

---

7. The bibliography on the Spirit in John is vast. Notable monograph-length studies include Cornelis Bennema, *The Power of Saving Wisdom: An Investigation of Spirit and Wisdom in Relation to the Soteriology of the Fourth Gospel*, WUNT 2/148 (Mohr Siebeck, 2002); Tricia Gates Brown, *Spirit in the Writings of John: Johannine Pneumatology in Social-Scientific Perspective*, JSNTSup 253 (T&T Clark, 2003); Gitte Buch-Hansen, *"It Is the Spirit That Gives Life": A Stoic Understanding of Pneuma in John's Gospel*, BZNW 173 (de Gruyter, 2010); Gary M. Burge, *The Anointed Community: The Holy Spirit in the Johannine Tradition* (Eerdmans, 1987); George Johnston, *The Spirit-Paraclete in the Gospel of John*, SNTSMS 12 (Cambridge University Press, 1970); David Pastorelli, *Le Paraclet dans le corpus johannique*, BZNW 142 (de Gruyter, 2006).

8. As this is a study of the role played by pneuma in the narrative epistemology of John, history-of-religion-informed questions about the proper background to understanding the spirit in John—whether Jewish, Stoic, or popularly Platonic, to the extent that these can be isolated from each other and used to illuminate what John says about the spirit—are mostly left to the side. The argument that the Stoics offer the most illuminating background for understanding John's pneuma-language has received

a critical role in the gospel's narrative epistemology, the gospel's account of *how people know what they know*, its account of *what gives people confidence in their knowledge*, and *the ways of knowing the gospel describes or implies in developing its narrative*.[9] The pneuma is integral both to the production of Jesus's revelatory words and to Jesus's hearers' ability to grasp the significance of those words.

The knowledge that especially interests John is knowledge of God. Programmatically in the prologue, the Evangelist announces that "no one has ever seen God" and that "God the only Son, who is close to the Father's heart, ... has made him known" (1:18). Jesus claims unique knowledge of God and insists that the world has not known God (10:15; 17:25). Jesus's claim to knowledge of God is set in contrast to other actors who presume (wrongly, from the Evangelist's perspective) to have knowledge of God. This is vividly illustrated in the dialogue between Jesus and Nicodemus in chapter 3, but it is developed in stark terms throughout the gospel, particularly in Jesus's conflicts with the Jews in chapters 7 and 8. It is in the midst of those conflicts that Jesus invites those who are thirsty for understanding

---

notable elaboration in recent years. I find this scholarship helpful, particularly in connection to Johannine epistemological discourse and the idea of a community of reason held together by a shared, material pneuma. On the Stoic pneuma, see Teun Tieleman, "The Spirit of Stoicism," in *The Holy Spirit, Inspiration, and the Cultures of Antiquity: Multidisciplinary Perspectives*, ed. Jörg Frey and John R. Levison, Ekstasis 5 (de Gruyter, 2014), 39–62. On the pneuma in the Fourth Gospel, see especially Buch-Hansen, *It Is the Spirit*. For a contrasting view, see Bennema, *Power of Saving Wisdom*.

9. While there are many studies of knowledge and wisdom in connection to the Fourth Gospel, there are relatively fewer studies of Johannine epistemology. Where these studies exist, they tend to focus on the knowledge of God. See Mary Redington Ely Lyman, *Knowledge of God in Johannine Thought* (Macmillan, 1925); Ignace de la Potterie, "Οἶδα et γινώσκω: Les deux modes de la connaissance dans le quatrième evangile," *Biblica* 40.3 (1959): 709–25; John Painter, "The Idea of Knowledge in the Johannine Gospel and Epistles" (PhD diss., University of Durham, 1968); Jerome H. Neyrey, "John III: A Debate over Johannine Epistemology and Christology," *NovT* 23 (1981): 115–27; Marianne Meye Thompson, *The God of the Gospel of John* (Eerdmans, 2001), 101–44; Howard Clark Kee, "Knowing the Truth: Epistemology and Community in the Fourth Gospel," in *Neotestamentica et Philonica: Studies in Honor of Peder Borgen*, ed. David E. Aune, Torrey Seland, and Jarl Henning Ulrichsen, NovTSup 106 (Brill, 2003), 254–80; Cornelis Bennema, "Christ, the Spirit and the Knowledge of God: A Study in Johannine Epistemology," in *The Bible and Epistemology: Biblical Soundings on the Knowledge of God*, ed. Mary Healy and Robin Parry (Paternoster, 2007), 107–33.

to come to himself and have a drink of "living water," a metaphor he uses to describe the Spirit (7:37–39).

Perhaps the most important epistemological function of the divine pneuma in the Johannine narrative is that it fills Jesus's words with revelatory potency. This principle is hinted at in 7:37–39 and developed more concretely at 3:34 and 6:63, texts that we will consider in more detail below. Consequently, the spirit is implicitly present whenever the Johannine Jesus speaks, whether or not pneuma is mentioned explicitly in the immediate context. Similarly, the spirit is present whenever divinely sanctioned testimony, confession, teaching, and conviction figure into the narrative. These functions are spelled out most explicitly in connection to the Paraclete that Jesus promises will be sent to guide the disciples after his own glorification/death and ascent to the Father. The Paraclete, who is identified explicitly with the Holy Spirit at 14:26, will take on some of Jesus's functions. This narrative dynamic has profound consequences for the status of the disciples' words in the postresurrection world. It suggests that the words of the disciples are buoyed up by the same spirit that rested on Jesus; it also means that the gospel's implied author, as a sharer in this divine spirit, understands his own testimony (i.e., the words of the gospel itself) to be inspired.

The pneuma with which John is most interested is the divine spirit, also called the Holy Spirit, the Spirit sent from the Father, and the Spirit of truth. The divine spirit may be distinguished from the mundane animating spirit found all breathing persons, including the incarnate Jesus (in Jesus: 11:33; 13:21; cf. 12:27; 14:1, 27). The activity of the Holy Spirit, as John presents it, is the necessary mechanism needed for human beings to become truly alive, spiritually alive, to possess eternal life.

The pneuma in the Fourth Gospel is an autonomous cognitive agent. It goes "where it chooses" (3:8) and is not subject to human control. One cannot simply opt into belief in Jesus and the privileged epistemological status dependent on that belief. The epistemological situation imagined by the Fourth Evangelist is one in which human actors have limited control over their own epistemological standing and destiny. Fortunately for those who desire to be counted in the company of believers, however, the desires of the Johannine pneuma are presented as aligned with the desires of God the Father. In this too the pneuma emulates and carries on Jesus's work. For Johannine believers beyond the narrative horizon, the spirit is offered as the model of rightly aligned desire and belief.

Upon encounter with the spirit-infused revelatory words of Jesus or, in the world beyond the text, words proceeding from the mouths of those to whom God has given the spirit, the Fourth Evangelist paints a situation in which hearers/readers should resist the urge to claim perfect understanding of what has been revealed. In the narrative world of the Fourth Gospel, even those who are most committed to God and Jesus as his anointed one struggle to comprehend the inspired words they hear. John encourages humility in his audience when it comes to claiming epistemological confidence regarding divine things.[10]

The Spirit and the Johannine Jesus

At the outset of Jesus's revelatory mission in the Fourth Gospel, the pneuma makes an initial and oblique appearance in the testimony of John the Baptist:

> And John testified, "I saw the Spirit descending from heaven like a dove, and it remained on him [viz., Jesus]. I myself did not know him, but the one who sent me to baptize with water said to me, 'He on whom you see the Spirit descend and remain is the one who baptizes with the Holy Spirit.' And I myself have seen and have testified that this is the Son of God." (1:32–33)

This scene has a clear parallel in the Synoptic tradition (cf. Matt 3:13–17; Mark 1:9–11; Luke 3:21–22), but the Fourth Evangelist artfully combines in this episode the arrival of the Spirit with the Johannine cognitive discourse of recognition (anagnorisis).[11] The descending spirit is the "sign" or "token" (*sēmeion*) that permits the water baptizer to recognize Jesus as the anticipated spirit baptizer.[12] Notably, John the Baptist does not take credit for the recognition ("I myself did not know him, but ..."), giving credit instead to "the one who sent me to baptize with water." The audience

---

10. In this respect, there is a tension between the epistemological tenor of the Fourth Gospel and that of 1 John, where the author is keen to shore up his recipients' confidence in their knowledge of divine things (cf. 1 John 2:3–5).

11. On this important motif, see Kasper Bro Larsen, *Recognizing the Stranger: Recognition Scenes in the Gospel of John*, BibInt 93 (Brill, 2008).

12. The first half of the gospel, in which Jesus's healings and other marvelous deeds are called "signs" (*sēmeia*) rather than "miracles," is sometimes referred to as the "Book of Signs." John's interest in signs, however, goes beyond what we would otherwise label miracles. Both words and narrative developments are significant, including this, the descent of the spirit upon Jesus.

should presumably understand the sender here as God the Father, but it is provocatively ambiguous. It could equally be the spirit or somebody speaking to John while possessed by the divine pneuma. At any rate, in the Johannine epistemological framework, these potentialities are not mutually exclusive. As in the Synoptic accounts, the appearance and resting of the Spirit upon Jesus evokes an Isaianic Messianic promise:

> The spirit of the LORD shall rest on him,
> the spirit of wisdom and understanding,
> the spirit of counsel and might,
> the spirit of knowledge and the fear of the LORD. (Isa 11:2)[13]

From this moment until 20:22, when he breathes the spirit into his disciples, Jesus is the primary locus and carrier of the divine spirit. That climactic moment in 20:22, when Jesus passes on the spirit, is signaled preemptively at several key prior moments in the narrative. The first is in John's testimony, where Jesus is referred to as the one who will "baptize with the Holy Spirit." A second foreshadowing moment comes in chapter 3, where the function of Jesus as "the one whom God has sent" is foregrounded: "He whom God has sent speaks the words of God, for he gives the Spirit without measure" (3:34).[14] And a third foreshadowing moment occurs when Jesus passes into death: "When Jesus had received the wine, he said, 'It is finished.' Then he bowed his head and gave up his spirit" (19:30).

Returning to John 20:22, we find Jesus sharing this spirit of wisdom and understanding with the disciples. He "breathes the spirit into" them in a scene richly evocative of Gen 2:27, where God breathed life into the dustman *'adam*. Life and knowledge are linked in the presence of the spirit[15]: "Jesus said to them again, 'Peace be with you. As the Father has sent me,

---

13. See also Isa 42:1; 61:1.

14. It is unclear whether the subject of the verb "he gives" (*didōsin*) is God or the sent one who speaks the words of God (i.e., Jesus). If one of the goals of the Fourth Gospel is to blur the lines between God the Father and Jesus the Son, however, the ambiguity may well be intentional.

15. See also 3 Kgdms 17:17–24 LXX, where Elijah breathes into the widow's son and asks God to restore his life, and Ezekiel's vision of the valley of dry bones, where the prophet says "Thus says the Lord God: Come from the four winds, o breath, and breathe upon these slain, that they may live" (Ezek 37:9–10). While it is impossible to say whether the Evangelist had one or several of these specific texts in mind when he

so I send you.' When he had said this, he breathed into them and said to them, 'Receive the Holy Spirit'" (20:21–22; NRSV modified).

Those who possess the Holy Spirit in John are epistemologically equipped to be sent out to bear witness to the work of God through Jesus Christ. Just as God sent his Spirit to rest upon Jesus and literally inspire him to speak the words of God (cf. 1:32; 3:34; 6:63), so here the disciples are literally inspired—the actions of Jesus and the desires of the spirit coalesce to put the spirit into their bodies—and thereafter sent. The Johannine sending motif—introduced already in the Baptist's testimony ("the one who sent me to baptize with water said to me")—is symbiotically connected to the motifs of teaching, testifying, convicting, and convincing, all of which are functions of the spirit/Paraclete.

How does the risen Jesus give the spirit to the disciples (20:22) if he has already "given up his spirit" in 19:30? The problem is solved if we allow for two perfectly conventional ways of talking about *the* spirit, distinguishing Jesus's personal spirit from the divine spirit. In the first case, the pneuma is what animates Jesus's body, what gives him breath, what gives him the capacity to be alive, and the site at which he registers emotion, as in the context of the Lazarus's death (11:33; cf. 13:21). The spirit that Jesus gives to the disciples in 20:22, on the other hand, is the divine spirit. Jesus refers to it in this scene as the "Holy Spirit." This is the spirit that John the Baptist sees descending and remaining upon Jesus in chapter 1 and is coextensive with the figure referred to by turns as the Paraclete, the Spirit of truth, and the Holy Spirit. There is a certain amount of (deliberate?) ambiguity about the relationship between Jesus's personal spirit and the divine pneuma, the Holy Spirit. By analogy to the play between conventional seeing and profound seeing in the Fourth Gospel (see esp. chapter 9), there is a play between the spirit that animates bodies and the Holy Spirit, given only by God's gift, which animates the spiritually reborn believer in Jesus. The one makes life possible; the other makes Life possible.

Jesus's possession of the divine spirit in the Johannine epistemological framework is what enables him to speak the words of God. We saw this hinted at already in 3:34 in the connection John draws between the spirit and the ability to share God's words; to that text we add another, even clearer identification of Jesus's words with spirit and (capital-L) Life

---

painted the scene in John 20, it is certain that the narrative world of the Fourth Gospel presupposes a general familiarity with Israel's scriptures.

in chapter 6: "It is the spirit that gives life; the flesh is useless. The words that I have spoken to you are spirit and life" (6:63).

Knowledge in the Fourth Gospel that comes through the senses (the aforementioned "useless flesh") is often unreliable, while knowledge that comes through true revelation is reliable but easily misunderstood. Jesus's words, the words of God, constitute the vehicle for that revelation. If the divine spirit is what gives Jesus the ability to proclaim this revelation, pneuma is also the cognitive agent or mechanism responsible for allowing the revelatory words to be understood. We have seen already how the spirit made John the Baptist's recognition of Jesus possible; we turn now to consider the spirit at work in some other encounters with Jesus.

The Spirit and the Johannine Cast of Characters

In John 3, Jesus confounds the Pharisee Nicodemus by saying:

> Very truly, I tell you, no one can enter the kingdom of God without being born of water and Spirit. What is born of the flesh is flesh, and what is born of the Spirit is spirit. Do not be astonished that I said to you, 'You must be born from above [*anōthen*].' The wind [*pneuma*] blows where it chooses, and you hear the sound [*phōnē*] of it, but you do not know where it comes from or where it goes. So it is with everyone who is born of the Spirit." (3:5–8)

Nicodemus's response, "How can these things be?" (3:9), indicates a failure to understand, a status which, in the Johannine epistemological framework, indicates that he has not been born of the Spirit. On one level, his misunderstanding concerns the polysemic adverb *anōthen*, which can mean "again" (the sense in which Nicodemus takes it) or "from above" (as translated). The ironic narrative reality is that Nicodemus, though rendered here as spiritually ignorant, began this dialogue with a claim to knowledge: "He came to Jesus at night and said, 'Rabbi, we know that you are a teacher who has come from God. For no one could perform the signs you are doing if God were not with him'" (3:2). This is one of the ironic sayings noted earlier, in which a character unwittingly says something that is profoundly true about Jesus: God *is* with Jesus, by means of the spirit Nicodemus lacks. That Nicodemus is speaking from a place of ignorance is hinted at also by the narrative detail that "he came to Jesus at night" in a story where the darkness of night and the darkness of the mind are correlated (cf. 1:5). Jesus highlights Nicodemus's failure to understand, perhaps with a note of outrage: "Are you a teacher of Israel, and yet you do not understand these things?" (3:10). Counterintuitive though it may seem to readers steeped in an individualist culture of autonomous self-determination, however, Jesus does not urge Nicodemus to change course, accept the spirit into his heart, and thereby come to a more perfect understanding. Nicodemus's inability to understand is explained, at least in part, by the fact that the spirit has not chosen to inspire his understanding. The pneuma blows where it chooses, and it has not elected to enlighten Nicodemus the Pharisee. In his conversation with Jesus, Nicodemus has heard the sound of the pneuma in Jesus's words, but the spirit has not equipped him to understand them.

Something comparable happens in Jesus's dialogue with the Samaritan woman in chapter 4. In response to her question about the proper place of worship, the Johannine Jesus broaches both (mis)understanding and the spirit:

> You [pl.; viz., Samaritans] worship what you do not know; we worship what we know, for salvation is from the Jews. But the hour is coming, and is now here, when the true worshipers will worship the Father in spirit and truth, for the Father seeks such as these to worship him. God is spirit, and those who worship him must worship in spirit and truth. (4:22–24)

As with Nicodemus, the Samaritan woman's response suggests to the epistemologically privileged audience that she does not grasp what Jesus is revealing—at least not at first. "The woman said to him, 'I know that Messiah is coming' (who is called Christ). 'When he comes, he will proclaim all things to us'" (4:25). This exchange features a cognitive failure to recognize Jesus as the Messiah, accompanied by another dose of Johannine irony, insofar as Jesus the Messiah *is* "proclaiming all things" to her, or at least those things which are necessary for her to understand what true worship consists in, namely, pneuma and truth. While no sign is given that Nicodemus in chapter 3 had an spirit-enabled aha! moment (he appears on two later occasions in the gospel, but in neither case is it clear that he has grasped Jesus's words in their profounder sense), and while the Samaritan woman is for the moment apparently bewildered, it may be that she ultimately comes around to a fuller recognition of Jesus and his revelatory words, at the point when she testifies to her fellow Samaritans about Jesus (4:28–29, 39–42). It is significant, in the Johannine narrative world, that Nicodemus is a Pharisee and a "teacher of Israel" and the spirit has not selected to revolutionize his thinking, while "many Samaritans" on the other hand, those who are defined in opposition to the Jews (4:9), *do* have their minds transformed by the spirit. That is, after hearing Jesus's inspired words for themselves, they can confess "we believe ... and we know that this is truly the Savior of the world" (4:42).[16]

Both the Samaritan woman and Nicodemus are ambiguous characters,[17] who "hear the sound" of Jesus's pneumatic words and do not know where the words come from or where they are going. The Samaritan woman, however, seems to lean into Jesus's words, and there is some suggestion that she is moving toward the cognitive status of recognition and belief that is the Johannine ideal. There is a sequence of double entendre in Jesus's remark to Nicodemus in the passage cited above, which supports such a reading: "The *pneuma* blows where it chooses, and you hear the *phōnē* of it, but you do not know where it comes from or where it goes" (3:7 NRSV modified). *Pneuma* in Greek can mean wind, breath, spirit, or the divine spirit that enables understanding. *Phōnē* is another polysemic word that can mean an impersonal "sound" or a personal "voice." Hearing, in the Fourth Gospel, can mean both the hearing that comes through the ears and also true understanding (cf. the two levels on which the blindness/sight language works in this gospel). Here, the polysemy of both *pneuma* and *phōnē* is in play. The strand of latent significance germane to our purposes concerns the ability of characters like Nicodemus and the Samaritan woman to hear in the more profound sense the voice of the divine pneuma as manifested in Jesus's words. The trouble is that, without the pneuma enabling them to hear in the more profound sense, without a baptism in the pneuma, they are trapped in confusion. And the uncomfortable reality that Jesus seems to be presenting here is one in which such people have very little control over their ability to come to a spirit-powered state of understanding, since the pneuma blows where it chooses. They may perceive its comings and goings, at least in the audible words pouring from Jesus's mouth, but they are powerless to grasp the totality of its divine origin or destination.

---

16. Again, the literature on the Gospel of John and the Jews is vast. See most recently Adele Reinhartz, *Cast Out of the Covenant: Jews and Anti-Judaism in the Gospel of John* (Lexington Books; Fortress Academic, 2018).

17. Susan Hylen, *Imperfect Believers: Ambiguous Characters in the Gospel of John* (Westminster John Knox, 2009).

This framing of understanding in the gospel also has implications for what Jesus says to the Samaritan woman about true worship. Jesus's saying that "God is spirit, and those who worship him must worship in spirit and truth" has generally been understood as an exhortation, a summons to a certain mode of worship. Thus it should come as no surprise that much ink has been spilled over what it means to worship "in spirit and truth"; if this is something a reader can choose to do, then they need to begin by figuring out what the desired mode of worship entails. In light of the gospel's larger account of the spirit and its activity, however, Jesus's remark to the Samaritan woman may be better understood as *descriptive* rather than hortatory. In other words, worshipers do not simply decide to become true worshipers and offer true worship; they *become* true worshipers when the spirit finds them and produces true worship.

Jesus, of course, interacts with many more characters than just Nicodemus and the Samaritans, both individual (Mary, Martha, the man born blind, individual disciples, et al.) and corporate (the Jews, the Pharisees, the disciples, crowds, et al.). These characters can be predisposed favorably or unfavorably to Jesus, though a favorable disposition is by no means a guarantee of being able to understand his words—that ability in John comes at the discretion of the spirit. This is demonstrated by the apparent failure of some of Jesus's closest disciples to understand his words in the profounder sense intended by Jesus and accessible to the implied author and audience (e.g., Martha in chapter 11; Peter in chapters 13, 18, and 21; Peter and the Beloved Disciple in 20:9; Mary in chapter 20). While the spirit is not invoked explicitly in every dialogue, the spirit is present implicitly whenever the spirit-anointed Jesus speaks, as the principle at 3:34 and 6:63 makes clear.

The Spirit and Those beyond the Narrative Horizon

The narrative of the Fourth Gospel constructs an epistemological paradigm that extends to the world beyond the text. In this section, we will consider two primary sites of interest: the implied author and the audience.

John 20:31 is often described as the purpose statement of the gospel. In that verse, the Evangelist presents his interest in transforming the epistemological status of the audience: Jesus did many signs in the presence of his disciples, and the gospel contains a selection of them, "written so that you may believe that Jesus is the Messiah, the Son of God, and that through believing you may have life in his name" (20:31 NRSV modified).

In the epistemological paradigm constructed in the chapters preceding this statement, what role does the Spirit play in making possible the knowledge that Jesus is the Messiah and transforming minds from unbelief to belief? On the one hand, it seems intuitive to infer an implied author in search of a reader who will read this testimony about Jesus and then choose belief in Jesus. But as we have seen above, there is an alternative and a more expansive reading that takes into account a fuller sweep of the Johannine spirit's role in initiating epistemological transformations. The pneuma blows where it wishes, and some people in the audience (like Nicodemus) may perceive the presence of the spirit only superficially—that is, they will see and hear the same spirit-infused words as everyone else, but not understand—while others in the audience (like the Samaritans) are expected to grasp and appreciate the profounder significance of what they have seen or heard. In other words, it is possible to be in the presence of the spirit and not to experience epistemological transformation, willing or unwilling. To be transformed requires that one be baptized with the spirit, and this is a gift one cannot simply opt into. Rather, it comes at the initiative of the spirit who is God's divine emissary. In this framework, a reader's choice to believe is secondary, and perhaps even illusory.

The implied author, on this reading, believes that he himself has been inspired by the divine spirit and that the production of this gospel narrative is itself an act of testifying to the work of God through Jesus Christ, the incarnate *logos* of the divine and true God (cf. 21:24). The implied author believes that the work of testifying, convincing, and convicting of sin are all epistemologically freighted speech acts in which the divine spirit plays an operative role. These functions are given their clearest expression in an important set of references to the divine spirit identifying him as the Paraclete (*paraklētos*; literally, "the one called alongside").[18] In the Farewell Discourses (14–16), Jesus refers to such a figure on four occasions:

> And I will ask the Father, and he will give you another Paraclete, to be with you forever. This is the Spirit of truth, whom the world cannot receive,

---

18. The term is often rendered in English as "Advocate," "Comforter," or "Helper." Of these, the strongest case can be made for "Advocate." Formally, the word is a passive verbal adjective, "the one called [*klētos*] alongside [*para*]." In ancient legal contexts, it was routine to have an advocate called upon for legal assistance (cf. Latin *advocatus*). This fits well with the Fourth Gospel's courtroom/trial motif, on which, see Andrew T. Lincoln, *Truth on Trial: The Lawsuit Motif in the Fourth Gospel* (Hendrickson, 2000).

> because it neither sees him nor knows him. You know him, because he abides with you, and he will be in you. (14:16-17 NRSV modified)

> I have said these things to you while I am still with you. But the Paraclete, the Holy Spirit, whom the Father will send in my name, will teach you everything, and remind you of all that I have said to you. (14:25-26 NRSV modified)

> When the Paraclete comes, whom I will send to you from the Father, the Spirit of truth who comes from the Father, he will testify on my behalf. (15:26 NRSV modified)

> It is to your advantage that I go away, for if I do not go away, the Paraclete will not come to you; but if I go, I will send him to you. And when he comes, he will prove the world wrong about sin and righteousness and judgment. (16:7-8 NRSV modified)

A further detail is added about this figure a few verses later, though the label Paraclete is not explicitly present:

> When the Spirit of truth comes, he will guide you into all the truth; for he will not speak on his own, but will speak whatever he hears, and he will declare to you the things that are to come. He will glorify me, because he will take what is mine and declare it to you. (16:13-14)

The Johannine Paraclete is cast as an agent with important cognitive work to do in the world imagined by the Fourth Evangelist. Some scholars have attempted to put a clear break between the degree of agency wielded by this post-Jesus Paraclete and the Holy Spirit at work during Jesus's ministry,[19] but to make such a distinction may be misguided. As we had occasion to see above, the spirit throughout John's Gospel blows where it chooses, and its desires are aligned with God the Father and Jesus as his emissary. The agentive continuity of Jesus's divine pneuma and the post-Jesus Paraclete is made even clearer if we consider the functions ascribed to it. The Paraclete will be "with you forever," just as the pneuma was with Jesus throughout his ministry, inspiring his revelatory words. The Paraclete will teach, as Jesus taught, and remind the disciples of what Jesus

---

19. See, e.g., Michael Becker, "Spirit in Relationship–Pneumatology in the Gospel of John," in Frey and Levison, *Holy Spirit*, 331–42.

had already revealed. The Paraclete will testify on Jesus's behalf, as various characters throughout the gospel—including John the Baptist and the Samaritan woman—testified on Jesus's behalf. The Paraclete will exercise a juridical function, proving the world wrong about sin and righteousness and judgment, just as the Johannine Jesus exercises a prosecutorial role in connection to the unbelieving world.[20]

Conclusion

The divine spirit's possession of Jesus is important not just for the role it plays in his ability to speak the inspired and revelatory words of God. It is important also for the effect it has on the understanding faculties of those who hear Jesus. Bodies in the world of the Fourth Gospel are not hermetically sealed containers that either possess the divine spirit or not; the spirit, rather, flows out from Jesus and into those who hear him.[21] When the resurrected Jesus "breathes the spirit into" the disciples at 20:22, he is continuing to do what he has been doing since he began speaking the words of God in chapter 1. This audible and visceral outflow of the spirit from one body to another, moreover, is not limited to a unidirectional relationship from Jesus to the disciples. Here it is instructive to recall what Jesus said earlier in the gospel, on the last day of the Feast of Tabernacles:

> "Let anyone who is thirsty come to me, and let the one who believes in me drink. As the scripture has said, 'Out of the believer's heart shall flow rivers of living water.'" Now he said this about the Spirit, which believers in him were to receive; for as yet there was no Spirit, because Jesus was not yet glorified. (7:37–39)

This text has occasioned some difficulty among interpreters because the narrative frame to the scriptural citation suggests that the living water/spirit comes out of Jesus, and yet the scripture citation makes it clear that the living water/spirit comes out of the heart of the believer. Again,

---

20. On the legal motif in the Fourth Gospel, see Lincoln, *Truth on Trial*; George L. Parsenios, *Rhetoric and Drama in the Johannine Lawsuit Motif*, WUNT 258 (Mohr Siebeck, 2010).

21. Such an understanding of the spirit is paralleled in a number of other ancient texts. See, e.g., Philo's comments on the divine spirit's possession of Abraham at *Virt.* 217.

we encounter a piece of productive ambiguity: the spirit, who is like the living water about which Jesus spoke with the Samaritan woman, flows verbally from his heart and out of his mouth in a manner that anticipates the believers' Paraclete-assisted verbal flow after Jesus's reascent to the Father. The explanatory note that "as yet there was no Spirit, because Jesus was not yet glorified" looks forward to that time beyond the narrative horizon, in which Jesus has been crucified in glory, raised from the dead, and returned to the Father above, a time in which the activity of the spirit will be seen and heard in the words and deeds of Johannine believers.

Among those deeds we are invited to count the Fourth Evangelist's decision to write a gospel, and among those words we are invited to consider the testimony in that gospel. As members of the audience, we have been primed to track and follow the words of Jesus on the profounder level of significance that is so often missed by characters in the Johannine drama. But John would not have us rest on our privileged epistemological laurels; his characters also warn the audience against overconfidence or complacency in claiming to understand the gospel's revelation. If there is anything in the Fourth Gospel that is confounding, the Evangelist's promise is that understanding may come through the work of the spirit. The logic of the gospel requires that not even the Evangelist himself can claim to have plumbed the significance of every word he has passed along, since every aspect of spiritual understanding is contingent on the desire of the life-giving spirit to make it possible. This is true even for those who believe Jesus and (like John the Baptist, the Samaritan woman, or the Beloved Disciple) testify on his behalf. No doubt the unsettling sense of not having everything figured out has played a major role in bringing readers back again and again to the words that make up the Johannine narrative.

3
IMAGINATION

Douglas Estes

The author of the Gospel of John—a self-declared witness to events in the life of Jesus (John 19:35)—knows about the story he tells through a variety of means. The author knows about Jesus from his personal testimony (John 1:14), from his immersion in Hebraic tradition (John 1:38), from his familiarity with Scripture (John 1:17), from his connection to the Spirit of God (John 7:39), and from his own personal identity and inner self (John 13:23), just to name a few. To write his story of Jesus, the author weaves together these strands of this knowledge—whether conscious or unconscious, and in varying measures—that bear on the story he wishes to tell. Some of these strands of knowledge are more obvious to the implied author; some strands are more powerful in shaping the story; some are closer to the surface; and some are hidden deep in the psyche of John.

In this chapter, we will contemplate how John's *imagination* shaped his telling of the story of Jesus. To us today, *imagination* typically conjures up a sense of the fantastic, the unreal, the untrue—but that is not what we mean here in this chapter, nor is it what Hellenistic culture understood this idea to mean, nor likely is it what John understood this idea to mean, either.[1] Readers may accept that certain genres of biblical literature such as apocalypse require imagination,[2] while assuming that other genres such as the gospels preclude it. Yet John's use of imagination makes no claim in and of itself either to truth or make-believe (cf. Aristotle, *De an.* 428a16–18).

---

1. Kevin Corrigan, *A Less Familiar Plato: From* Phaedo *to* Philebus, CSRP (Cambridge University Press, 2023), 140.
2. See, for example, John J. Collins, *The Apocalyptic Imagination: An Introduction to Jewish Apocalyptic Literature*, 2nd ed. (Eerdmans, 1998).

Whether history or fiction or somewhere in between, a storyteller cannot create a story without using their imagination.[3] Imagination is an integral but implicit part of knowledge assimilation and reproduction.

The medieval theologian Richard of Saint Victor (twelfth century) famously explained imagination this way:

> We have seen gold and we have seen a house, but we have never seen a golden house. However, if we wish, we can imagine a golden house.[4]

Everyone who reads Richard's example can readily imagine a golden house—as long as they have seen a house and they have seen gold. Richard builds his example on the way the human mind processes visualizations, where seeing leads to abstract understanding that leads to assimilation that leads to creative output. Once we see gold for the first time, we learn what gold is, we adapt it into usage in our mind, and then can apply it to both old and new situations. Richard uses this example in his discussion of the Apocalypse, demonstrating that even if a person has never seen a golden house, he or she can understand what it is and reasonably believe it exists (Rev 21:18). We can apply Richard's example to John's storytelling in the gospel:

> We have seen a man walk and we have seen water, but we have never seen a man walk on water. However, if we wish, we can imagine a man walking on water.

When Jesus realizes that the crowds will try to make him a king forcibly, he withdraws to a nearby high place alone (John 6:15). For reasons the narrator does not reveal, when night falls the disciples leave that side of the sea and sail to Capernaum (John 6:16–17). After setting sail, a storm arrives, and as the disciples continue to row, they suddenly see Jesus walking on the water toward them (John 6:18–19). As one of the gospel's hearers/readers, we *can* imagine Jesus walking on the sea—even

---

3. Adele Reinhartz, *Cast Out of the Covenant: Jews and Anti-Judaism in the Gospel of John* (Lexington Books; Fortress Academic, 2018), xxviii.

4. *BMIN* 16:132.10–13: "Verbi gratia: aurum uidimus, domum uidimus, auream autem domum nunquam uidimus, auream tamen domum imaginari possumus, si uolumus." English translation (and appreciation for this example) from Ritva Palmén, *Richard of St. Victor's Theory of Imagination*, IMP 8 (Brill, 2014), 1.

though we have never seen a man walk on the sea (or Jesus, either). If we were able to capture a digital image of this imaginary, water-walking Jesus who exists in readers' minds, there would be an unlimited number of superficial differences (your Jesus might have long hair and wispy beard, while my Jesus has short hair and bristly beard), but the similarities would be strong enough that readers everywhere would understand these images to be Jesus walking on the sea. In fact, visual variances would not scuttle truth claims.

However, it is not merely readers of the Fourth Gospel who need to use their imagination to *see* Jesus walk on water. It is the implied author also. Just like his readers, the implied author—sitting in the boat on a dark and stormy night—had seen a man walk and had seen water but had never before seen a man walking on water. To understand what he was seeing, something miraculous, impossible, fantastic, the implied author had to rely on more than just his eyes. He had to rely on his imagination to process (in a state of fear), understand (enough to steel himself [ἤθελον] to help Jesus into the boat), and later communicate the vision.[5] However, there is a limit to this ability to understand and process: John also records that when Jesus got in or near the boat, εὐθέως ἐγένετο τὸ πλοῖον ἐπὶ τῆς γῆς εἰς ἣν ὑπῆγον (loosely: "immediately he boarded the boat, and they arrived at the destination"). This is a curious clause which interpreters often take to suggest a second miracle.[6] If so, John is not able to narrate this miracle because he had not seen the elements of boats with fast travel or teleportation before (John 20:19, 26;

---

5. The water walking story is retold in three of the four canonical gospels (Matt 14:22–27 // Mark 6:45–52 // John 6:15–21). In Matthew, Peter also begins to walk on water, but out of fear he begins to lose faith and sink. Peter imagined himself walking on the water to Jesus but could not maintain the image in his mind due to the loss of faith. In Matthew and Mark, the narrators explain that the disciples thought Jesus was a φάντασμα ("phantasm"), but since the disciples had presumably never seen a phantasm before, it is the idea to which they were led by their imagination, and then corrected, as their vision became clearer.

6. Commentators who believe John narrates a second miracle in John 6:21 include C. K. Barrett, *The Gospel according to St John: An Introduction with Commentary and Notes on the Greek Text*, 2nd ed. (Westminster, 1978), 281; Rudolf Bultmann, *The Gospel of John: A Commentary*, trans. G. R. Beasley-Murray et al. (Westminster, 1971), 216; Siegfried Schulz, *Das Evangelism nach Johannes*, NTD 4 (Vandenhoeck & Ruprecht, 1987), 100; and Jean Zumstein, *Das Johannesevangelium*, KEK 2 (Vandenhoeck & Ruprecht, 2016), 252.

Acts 8:39).[7] Though he has seen, he cannot understand; he cannot narrate what he cannot imagine.

Imagination Isolated

The rhetorician and literary critic I. A. Richards surmises that there are six distinct forms of imagination.[8] Consequently, the academic study of human imagination is vast, covering diverse fields that include philosophy, literary theory, psychology, cognitive science, art, philosophy of science, and theology. This contrasts with the study of imagination within biblical studies, a field that has paid it scant attention.[9] This is likely due to the tendency in Western culture to equate imagination with fiction and the negative connotations that arise as a result when applied to biblical literature.[10] Thus, to answer the question suggested by this book, "What does John know?"—when it comes to imagination, we must first isolate the relevant parts of the expansive idea. Many of the observations that Richards makes about imagination do not apply to ancient writers—at least, in a way that these writers would have understood it, as far as we can tell from extant writings. For example, of the six forms that Richards details, only two are relevant to what John knows. The *first* is the experiential sensing and mental assimilation of visual images for processing by the mind. This type of imagination I define as "a means of knowing that results from visual sensations." Richards labels this "the commonest and least interesting" part of imagination—but it is the most essential part for this chapter.[11] It is also the most significant part of ancient discussions on imagination and the most significant for the study of historiography. The *second* is the power to create new ideas, whether *new* refers to the mundane (golden houses) or fantastic (telepor-

---

7. Another example of a nonnarrated miracle is Jesus's distribution of five loaves of bread and two fish to many thousands; the narrator cannot narrate it because the narrator cannot imagine (process the visuals of) what happened (John 6:9–12).

8. I. A. Richards, *Principles of Literary Criticism* (Harcourt, Brace, 1928), 239–43.

9. More often than not, biblical scholars use *imagination* in a negative way; among numerous examples, see Dale C. Allison Jr., *Constructing Jesus: Memory, Imagination, and History* (Baker, 2010), 2, 440.

10. Gerard Watson, "Imagination: The Greek Background," *ITQ* 52 (1986): 54. For an example of the uncritical use of imagination in a pejorative sense, see Augustus Tholuck, *Commentary on the Gospel of John*, trans. Charles P. Krauth (Smith, English, 1859), 23.

11. Richards, *Principles of Literary Criticism*, 239.

tation). This is the part of imagination most familiar to modern culture at large, and it is the one of most interest to literary theorists today. These two forms of imagination bring us to two critical distinctions that shape what we can learn about what John knew when using imagination in the creation of the Fourth Gospel.

Expressive versus Creative

The first differentiation is between the *expressive* and *creative* uses of imagination. At the root of the tree of imagination in the West is the classical use of the word *phantasia* (φαντασία).[12] The predominant sense of *phantasia* prior to the second century CE was "visualization."[13] Plato was the first to discuss *phantasia* as a means of visualization (*Soph.* 264a), and Aristotle expanded greatly on his discussion (see especially *De an.* 424b22–435b25).[14] To most classical Greek philosophers, *phantasia* was specifically epistemological.[15] Still there was an awareness that knowing a visual sensation was not the same as understanding the visual sensation and, even less, expressing for others this sensation. To this end, Aristotle argues decisively that while imagination is made of sensations, sensations are not the same as imagination (*De an.* 428a).[16] When a person experiences a visual sensation, that person must translate the visual input to make a coherent image within their minds, and this translation and resulting image is the early sense of *phantasia*.[17] This is the meaning that the rhetorician Quintilian (35–96 CE) uses (*Inst.* 6.2.29–30). This is

---

12. Joseph B. Juhasz, "Greek Theories of Imagination," *Journal of the History of the Behavioral Sciences* 7 (1971): 51. Greek philosophers also used other words, most notably the near synonymous φάντασμα.

13. Douglas Estes, "The Tree of Life in the Apocalypse of John," in *The Tree of Life*, ed. Douglas Estes, TBN 27 (Brill, 2020), 187; and cf. R. J. Hankinson and Marguerite Deslauriers, "Aristotle on Imagination and Action: Introduction," *Dialogue* 29 (1990): 4.

14. Aristotle employed *phantasia* broadly, though here we focus on visualization narrowly, instead of, for example, the relationship between imagination and dreaming; see for example, Deborah K. W. Modrak, "Aristotle on *Phantasia*," in *The Routledge Handbook of Philosophy of Imagination*, ed. Amy Kind (Routledge, 2016), 15; and Joyce Engmann, "Imagination and Truth in Aristotle," *JHP* 14 (1976): 264.

15. Watson, "Imagination," 58.

16. See Tony Roark, *Aristotle on Time: A Study of the Physics* (Cambridge University Press, 2011), 134–35.

17. Ruth Webb, "Sight and Insight: Theorizing Vision, Emotion and Imagination

not to say that the ancients were not aware of creativity and fantasy in the human mind; Plato was a truly unique thinker, poets concocted highly original mythologies—such as Callimachus's (305–240 BCE) *Hymn to Delos*—while rhetoricians and orators were keenly aware of the importance of *ekphrasis* (ἔκφρασις) and *enargeia* (ἐνάργεια) to paint a visual for their respective readers.[18] Longinus (first century CE) in *On the Sublime* is perhaps the first to connect these two ideas—the expressive and the creative:

> Weight, grandeur, and urgency in writing are very largely produced, dear young friend, by the use of "visualizations" [*phantasiai*]. That at least is what I call them; others call them "image productions." For the term *phantasia* is applied in general to an idea which enters the mind from any source and engenders speech, but the word has now come to be used predominantly of passages where, inspired by strong emotion, you seem to see what you describe and bring it vividly before the eyes of your audience. That *phantasia* means one thing in oratory and another in poetry you will yourself detect, and also that the object of the poetical form of it is to enthral, and that of the prose form to present things vividly, though both indeed aim at the emotional and the excited. (Longinus, *Subl.* 15 [Fyfe, LCL])

Yet these two concepts did not merge until sometime at or before the start of late antiquity (third century CE), notably in the works of Philostratus.[19] From this point, *phantasia* (and its semantic offshoots) increasingly came to signify the creative form of imagination.

Although today imagination more often indicates the creative use of the mind, in the ancient world its main focus was on the expression of experiences, especially those hard to understand. It is possible to see this differentiation on a spectrum, where a writer can use imagination

---

in Ancient Rhetoric," in *Sight and the Ancient Senses*, ed. Michael Squire, Senses in Antiquity (Routledge, 2016), 208.

18. Anthony W. Bulloch, "The Future of a Hellenistic Illusion," in *Greek Literature in the Hellenistic Period*, vol. 7 of *Greek Literature*, ed. Gregory Nagy (Routledge, 2001), 218–19; and Rhet. Her. 4.39.51, respectively. On the multiplicative power of visual images to stir the imagination in ancient literature, see for example, Estes, "Tree of Life," 183–216.

19. Gerard Watson, "Discovering the Imagination: Platonists and Stoics on *phantasia*," in *The Question of "Eclecticism": Studies in Later Greek Philosophy*, ed. John M. Dillon and A. A. Long (University of California Press, 1988), 208–33.

to merely process and express a visual sensation (e.g., house with golden trim), process and embellish the visual sensation (e.g., a golden house), or turn said visible sensation into something entirely new (e.g., a house made of gold). An example of this differentiation is the example of "the angel and the alien." On the one hand, an angel is a credible creature in the minds of biblical authors. If a person believes they see an angel, there are visual (and other) sensations that accompany the encounter, but it is not possible for the person to understand or express the sense of the angelic (to oneself, or especially, to others) without using their imagination. What that person sees is indescribable, and they must come to terms with what they see in a way that is comprehensible to their accumulated understanding. On the other hand, an alien from outer space is a fictitious device in stories; for a person to imagine an alien in most cases requires a great deal of creative imagination. Yet, the writer still visualizes this alien using adapted visuals from their own world. It is not possible for someone to imagine an alien that is unimaginable (i.e., not based to any degree on visual sensations experienced by humans). In this chapter, our discussion will focus on the angel, not the alien. John's imagination creates a unique and powerful story of Jesus based upon what John believes he witnessed. That witness requires imagination to take his experiences (such as Jesus's walking on the water) and turn them into meaningful narrative events embedded within the larger story. This is because the norm for humans is to turn everything they experience into stories.[20]

Author versus Reader

The second differentiation is between *author-derived* and *reader-focused* imagination in the Fourth Gospel. This differentiation falls in a similar fashion to the two definitions offered by Richards above.[21] Richards's first definition covers the ability of a person to receive visual stimuli and to translate these into a meaningful image. When we apply this definition to the Gospel of John, imagination affects both the implied author and real reader: the implied author sees Jesus walk on the water and must trans-

---

20. Jerome Bruner, "The Narrative Construction of Reality," *Critical Inquiry* 18.1 (1991): 4.

21. For a similar take on this differentiation from a different field, see Christopher Comer and Ashley Taggart, *Brain, Mind, and the Narrative Imagination* (Bloomsbury Academic, 2021), 16.

late this visual sensation into a meaningful image in their mind before turning it into an event on papyrus; the real reader reads of Jesus walking on the water and must translate these words into a meaningful image in their mind's eye.[22] For imagination, understanding is only part of the process; the receiver must be able to see what they experienced/read in order to imagine. Within this first definition, there are two receivers; however, the reception by the implied author is more significant because the author purports to convey actual images into meaningful text that makes believable truth claims.[23]

We can also apply Richards's second definition to both implied author and real reader. When the implied author writes his story of Jesus, it is a creative output meant to persuade hearers and readers that Jesus is the Messiah and that they may have eternal life (John 20:31). Readers, both implied and real, engage with this story through their imagination; the more rhetorical and creative the implied author is, the more the audience can engage with their minds and recommunicate these images to others. The symbols in the gospel are examples of intentional visuals supplied by the narrator for this very reason.[24] Ultimately, the implied author's goal is to engage the audience dialogically with the Johannine Jesus.[25] The author accomplishes this primarily by means of rhetorical hooks that snare the imagination—and emotions—of the gospel's readers.[26] Therefore, by this second definition, there are two creatives; however, the reception of cre-

---

22. Characters within the narrative, who form groups of internal audiences, must do the same also. When the Johannine Jesus asks the long-suffering invalid, "Do you want to become healthy?" (John 5:6), he is asking the man to imagine a possibility that the man cannot—that he could become well simply by Jesus making him well. Instead, he misses the point of Jesus's question and focuses on getting into the pool (John 5:7).

23. Cf. Susanne Luther, "The Authentication of the Past: Narrative Representation of History in the Gospel of John," *JSNT* 43 (2020): 68.

24. Dorothy Lee, *Flesh and Glory: Symbol, Gender, and Theology in the Gospel of John* (Herder & Herder, 2002), 28.

25. Paul N. Anderson, "Bakhtin's Dialogism and the Corrective Rhetoric of the Johannine Misunderstanding Dialogue: Exposing Seven Crises in the Johannine Situation," in *Bakhtin and Genre Theory in Biblical Studies*, ed. Roland Boer, SemeiaSt 63 (Society of Biblical Literature, 2007), 137, 142. For an example of how the narrator pulls the audience in, see the works of Tom Thatcher and Paul Anderson, plus my own, *The Questions of Jesus in John: Logic, Rhetoric, and Persuasive Discourse*, BibInt 115 (Brill, 2012).

26. Walter Reinsdorf, "How Is the Gospel True?" *SJT* 56 (2003): 343; and for example, see Douglas Estes, "Unasked Questions in the Gospel of John: Narrative,

ativity (the audience's experience of hearing/reading an imaginative text) by real readers is more significant because it defines how and with what skill the author conveyed the images visualized.[27]

Thus, for the purpose of this chapter, our focus is solely with the imagination of the implied author: What visual experiences did John have that created the images in his mind that were the basis for this text?[28] This is the reverse of most literary studies of the Fourth Gospel, since most studies evaluate the qualities of the text for the sake of the reader. (And in fact, studies on how John uses imagination to reach his audience would be worthwhile!) Moreover, it would be better for us to speak not of John's imagination (as a substantive), but of John's imagining (as an act or process), since "these relatively unconscious processes have been hidden from any direct examination and only glimpsed obliquely or inferred from their finished creative products," which, in this case, is the gospel.[29] Here, however, the question before us sits on the nebulous issue of how John perceived what he saw and turned those visualizations into a story about Jesus.

John, Imagining

It is not uncommon for stories to contain multiple temporalities. This is especially true of texts that claim to be based on actual events, as the Fourth Gospel does. Historiography, then, requires an awareness by the reader of at least two temporalities: The temporality in which the events take place and the temporality in which the narrator writes. Modern historiography often hides both the narrator and her temporality, feigning neutrality, but ancient historiographers held no such compunction. They

---

Rhetoric, and Hypothetical Discourse," in *Asking Questions in Biblical Texts*, ed. Archibald L. H. M. van Wieringen and Bart J. Koet, CBET 114 (Peeters, 2022), 229–45.

27. On the impact on the reader, see Sunny Kuan-Hui Wang, *Sense Perception and Testimony in the Gospel According to John*, WUNT 435 (Mohr Siebeck, 2017); Rainer Hirsch-Luipold, *Gott wahrnehmen: Die Sinne im Johannesevangelium (Ratio Religionis Studien IV)*, WUNT 374 (Mohr Siebeck, 2017), and passing mentions in the works of Robert Kysar.

28. As G. L. Phillips observes, "the imagination of the writer can be shown to be visual rather than aural." G. L. Phillips, "Faith and Vision in the Fourth Gospel," in *Studies in the Fourth Gospel*, ed. F. L. Cross (Mowbray, 1957), 83.

29. Stephen T. Asma, *The Evolution of Imagination* (University of Chicago Press, 2017), 5–6.

often made explicit their presence, creating texts with two or more *diegesis*, or stories, that exist on distinct levels of the greater narrative—most commonly one story framing, one story embedded.[30] The stories can represent much more than stories; they represent and point to possible narrative worlds that exist within the greater narrative. Readers may not be able to see much of these worlds, but upon exploration they do become aware that these worlds are much, much larger than the narrator of each lets on.

The Fourth Gospel contains two such possible worlds—the *witness world* and the *epic world*.[31] The witness world is the embedded world; it is the world in which Jesus walks on water (John 6:16–24), and there is presumably an unnamed and unnoticed disciple who is a witness to this world (John 19:35). This is also the world where most of the visualizations occur. The epic world is the framing world; it is the world in which a Beloved Disciple of Jesus speaks to the audience explicitly (John 4:9b) and uses hyperbole (and paradox) as a rhetorical flourish to convince the reader that Jesus's great works were essentially unlimited (John 21:25).[32] When these worlds collide, *metalepsis* occurs. Perhaps the most famous example of metalepsis in John's Gospel is when the narrator, after depicting Jesus telling some from within one of the antagonistic groups that inhabit the story that he could rebuild the temple in three days, then states that the disciples remembered his words after Jesus was raised from the dead (John 2:17). At the time, the disciples could remember no such thing; the narrator of the epic world is interfering in the witness world. In historiography, metalepsis is nothing unusual, and in fiction, it can be an important literary device. For both, the factor that holds these two worlds at bay is time—these worlds occur in different temporalities. Thus, there is a *temporal distance* between the witness world and the epic world, which creates a time when the epic world influences or shapes the witness world. In the witness world, the indexical now is one when Jesus

---

30. For the classic description, see Gérard Genette, *Narrative Discourse: An Essay in Method*, trans. Jane E. Lewin (Cornell University Press, 1980), 227–31.

31. Douglas Estes, "Time," in *How John Works: Storytelling in the Fourth Gospel*, ed. Douglas Estes and Ruth Sheridan, RBS 86 (SBL Press, 2016), 56; and for extended discussion, see Douglas Estes, *The Temporal Mechanics of the Fourth Gospel: A Theory of Hermeneutical Relativity in the Gospel of John*, BibInt 92 (Brill, 2008), 234–49.

32. On the paradox in John 21:25, see Douglas Estes, "Dualism or Paradox? A New 'Light' on the Gospel of John," *JTS* 71 (2020): 90–118.

is present on Earth and the Beloved Disciple is young(er); in the epic world, the indexical now is one when Jesus is ascended to the Father and the Beloved Disciple is old(er). It is in this realm, this limbo, that imagination must work, yet it works just over the cusp of the witness world, processing the visualizations that occurred in this world for expression now and later.[33] This is in contrast to memory, which works just inside the cusp of the epic world.[34] While both imagination and memory are constructive, imagination processes sensations into depictable images, and memory connects those images into story, with memory acting as a massive treasure room for the images experienced and processed over a lifetime (Augustine, *Conf.* 10.8).[35] Of course, the conventional view holds that if there is no memory, or memory is skipped, as in the case of fiction, then the imagination continues the process of connecting those images into story.[36] Yet there is overlap between imagination and memory in all narratives, fiction or not, as both are mimetic (Plato, *Soph.* 266d–267e).[37] Hayden White, reflecting his reading of Georg Hegel, comes to a similar conclusion through a slightly different (spatial) route, explaining that a historiographer's

---

33. Cf. Anders Schinkel, "Imagination as a Category of History: An Essay Concerning Koselleck's Concepts of *Erfahrungsraum* and *Erwartungshorizont*," *HT* 44 (2005): 48.

34. Paul Ricoeur notes "the problem posed by the entanglement of memory and imagination is as old as Western philosophy." See Paul Ricoeur, *Memory, History, Forgetting*, trans. Kathleen Blamey and David Pellauer (University of Chicago Press, 2004), 7.

35. Comer and Taggart, *Brain, Mind, and the Narrative Imagination*, 17; and Tory S. Anderson, "From Episodic Memory to Narrative in a Cognitive Architecture," in *Sixth Workshop on Computational Models of Narrative (CMN 2015)*, ed. Mark A. Finlayson et al., OASIcs 45 (Schloss Dagstuhl, 2015), 2–11. Felipe De Brigard observes there are four theories that explain how memory and imagination are different. Felipe De Brigard, *Memory and Remembering*, CE (Cambridge University Press, 2023), 2–3. Fine-tuning this distinction is beyond the scope of this brief chapter.

36. Arthur C. Danto, *Narration and Knowledge* (Columbia University Press, 1985), 67; cf. Frances A. Yates, *The Art of Memory* (Routledge & Kegan Paul, 1966), 3.

37. Didier Coste, *Narrative as Communication*, THL 64 (University of Minnesota Press, 1989), 324; and Ricoeur, *Memory, History, Forgetting*, 7. For a slightly different take, see Mark W. G. Stibbe, *John as Storyteller: Narrative Criticism and the Fourth Gospel*, SNTSMS 73 (Cambridge University Press, 1992), 52. See also Bo Pettersson, *How Literary Worlds Are Shaped: A Comparative Poetics of Literary Imagination*, Narratologia 54 (de Gruyter, 2016), 41.

imagination must strain in two directions simultaneously: *critically*, in such a way as to permit him to decide what can be left out of an account (though he cannot invent or add to the facts known); and *poetically*, in such a way as to depict, in its vitality and individuality, the medley of events as if they were present to the sight of the reader.[38]

Recent decades have produced strong scholarship on memory in biblical studies, but less so on imagination.[39] Although there is much more we could say about imagination, with this in mind, we turn now to two examples of John's use of imagination in his gospel.

Broad Imagination

The Fourth Gospel famously opens with a prologue (John 1:1–5) followed by an extension of the prologue (John 1:6–18), a vestibule followed by a foyer that welcomes the audience. The construction of the vestibule suggests that it is highly polished prose meant to introduce the audience to the narrative's foundational myth.[40] One of the features of the prologue is that it brings its audience to the topic of the story through *peristaseis*, a rhetorical device designed to answer the audience's immediate questions of when, where, who, in what way, by what means, what, and why for their reading of the story.[41] Upon entering the vestibule, the audience is struck

---

38. Hayden White, *Metahistory: The Historical Imagination in Nineteenth-Century Europe* (Johns Hopkins University Press, 1973), 91.

39. Among numerous examples, see Tom Thatcher, "Why John Wrote a Gospel: Memory and History in an Early Christian Community," in *Memory, Tradition, and Text: Uses of the Past in Early Christianity*, ed. Alan Kirk and Tom Thatcher, SemeiaSt 52 (Society of Biblical Literature, 2005), 79–97; and Jörg Frey, "The Gospel of John as a Narrative Memory of Jesus," in *Memory and Memories in Early Christianity*, ed. Simon Butticaz and Enrico Norelli, WUNT 398 (Mohr Siebeck, 2018), 261–84. Only a few recent scholars—Mark W. G. Stibbe, Adele Reinhartz, Jörg Frey, and James Charlesworth—make passing mention of the importance of authorial imagination for historiographical interpretation.

40. Here *myth* does not make any claims factual or fictional; myth is "a story that helps us make sense of the world." See Neville Morley, *Writing Ancient History* (Duckworth, 1999), 52; and also Paul Veyne, *Did the Greeks Believe in Their Myths? An Essay on the Constitutive Imagination*, trans. Paula Wissing (University of Chicago Press, 1988), 66.

41. Douglas Estes, "Rhetorical *Peristaseis* (Circumstances) in the Prologue of John," in *The Gospel of John as Genre Mosaic*, ed. Kasper Bro Larsen, SANt 3 (Vandenhoeck & Ruprecht, 2015), 191–207.

with a primordial vision that begins before the creation of the universe. The narrator offers a glimpse of the divine and a new telling of the creation story: At creation the Word already is and is with God but also is God; as creation begins, the Word produces everything that will be in creation and nothing that will not; and from creation, life comes from the Word and this life is a light to people that overcomes the darkness. Although the figurative and symbolic language evokes a sense of the visual, this telling of creation is completely abstract (in contrast to other versions, notably Gen 1:1–5, which also contains God, light, and darkness). What does John know about creation—what does he see—that permits him to write this opening myth?

There is no indication that the narrator has a divine vision that allows him to see creation. Circumstantial evidence suggests that the narrator would not hesitate to cite a visionary experience in support if such had occurred (e.g., Isa 6:1; Rev 4:1–2). It is possible that the Word, while dwelling among people, taught secrets of creation to the Beloved Disciple—but this seems uncharacteristic of John's version of Jesus (cf. John 18:20). Instead, Jesus merely explained who God was to his disciples (John 1:18). Seeing and hearing Jesus sparked the disciples' imagination enough to visualize the Word's role at creation—and this visual would not be of a general creation (primordial world) but of the Word becoming flesh, as his glory is the same glory as that of the Father (John 1:14).[42] This glory is not a glory achievable by humans, but a kind of glory that is unique to the Father.[43] This is the glory that the disciple meditates on, dreams about, and imagines as the basis for his depiction of creation.[44] The Word made flesh is the visual in his mind's eye.

The Beloved Disciple's interest is to tell the truth about Jesus, but in this story, truth does not mean "accurate knowledge" as much as it does "God's perspective." Thus, the creation account imagined is true if it

---

42. Cf. Barnabas Lindars, "The Fourth Gospel an Act of Contemplation," in Cross, *Studies*, 23.

43. Douglas Estes, "Isaiah's Glory in John's Gospel: Isaiah versus Caesar for John's Text-Immanent Reader," in *The Function of the Reader in the Formation and the Reception of the Book of Isaiah*, ed. Sehoon Jang and Archibald L. H. M. van Wieringen, SCCB 11 (Brill Schöningh, 2024), 285–302.

44. Thomas Aquinas emphasizes that no one "has seen God, that is, the divine essence, with the eye of the body or *of the imagination*" (emphasis mine). See Thomas Aquinas, *Commentary on the Gospel of John: Chapters 1–5*, trans. Fabian Larcher and James A. Weisheipl (Catholic University of America Press, 2010), 88.

reflects God's perspective on creation, even if the account remains highly abstract (and short on details). It may reflect truth more accurately to omit details, because no one can see the creation event and live (cf. John 1:18).[45] More significantly, the narrator's familiarity with the Hebraic creation story (Gen 1), combined with his experiences with the Word, allow the narrator to imagine creation as truth that he can pass on to his audience.[46] This, actually, is not unusual. Just as Mark's Gospel "calls the reader to imagine Jesus in light of the larger context of Isa 40, as the divine Warrior who comes to ransom God's people from the nations,"[47] so too does John call his reader to imagine the glory of Jesus in the light of creation.

There is another myth in the Fourth Gospel in which the narrator also relies on his faculty of imagination, albeit one that reaches into the future instead of into the past. This is the final scene of the gospel, when the Beloved Disciple hears Jesus's prophecy of Peter's life (John 21:18–23). Similar to the prologue, the narrator cannot see Peter's future just as he could not see creation; he can only see the people involved (the Word; Peter) and understand the events in a general way (God created the world; Peter will be martyred for his faith). This still allows the disciple in the witness world to visualize and calculate the possibilities of Peter's future.[48] Different, however, between the two is the conflation of temporalities in John 21. The disciple in the epic world conflates his understanding of the prophecy with the understanding that the disciples possesses in the witness world. Thus, the imagination activated by Jesus's prophecy in the

---

45. According to Philostratus (*Vit. Apoll.* 6.19), Apollonius of Tyana debated Thespesion over how to best sculpt the divine; Thespesion held the highest expression was imitation (μῑμησις), but Apollonius ridiculed this view because the sculpting always included inferior (earthly) parts. Apollonius believed only imagination (φαντασία), filled with wisdom and artistic devotion, could capture the divine. See Watson, "Imagination," 58.

46. Marie-Laure Ryan, *A New Anatomy of Storyworlds: What Is, What If, As If*, TIN (Ohio State University Press, 2022), 31: "Myth is the voice of Truth itself, the foundation of a culture, a definitive representation that refuses to acknowledge the existence of any other version. Its truth is so secure that the narrators of myth never need to justify the source of their information." See also Wayne C. Booth, "Where Is the Authorial Audience in Biblical Narrative—and in Other 'Authoritative' Texts?," *Narrative* 4 (1996): 240–44.

47. Elizabeth E. Shively, *Apocalyptic Imagination in the Gospel of Mark: The Literary and Theological Role of Mark 3:22–30*, BZNW 189 (de Gruyter, 2012), 36.

48. Watson, "Imagination," 57.

mind of the disciple in the witness world is remembered and augmented with additional understanding in the epic world. The original visualization, one of many "relics" of the past that "remain inert matter until we breathe our reanimating life into them,"[49] meshes with later visualizations. The disciples' imagination and memory fuse into one powerful mimetic scene that he captures in the epilogue to his story.

Narrow Imagination

Whether acknowledged or not, narrators employ imagination throughout their narratives—not just in obvious micro-genres such as miracles stories or creation myths, but also in the construction of everyday scenes—scenes that do not seem to be imaginative (creative) at all. Unseen, imagination is still most critical in these scenes. Taking the story of Jesus walking on water again as an example, the audience assumes the Beloved Disciple is in the boat and sees Jesus walk through the waves. It is possible the narrator confirms the disciple saw and heard Jesus through the use of the historical present; either way, his overall claim of witness remains (John 19:35).[50] What is *impossible*, however, is for the disciple to see all that happens in an event, even if he is present and aware. Although the narrator writes with a certain omniscience, the audience knows the disciple in the witness world is cold, wet, tired, and afraid (John 6:19). The witness may take his eye off of Peter or another disciple for a minute or two and miss a key part of the story. The disciple may play little or no role in this event, even though he is still present, still a witness to this story about Jesus.[51] This raises the question of how witnesses experience events and what role imagination plays in stitching together the lost details of witness accounts.

There are a number of events recorded in the Fourth Gospel where it is not clear if and to what degree the Beloved Disciple is personally

---

49. Alan Robinson, *Narrating the Past: Historiography, Memory and the Contemporary Novel* (Palgrave Macmillan, 2011), 7.

50. For example, Raymond E. Brown, *The Gospel according to John I–XII*, AB 29 (Doubleday, 1966), 252.

51. Modern scholars maintain that the less detailed depiction in John is because the Evangelist bases his story on an earlier, more primitive version; see for example, Brown, *Gospel according to John*, 254. However, it is possible that the narrator limits the description because the disciple is too frightened to see the events that take place and does not bother to use his imagination to fill in the rest of the story.

present.[52] In some cases, it seems highly improbable (e.g., the council of the chief priests in John 11:47–53), while others seem possible but not probable (e.g., the discussion with Nicodemus at night in John 3:1–21). From the perspective of the narrator, this distinction probably matters little. The Beloved Disciple is a witness both as an eyewitness as well as an earwitness to the events of the story in real time (the indexical now of the witness world).[53] As we investigate what John knows by way of imagination, there exists the possibility that John uses his imagination to blend both eyewitness and earwitness experiences of the Beloved Disciple. Thinkers in the ancient world were aware of this by the time of the gospel. For example, Quintilian discusses a scenario where a rhetor must take up the argument of a citizen that they will represent (*Inst.* 6.2.26–31). In order to convince others that the citizen is speaking the truth, the orator must speak with passion and conviction. But how can the orator speak with these emotions, when they themselves did not see the event? Quintilian argues that, once the facts are known, the rhetor must now use their *phantasia* to place themselves in the event as accurately as possible. Once they experience the event, they can come to possess the emotions of the citizen needing their counsel.[54] The rhetor is an earwitness to the event and can speak truth more plainly than perhaps even the citizen eyewitness.

One event where it is unclear if the Beloved Disciple is present or absent is Jesus's conversation with the woman at Jacob's well near Sychar (John 4:5–26). In relaying the scene, the narrator firmly affixes his narratorial lens right on the conversation between Jesus and an anonymous woman, narrating as if the Beloved Disciple is transfixed on the scene. The narrator even narrates with numerous historical present tenses in order to enhance the vibrancy of the dialogue. The two characters speak against the backdrop of the

---

52. Other notable examples include the stylized introduction of John the Baptist (John 1:6–8, 15), the journey of the royal official (John 4:50–53), the conversation between the officers of the chief priest and the chief priests and the Pharisees (John 7:45–52), the nosy neighbors (John 9:8–12), the interrogation of the man healed from blindness and his parents (John 9:13–34), Martha and Mary's conversation (John 11:28–31), the interrogation of Jesus in the Praetorium (John 18:33–38), the intercession of Nicodemus and Joseph of Arimathea (John 19:38–42), and the revelation of the risen Jesus to Mary (John 20:11–18).

53. Cf. Booth, "Authorial Audience," 240–44.

54. Webb, "Sight and Insight," 209–11.

well. There are no external descriptions of the characters or setting.⁵⁵ Unlike most scenes in the gospel, there are also no groups positioned in the wings with comment or criticism that interrupts the protagonist. In fact, the narrator tells the audience that the disciples have left, implying that Jesus and the woman are alone (John 4:8). Could the Beloved Disciple somehow have remained behind? Tenses aside, it seems unlikely; the witness has departed (or remains fully hidden). This is the place for the implied author to lean in to the story with imagination—an imagination, visualized and mimetic, that sharpens the story in the way that Quintilian suggests. According to the narrator, the only prop on stage is the well—just Jesus, the woman, and the well—no waterpot, no stool, no rock. The audience is aware that the disciples saw the well before heading to the city to purchase food (John 4:8). The disciple knows Jesus, how he looks, how he talks; the disciple sees the woman when he returns with the rest of the disciples, all of whom are in amazement at whatever part of the conversation they catch between Jesus and the woman. As a consequence, the disciple can visualize the conversation even if he were not present; he can see the well, he can see Jesus, and he can see the woman. He can discern the gist of their words. The Beloved Disciple becomes an ideal orator, able to speak with passion and understanding about the event, even if he was an earwitness more than an eyewitness. His experience is "a fully rounded and embodied virtual experience, one which brings with it knowledge, both intellectual and sensory, of the experience."⁵⁶ For the implied author, "imagination plays an indispensable role in the interpretation of evidence, helping [him] to make connections, fill in gaps and build up a wider picture of the [event]."⁵⁷ Just as memory summarizes many actions into coherent, demarcated wholes, so too does imagination synthesize many existents from events into similarly coherent, demarcated wholes.

Conclusion

As evidenced by its reception, the Gospel of John is a meaningful story. To create a meaningful story requires imagination, not merely creativity

---

55. Ruben Zimmermann, "Figurenanalyse im Johannesevangelium: Ein Beitrag zu Sinn und Wahrheit narratologischer Exegese," *ZNW* 105 (2014): 39.

56. Webb, "Sight and Insight," 219; and Pettersson, *How Literary Worlds Are Shaped*, 40.

57. Morley, *Writing Ancient History*, 32; and cf. William H. Dray, *History as Reenactment: R.G. Collingwood's Idea of History* (Clarendon, 1995), 37.

but more so the ability to visualize existents and events in such a way as to communicate meaningfully to an audience.[58] The narrative turn in the study of biblical literature allows us to acknowledge the role of imagination without parsing truth claims, although as we have defended, historical "truths are already products of the imagination."[59] In this chapter, we briefly examined how the implied author of the Fourth Gospel applied the faculty of imagination to appreciate, express, and convey the experiences surrounding the life of Jesus to tell the author's story. We considered two uses of imagination, broad and narrow, that connect the original witnessed visuals with the enfleshed story. Although the implied author's knowledge of Jesus is critical, it is his imagination that makes the knowledge meaningful. Just as "apocalyptic discourse functions to fire the imagination of the oppressed by helping them imagine a world where spiritual forces are at work beyond what is visible to the human eye,"[60] so too do narratives of the life of Jesus function to fire the imagination of believers by helping them imagine a world where the Word has given people the right to become children of God (John 1:12). John's story of Jesus fires our imagination, but only because it first fired John's imagination.[61]

---

58. J. J. A. Mooij, *Fictional Realities: The Uses of Literary Imagination*, UPGCL 30 (Benjamins, 1993), 76; and also, Stibbe, *John as Storyteller*, 16.

59. Veyne, *Did the Greeks Believe in Their Myths*, xii; and also Brian Larsen, *Archetypes and the Fourth Gospel: Literature and Theology in Conversation* (T&T Clark, 2018), 57.

60. Shively, *Apocalyptic Imagination in the Gospel of Mark*, 260.

61. "For the specialists of ancient rhetoric, then, mental images, their verbal communication, and their impact on the audience were difficult to separate. The whole was conceived as a single process binding together speaker and audience in a shared process of imagining"; see Webb, "Sight and Insight," 219.

4
Tradition

Edward H. Gerber

Although it is widely agreed that the Fourth Gospel is the work of a highly skilled artist, questions remain about the final form of John's narrative. Specifically, how would (or could) an author like John manage to produce a final product as artfully structured and deployed as the one that lies before us? What compositional tools were available to him to conceive and produce the whole? More specifically, given that John had more memories about Jesus to tell than could be "written down" (John 20:30; 21:25), what sort of comprehensive master structure might have guided his narrative selections?

Doubtlessly because of the material texts that lay before us and the mass print and word-processing culture in which we are today situated, we tend to think about the media of ancient scriptural texts in explicitly physical and literary terms or according to what John Miles Foley calls a "textual ideology."[1] So, too, do we think about the nature of their production in authors' minds.[2] When it comes to trying to work backward, then, and ascertain what sort of structural building blocks might best account for frequently complex interwoven textual wholes, we tend to look for what we take to be sophisticated signs of literary interweaving and patterning: geographical movements, time indications, number pat-

---

1. See John Miles Foley, *Oral Tradition and the Internet: Pathways of the Mind* (University of Illinois Press, 2012), 117–25.
2. Physically, we think about texts as material objects in space that, by various forms of intertextuality, interact with one another. Literarily, we think about discrete authors—likely sitting at desks, paper before them, pens in hand—engaged in a solitary and dialectical process of thinking and then writing and then rewriting in order to confer meaning into a self-contained artifact.

terns, cycles, repetitions, chiasmus, and the like.³ Overwhelmingly, this has been the method de rigueur within Johannine studies, a method that has led to a vast proliferation of proposals about John's master structure.⁴ As a result, nothing approaching a consensus has been reached, except at the most general levels of analysis.⁵ While not in any way wanting to dismiss John's literary ability or the likelihood that many of the structures hitherto proposed are indeed observable,⁶ the current chapter will argue that a central—if not the central—tool in John's narrative epistemological toolbox, and one that may well point to the most plausible master structure, was tradition. More specifically, what John knew as an orally situated composer within a rich Jewish tradition of storytelling when premeditating the broad contours of his narrative about Jesus was the "oral-traditional form."⁷

John's Syncretic Poetics

Biblical scholars are becoming increasingly aware that the media environment (or "marketplace") within which scriptural authors composed was complex.⁸ Neither exclusively literary/textual or oral/aural, compositions were conceived and produced in bifid (oral *and* written) media

---

3. The English word *text*, comes from the Latin *textus*, meaning "fabric" or "structure." In the nature of the case, we tend to think of texts as "something that has been woven … the tangible product of craftmanship" (Foley, *Oral Tradition and the Internet*, 119).

4. See the survey in George Mlakuzhyil, *The Christocentric Literary Structure of the Fourth Gospel*, AnBib 117 (Editrice Pontificio Istituto Biblico, 1987).

5. See Mlakuzhyil, *Christocentric Literary Structure*, 137–68.

6. On the concept of interwoven or combined structures see Thomas L. Brodie, *The Gospel according to John: A Literary and Theological Commentary* (Oxford University Press, 1997), 23; and Mlakuzhyil, *Christocentric Literary Structure of the Fourth Gospel*, 87.

7. For a much fuller discussion and substantiation of what will be discussed in this chapter, please see Edward H. Gerber, *The Scriptural Tale in the Fourth Gospel: With Particular Reference to the Prologue and a Syncretic (Oral and Written) Poetics*, BibInt 147 (Brill, 2016), especially chapters 3–5 and 7.

8. On media "marketplaces" or "agoras," see Foley, *Oral Tradition and the Internet*, 40–41, who distinguishes between three media "technologies" or "marketplaces" that fuel the exchange of ideas: t-agora (textual marketplace), o-agora (oral marketplace), and e-agora (electronic marketplace).

environments (or "biospheres").[9] Written texts and oral compositions/performances coexisted in a variety of forms.[10] The hermeneutical implications of this blended media marketplace are important to highlight—especially since, in John's context, as in most pre-Gutenberg antiquity, the spoken word, especially among the peasantry, was predominant.[11]

One might initially think that an awareness of the Fourth Gospel's hybrid media nature and the overwhelmingly oral/aural environment in which he was situated merely suggests that interpreters must now lament that we "only have a text" and ruefully acknowledge that layers of meaning that once resonated through orators in live performance arenas have gone silent with the performative moment.[12] This is, however, to miss the critical discovery of folkloric and ethnopoetic scholars examining verbal art within highly oral/aural cultures. Namely, *although literary and oral poetics may overlap, their compositional poetics are distinct.*[13] In particular, the building blocks that an orally situated author may be predisposed to use will be different than an author steeped in literacy.[14] Naturally

---

9. John Miles Foley, "Words in Tradition, Words in Text: A Response," *Semeia* 65 (1994): 171.

10. To be sure, the mutual interactions and infusions among oral and written texts could be many and complex. For of a wide range of possibilities, see Vernon K. Robbins, "Progymnastic Rhetorical Composition and Pre-Gospel Traditions: A New Approach," in *The Synoptic Gospels: Source Criticism and the New Literary Criticism*, ed. Camille Focant, BETL 110 (Leuven University Press, 1993), 111–48.

11. Cf. William V. Harris, *Ancient Literacy* (Harvard University Press, 1989); Werner Kelber, *The Oral and the Written Gospel: The Hermeneutics of Speaking and Writing in the Synoptic Tradition, Mark, Paul, and Q* (Indiana University Press), 1997; Catherine Hezser, *Jewish Literacy in Roman Palestine*, TSAJ 81 (Mohr Siebeck, 2001). "Even today, barely half of the world population masters reading and writing beyond the basics"; see Mihailo Antovic and Cristóbal Pagán Cánovas, *Oral Poetics and Cognitive Science*, Linguae & Litterae 56 (de Gruyter, 2016), 2.

12. As Foley expresses: "We lose vocal features such as intonation ... visual signals such as gesture and facial expression ... musical and rhythmical dimensions of performance. Critically, we lose ... the network of potentials out of which any single performance emerges. Just as importantly, we lose the contribution of the audience" (Foley, *Oral Tradition and the Internet*, 122).

13. "Poetics," as Adele Berlin defines it, "is not an interpretive effort—it does not aim to elicit meaning from a text. Rather it aims to find the building blocks of literature and the rules by which they are assembled." See Adele Berlin, *Poetics and Interpretation of Biblical Narrative*, BLS (Almond, 1983), 15.

14. This appears to be attested by early readers of the Fourth Gospel like Origen who could detect that the Fourth Gospel was not composed according to literate

then, if interpreters are to discover the building blocks by which textual artefacts like John were composed, their method of exploration must be calibrated to this hermeneutical complexity. A "syncretic poetics," wherein the nuances of *both* oral and written dynamics are appreciated, must be recognized.[15]

It is not unreasonable to suggest that if John's context was indeed primarily oral/aural, then scholars should give a priority of investigation to oral poetic influences. A brief synopsis of the pioneering work of Milman Parry, Albert Lord, and John Miles Foley will establish why this is so.

The Oral-Traditional Form

Taking it as axiomatic that orally situated authors of all time periods will share the same compositional needs, Harvard professor Milman Parry (1902–1935), along with his protégé Albert Lord, set out in the early 1930s to study the compositional methods of illiterate Yugoslavian storytellers—consummate "singers" of traditional tales. The goal of their field work was to be able to ascertain "how the form of the [Yugoslavian singers'] songs hangs upon their having to learn and practice their art without reading and writing" and then to apply this new understanding backwards to uncover Homer's own compositional method.[16] Key among Parry and Lord's discoveries was that storytellers' ability to learn, recite, and even improvise on traditional tales was irreducibly related to traditional forms, or "integers," as Foley coins them. Specifically, these oral tales were comprised of: (1) formulaic language, (2) themes ("type scenes"), and (3) story

---

standards of the day. As Richard Horsley observed, fifty years after the gospels were written, "Origen proudly admitted that the apostles possessed 'no power of speaking or of giving an ordered narrative by the standards of Greek dialectical or rhetorical arts' (*Cels.* 1.62)" and "had to agree with Celsus that the evangelists were, as the Jerusalem 'rulers, elders, and scribes' in the second volume of Luke's 'orderly account' said about Peter and John, 'illiterate and ignorant' (*agrammatoi kai idiotai* Acts 4:13)." See Richard A. Horsley, "Oral and Written Aspects of the Emergence of the Gospel of Mark as Scripture," *Oral Tradition* 25 (2010): 94. In all probability, they were assessed this way because, while their poetic techniques did not coincide with Greek literary standards, they betrayed the less arabesque—but no less artful—contours of oral traditional art forms.

15. The phrase *syncretic poetics* is Foley's. See John Miles Foley, *The Singer of Tales in Performance*, Voices in Performance and Text (Indiana University Press, 1995), 207.

16. Albert B. Lord, *The Singer of Tales* (Harvard University Press, 1960), 3.

patterns ("tale types"). Akin to the way people tend to learn music, Yugoslavian bards would learn the stories not so much by memorization as by the absorption of the traditional forms through repeated listening.

Akin to a Russian matryoshka doll, Parry and Lord also came to see that the Yugoslavians' oral art was, as we might summarize it, both concatenated and hierarchical. It was concatenated insofar as the story patterns were built up by the interlocking of traditional themes/type scenes, even as the themes/type scenes were themselves built up by the interlocking of formulaic language. In this way, just as the largest shell of a nesting doll will be built up (and indeed become a proper matryoshka doll) by being stuffed full of smaller figures, so in Yugoslavian storytelling are the story patterns themselves populated by the smaller formulaic integers. Traditional lore would thus be constituted of content held together by what Lord calls a "tension of [traditional/familiar] essences," or "habitual associations."[17]

This is not to say that all integers shared the same traditional value or would need to be used in a stuffy, restrictive, or verbatim way. As Parry and Lord also discovered, when it came to the traditional repertoire, the story patterns or tale types stood at the top of the hierarchy of conservational importance. A singer might, therefore—and, in fact, once accomplished was *expected to*—improvise on formulaic language and type scenes without a fastidious concern for verbal equivalences,[18] but the story pattern itself would remain stable across time. The singer could artfully rearrange thematic components of the story pattern and dischronologize events, but the story pattern itself—the core thematic components of plot—would be reproduced.[19] In this way, besides providing storytellers with an indispensable mnemonic, singers would conserve the tradition even while meeting the rhetorical needs of listening audiences.[20]

---

17. Lord, *Singer of Tales*, 97–8.

18. Lord, *Singer of Tales*, 36–37. It is precisely the improvisational elements and jazz-like dynamic, Lord insists, that made some singers better than others.

19. Lord, *Singer of Tales*, 120–23. See also John Miles Foley, *Traditional Oral Epic: The Odyssey, Beowulf, and the Serbo-Croatian Return Song* (University of California Press, 1990), 363.

20. In brief, audiences generally require variation within sameness for both comprehension and delight. Too much of the unfamiliar or complex unduly taxes audiences and stymies attentional focus; too much sameness likewise fails to enthrall. Freedom within familiar form, however, tends to be most captivating. See Patrick Colm Hogan, *Cognitive Science, Literature, and the Arts: A Guide for Humanists* (Routledge, 2003), 7–28.

In terms of the method of composition, Parry and Lord concluded that Yugoslavian singers began with the "stable skeleton of narrative" and built up their compositions by the creative addition of type scenes and formulaic language.[21] Following their ground-breaking work, Foley and other scholars have determined that the same is true for other living oral traditional cultures.[22] To highlight the most important discovery: *Story pattern is king in the compositional poetics of oral-traditional societies.* The story pattern marks the well-known and premeditated master structure of a performance; it is conscientiously conserved.[23]

The reason this discovery is important for understanding what the writer of John knows is because there is good evidence that John tells his story of Jesus in accord with a traditional story pattern. This should not surprise us. Writers like John were *inclined* to use traditional story patterns in the composition of new narratives, whether these narratives were fictional or historical. To be sure, in an atmosphere where authors were largely unlettered or writing materials were expensive or rare, a preformed story pattern would be helpful (and perhaps even necessary) in the act of composition and memory retention.[24] The project of telling a new *true* story, too—which is to say, a piece of history—would also incline the orally situated composer to tell the story with reference to pre-formed narrative patterns since, by necessity, a story told is a story emplotted, and

---

21. Lord, *Singer of Tales*, 123.

22. See, for example, John Miles Foley, "Analogues: Modern Oral Epics," in *A Companion to Ancient Epic*, ed. John Miles Foley, BCAW (Blackwell, 2005), 204.

23. With reference to African, Finnish and other epic works, Robert Kellogg notes that "every performance of a traditional narrative takes place in a vast context of story and must be understood so by the critic, to exactly the same extent that the opposite assumption must be made about 'high' narrative art." Quoted in John Miles Foley, *Immanent Art: From Structure to Meaning in Traditional Oral Epic* (Indiana University Press, 1991), 11.

24. This is true because while a composer working her thoughts out on paper may painstakingly build her composition up into a coherent whole by pausing and pondering and drafting and redrafting in the act of writing, a composer in a predominately oral environment will not have the benefit of such coherence-building compositional techniques. Instead, unless stunningly gifted, a composer whose medium of communication is the performative moment must conceptualize the whole *prior* to performance and be able easily to recall it *within* performance. A preformed narrative skeleton that provides a prepackaged and highly memorable movement of thought would thus be a most natural and handy resource for an orally situated composer setting out to tell a new tale.

plot structures are more learned than invented. A composer seeking to tell a new story about an historical event, then, will be predisposed by preexisting cognitive structures to package the telling of the event according to already known plot structures.[25]

Perhaps the greatest reason, however, that an orally situated composer like the Fourth Evangelist might be inclined to use a traditional story pattern for the composition of a new narrative is because, in addition to being compositionally and mnemonically useful, all formulaic integers, including story patterns, provide an immanent context—a referentially preloaded landscape—for generating meaning. Oral composers could, for ideological and rhetorical purposes, use a story pattern in new works, therefore, to spark worlds of shared meaning and thought in listeners' minds with the utmost of verbal economy: worlds of thought and meaning that could then be either confirmed, updated, or subverted. Foley labels this power of traditional integers *pars pro toto* speech or "metonymic referencing."[26]

A metonym represents a part that stands in for the whole. Foley's central insight is that, unlike a written text, which is usually thought to reference another (and usually singular and specific) written text by means of "quotation," "allusion," or "echo," an oral traditional integer refers not simply to one text or performance but metonymically to every instance in the tradition in which the integer has been used. The part—the integer— stands in for the whole—its multiform use in the tradition. The meaning of the integer, therefore, is inherent and aggregative because its meaning has been built up by repeated usage within the tradition. When it comes to evoking a tale type, the familiar tale type, once evoked, will automatically provide listeners with a filter or template for catching more specific nuances of referential meaning: "Story patterns can also enable reception by providing a large-scale 'map' to complement the finer, inset details of formulas and themes."[27]

---

25. See, e.g., the discussions in Paul Connerton, *How Societies Remember*, Themes in the Social Sciences (Cambridge University Press, 1989); Hayden White, "The Historical Text as Literary Artifact," in *The History and Narrative Reader*, ed. Geoffrey Roberts (Routledge, 2001), 223; Alan Kirk and Tom Thatcher, "Jesus Tradition as Social Memory," in *Memory, Tradition, and Text: Uses of the Past in Early Christianity*, ed. Alan Kirk and Tom Thatcher, SemeiaSt 52 (Society of Biblical Literature, 2005), 37.

26. "Pars pro toto logic extends from the macrostructure of the tale as a whole to the microstructure of its smallest parts" (Foley, *Immanent Art*, 13).

27. Foley, *Singer of Tales*, 92. To suggest a scriptural example, the often repeated and wide-ranging Hebrew phrase וידעתם כי אני יהוה—"and you will know that I am

For an author such as John, then, situated in an oral-traditional context where scriptural language, figures, and stories were constitutive of identity and, therefore, by all appearances very important and well known, utilizing an oral-traditional story pattern, and packing it with a host of meaning-generating referential integers, could indeed be most useful: compositionally, performatively, ideologically, and pedagogically. By this subtle yet powerful form of pars pro toto referentiality, John could systematically unveil just how it is that Scripture points to Jesus and how Jesus fulfils Scripture, even while teaching wider audiences the ABCs of scriptural knowledge.[28] Another factor that may have motivated John is that a large scale and resonant framework would function as a potent community-building tool.[29]

The Oral-Traditional Form in Biblical Literature

There is broad tradition of rehearsing and reimplementing the basic figures and movements of Israel's story within Second Temple Judaism. A great number of "rewritten Bible" texts and "summaries of Israel's story" attest to this in a most basic way.[30] Popular movements among the (largely

---

the LORD"—appears to be a traditional integer that had the power to evoke the idea that the Lord is and will be revealed in and through acts of judgment. Cf. Exod 6:7; 7:5, 17; 10:2; 14:4, 18; 16:12; Deut 29:6; 1 Kgs 20:13, 28; Isa 45:3; 49:23; Ezek 6:7, 10, 13–14; 7:4, 27; 11:10, 12; 12:15–16, 20; 13:14, 21, 23; 14:8; 15:7; 16:62; 20:20, 26, 38, 42, 44; 22:16; 24:27; 25:5, 7, 11, 17; 26:6; 28:22–23, 26; 29:6, 9, 21; 30:8, 19, 25–26; 32:15; 33:29; 34:27; 35:4, 9, 15; 36:11, 23, 38; 37:6, 13; 38:23; 39:6, 22, 28. Were this evocative phrase used in the midst of a well-known story pattern that included Israel's exodus from Egypt as one of its major moves, the phrase may properly be heard to evoke the more specific instance of God's self-revealing showdown with Pharaoh; for example, "And the Egyptians will know that I am the LORD when I stretch out my hand against Egypt and bring the Israelites out of it" (Exod 7:5; cf. 6:7; 10:2).

28. See, e.g., John 2:22; 5:39; 7:38, 42; 17:12; 19:24, 28, 36–37; 20:9.

29. For further discussion, see Catherine Quick, "The Metonym: Rhetoric and Oral Tradition at the Crossroads," *Oral Tradition* 26 (2011): 597–600.

30. On rewritten Bible texts, see Sidnie W. Crawford, *Rewriting Scripture in Second Temple Times* (Eerdmans, 2008); George J. Brooke, "Biblical Interpretation in the Qumran Scrolls and in the New Testament," in *The Dead Sea Scrolls: Fifty Years after Their Discovery*, ed. Lawrence H. Schiffman, Emanuel Tov, and James C. VanderKam (Israel Exploration Society 2000); and Andrew Chester, "Citing the Old Testament," in *It Is Written: Scripture Citing Scripture: Essays in Honor of Barnabas Lindars*, ed. D. A. Carson and H.G.M. Williamson (Cambridge University Press, 1988). On summaries

illiterate) peasantry around the time of Jesus also attest to a knowledge and symbolic reappropriation of traditional figures and stories of Scripture in shorthand but referentially explosive ways. As Richard Horsley has shown, collective memories of key figures such as Moses, Joshua, and David, and actions such as "crossing the Jordan" and "going into the desert" regularly animated and gave tacit interpretation to these popular movements.[31] Gospel scholars are increasingly aware of the imprint of older narratives operating as frameworks for newer works at both micro and macro levels.[32]

---

of Israel's story, see Jason B. Hood, "Matthew 1:1-17 as a Summary of Israel's Story: The Messiah, His Brothers, and the Nations" (PhD diss., University of Aberdeen, 2009), 67-68. For examples of summaries of Israel's story, see Exod 15; Lev 26:4-13; Deut 26:5a-10a; 29; 32; Josh 23:2-4; 24; Pss 78, 105, 106 [104–106] 135, 136 [135–137]; 1 Sam 12:7-15; 1 Kgs 8; 1 Chr 1–9; 16:8-36; Ezra 5:11-17 (1 Esd 6:13-20); Neh 9 (2 Esd 19); Isa 5:1-7; Jer 2:2-9; Ezek 16, 20, 23; Dan 9:1-27; Hab 3:1-16; Jdt 5; Wis 10–19; Sir 44–50; 1 Macc 2:50-61 [2:49-68]; 3 Macc 2:1-20, 6:1-15; 4 Ezra 3–6; 7.106–111; 4 Macc 16:18–23, 18:11-19; 2 Bar 53–74; 1 En. 85–90 (Animal Apocalypse); Apoc. Ab. 23–31; Ascen. Isa. 3.13–4.18 (= Testament of Hezekiah); As. Mos. 1–10; LAB 32.1-17; Song of Songs Targum; T. Mos 1–10; T. Lev 14–18; 1QS I, 21–II, 6; 4Q504 1-2, IV, 5-14; CD, "The Exhortation"; Matt 1:1-17; Mark 12:1-12, Matt 21:33-46 and Luke 20:9-18; Acts 7; Acts 13:16-41 (or 13:16-48); Rom 9–11; Heb 11:1–12:2; Rev 12:1-12 [or 12:1-9, 13-17]; Philo, *Praem.* 11–56; Philo, *Virt.* 199-227; Philo, *Hypoth.* 8.5.11–6.8 (= Eusebius, *Praep. ev.* 8.5.11–6.8); Josephus, *B.J.* 5.8.4, 5.9.4, 6.2.1.

31. Whether by approaching enemies as new Philistines, entering into the desert, symbolically crossing the Jordan, or ascending Mount Olives to wait for the collapse of the walls of Jerusalem, prospective prophets and messianic figures would stylize themselves by symbolically resonant actions as new David's, Moses's, and Joshua's. See Richard A. Horsley, *Bandits, Prophets, and Messiahs: Popular Movements at the Time of Jesus* (Harper San Francisco, 1985); Horsley, "A Prophet Like Moses and Elijah: Popular Memory and Cultural Patterns in Mark," in *Performing the Gospel: Orality, Memory, and Mark: Essays Dedicated to Werner Kelber*, ed. Richard A. Horsley, Jonathan A. Draper, and John Miles Foley (Fortress, 2006), 180–83; and Horsley, "Oral and Written Aspects," 99–101.

32. See, for example, Kenneth Bailey, *Jacob and the Prodigal Son: How Jesus Retold Israel's Story* (InterVarsity Press, 2003); Rikki E. Watts, *Isaiah's New Exodus in Mark*, BSL (Baker Academic, 1997); Thomas L. Brodie, "Luke the Literary Interpreter: Luke-Acts as a Systematic Rewriting and Updating of the Elijah-Elisha Narrative" (PhD diss., University of St. Thomas, 1981); Brodie, *The Crucial Bridge: The Elisha-Elisha Narrative as an Interpretive Synthesis of Genesis-Kings and a Literary Model for the Gospels* (Liturgical, 2000); Joel Kennedy, *The Recapitulation of Israel: Use of Israel's History in Matthew 1:1–4:11*, WUNT 257 (Mohr Siebeck, 2008); Leroy A. Huizinga, "The Matthean Jesus and Isaac," in *Reading the Bible Intertextually*, ed. Richard B. Hays, Stefan Alkier, and Leroy A. Huizenga (Baylor University Press, 2009); Huizinga, *The*

This suggests that however much the Fourth Gospel is a "maverick gospel,"[33] if the Fourth Evangelist chose to structure his story of Jesus according to a pre-formed scriptural story, it was not *this* decision that made him a maverick. Instead, it was the choice to underpin his gospel with a story pattern that was theologically distinctive and more comprehensive than the others—beginning "in the beginning" and then moving through the major stages of Israel's (hi)story prior to ending at the telic end, a new beginning—that truly made John a maverick among the gospel writers.

Story Patterning in the Fourth Gospel

The Prologue

The first clue that the Fourth Evangelist may indeed have patterned his gospel after a traditional (scriptural) story pattern is discernible in the prologue (vv. 1–18). Whatever its prehistory or diachronic relationship to the rest of the gospel, the prologue has been deemed a "gateway," "overture," "preamble," and "preview" to what follows; the prologue *tells* what the rest of gospel more expansively *shows*.[34] This is significant when considering a possible oral traditional story patterning of the gospel given indications a highly condensed traditional story pattern in the prologue.

In terms of this traditional story pattern, a host of traditional stories revolving around the primordial Adam and/or people of Israel (or figures therein) portray the fate of the world (God's temple) being wrapped up

---

New Isaac: Tradition and Intertextuality in the Gospel of Matthew, NovTSup 131 (Brill, 2009). Stories about Isaac, Jacob, Moses, the Exodus from Egypt, the Elijah-Elisha narratives, along with the story of Israel as a whole have all credibly been seen to underpin stories told by or about Jesus.

33. See Robert Kysar, *John: The Maverick Gospel* (John Knox, 1993).

34. For the historical relationship with the rest of the gospel, see the discussion in Rudolf Schnackenburg, *The Gospel according to John*, trans. Kevin Smyth (Herder & Herder, 1968), 1:221–23. For different characterizations, see, e.g., Edwyn Clement Hoskyns, *The Fourth Gospel*, rev. ed. (Faber & Faber, 1950), 137; Schnackenburg, *Gospel according to John*, 1:221–23; Lesslie Newbigin, *The Light Has Come: An Exposition of the Fourth Gospel* (Eerdmans, 1982), 1; Elizabeth Harris, *Prologue and Gospel: The Theology of the Fourth Evangelist*, JSNTSup 107 (Sheffield Academic, 1994), 189–95; and Morna D. Hooker, *Beginnings: Keys that Open the Gospels* (Trinity Press International, 1997), 83.

with the functioning of human beings.[35] Protology and eschatology are inextricably linked. In particular, the goal of history is for God's world to be filled with the glory of the Lord as the waters cover the sea. This will be mediated by fully alive human beings: image-bearers who, filled with the life-giving Spirit/presence/glory of God will themselves be glorious and light-filled; as they are fruitful and multiply, the glory of God in them will progressively fill the earth (his cosmic temple). These traditional stories continue by clarifying that this can only happen if Adam/Israel obey the word (law, wisdom, commands) of God. Disobedience leads to a loss of glory/light in them (i.e., "darkness") and, by implication, the same loss for the micro and/or macro-cosmic temple. God's designs for history are not consummated.[36] Interacting with this story pattern, several texts articulate the hope for a renewed glorious humanity or human figure to arise who will not disobey the Word/love the darkness and thus, as an enduring glorious/Spirit-filled figure, will bring God's project to completion.[37]

This background is intriguing when one becomes aware that the prologue of the Fourth Gospel can be understood as a retelling of the history of the Logos, pivoting on the Logos becoming flesh.[38] The history of

---

35. To summarize a vastly more in-depth treatment of the subject, see Gerber, *Scriptural Tale in the Fourth Gospel*, especially 117–59.

36. Many of the stories rehearse this sad end: Adam disobeys, his glory departs, and he and the world are plummeted into darkness. Israel disobeys, the glory departs the temple, and darkness covers the land. For texts rehearsing the fall (or better, divestiture) of Adam in this regard, cf. 2 En. 30.14; T. Levi 18.10; 19.1; Apoc. Adam, 1.5, 12; 1QS III, 13–24; Philo, *Leg.* 3.1; and cf. Philo, *Leg.* 3.54.

37. Cf. Isa 40–66; Ezek39:25–48:35; Sir 24, 50; Joseph and Aseneth; 1 En. 85–90. On the Dead Sea Scrolls, see also George J. Brooke, "Miqdash Adam, Eden, and the Qumran Community," in *Gemeinde ohne Tempel/Community without Temple: Zur Substituierung und Transformation des Jerusalemer Tempels und seines Kults im Alten Testament, antiken Judentum und frühen Christentum*, ed. Beate Ego, Armin Lange, and Peter Pilhofer, WUNT 118 (Mohr Siebeck, 1999), 285–301; Brooke, "The Ten Temples in the Dead Sea Scrolls," in *Temple and Worship in Biblical Israel: Proceedings of the Oxford Old Testament Seminar*, ed. John Day, LHBOTS 422 (T&T Clark, 2007), 417–34.

38. C. H. Dodd, *The Interpretation of the Fourth Gospel* (Cambridge University Press, 1953), 263–85; Daniel Boyarin, "The Gospel of the Memra: Jewish Binitarianism and the Prologue to John," *HTR* 94 (2001): 243–84; Boyarin, "*Logos*, A Jewish Word: John's Prologue as Midrash," in *The Jewish Annotated New Testament*, ed. Amy-Jill Levine and Marc Zvi Brettler (Oxford University Press, 2011); Martin Hengel, "The Prologue of the Gospel of John as the Gateway to Christological Truth," in *The Gospel*

the Logos *asarkos* ("un-fleshed") is retold in verses 1–13, and the history of the Logos *ensarkos* ("enfleshed") is retold in verses 14–18. It is even more intriguing to notice that this history of the Logos is retold with what appears to be the same habitual associations/tension of essences manifest in the stories about Adam and Israel. John emphasizes the images and ideas of light and glory and darkness as they relate to humanity's creation (vv. 1–4) and repeated rejection of the Logos (vv. 5, 10, 11).[39] The Logos then becomes flesh filled with a glory that resembles the glory and nature of the Father: the enfleshed Logos is portrayed, in other words, as a true image-bearer, a glory-filled tabernacle (σκηνόω, v. 14),[40] who *does* obey the grace-filled law of Moses (vv. 16–17). In the Logos, then—the divinely embodied protological man situated in this immanent context—John leads us to anticipate that God's purposes for cosmic history that are dependent on the right functioning of a glory-filled flesh are at long last about to be fulfilled. The Spirit of God will be unleashed, glory/light will return to humanity, and thus, ultimately, the cosmic temple—God's heavens and earth—will be restored. Creation will be regained. Put otherwise, Jesus will at long last fulfill the vocations of Adam and Israel.

Body of the Gospel

The body of the gospel picks up what the prologue anticipates: Jesus, as the embodiment of a truly light-filled/glorious humanity (i.e., new Adam/Israel), will reenact in his own person the broad sweep of the primary history (Genesis–Kings) as interpreted and retold in Jewish tradition thereby living out the vocation of Adam/Israel and, as John 20 will evoke, fulfilling eschatological hopes.

A review of extant texts where the story of Scripture is told in whole or part reveal a consistent framework consisting of seven basic movements:

---

of John and Christian Theology, ed. Richard Bauckham and Carl Mosser (Eerdmans, 2008). Cf. also, Hartmut Gese, *Zur biblischen Theologie: Alttestamentliche Vorträge*, BEvT 78 (Kaiser, 1977); and Herman C. Waetjen, *The Gospel of the Beloved Disciple: A Work in Two Editions* (T&T Clark, 2005), 61–87.

39. This rejection of the Logos also appears to be narratively expansive, focalizing on humanity/Adam, first (v. 5); the "world" after Adam, second (v. 10); and then the Logos' "own," meaning Israel, third (v. 11).

40. For the cultic overtones of the Greek, see Jan-Adolph Bühner, "σκηνόω," *EDNT*, 3:252.

creation and fall; establishment of an elect people; rescue out of Egypt; provided for in/led through the wilderness; settlement through conquest; exile; return/restoration. Packaged even more tightly, these seven movements could be conceptualized as fitting within three distinct epochs or periods of time: the time of (1) *beginnings* (creation/fall and establishment of God's chosen people; vis-à-vis Genesis); (2) *the campaign of Moses* (which led Israel out of Egypt, through the wilderness, and to the threshold of the promised land by the Jordan; vis-à-vis the Pentateuch); and (3) *the campaign(s) of Joshua/David* (including conquest/settlement and exile; vis-à-vis Deut–Kings). Similarly, John consists of three overarching units including a front portion (1:1–51), a middle portion (2–11), and an end portion (12–20).[41] These sections are joined by hinge or Janus passages (e.g., 2:1–11; 12:1–50)—a feature of oral traditional poetics.[42] There is also a deliberate number patterning binding these sections together—another staple feature within oral traditional poetics.[43] What is significant about this is that each of these sections correspond to the three epochs within Israel's story. They also recapitulate the seven basic narrative moves along with associated language and type scenes that populate and make up the broadest skeleton of the story of Israel. Since space does not permit a full exposition of this claim, we will demonstrate this thesis with two examples. Specifically, we will look at how the narrator frames the first two architectonic sections of John's narrative (1:1–51 and 2:1–11:57) and how the content within these frames shows evidence of formulaic language, themes, and movements of thought relevant to the epochs after which they are patterned.

---

41. The nomenclature used to describe these three sections is not always the same. Chapter 21 is usually considered an epilogue that was added some time after the preceding narrative was established. Again, compare the various proposals summarized in Mlakuzhyil, *Christocentric Literary Structure of the Fourth Gospel*, 137–68.

42. For more on Janus passages, see Bruce K. Waltke, *An Old Testament Theology: An Exegetical, Canonical, and Thematic Approach* (Zondervan, 2007), 122. For this usage of Janus or interlocking sections within oral traditions, see Dell Hymes, "Ethnopoetics, Oral-Formulaic Theory, and Editing Texts," *Oral Tradition* 9 (1994): 332.

43. See e.g., M. Dale Kinkade, "Native Oral Literature of the Northwest Coast and Plateau," in *Dictionary of Native American Literature*, ed. Andrew Wiget, GRLH (Garland, 1994), 40; Jan Vansina, *Oral Tradition as History* (University of Wisconsin Press, 1985), 132–33. On proposals for number patterning in the Fourth Gospel, see summary in Mlakuzhyil, *Christocentric Literary Structure of the Fourth Gospel*, 26–27. For my own proposal, and how it fits with the story patterning of the gospel, see Gerber, *Scriptural Tale in the Fourth Gospel*, chapters 6 and 7.

John 1:1–51

The first section of John's narrative in 1:1–51 moves rather conspicuously from an association with the original creation narrative in 1:1 to an aggregated association with Jacob in 1:42–51, capturing the outer frames of Israel's story of beginnings (Gen 1–50).[44] Jacob, having departed his father's house, was a man in whom was much "guile" (δόλος, Gen 27:35 LXX). Nonetheless, when Jacob slept on a stone, he had a dream of angels ascending and descending from heaven upon the earth and was told by God that he would be heir to a great people. The stone was set up as an *axis mundi*, an anticipatory temple, a gate of heaven, Bethel—the "house of God" (28:10–21). Eventually Jacob, who "sees God face-to-face," is renamed Israel (32:22–30).

After John introduces Jesus as the glory-filled Logos-become-flesh and Jesus begins gathering disciples, reestablishing the people of Israel around himself as God become flesh, he renames Simon "Cephas" (Aramaic) or "Peter" (Greek), both meaning "rock."[45] The naming, reminiscent of Jacob's rock, is proleptic, anticipating a destiny yet to be fulfilled: the church, filled with the Spirit as God's new humanity, will become the new *axis mundi* and temple of God once the Spirit is given (cf. 1:33; 19:30; 20:22). Jesus then takes one look at Nathanael and declares that he, unlike the first Jacob-become-Israel, is an Israelite without "guile" (δόλος, 1:47). Like Jacob who saw angels of God ascending and descending, Nathanael, as a member (and representative) of the newly (re)established people of God, will see angels ascending and descending upon the *Son of Man*, the new locus of God's presence on earth (1:51). In addition to this framing, the Fourth Evangelist also evokes the figures of Abraham, Isaac, and Joseph within this first introductory section of the Fourth Gospel.[46] Given that—after Adam—Abraham, Isaac, Jacob and Joseph (along with Judah) were those with most prominence in establishing the people of God, their subtle evocation suggests intentional story patterning from Israel's story of beginnings.

---

44. The book of Genesis ends with Jacob's, and then Joseph's, death.
45. See Schnackenburg, *Gospel according to John*, 1:311–12. The implication is that the church, which springs up around the leadership of Peter most prominently, will be the new *axis mundi* in the world.
46. See, again, Gerber, *Scriptural Tale in the Fourth Gospel*, 188, 293–96, 304.

John 2:1–11:57

Continuing in 2:1–11 with a sign of turning water into wine and ending in 10:40 and 11:54 with a double notation about Jesus's being across the Jordan or in the desert, the second major section of the Fourth Gospel recapitulates the frames of the story of Moses, which similarly begins with Moses's turning water into blood and ends with Moses across the Jordan, in the desert, on the threshold of the promised land, ready to hand the mantle of leadership to Joshua.[47] Multiple strong thematic associations with the campaign of Moses also occur within these sectional end-posts, including that: Jesus is a man who engages in a ministry of signs; these signs reveal glory; these signs are creatively reconfigured; belief in Jesus is requisite; Jesus was sent by God; and enemies threaten Jesus with stoning.[48] All of this seems to attest to the presence of the habitual associations/tension of essences that is common in oral traditional contexts.

The narrative movements of this section likewise echo key moments and habitually associated elements in Second Temple narrations of scriptural stories. For example, 2:1–3:36 appears to be a creative recapitulation of Israel's redemption from Egypt. As Moses's signs in Egypt climax with the death of the firstborn sons in the context of Passover, so does the Fourth Evangelist move from Jesus's first sign to predict his

---

47. Moses turned water into blood at the beginning of his ministry and hands the mantle of leadership to Joshua in the desert "across the Jordan" at the end.

48. Ministry of signs: cf. John 2:11, 18, 23; 3:2; 4:48, 54; 6:2, 14, 26, 30; 7:31; 9:16; 10:41; 11:47; 12:18, 37; and for additional background and parallels, see Exod 3:12; 4:8–9, 17, 28, 30; 7:3, 9; 8:19; 10:1–2; 11:9–10; 12:13; 31:13; Num 14:11, 22; Deut 4:34; 6:22; 7:19; 11:3; 26:8; 28:46; 29:2; 34:11; Neh 9:10; Ps 73:9; 77:43; 104:27; 134:9; Jer 39:20–21; Mic 7:15; Wis 10:16; Sir 36:5; 45:3; Bar 2:11; Acts 7:36; LAB 9.10b, 16b; 10.1; T. Sol. 25.4; Jan. Jam. 3.8; Ezek. Trag. 1.224–6; Artap. 3.27; 4Q422 III, 5–13 [A Paraphrase of Genesis and Exodus]; Josephus, *B.J.* 5.9.4. Signs reveal glory: cf. John 2:11; 11:4, 40; 12:41; and for additional background and parallels, see Exod 7:3–5; Deut 32:6, 18b; 2 Sam 7:23; Isa 63:12–17; Ezek 20:5–9; Sir 45:3; LAB 10.7. Signs are creatively reconfigured: Ps 78:43–51 and Wis 11–19. Belief in Jesus is requisite: see Ulrich W. Mauser, "God in Human Form," *Ex Auditu* 16 (2000): 81–99. Jesus was sent by God: cf. John 3:34; 4:34; 5:23–24, 30, 36–38; 6:29, 38–39, 44, 57; 7:16, 18, 28–29, 33; 8:16, 18, 26, 29, 42; 9:4; 10:36; 11:42; 12:44–45, 49; 13:20; 14:24; 15:21; 16:5; 17:3, 8, 18, 21, 23, 25; 20:21; and for additional background and parallels, see Exod 3:13–15; 4:13, 28; 5:22; Num 16:28; Jos. 24:5; 1 Sam 12:8; Ps 105:26; Isa 63:12; Mic 6:4; Acts 7:35. Enemies threaten Jesus with stoning: cf. John 5:16; 7:1, 23, 30, 44; 8:20, 40, 59; 10:31, 39; 11:53; 12:10; and for additional background and parallels, see Exod 17:4; Num 14:10.

death as God's Son in the context of Passover. As the following deliverance comes by way of water, wind/spirit, a division between light and dark, and is metaphorized in Jewish tradition most memorably as the birth of the Lord's "wife,"[49] so does the Evangelist tell us that no one can enter the kingdom of God unless they are born again/from above by water and wind/spirit as one willing to flee the darkness for the light (3:3–21) in a passage that speedily moves from a scenic depiction of John baptizing (v. 23) across the Jordan (v. 26) to speak about baptism and Christ, the bridegroom of his bride (vv. 29–30). As light and darkness, death and life, belief and unbelief feature prominently in memories of God's rescue through Moses, so too do these elements reappear in this span of John's narrative.

As with the flow of Israel's history, John 4–11 also appears to pick up on a host of memories from Israel's wilderness period. To put it most succinctly, as in Jewish memory, so now in John's Gospel: wells spring up, manna and meat reign down, Israel is given sabbaths, promises of rescue from disease are made, Israel grumbles and suffers for it, the law is given, Israel's idolatry at Sinai is characterized as the sheep becoming "dim sighted" and "blind in their eyes," the need for a shepherd is emphasized, and (re)entry into the land due to exile is reconfigured in Ezekielian terms as a "resurrection."[50] Again, the poetics of this section betray the tension of essences and stockpiling of language and themes consistent with orally-situated artists using preexisting story patterns and their habitually associated elements to compose their works.[51]

---

49. For the division between light and dark, cf. Exod 13:21; 14:19–20; 15:8–10; Josh 24:7; Ps 78:13–14; 105:39; Neh 9:11–12; Wis 10:17–18; 1 En. 89.24–27; Heb 11:29; Esd 1:14; LAB 10.5. For the birth of the Lord's "wife," cf. 4 Ezra 2:1–2; Hos 2:2–3. On Israel's being "born" of God, see Isa 1:2; 45:4–12; 46:3–9; Jer 2:26–7; Ezek 16:1–9.

50. See Gerber, *Scriptural Tale in the Fourth Gospel*, 318–27.

51. The final section of John's narrative does likewise, most conspicuously by mapping out Jesus's preparation for and then victory over sin and death as an ironic and synthesized "re-enactment of the signature campaigns of Israel's most legendry shepherd leaders, Joshua and David." See Gerber, *Scriptural Tale in the Fourth Gospel*, 327–46. Since Jesus fulfills God's protological designs, the eschaton arrives in embryo, as marked by a new man and new woman in a reminted garden. Until the new creation arrives in fullness, the disciples of Jesus—his reinsufflated new humanity—are sent into the world with a task conceived in irreducible temple terms: the forgiveness of sins (20:21–22). Such a task betokens the immanence of cosmic destiny. For, as repentance is made, forgiveness is granted, and the Spirit reanimates humanity to live

Conclusion

Blaise Pascal (1623–1662) once said that objects of intuition are "scarcely seen; they are felt rather than seen."[52] Story patterns are intuited objects and therefore difficult to verify or prove to others. Even still, as proposed in the present chapter, several realities make intuiting such an object in John's Gospel less difficult and more palatable. First, John was embedded in a rich tradition of scriptural knowledge and storytelling. Second, John was also situated in an orally saturated environment where using traditional, prefabricated narrative structures in the composition of new works was conventional. Finally, John's Gospel betrays strong intimations of such a resonant storytelling. Thus, we may fairly suspect—what did John know? John knew Israel's traditional story and how to compose his gospel about the glory-filled Jesus as a referentially explosive retelling of it.

---

out its original light/glory/glorifying purpose. According to the story pattern, history will thus proceed to its consummation.

52. Blaise Pascal, *Pensées* (Dutton, 1958), 2.

5
Philosophy

George L. Parsenios

Troels Engberg-Pedersen's *John and Philosophy: A New Reading of the Fourth Gospel* attempts at every turn to connect the philosophical ideas that drive the Gospel of John with the literary form in which those ideas are presented. Engberg-Pedersen writes near the end of his volume, "The point here is the exceedingly banal one that any analysis of a given literary feature should never be left alone, but always connected with other aspects of the text."[1] The "other aspects" of which he speaks are the philosophical underpinnings of narrative decisions. The medium is part of the message. Attending to the narrative, therefore, is an essential way to understand the ideas that drive the text, especially its philosophical influences. Engberg-Pedersen argues that Stoicism provides the best philosophical background for the gospel and energetically opposes those, like C. H. Dodd and others, who have tried to place John in the world of Middle Platonism, alongside figures like Philo and Plutarch.[2] The present essay is more amenable to the

---

1. Troels Engberg-Pedersen, *John and Philosophy: A New Reading of the Fourth Gospel* (Oxford University Press, 2017), 345–46.
2. C. H. Dodd, *The Interpretation of the Fourth Gospel* (Cambridge University Press, 1951). For more recent efforts, see Harold W. Attridge, "The Cubist Principle in Johannine Imagery: John and the Reading of Images in Contemporary Platonism," in *Imagery in the Gospel of John: Terms, Forms, Themes, and Theology of Johannine Figurative Language*, ed. Jörg Frey, Jan G. van der Watt, and Ruben Zimmermann, WUNT 200 (Mohr Siebeck, 2006), 47–60; Rainer Hirsch-Luipold, "Klartext in Bildern: ἀληθινός κτλ., παροιμία – παρρησία, σημεῖον als Signalwörter für eine bildhafte Darstellungsform im Johannesevangelium," in Frey, van der Watt, and Zimmermann, *Imagery in the Gospel of John*, 61–102; and Hirsch-Luipold, *Gott wahrnehmen: Die Sinne im Johannesevangelium (Ratio Religionis Studien IV)*, WUNT 374 (Mohr Siebeck, 2017).

Platonic side of this equation, but not by any association with Middle Platonism. The dialogues of Plato himself will be our concern in what follows here and not the writers of Middle Platonism, because Plato helps us to see the significance of an often-ignored literary aspect of the Fourth Gospel. It is impossible, despite the title of this essay, to say whether or not John actually *knows* Plato's dialogues. But Plato provides an ancient analogy to what is seen in John, and reading Plato helps us to read John more clearly. In several places, the Gospel of John suppresses the voice of its narrator. The dialogues of Plato also diminish or silence the voice of the narrator in several places, and this essay will explore the significance of this feature in the Gospel of John by comparison with the philosophical significance of this feature in Plato.

Plato's *Theaetetus* informs its readers at the outset that no narrator's voice will be heard in this dialogue. Euclid opens the text by explaining that he will relate a conversation with Socrates but that he will remove the conversational markers. He will suppress the voice of the narrator. Euclid says,

> Now in order that the explanatory words between the speeches might not be annoying ... such as "and I said," or "and I remarked," ... I omitted all that sort of thing and represented Socrates himself as talking with them. (*Thaet.* 143C [Fowler, LCL])

In several key places in the Fourth Gospel the narrator's voice is also suddenly and surprisingly silent, giving the gospel a "dramatic" effect.[3] By reading John in conversation with texts like the *Theaetetus* of Plato, I believe that we can shed new light on the relationship between theological content and narrative form in the Gospel of John. This will also give us an indication of what philosophical ideas might underpin the Gospel of John.

The best place to begin discussing the role of the narrator in John and Plato is found in a passage in Plato's *Republic* where Socrates famously

---

3. For previous discussion on this issue, see George Parsenios, "The Silent Spaces between Narrative and Drama," in *The Gospel of John as Genre Mosaic*, ed. Kasper Bro Larsen, SANt 3 (Vandenhoeck & Ruprecht, 2015), 85–98; Parsenios, "The Testimony of John's Narrative and the Silence of the Johannine Narrator," in *The Opening of John's Narrative (John 1:19–2:22): Historical, Literary, and Theological Readings from the Colloquium Ioanneum 2015 in Ephesus*, ed. R. Alan Culpepper and Jörg Frey, WUNT 385 (Mohr Siebeck, 2017), 1–18; and Parsenios, "Anamnesis and the Silent Narrator in Plato and John," *Religions* 8.47 (2017): 1–11.

defines three different forms of literature.[4] Each is distinguished by the presence or absence of a narrator's voice. The well-known passage reads as follows:

> So don't they achieve this either by a simple narrative [ἁπλῇ διηγήσει], or by means of imitation [μιμήσεως], or a combination of both [δι' ἀμφοτέρων]?... Of poetry and storytelling: the one is done entirely by means of imitation, i.e., tragedy and comedy ... the other is the recital of the poet himself, and you would find it in particular ... in the dithyramb. Where it is a combination of the two, you would find it in the composition of epic poetry. (Plato, *Republic* 392d, 394b–c [Emlyn-Jones and Preddy, LCL])

Thus, a text that is the product entirely of the description and narration of a narrator's voice would be found in a dithyramb and functions as a simple narrative (ἁπλῇ διηγήσει). Dramatic texts like tragedy and comedy represent the opposite end of the spectrum and involve no narrator's voice at all but present the characters speaking to one another without interruption or explanation. These are mimetic texts (μιμήσεως), while the final category blends the narrator's narration and the direct speech of characters. It is a mixed form (δι' ἀμφοτέρων). If we were to assign the Gospel of John to one of these three options, the most likely candidate would be the "mixed" category (δι' ἀμφοτέρων), since John includes both the direct speech of its characters as well as a narrator's voice. But this assignment is not complete. There are a few key places where the Fourth Gospel lapses into something closer to what Plato would call "mimetic" and where the suppression or absence of the narrator's voice gives the text a dramatic quality. These are the places where the narrator disappears, and they are the places where our attention can now turn.

The first such passage appears in the opening scene of the gospel, in the interrogation of John the Baptist in 1:19–22, which reads as follows:

> 19 a: This is the testimony given by John
> b: when the Jews sent priests and Levites from Jerusalem
> c: to ask him,
> d: **"Who are you?"**

---

[4]. The next several pages present a slightly updated and modified version of the argument presented in Parsenios, "Silent Spaces between Narrative and Drama," mentioned in the previous note.

20 a: He confessed and did not deny it,
   b: but confessed,
   c: "**I am not the Messiah.**"
21 a: And they asked him,
   b: "**What then?**
   c: **Are you Elijah?**"
22 a: He said,
   b: "**I am not.**"
   c: "**Are you the prophet?**"[5]

The descending length of the lines draws our attention to the suppression of the narrator. As the lines get shorter, the feature that is actually slowly disappearing is the voice of the narrator. The first narrator's comment in verse 19 a–c is: "This is the testimony given by John when the Jews sent priests and Levites from Jerusalem to ask him." That lengthy comment is followed by a slightly shorter narrator's comment in verse 20 a–b, "He confessed and did not deny, but confessed." The next comment in verse 21a is even briefer: "And they asked him." The narrator's comment is even more brief in verse 22a: "He said." The narrator's presence in the conversation has been slowly and gradually diminished. By the end, the narrator completely disappears. As soon as John answers in 22b, "I am not," the next question of his interrogators has no narrator's introduction at all. John says, "I am not," and immediately we read, "Are you the prophet?" The narrator has disappeared. The gradual tapering of the narrator's presence concludes in a total retreat of the narrator from the discussion. The careful construction of the interrogation demonstrates that the utter disappearance of the narrator's voice with the question "Are you the prophet?" is not some irrelevant or chance fact. It is the culmination of the structure of the passage. It appears to be an intentional narrative move.

To defend the claim that this is an intentional literary move, we can find the same device in Thucydides's *History of the Peloponnesian War*, in at least two places. The two relevant passages are the Melian dialogue in book 5 and the report of the Ambraciot herald in book 3. The famous Melian dialogue (*P.W.* 5.85–113) contains a series of dueling arguments delivered back and forth between the Athenians and the people of the island

---

5. I have followed here the presentation of the passage and the emphasis on the architecture of the lines in Michael Theobald, *Das Evangelium nach Johannes: Kapitel 1–12* (Pustet, 2009), 146–52.

of Melos. The opening speeches of both sides are introduced by a narrator's comment, such as "they said." Thereafter follows a purely mimetic, dramatic presentation. The first speeches of both parties—the Athenians in *P.W.* 5.86 and the Melians at *P.W.* 5.87—are introduced with narrator's comments, but the next speech of the Athenians at *P.W.* 5.88 and that of the Melians at *P.W.* 5.89 are spoken with no narrator's introduction. The narrator is silent until the end of the dialogue many sections later.

The Melian dialogue, of course, is massive in scale and extends over several pages of text. In this sense, it is very different from John 1. But this is not the first time that Thucydides writes like this.[6] It is the most famous example, but there is another example that is more similar to what we find in John in terms of scale. This other episode appears in book 3. After the Athenian general Demosthenes defeats a force consisting of both Spartans and Ambraciots in 426 BCE near the city of Olpae, the Ambraciots send a herald to request that they might recover their dead (*P.W.* 3.113). The ensuing conversation between the herald and those at the battle takes the form of the Melian Dialogue. The first several lines of the conversation are introduced with narrator's comments, but then suddenly and briefly, the text shifts to direct conversation.[7] Commentators both ancient and modern recognize that this gives a dramatic quality to the conversations.[8] Both the interrogation of John the Baptist and the interrogation of the Ambraciot Herald look like the device from ancient drama labeled sticho-

---

6. For a similar comparison to Thucydides on the subject of temporal mechanics, though more on the subject of style than narratorial structuring, see Douglas Estes, *The Temporal Mechanics of the Fourth Gospel: A Theory of Hermeneutical Relativity in the Gospel of John*, BibInt 92 (Brill, 2008), 142–46.

7. Hornblower suggests that this briefer passage might have been a trial effort for the Melian dialogue. Simon Hornblower, *A Commentary on Thucydides* (Oxford University Press, 2008), 3:219.

8. Hornblower underscores the dramatic character of the scene of the Ambraciot herald by saying, "This [chapter], exceptionally, contains some rapid dialogue (the Melian dialogue is the only other example of this in [Thucydides]). This is a tragic feature" (Hornblower, *Commentary on Thucydides*, 1:533). His comments are anticipated by and follow those of Dionysius of Halicarnassus, who writes on the Melian Dialogue, "Thucydides begins by stating in his own person what each side said, but after maintaining this form of reported speech for only one exchange of argument, he dramatizes [δραματίζει] the rest of the dialogue and makes the characters speak for themselves" (*Thuc. id.* 37 [Usher, LCL]). Dionysius later adds, "After this, [Thucydides] changes the style of the dialogue from narrative [διηγήματος] to dramatic [δραματικόν]" (*Thuc. id.* 38 [Usher, LCL]).

mythia. *Stichomythia* is the device by which tragic characters speak to one another in alternating one-line exchanges. It is a form of rapid and forceful conversation. The following conversation between Electra and the Chorus in Aeschylus's *Libation Bearers* is a famous example of *stichomythia* (168–178, my translation):

> Electra: I see cut here on the tomb a lock of hair.
> Chorus: From some man? Or from a slim-waisted girl?
> Electra: This is an obvious clue for anyone to judge.
> Chorus: Let me, then, learn how so—older learning from younger.
> Electra: There is no one but me who could have cut it.
> Chorus: Indeed, the ones for whom it would be appropriate to cut their hair are enemies.
> Electra: And, likewise, it appears to be so very similar to …
> Chorus: —to which tresses? For, I want to learn this.
> Electra: … to my hair it bears a close resemblance.
> Chorus: It couldn't be a veiled gift from Orestes, could it?
> Electra: It most definitely resembles his locks.

Notice the urgency of the conversation when the chorus interrupts Electra and asks, "to which tresses?" The one-line interrogations in *stichomythia* mimic trial debates in the Athenian law courts and are a common feature of Greek drama.[9] The interrogation in John 1, thus, lapses into a dramatic mode.

In John 14, a similar silence occurs when the voice of the narrator drops out of view in the midst of the Farewell Discourses. As chapter 14 draws to its conclusion, Jesus says (John 14:30–31):

> I will no longer talk much with you, for the ruler of this world is coming. He has no power over me; but I do as the Father has commanded me, so that the world may know that I love the Father. Rise, let us be on our way.

The important phrase is the last one: "Rise, let us be on our way." The passage is important because Jesus is describing his own movements. This

---

9. Jennifer Wise argues that this mode of communication arises at least partly from the move to written texts in tragedy, which explains why *stichomythia* does not occur in the oral world of epic poetry. See Jennifer Wise, *Dionysus Writes: The Invention of Theatre in Ancient Greece* (Cornell University Press, 2000), 94. After asserting this, however, she adds, "As a poetic mode of representing human speech, however, it owes an equal debt to the model of forensic speech" (138–40).

is a place where a narrator would generally say, "He got up and left." But not only does Jesus give his own stage directions; these directions also have no accompanying narrator's comment. Like the example in John 1, this example, too, has a dramatic quality. A defining quality of dramatic technique is that a character must give his or her own stage directions. A scholion passed down as a comment on Aeschylus's *Eumenides* makes this clear. At line 29 of the Eumenides, the priestess says, "I take my seat upon my throne." A scholion for this verse teaches us something about the difference between a prose text and a drama. The scholion says,

> [The priestess] says this herself, since the work is a dramatic one [δραματική]. If, on the other hand, it had been a narrative one [διηγηματική], the poet would have said, "Saying these things, she sat upon the throne." (my translation)[10]

The priestess has to explain her own stage directions, since, in a dramatic mode, there is no narrator to explain them for her. If the character does not speak the stage directions, then there are no stage directions.[11]

A final example of the silent narrator appears in the contested and confusing case of John 3. The reader struggles to understand who speaks in John 3:31–36.[12] The last-mentioned speaker is John the Baptist, who is identified at 3:27, and his words clearly extend to 3:30, where he says, "He must increase, while I must decrease." Some interpreters believe, therefore, that the Baptist continues speaking in verses 3:31–36. Other commentators believe that the content of the discourse accords more closely with the words of Jesus himself earlier in the dialogue with Nicodemus and assume that these are the words of Jesus. Still others argue that we have here the

---

10. For this scholion, see *Scholia Graeca in Aeschylum quae exstant Omnia*, ed. Ole Langwitz Smith, 2 vols. (Teubner, 1976), 1:44.

11. Whether this circumstance arose from sloppy editing or careful *relecture*, the device appears in the text. Further, absence of the narrator here is not an isolated dramatic feature of these discourses, but part of a larger dramatic program. For discussion, see Parsenios, "Silent Spaces"; Parsenios, *Departure and Consolation: The Johannine Farewell Discourses in Light of Greco-Roman Literature*, NovTSup 117 (Brill, 2005), especially chapters 1 and 2; and Parsenios, "'No Longer in the World' (John 17:11): The Transformation of the Tragic in the Fourth Gospel," *HTR* 98 (2005): 18.

12. For full discussion of the problems in these verses and the solutions proposed, see Raymond E. Brown, *The Gospel according to John I–XII*, AB 29 (Doubleday, 1966), 159–62.

words of the Evangelist in the role of narrator. It is not our purpose to resolve this confusion, but only to recognize the fact of the confusion and the cause of the confusion: the absence of a clear comment from the narrator identifying the speaker of these lines.

Before moving to philosophical questions proper, we can pause for a moment to recognize that both John and Thucydides suppress the voice of their narrators, rendering their prose narratives more dramatic in these particular examples. Before reflecting on a possible philosophical purpose for this decision, we can recognize that this device has a historiographic purpose. Such a turn toward drama can be seen as inherent to the writing of history.[13] David Aune writes, "The historian ... created the illusion that he was an observer of the events he depicts."[14] Scholars like Richard Bauckham have connected John in various ways to ancient historiography, and the occasional silencing of the narrator in John could be part of that effort.[15] Thus, by suppressing occasionally the voice of the narrator, the Evangelist is able to underscore that he was an eyewitness of the events described. The concern for eyewitness status is obvious at the cross, when the testimony of the blood and water flowing from Jesus's side is followed by the notice, "He who saw this has testified so that you also may believe. His testimony is true, and he knows that he tells the truth" (19:35). The author is describing events as in a newsreel, as an eyewitness.

If the phenomenon of silencing a narrator were confined to historiography, our work would be done. But the same device operates in the dialogues of Plato. Plato's use of the device can help us to reflect further on John. This is not to suggest that literary questions are simple in regard to Plato. Even more debates rage in Platonic scholarship than in Johannine about the relationship between the form of the dialogues and their content, with the last several decades seeing sustained efforts to connect the literary form of the dialogues to their philosophical content.[16] Even in

---

13. Rhetoric and historiography are joined in various ways in various works. For a quick description of the relevant issues, see Charles William Fornara, *The Nature of History in Ancient Greece and Rome* (University of California Press, 1983), 169–75.

14. David E. Aune, *The New Testament in Its Literary Environment* (Westminster, 1987), 86.

15. Richard Bauckham, "Historiographical Characteristics of the Gospel of John," *NTS* 53 (2007): 17–36.

16. The *Symposium* has received particular attention for its literary artistry. See especially J. L. Penwill, "Men in Love: Aspects of Plato's *Symposium*," *Ramus* 7 (1978): 143; Diskin Clay, *Platonic Questions: Dialogues with the Silent Philosopher* (Pennsyl-

antiquity people wondered how Plato's three categories of literature in the *Republic* applied to Plato's own dialogues. In his *Lives of Eminent Philosophers*, Diogenes Laertius records the traditions of people with whom he disagrees as follows (3.50):

> I am not unaware that there are other ways in which certain writers classify the dialogues. For some dialogues they call dramatic [δραματικούς], others narrative [διηγηματικούς], and others again a mixture of the two [μεικτούς]. But the terms they employ in their classification of the dialogues are better suited to the stage than to philosophy. (Hicks, LCL)

Plato's *Theaetetus* is a particularly rich place to focus our discussion of the relevant issues, since it opens with a conversation where Euclid is explaining to Terpsion how he came to record the conversation between Socrates and Theaetetus, even though he had not been present. Euclid had the conversation described to him by Socrates, wrote it down, and then corrected his text later by further conversation with Socrates. The interesting fact is that he does not merely transcribe what Socrates tells him. Rather, he says (*Theaet.* 143c),

> Now this is the way I wrote the conversation: I did not represent Socrates relating it to me as he did, but conversing with those with whom he told me he conversed. And he told me they were the geometrician Theodoras and Theaetetus. Now in order that the explanatory words between the speeches might not be annoying in the written account, such as "and I said" or "and I remarked," whenever Socrates spoke, or "he agreed" or "he did not agree," in the case of the interlocutor, I omitted all that sort of thing and represented Socrates himself as talking with them. (Fowler, LCL)

Commenting on this reality, Diskin Clay writes, "In the *Theaetetus*, the editorial suppression of narrative links creates the illusion of dramatic immediacy."[17] Further, this suppression of narrative links is not merely a

---

vania State University Press, 2000); Charles H. Kahn, *Plato and the Socratic Dialogue: The Philosophical Use of a Literary Form* (Cambridge University Press, 1996); Kenneth Dorter, "The Significance of the Speeches in Plato's *Symposium*," *Philosophy and Rhetoric* 2 (1969): 215–34; Henry G. Wolz, "Philosophy as Drama: An Approach to Plato's *Symposium*," *PPR* 30 (1970): 323–53.

17. Clay, *Platonic Questions*, 26.

literary move. According to Clay, Plato develops this dramatic immediacy for a very clear purpose, or rather two closely related purposes, and both are suggestive for interpreting John.

First, the conversation between Euclid and Terpsion is a frame dialogue set in the present day that introduces the older conversation with Socrates from the past. By presenting the past conversation with Socrates within the frame of the new conversation between Terpsion and Euclid, Plato creates a memorial of the speaking Socrates. The two contemporary conversation partners (in this case, Euclid and Terpsion) are creating a memorial to the conversation that Socrates had in the past. Euclid makes this commemorative purpose plain when he describes his work as follows (*Thaet.* 143a):

> I made notes [ὑπομνήματα] at the time as soon as I reached home, then afterwards at my leisure, as I recalled things [ἀναμιμνῃσκόμενος], I wrote them down, and whenever I went to Athens I used to ask Socrates about what I could not remember [ἐμεμνήμην], and then I came here and made corrections; so that I have pretty much the whole talk written down.

His purpose is to remember the dialogue correctly.

Furthermore, the concern for producing an accurate memorial as it is expressed in the opening lines of the dialogue is not unconnected to the content of the dialogue that follows. Not long after the conversation begins, Socrates insists that a central aspect of knowledge is memory (*Thaet.* 163d), and the discussion here in the *Theaetetus* evokes the relationship between recollection and knowledge in the *Phaedo* (72e–78b). Thus, the literary frame conversation between Euclid and Terpsion emphasizes the central importance of recollection in a dialogue that will soon explain why recollection is important for acquiring true knowledge. The concern for memory in the opening conversation is, thus, not a random or a meaningless concern. The mimetic move is a mnemonic move.

The Gospel of John shares this mnemonic purpose. Jesus urges his followers, for instance, to remember and to keep his words. He does so in the midst of his Farewell Discourses. He twice commands them to remember what he says to them:[18]

---

18. In addition to these two examples, see also Jesus's promise that the Paraclete will remind (ὑπομνήσει) the disciples of Jesus's words (14:26). For more on the relevant issues, see Parsenios, *Departure and Consolation*, 111–49.

Remember [μνημονεύετε] the word that I said to you.... (15:20)

But I have said these things to you so that when their hour comes you may remember [μνημονεύητε] that I told you about them. (16:4a)

Because Jesus's words are so valuable, the disciples must not only remember them. They must also "keep" them (John 14:21–26). But, what does it mean to *keep* the word(s) of Jesus? In the most obvious sense, one keeps the word of Jesus by performing the acts that he prescribes. At another level, the disciples must keep Jesus's word by transmitting his message (15:20) and by testifying on his behalf (15:26). But, even more basically, the disciples keep the word of Jesus by enshrining it in the Gospel of John.[19] The very production of the gospel, then, is a response to Jesus's injunction to keep his words.

But in the cases of both John and Plato, there is more at work than a mere memorial to the past. This is the second point that Clay stresses. The purpose of writing dialogues as Plato does is not only to commemorate the past, but to view the past from a particular perspective, and to understand the past through recent events. Euclid and Terpsion are speaking in the town of Megara long after Socrates's death, and they describe a conversation that Socrates had had years before in Athens. In the dialogue, that conversation is enacted again, as though onstage. But this time it plays out not in Athens, but in Megara. Clay adds,

> If Plato produces the illusion that his intellectual life remained fixed with Socrates in the fifth century, he also reminds us that his dialogues speak to another age—his own. The other Socratics evoked the memory of Socrates by bringing him into contact with the large and varied cast of his contemporaries. Plato did more. He not only provided his dialogues with recognizable historical settings, he also fashioned frame dialogues for the canvas of his dialogues that belong to another age.[20]

The past is read in such a way that it has a purchase on the present and can only be understood in light of present concerns. The sense of dramatic immediacy that is created by the absence of a narrator makes it appear as though the conversation with Socrates is not confined to Athens but is

---

19. John Ashton, *Understanding the Fourth Gospel* (Oxford University Press, 1991), 459.
20. Clay, *Platonic Questions*, 23.

taking place in Megara, miles away and years later. The life of Socrates is read from a later perspective, from the perspective of his followers after his death, who remember him through the prism of his death.

The Gospel of John, of course, does the same, especially in places like the comments of the evangelist in chapter 2, where we read that the memory of Jesus's earthly life is filtered through later experience, most particularly the resurrection on the third day. After the cleansing of the temple, we read, "But he was speaking of the temple of his body. After he was raised from the dead, his disciples remembered [ἐμνήσθησαν] that he had said this; and they believed the scripture and the word that Jesus had spoken" (2:20-22). The same sentiment is repeated at 12:16. The power of the resurrection has a profound hermeneutical value that is connected to the gift of the Spirit that is also present only after Jesus is glorified (7:39).[21] If the *Theaetetus* is read within the context of a different and later place, the Gospel of John is read in light of a different and later time. But in both, we are reminded that the past discourses are directed to a later audience, and specifically so.

There is nothing exactly like the Johannine postresurrection perspective in the case of Plato, but there is a related device. As was just said, John tells the earthly life of Jesus from the later perspective of the resurrection. Even before Jesus is risen from the dead, John speaks of him as such, as in chapters 2 and 12. The postresurrection perspective intrudes on the preresurrection life of Jesus. The same is true of Socrates, only if we recognize that it is his mortality, his death, that hangs over several dialogues and colors how they are read. In other words, if John has a postresurrection perspective, many of Plato's dialogues operate with a postexecution perspective. If the life of Jesus is told from behind the glow of the resurrection, the dialogues of Socrates often take place under the shadow of his impending death. For example, as Socrates finishes telling his allegory of the cave in book 7 of the *Republic*, he describes the anguish of people chained to a false reality within their cave, where they have grown comfortable and accustomed to their falsehood and do not want to leave it. After describing the effort required to be released from this fate, Socrates asks Glaukon how people would respond to the person who had forced them to leave the darkness and stretch toward the light, "And if they

---

21. See Jörg Frey, *Das johanneische Zeitverständnis*, vol. 2 of *Die johanneische Eschatologie*, WUNT 110 (Mohr Siebeck, 1998), 247-52; and Marianne Meye Thompson, *The Humanity of Jesus in the Fourth Gospel* (Fortress, 1988).

were somehow able to get their hands on and kill the man who attempts to release and lead them up, wouldn't they kill him?" Glaukon responds, "No question, they would" (Plato, *Resp.* 517a [Bloom]), and we know that the Athenians responded precisely in this way to Socrates when he endeavored to lead them from falsehood to truth. Socrates's own career is in view. Likewise, in the *Meno*, the figure Anytos warns Socrates to be careful with his teaching by saying, "Socrates, it seems to me you slander men lightly. If you will be persuaded by me, I would advise you to beware" (Plato, *Meno* 94d [Allen]). Socrates responds by saying, "Anytus seems angry, Meno. I'm not surprised" (Plato, *Meno* 95a [Allen]). This warning from Anytos is not in vain, and the anger of Anytos does not abate. Anytos will be one of the three chief accusers who prosecute Socrates in the trial that leads to his death. The *Gorgias*, in the same vein, includes a conversation about the failure of the philosopher to be able to defend himself in court (486a–b). Finally, this same theme appears in the dialogue most of interest for the present paper, the *Theaetetus* (173 CE). The *Theaetetus* ends with Socrates referring to the charges that will lead to his execution. He says, "Now I have an appointment at the King's Porch to face the indictment which Meletus has brought against me. But let's meet here again tomorrow morning, Theodorus" (Plato, *Theaet.* 210d [Waterfield]). If they ever do meet again, their meeting takes place under the shadow of trial and death. To explain the significance of the shadow of death that hangs over the Socratic dialogues, Clay is again instructive. He writes,

> The courtroom drama of the *Apology* helps us understand the moments in the Platonic dialogues where the shadow of Socrates' death passes over the scene. This is the moment to which they all lead and from which they all radiate.[22]

The trial of Socrates intrudes into the dialogues in various ways, and if these dialogues are memorials of past conversations, they are memorials, therefore, filtered through the trial and execution of Socrates. The same mnemonic mechanism, thus, drives both John and Plato. A key aspect of this memorializing tendency is the turn to mimesis and the silence of the narrator.

At this point, a point of correction is in order, of course. To say only this much is to say too little and to misrepresent both John and Plato. Up

---

22. Diskin Clay, *Platonic Questions*, 38.

to this point, it appears as though both Plato and John saw the memorialization of the past in a written record as an uncomplicated and uncontroversial matter. This is not true. A concluding thought at this point can signal the path in which my work will take me in the future, with an example drawn from the *Symposium*. David Halperin has recognized that the *Symposium* has both an official philosophical perspective as well as an unofficial one regarding the preservation of the words of Socrates.[23] On the one hand, in its official position, the dialogue reinforces the value of recalling and remembering the words of Socrates. The dialogue famously opens with Apollodorus explaining the circuitous path by which the words of Socrates passed down to him from the original conversation in the house of Agathon (*Sym.* 172b–174a). Apollodorus hears the words of Socrates as passed down through many generations of transmitters. This shows the importance of remembering Socrates's words, even if only dimly and as reported imperfectly over a long period of time.[24] But the very complexity of the process of transmitting Socrates's original speech to Apollodorus, as the original discourse passes from person to person, also shows the impossibility of accurate recollection. This gives rise to what Halperin calls the unofficial position of the dialogue, which privileges inscription over recollection.

The Gospel of John has a similar tension. The gospel draws to a close in chapter 20 with the famous comment on the insistence of seeing, remembering, and preserving Jesus's deeds when it says, "Now Jesus did many other signs in the presence of his disciples, which are not written in this book. But these are written so that you may come to believe that Jesus is the Messiah, the Son of God, and that through believing you may have life in his name" (20:30–31). This statement emphasizes the need to preserve the words of Jesus in a written gospel and to read them and to see his signs in the way that his original audiences saw them. This, to borrow a phrase from Halperin, is the book's official position.

But the comment in John 20 about the importance of seeing and remembering Jesus's earthly ministry and his signs is undercut by an unofficial position. If seeing the signs is essential for believing, seeing is not

---

23. David M. Halperin, "Plato and the Erotics of Narrativity," in *Oxford Studies in Ancient Philosophy: Supplementary Volume 1992, Methods of Interpreting Plato and His Dialogues*, ed. James C. Klagge and Nicholas D. Smith (Oxford University, 1992), 93–129.

24. Halperin, "Plato and the Erotics of Narrativity," 106.

always so clearly a positive thing in John. In John 6:40, Jesus states that his disciples must see in order to believe, affirming a positive connection between seeing and believing. But in John 6:36, some people are said to see, but they still do not believe. To make matters even more complicated, in John 20:29, Jesus tells Thomas that the most blessed people are those who do *not* see, and yet believe: "Blessed are those who have not seen yet believe" (20:29). Reading the gospel and seeing its signs, therefore, is essential but problematic. C. K. Barrett explains the matter well and in a manner that connects what John does to what Halperin sees Plato doing. Barrett writes,

> The Fourth Gospel could only have been written by one who regarded the life, death, and resurrection of Jesus as the indispensable turning-point in God's dealing with mankind; but the evangelist does not look upon this complex event in a historicist way ... [Believers] live under the necessity of that same decision of faith which was once evoked by sight and is now demanded by the apostolic testimony and the witness of the Spirit.[25]

Plato and John are motivated by very different purposes, but their respective theological and philosophical concerns find expression in the literary decisions they make and in the ways that they problematize the recollection of Jesus and Socrates, respectively.

---

25. C.K. Barrett, *New Testament Essays* (SPCK, 1972), 66–67.

6

Rhetoric

Jo-Ann A. Brant

In the quest to ferret out what John knows, this investigation poses the question what, or perhaps more accurately how, does John attempt to persuade his audience to think. This question immediately presents a challenge. Persuasion is the domain of rhetoric, and rhetoric is the act of an occasion. A president addresses the nation seeking support for a particular policy. A defense attorney addresses the jury and sums up the evidence that exonerates his or her client or mitigates against a guilty verdict. A leader stands before a grieving community and praises the virtues of the departed in words of consolation. The Gospel of John is a narrative. Nevertheless, the narrator makes clear that its end is rhetorical by stating that the narrative presents a series of episodes that will cause its audience to have confidence that Jesus is the Messiah who will give them life everlasting (20:30–31). To do this, the gospel writer borrows heavily from the art of rhetoric in both constructing the speeches of the various characters within the narrative and arranging the constitutive components of his narrative in a manner designed to persuade. The lines of argument and rhetorical narrative strategies endeavor to solicit from the audience a variety of cognitive states conducive to their believing that they share a clear picture of Jesus's identity and capabilities. These include nudging them into a cognitive space furnished with metaphors and abstractions that point to transcendent realities that cannot be captured with conventions and toward an ethos of confidence in the credibility of the gospel's witness to Jesus. In looking at how John persuades, we find the process that pulls both writer and reader deep into a space in which to strengthen the identity of a new community while severing the ties with the Jewish community from which the Johannine narrative sprang. As a result, this rooting out of rhetorical strategies brings to light both marvels in the art of persuasion and strategies with which we may not be comfortable as modern readers.

Aristotle identifies three types of contexts for rhetorical speech: the courtroom (forensic) and the legislature (deliberative) in which the audiences are called to judge, and a catchall category (epideictic) for occasions for praise or blame such as funerals or victory celebrations in which the audience is called to be spectators who judge the ability (*dynamis*) of the speaker to match eloquence with the merits of the subject of the speech (*Rhet.* 1358b). In his tidy process of classification, analysis of narrative falls under the category of poetics rather than rhetoric. Modern critical studies recognize that the boundaries between poetics and rhetoric are porous and that tales, no less than speeches, can be told to persuade. Wayne C. Booth draws attention to how authors can choose literary techniques to sway their readers to see events, institutions, and people as the authors do by showing and not just telling us the foundations of various commitments.[1] Epideictic, the category that Aristotle neglects but in which current scholars of rhetoric take great interest, may provide the most helpful lens through which to study Johannine rhetoric in answer to this volume's question.[2] The audience of epideictic rhetoric expects not just that the rhetor will tell them with what they ought to agree but, for the rhetor to succeed, that they will hear a story that both reinforces consensus by inspiring and plumbing the depths of their convictions.[3] In doing so, the rhetor stretches prior understandings to shape, as Jeffrey Walker puts it, "the ideologies and imageries with which, and by which, the individual members of a community identify themselves and ... the fundamental grounds, the 'deep' commitments and presuppositions, that will underlie and ultimately determine decision and debate in particular pragmatic

---

1. Wayne C. Booth, *The Rhetoric of Fiction*, 2nd ed. (University of Chicago Press, 1983), 1–20.

2. For forensic rhetoric see George L. Parsenios, *Rhetoric and Drama in the Johannine Lawsuit Motif*, WUNT 258 (Mohr Siebeck, 2010); Andrew T. Lincoln, *Truth on Trial: The Lawsuit Motif in the Fourth Gospel* (Hendrickson, 2000); Per Jarle Bekken, *The Lawsuit Motif in John's Gospel from New Perspectives: Jesus Christ, Crucified Criminal and Emperor of the World*, NovTSup 158 (Brill, 2015). Jerome H. Neyrey, S.J., *The Gospel of John in Cultural and Rhetorical Perspective* (Eerdmans, 2009), 396–401, points out places where deliberative rhetoric prevails such as John 15–16.

3. Jonathan Pratt, "The Epideictic *Agōn* and Aristotle's Elusive Third Genre," *AJP* 133.2 (2012): 191.

forums."⁴ The following analysis will begin by examining the rhetorical strategies by which John expands the horizons of the reading audience and then the rhetorical strategies by which he seeks to inspire confidence in his witnesses and ultimately in Jesus.

Before beginning, three qualifications are in order. First, what an audience member is supposed by a rhetor to feel or think is quite different from what an actual individual feels or thinks. Just as speeches can fail to persuade so too narratives may be ineffective. While an audience may find a story absorbing and allow it to transport them to another reality for a time, studies indicate that those who tend to find a story meaningful meet these preconditions: emotional engagement with characters and longing for meaningfulness.⁵ Given that the narrator seems to presuppose an audience familiar with Jesus's stories, I will discuss the audience predisposed to identify with Jesus and his followers. Just as Jesus's rhetoric in the gospel fails to persuade those in the narrative audience who are not predisposed to believe that he is the Son of God, the gospel can also fail to persuade real readers about Jesus's identity while succeeding in earning points for his rhetorical art. Second, the sort of knowledge or understanding to which I will refer is best understood as a form of social epistemology rather than the sorts of certitude that can be proven universally valid. The gospel's knowledge is shaped by social relationships and institutions and depends upon testimony and authority. Third, the authorship of the Gospel of John is a tangle of voices. For simplicity's sake, I will refer to the voice that tells the story as the *narrator*, the author who wrote the work as the *gospel writer*, and the gospel as *John* or *the gospel*.

Narratologists have adopted the word *rhetoricalization* to describe the way that narratives indirectly answer ideological questions and lead the reading audience to look at experience in a particular way that turns conventional certitudes upon their head.⁶ Examining techniques of rhetoricalization evident in John reveals strategies by which the gospel opens

---

4. Jeffrey Walker, *Rhetoric and Poetics in Antiquity* (Oxford University Press, 2000), 9.

5. Mary Beth Oliver et al., "Absorption and Meaningfulness: Examining the Relationship Between Eudaimonic Media Use and Engagement," in *Narrative Absorption*, ed. Frank Hakemulder et al., Linguistic Approaches to Literature 27 (Benjamins, 2017), 257.

6. E.g., Michel Meyer, *Meaning and Reading: A Philosophical Essay on Language and Literature*, P&B 4.3 (Benjamins, 1983), 158.

up a cognitive space that admits new concepts and language, such as living water and bread of life, for describing Jesus's status. Through narrative, problems can be implied and answers given to questions in a way that invites assent without discussion by showing the audience that something is true. The narrative deals with the unanswered questions raised by a thought system and through the experience of the audience that must be faced by showing their solution as reasonable. In the case of John's thought system, many of the questions that revolve around the person of Jesus spring from the lips of characters within the narrative:

> Is not this Jesus, the son of Joseph, whose father and mother we know? How can he say, "I have come down from heaven"? (6:42)
>
> How does this man have such learning, when he has never been taught? (7:15)
>
> What do you mean by saying, "You will be made free"? (8:33)
>
> Are you greater than our father Abraham, who died? The prophets also died. Who do you claim to be?" (8:53)
>
> We have heard from the law that the Messiah remains forever. How can you say the Son of Man must be lifted up? (12:34)[7]

Such questions within the action of the narrative serve varied purposes such as challenges or prompts for further interaction but within the overall rhetorical strategy of the narrative serve as a sign of the ignorance or incomplete understanding of those who put their questions to Jesus. The prologue addresses several of these questions in advance of the narrative presumably as a way to encourage the reader to adopt a priori the conviction that Jesus is all that he claims to be. Casting truth claims in a grand style fraught with figurative language plays upon a cultural literary convention that allows hyperbole or an unfamiliar perspective when receiving assertions through poetry.

One of the most consistent questions to which the narrator frequently returns is Jesus's relation to the prophets. The Samaritan woman responds to Jesus's display of prescience about her marital status, "Sir, I see that you

---

7. All biblical quotations are taken from the NRSV.

are a prophet" (4:19). The crowd responds to the miraculous supply of bread and fish, "This is indeed the prophet who is to come into the world" (6:14). At the festival of Sukkoth, the crowd's deliberation about Jesus's identify begins with the assertion, "This is really the prophet" (7:40), and the man whose sight Jesus restores defends Jesus before the Pharisees with the claim, "He is a prophet" (9:17). Wayne Meeks has demonstrated the prevalence of a Jewish tradition that saw Moses as a prophet-king and that hoped for a messiah of the same status.[8] Looking at this from the perspective of rhetorical criticism, it seems that the narrator is showing the inadequacy of depending upon familiar categories. Jesus responds to the Samaritan woman, "the hour is coming when you will worship the Father neither on this mountain not in Jerusalem ... the hour is coming, and is now here, when the true worshipers will worship the Father in spirit and truth" (4:21, 23). The contested space of conflicting traditions is replaced by an abstraction that invites discussion rather than disagreement. Jesus corrects the previously blind man's broad but human category of prophet with the more ambiguous term *Son of Man* that can signify either a human being or a heavenly agent.

Narrative sometimes persuades its audience to look at experience in a particular way that turns conventional certitudes upon their head. With *To Kill a Mockingbird* (1960), Harper Lee succeeded in persuading many of her readers to question the justice of the execution of justice in the Jim Crow south. With *Oliver Twist* (1837–1839), Charles Dickens invited readers to question the charity of houses of charity. John's narrative presents a number of such inversions. Washing the feet of another is an act of participating in Jesus's glory rather than an act of hospitality signifying the subservience of the one washing the feet of the guest. Crucifixion is a sign of glory rather than shame.[9] Being kicked out of the synagogue becomes a sign of faithfulness to God rather than infidelity. Calamities become hopeful signs. Jesus displays such optimism by saying "[the blind man] was born blind so that God's works might be revealed in him" (9:3) and "unless a seed of grain falls into the earth and dies, it remains just a single grain; but if it dies, it bears much fruit" (12:24). The audience, in turn, is invited to adopt such optimism about their own experiences.

---

8. Wayne Meeks, *The Prophet-King: Moses Traditions and the Johannine Christology*, NovTSup 14 (Brill, 1967).

9. See Neyrey, *Gospel of John in Cultural and Rhetorical Perspective*, 412–38.

The episode of the blind man betrays a careful design aimed at persuading the audience to be sanguine about their experience of any negative consequences arising from fidelity to Jesus. In a gospel centered on Jesus, the gospel writer gives over an unprecedented twenty-seven verses to a scene in which Jesus is not present. The Synoptic writers dare keep Jesus off-page for so long only prior to his birth. The narrator uses the rhetoric of the dialogue with the blind man to represent him as a parallel character to Jesus. Both his inquisition before the Pharisees (9:13–34) and Jesus's trial before Pilate (18:38–19:16) consist of a series of exits and entrances. The blind man is the only other character in the gospel to make an "I am" (*egō eimi*) assertion. When the crowd disputes that he is the same man who use to be a blind beggar, he states simply *egō eimi* (9:9). Both are accused of being invalid witnesses (8:13; 9:18), sinners (9:24, 34), and teaching without authority (7:15; 9:34). Both speak frankly (10:25–30; 9:25, 7, 30–33) and logically (8:39-40; 9:31-34), and both sarcastically express astonishment at the Pharisees' lack of understanding (3:10; 9:3). The Pharisees throw (*exebalon*) the man out of the assembly (9:34), and, in the language of the prologue, Jesus's own did not receive/accept (*parelabon*) him (1:11). The blind man becomes a model for the believer illustrating that it is possible to witness to Jesus even in extreme duress and even as one who is not typically called upon as a witness. The man's parents provide a foil for their son's courage by evading frank speech for fear, according to the narrator, of being *aposynagōgos* (9:22). This term, unique to John, is used again in 12:42 to describe leaders who believed in Jesus but remained silent for fear of being put out of the synagogue and then in 16:2 when Jesus warns the disciples that they will be put out of the synagogue "when those who kill you will think that by doing so they are offering worship to God." When fear becomes the motivation for remaining in the synagogue and imitation of Jesus becomes the cause for exclusion, exclusion or separation becomes honorable and fidelity becomes courage. This view is reinforced when Jesus's supposed humiliation on the cross is rhetorically rendered as glorification.

When Jesus reclaims his central place in the narrative, the formerly blind man's insistence upon trusting in the goodness of his benefactor and his predilection of associating him with divine agency makes him receptive to believing in the Son of Man, although his words suggest that he has no clear idea of what the title entails (9:36). Belief does not signify assent to truth claims so much as accepting Jesus as the source of truth claims. Some Pharisees quickly displace the man as Jesus's conversation partners, but the narrative pursues the same rhetorical end of representing disassociation from Jewish social institutions and their authorities as positive:

> Jesus: I came to this world for judgment so that those who do not see may see and those who do see may become blind.
> Pharisees: Surely we are not blind, are we?
> Jesus: If you were blind, you would not have sin, but now you say "We see," your sin remains. (9:39–41)

The Pharisees now stand in the position first marked by the disciples in their assertion that blindness signifies sin. The reading audience is not called to work out the verbal puzzle but rather to observe the puzzle acting upon the narrative audience. Such paradoxes become reassuring statements for those who have abandoned prior reliance upon traditional authorities and conventional knowledge. Similarly, the extended metaphor of the good shepherd frustrates the Pharisees while providing positive emotional associations for the reading audience members who are intended to identify with the sheep. As Jonathan Charteris-Black points out, by representing issues metaphorically, the speaker conjures a mental representation that occupies the mind making it more difficult to understand issues differently.[10] The complexity of the biblical metaphor of God the father illustrates how deeply entrenched a metaphor can be in the way that many in the biblical tradition understand reality. The metaphoric identification of Pharisees with wolves and hirelings (John 10:12–13) has helped the negative portrayal of Pharisees become deeply rooted in many Christian minds. Furthermore, the stewardship metaphor establishes Jesus's moral authority. In John, the good shepherd "lays down his life" when the wolf threatens the flock whereas the hired hand "runs away" (10:12).

Given that the narrator's goal is not simply to engage an audience but to share confidence in the certitude that Jesus is the Son of God and given that the invitation is to a social epistemology that provides individual members within a group a sense of shared understanding, much of Johannine rhetorical energy is devoted to matters of *ethos*. This is achieved, in part, by putting on display the false bravado and flaws in the thinking of Jesus's narrative opponents when they claim certitude and authority as well as displaying the virtues of Jesus and his witnesses by which they

---

10. Jonathan Charteris-Black, *Politicians and Rhetoric: The Persuasive Power of Metaphor*, 2nd ed. (Palgrave Macmillan, 2011), 28.

gain greater credibility. Narrative, thereby, rewards its audience with the pleasure of access to people's minds and a sense of superior discernment.[11] Liesbeth Korthals Altes describes the flip side of this coin as "the more melancholy, yet just as familiar, confrontation with characters' and our own opacity, obtuseness, inconsistency, and duplicity."[12] Aristotle describes a propensity of reasoning called *akrasia* by those who commit evil (*kakos* or *phaulos*) that seems particularly applicable in the characterization of the Jewish authorities' thoughts. *Akrasia* is manifest when decisions and actions are guided by weak emotions such as fear, when one utters words without fully understanding what one is saying, and when one comes to regret what one has done (Aristotle, *Eth. Nic.* 1147).

Within the broad population of the narrative audience, to which the narrator frequently refers to as the Jews that with one voice rejects Jesus (2:18–20; 5:16–18; 7:13; 9:22; 10:31–39; 18:38–40; 19:7; 19:38; 20:19), two authoritative bodies are singled out, the Pharisees and the priests. The narrator lines up the authority of the Pharisees for first inspection. Nicodemus opens by claiming certainty and the ability to recognize whether someone is from God or not: "Rabbi, we know that you are a teacher who has come from God; for no one can do these signs that you do apart from the presence of God" (3:2). Nicodemus's praise of Jesus may be sincere, but the narrative setting of a private interview at night suggests that, while Nicodemus may feel confident in his knowledge, he is not ready to defend it publicly. In the subsequent dialogue, he seems to lose his confidence about being in the know when Jesus comments upon Nicodemus's mental state, "Do not be astonished because I said to you, it is necessary for you [pl.] to be born from above!" (3:7), to which Nicodemus responds, "How can these things be?" (3:9). Jesus then wryly plays on Nicodemus's pretentious opening, "Are you a teacher of Israel, and yet you do not understand these things?" (3:10). When his fellow Pharisees allege that Jesus is a deceiver (7:47–49; see Deut 13:6–11), Nicodemus's next question might betray a retreat from former certitude and only a little confidence in speaking for the group, "Our law does not judge people without first giving them a hearing to find out what they are doing, does it?" (7:51). His valid argument by Pharisaic standards is dismissed by his associates with a lazy argument

---

11. See Lisa Zunshine, *Why We Read Fiction: A Theory of Mind and the Novel* (Ohio State University Press, 2006), 72.

12. Liesbeth Korthals Altes, *Ethos and Narrative Interpretation: The Negotiation of Values in Fiction* (University of Nebraska Press, 2014), 35.

in the form of the logical fallacy of guilt by association, "Surely you are not also from Galilee, are you?" (7:51). The righteous application of the law upon which Pharisaic authority rests is not evident in their summary judgement of Jesus. While John in general is rather careless about drawing distinctions between types of late Second Temple Judaism, he seems to be sufficiently familiar with the Pharisaic tradition to parody them.

Next on deck is the priesthood. The authority of the priesthood should rest upon their autonomy from the political interests of earthly power and their role as mediators between humanity and God who alone holds dominion over them. The Johannine priests' words and actions betray their lack of confidence in God's power to preserve them and that they have replaced God with Rome. The plan to eliminate Jesus is put into action because, if he continues, "everyone will believe in him, and the Romans will come and destroy both our holy place and our nation" (11:47). Ought not their primary concern be God's judgement? Their downbeat words of destruction form a counterpoint to Jesus's upbeat challenge, "Destroy this temple, and in three days I will raise it" (2:19). The Jerusalem authorities' references to defeat stand in contrast with Jesus's language of victory. Jesus consistently motivates his followers with positive representations of the future with his repeated play on the verb *hypsoō* ("lift up") to treat his death as an exaltation (3:14, 8:28; 12:32), his claims to victory, "take courage, I have conquered the world" (16:33; see also 14:30), and his promises that suffering with turn quickly to joy (16:20–22; see also 16:7). Caiaphas's ironic prophecy, "You do not understand that it is better for you to have one man die for the people than to have the whole nation destroyed" (11:49), underscores how an appeal to fear invites its audience to sacrifice justice for short term survival. His motive stands in counterpoint to Jesus who sacrifices his security for Lazarus and surrenders himself so that no one else will be harmed (18:8). He also fulfills Aristotle's definition of an *akratic* man who like actors on stage can speak lines filled with facts and concepts about which they have no understanding (*Eth. Nic.* 1147a8).

When the priests hand Jesus over to Pilate, they provide the dodgy charge, "If this man were not a criminal, we would not have handed him over to you" (18:30). Pressed by Pilate for something more substantial, they provide covenantal grounds, "We have a law, and according to that law he ought to die because he has claimed to be the Son of God" (19:7), which they all too quickly replace with Roman law, "If you release this man, you are no friend of the emperor. Everyone who claims to be a king sets himself against the emperor" (19:12). The gospel writer's construction of this progression culminates with the line, "We have no king but the emperor" (19:15). Whereas Matthew and Mark's priest make blasphemy the consistent charge and render their concession to Roman authority as merely administrators of executions, John makes apparent that such a concession is itself blasphemy. Luke's priests know to add offences indictable under Roman law by claiming that Jesus forbids payment of Roman taxes (23:2), but they do not overtly jeopardize their covenantal authority. Aristotle's akratic man whole-heartedly endorses a plan but comes to regret it over the course of time (*Eth. Nic.* 1166b5–29). When John's priests gaze upon the sign that Pilate posts on the cross, they quickly come to see that their means of achieving their goal lacked prudence, a virtue that I will discuss in the context of the representation of Jesus's authority.

Woven between the episodes that rhetorically undermine the authority of the Jewish leaders stand a series of short dialogues in which the crowd manifests its confusion and two-mindedness about Jesus's identity. In these anonymous utterances, John skillfully engages a subtler authority that can undermine his Christological agenda, the authority of conventional knowledge. Whenever the crowd appeals to collective experience and tradition to make sense of what they have witnessed, they give voice to conflicting traditions. Shortly after stating that no one is supposed to know where the Messiah comes from (7:27), the crowd points out that Scripture says that the Messiah will come from Bethlehem (7:42). John shows the limitations of common sense by having the Jews point out that raising the temple in three days is an impossibility if it has taken forty-six years of renovation to reach its present form (2:20) and puzzle over how Jesus can come down from heaven when they know Joseph (6:42). Watching the crowd's befuddlement signals the reader that the solution is to accept the authority of Jesus's witness.

Johannine rhetoric displays quite prominently a disturbing aspect of epideictic rhetoric.[13] Andreea Deciu Ritivoi contends that epideictic discourse "lies on the verge of propaganda" by creating a mythical and glorious "us" that justifies exclusion of a mythically constructed "them."[14]

---

13. Celeste M. Condit, "The Functions of Epideictic: The Boston Massacre Orations as Exemplar," *Communication Quarterly* 33.4 (1985): 289.

14. See Michael Schandorf, "A Gesture Theory of Communication" (PhD diss., University of Illinois at Chicago, 2015), 236–37, who cites Andreea Deciu Ritivoi, *Paul Ricoeur: Tradition and Innovation in Rhetorical Theory* (State University of New York Press, 2006), 97.

In response to the expulsion theory that the Fourth Gospel reflects a past in which Jews forced Christians out of the synagogue, Adele Reinhartz contends that the rhetoric of the Fourth Gospel supports a propulsion theory. By telling stories like that of the blind man, the gospel provides grounds for Christ-confessors to distance themselves from Jews.[15] The examination above supports her hypothesis by presenting Jewish authorities appealing to fear and failing to fulfill their own virtues. The question that cannot be answered without a before and after measure of the gospel writer's own perception of his relationship with Jews is the degree to which he is writing himself out of a relationship. Recent studies of the pedagogy of composition known as cognitive rhetoric demonstrate that writing is a process of working out problems that transforms knowledge.[16] John does not reject Jewish heritage. The line "You worship what you do not know; we worship what we know, for salvation is from the Jews" (4:22) appears early in the narrative. The gospel writer appropriates, or as Reinhartz puts it exproperiates, Jewish signifiers to describe Jesus and a new socioreligious community.[17] Cognitive rhetoric studies the writing and verbalized thoughts of a writer in action. Without this data or a baseline, we can only speculate to what degree John is reconciling himself to the idea of community in relation with God that does not include most ethnic Jews. In the *Phaedrus*, Socrates observes that those who write rhetoric handbooks are "cunning folk" who "know all about the soul but keep their knowledge out of sight" (271c [Hackforth]). Socrates is troubled by a rhetorician's power to persuade an audience about matters that the speaker knows to be false because the art of persuasion requires one knows what is true (261d–262d). Socrates's warning seen in the context of what Reinhartz calls a "rhetoric of disaffiliation" suggests that John knows that the Jewish authorities to which Jews attend in the aftermath of the destruction of the temple in fact possess the three properties that Aristotle describes as necessary for gaining an audience's trust: practical wisdom (*phronēsis*), virtue (*aretē*) and goodwill (*eunoia*) (*Rhet.* 1378a112).

Jerome H. Neyrey has discussed how John handles the standard encomiastic topoi—origins, education, deeds of the soul, and noble death—to

---

15. Adele Reinhartz, *Cast Out of the Covenant: Jews and Anti-Judaism in the Gospel of John* (Lexington/Fortress Academic, 2018), 119.

16. E.g., Linda Flower, *The Construction of Negotiated Meaning: A Social Cognitive Theory of Writing* (Southern Illinois University Press, 1994), 36–43.

17. Reinhartz, *Cast Out of the Covenant*, 51–66.

demonstrate that Jesus is worthy of being called the Son of God.[18] I will focus upon the demonstration of practical wisdom (*phronēsis*), virtue (*aretē*), and goodwill (*eunoia*). The credibility of the gospel relies upon Jesus's authority, as well as the solidity of the witness of the Beloved Disciple and then the reliability of the narrator to share what has been received. If one rejects the wisdom, virtue, and goodwill of any of these, the act of persuasion fails. The gospel constructs a shared social reality by which authority is extended to the gospel's witnesses by emphasizing the close relationship of the Beloved Disciple to Jesus. As if the designation "beloved" is not enough, he is represented reclining at the bosom of Jesus (13:23) and as one known to the high priest yet prepared to follow Jesus after his arrest—in contrast to Peter who stands outside the gate and denies his affiliation (18:15–18); he is also charged with caring for Jesus's mother as if he were a son (19:26–27), is said to believe before the empty tomb (20:8), and is the first to recognize Jesus when he stands at the seashore (21:7). Jesus's own claims to his authority by virtue of his unity with the Father are numerous and are substantiated through his signs. The narrator participation in this unity is signified by participation in the designation "children of God" and the metaphor of the vine and expression of certitude about the testimony of the Beloved Disciple.

The prologue presents Jesus as the personification of *logos* and in possession of wisdom about divine matters. *Phronēsis*, in contrast, is a more pragmatic kind of wisdom manifest in the capacity to be single minded about what action to take and to be discriminating about in what context to act.[19] It is distinct from shrewdness in which one understands what is good for oneself. *Phronēsis* comprehends what is good for other human beings. An obvious example of Jesus's *phronēsis* becomes all the more apparent in contrast with the Synoptic Jesus who falters just before his arrest asking God "to remove this cup" (Mark 14:36 par.). The gospel writer seems to know this tradition because his Jesus says, "Am I not to drink the cup that the Father has given me?" (18:11). Earlier Jesus parodies *akrasis* by imagining himself in doubt, "Now my soul is troubled. And what should I say—'Father, save me from this hour'? No, it is for this reason that I have come to this hour" (12:27). Aristotle's virtuous person is unified and not torn by conflict (*Eth. Nic.* 1102b28).

---

18. Neyrey, *Gospel of John in Cultural and Rhetorical Perspective*, 5–28.

19. See Eve Rabinoff, *Perception in Aristotle's Ethics* (Northwestern University Press, 2018), 114.

Jesus practices prudent deception by refraining from being baited by his brother's goading him to be candid (*parrhēsia*) and to go up to Jerusalem with them by going up covertly (7:3–10). He exercises judicious caution by hiding and slipping out of the temple when the crowd is ready to stone him (8:59, see also 6:15). When others try to force Jesus's hand, he takes care to choose his own opportune moment (see Aristotle, *Eth. Nic.* 1096a23; 1104a8–9, 14). The concept of timing (*kairos*) is a significant theme in both classical rhetoric and philosophy.[20] Even when Jesus seems to bow to the pressure of pleasing his mother at Cana, the witnesses to the sign are the disciples and servants rather than beneficiaries. Jesus's deliberateness is evident in the handling of the resurrection of Lazarus. The setting of previous restoration miracles has been intimate (5:8–9) or at a distance (4:49–53; 9:7). Jesus intentionally delays his arrival in Bethany so that Lazarus is dead (11:6) and a crowd has gathered (11:42) and then speaks loudly, "Lazarus, come out!" (11:43). Jesus displays *phronēsis* when he perceives the blind man not as the victim of sin but rather as the occasion for God's goodness, a perception that is made possible by the goodness of his own aims.[21]

Aristotle calls *phronēsis* the "eye of the soul" that sees how the motivation provided by virtue can be enacted (*Eth. Nic.* 1144a29–30). From the four cardinal virtues of the Greco-Roman world, wisdom, justice, courage, and temperance, Neyrey singles out justice in the form of piety to God as one of the Johannine Jesus's qualities of character that best fits Greco-Roman and Jewish notions of cardinal virtues.[22] Jesus's claims of his relationship with God (e.g., 5:19–24), that strike the ear of his hostile narrative opponents as arrogant or blasphemous, would strike the ear of the ancient intended reading audience as evidence of piety. John repeats the refrain that Jesus is God's faithful agent throughout the gospel (e.g., 10:17–18; 14:31; 15:10) and uses it as emphasis in the Farewell Address (17:4, 8, 14, 24). We have already seen how John implicitly criticizes Jesus's opponents by showing that piety toward God is not the virtue that motivates their actions.

---

20. See Phillip Sipiora, introduction to *Rhetoric and Kairos: Essays in History, Theory, and Praxis*, ed. Phillip Sipiora and James S. Baumlin (State University of New York Press, 2002), 1–22.

21. See Rabinoff, *Perception in Aristotle's Ethics*, 133, on *Eth. nic.* 1113a22–31.

22. Jerome H. Neyrey, S.J., *The Gospel of John*, NCBC (Cambridge University Press, 2006), 20. He cites Menander Rhetor, 1.361.17–25.

Although Aristotle lists *eunoia* as essential to the ethos of a credible speaker, he does not explicitly address the topic in his *Rhetoric* but picks it up in his discussions of friendship (e.g., *Eth. eud.* 1241a5–10). *Eunoia*, in modern rhetorical handbooks, is the goodwill that a speaker cultivates with an audience by identifying with them. US presidential addresses attempt to do this with the words, "My fellow Americans." Guest speakers begin with words of thanks for being invited. For Aristotle, a speaker demonstrates goodwill by providing those things that are to the benefit of the audience (*Eth. Nic.* 1378a6). In John, *eunoia* is encoded in the promises that are made within the narrative by Jesus to his followers and by the narrator to the reading audience—Reinhartz characterizes this as a rhetoric of "desire and fulfillment"—as well as in references to the sincerity of Jesus and the narrator's motives.[23] The prologue states that Jesus offers his followers the "ability to become children of God" (1:12). The metaphors that Jesus uses to describe himself—bread, living water, and life—describe what he offers his followers rather than his own status. The act of receiving or trusting Jesus and his teachings is treated metaphorically with objects of desire such as eating, drinking, rebirth, and bearing fruit.[24]

Jesus and the narrator frequently imply that their motives are in the best interests of their audience. The gospel writer indicates that his own editorial selections from the many Jesus stories with which he is familiar are made on behalf of the reader, "Now Jesus did many other signs in the presence of his disciples, which are not written in this book. But these are written so that you may come to believe [that Jesus is the Messiah], the Son of God, and that through believing you may have life in his name" (20:30–31). When Jesus describes his own motives and God's motives, he emphasizes they both are driven by love in order to provide life rather than judgement (3:16–17; 12:47). In his self-defense after the first Sabbath healing, Jesus provides a commentary on his testimony, "I say these things so that you may be saved" (5:34b). In the Farewell Address, Jesus stops to explain himself, "I have said these things to you so that my joy may be in you, and that your joy may be complete" (15:11). The most critical sign of the goodwill or sincerity of a speaker necessary to their credibility is the proof of their own personal commitment to what they are espousing. The narrator encodes this in the enthusiastic language of the prologue, "we

---

23. Reinhartz, *Cast Out of the Covenant*, 3–22.
24. Nourishment and food are common metaphors for teaching in Greco-Roman and early Christian literature (e.g., Quintilian, *Inst.* 2.4.5, 2.5.18, and Heb 6:4–5).

have seen his glory, the glory as of a father's only son, full of grace and truth" (1:14) and the confident assertion, "From his fullness we have all received, grace upon grace" (1:16). Jesus makes claim to his convictions by fulfilling his own definition of love, "No one has greater love than this, to lay down one's life for one's friends." (15:13; see also 10:17).

If one is looking for knowledge of facts such as the accuracy of John's topography or his representation of the Pharisee/priest relationships, an examination of Johannine rhetoric is probably not the best tool. If one is looking for evidence of the gospel writer's knowledge of rhetoric, the ease with which one may find examples of Greco-Roman rhetorical conventions in John suggests significant familiarity with these conventions. Where he learned them—in the classroom or on the street—may have to be answered with the toss of a coin. In his handling of controversy, he seems well aware of the potential for a high Christology to lead to divisive debates and is cognizant of the potential for dramatization of such debates in narrative to create a sense of agreement and shared social identity in the minds of his audience. He may not have anticipated how his technique of using metaphor and abstraction to make room for new or deeper reflection would itself generate doctrinal conflicts. Did he know Aristotle? Whereas I have had to rely upon Aristotle for the categories with which I can analyze John's construction of Jesus's authority and the weakness of his opponents' claims to authority, John seems to be as keen an observer of the dynamics of human discourse as the philosopher. The question that remains unanswered is the degree to which the gospel writer recognized that the rhetorical strategies, including the rhetorical construction of Jews and their leaders, to create a social epistemology contained the capacity to motivate subsequent deliberations and actions against the Jews. I began this essay by describing its activity as ferreting, a metaphor designed to conjure up images of fiercely pulling into the light understandings that lie in the dark. By laying bare Johannine persuasive strategies, modern readers hopefully can with greater intentionality determine how best to respond to the gospel as a rhetorical act.

7

Scripture

Catrin H. Williams

While the exact scope and depth of engagement with the Jewish Scriptures may be difficult to determine, there are numerous indicators in the Gospel of John that Scripture was an important source for and probably formed much of what underpinned the cultural encyclopaedia of its author. In contrast, therefore, to many of the other topics examined in this collection of essays, Scripture is overtly and methodically signposted within the text as having played a pivotal role in relation to *what John knows*. At regular intervals, attention is drawn to the content of Israel's Scriptures and, invariably, to how they bear witness to Jesus's identity, mission, and significance. An assortment of vocabulary is used for this purpose.[1] "The scripture" (ἡ γραφή) is the designation that features most prominently in the narrative, often in relation to a quotation (John 7:38; 10:35; 13:18; 19:24, 28, 36, 37; cf. 17:12) or paraphrastic allusion (7:42); sometimes it occurs without reference to specific passages (2:22; 20:9), pointing in all likelihood, as in the case of the plural "the scriptures" (αἱ γραφαί; 5:39), to Scripture in its entirety.[2] Reference is also made to "the writings" (τὰ γράμματα) to denote the Pentateuch (5:47) and an unnamed collection of scriptural texts (7:15), as well as to "the prophets" (οἱ προφῆται) in connection with a

---

1. For a helpful discussion of John's application of the relevant terminology, see Andreas Obermann, *Die christologische Erfüllung der Schrift im Johannesevangelium: Eine Untersuchung zur johanneischen Hermeneutik anhand der Schriftzitate*, WUNT 2/83 (Mohr Siebeck, 1996), 38–63. See also Wolfgang Kraus, "Johannes und das Alte Testament: Überlegungen zum Umgang mit der Schrift im Johannesevangelium im Horizont Biblischer Theologie," *ZNW* 88 (1997): 2–3.

2. In John 10:35 and 19:24, "the scripture" (ἡ γραφή) may be used to denote a particular quotation and the whole of Scripture at the same time.

direct quotation (6:45) and the prophetic books more widely understood (1:45). In the latter case, the Jesus-witness provided by "the prophets" is tied to the testimony of "the law" (ὁ νόμος), a term used by John on various occasions and with numerous possible connotations, either to refer to the torah given by Moses on Sinai (1:17, 45; 7:19 [2x], 49; 18:31), its individual commandments (7:23, 51; 8:17; 19:7[2x]) or, once again, as a synonym for Scripture (10:34; 12:34; 15:25). To be noted also are the many cases in which the law is explicitly attributed to Moses as writer and/or mediator,[3] while the spoken witness of the prophet Isaiah is strikingly adduced to frame the account of Jesus's public ministry (1:23; 12:38–41).

Both individually and collectively, these numerous references to the Jewish Scriptures and their content afford more than ample confirmation *that* John knows Scripture and repeatedly highlights its recognized authoritative significance. Drawing attention to this particular set of data, however, represents only one of several possible approaches to the subject of John's knowledge of and engagement with scriptural resources. In fact, it does no more than skim the surface of any attempt at probing the *extent* and *implications* of such an undertaking. As is widely acknowledged, the Gospel of John also appears to be steeped in a rich and often deeply embedded deposit of references to a range of scriptural themes and motifs, many of which play an integral role in John's shaping and (re)telling of the Jesus story. To cite one well-known example: it is evident, from the choice of ἐν ἀρχῇ as the opening words of the prologue (John 1:1; cf. Gen 1:1 LXX) and also the evocative reference to the risen Jesus breathing (ἐνεφύσησεν) life-giving spirit into his disciples (John 20:22; cf. Gen 2:7 LXX),[4] that the gospel narrative is structured in such a way that it begins with first creation and draws to an end with images of new creation and eschatological life and that it also alerts readers/hearers from the outset to how, "starting with the Old Testament, they should

---

3. All occurrences are to be found in John 1–9 and in relation to the question of Jesus's authority (1:17, 45; 3:14; 5:45, 46; 6:32; 7:19, 22, 23; 9:28, 29).

4. That other scriptural evocations may also be at work is suggested by the fact that the precise verbal form ἐνεφύσησεν is also used to describe Elijah's raising of the son of the widow of Sarepta (3 Kgdms 17:21); cf. also the divine command for life to be breathed (ἐμφύσησον) into the dry bones in Ezekiel's vision (Ezek 37:9 LXX). See further Martin Hengel, "Die Schriftauslegung des 4. Evangeliums auf dem Hintergrund der urchristlichen Exegese," *JBT* 4 (1989): 273–74; Carlos R. Sosa Siliezar, *Creation Imagery in the Gospel of John*, LNTS 546 (Bloomsbury T&T Clark, 2015).

read the story of Jesus."[5] This immediately raises expectations that Israel's Scriptures contribute in significant ways to the emplotment of that story.

The aim of this essay is to examine how and, to some extent, why the Jewish Scriptures inform the composition of John's Gospel. To carry out that task, three questions will guide the ensuing discussion. First, what can be learned from John's Gospel as to what the author knew of Israel's Scriptures? Second, how could that knowledge have been acquired and also how was it fashioned by John for the purpose of communication to others? Third, how does Scripture work within the narrative and contribute to the design and message of John's Gospel?

What John Knows of Scripture

To enquire about John's familiarity with, and access, to the Jewish Scriptures, one must inevitably begin with the gospel's explicit quotations. To establish, for this purpose, what qualifies as a direct scriptural quotation, two criteria must be tested: (1) readers/hearers need to be alerted to the presence of a quotation by the author's use of a citation formula, although—as we shall see—this is not invariably the case in John; (2) one must search for evidence of the use of word combinations that are clearly recognizable from their occurrence in an antecedent text or texts.[6] If these criteria are applied fairly rigidly, it is possible to isolate fourteen explicit quotations in John's Gospel,[7] all of which are accompanied by a citation

---

5. Richard Bauckham, *Gospel of Glory: Major Themes in Johannine Theology* (Baker, 2015), 50. Cf. also Alicia D. Myers, *Characterizing Jesus: A Rhetorical Analysis of the Fourth Gospel's Use of Scripture in Its Presentation of Jesus*, LNTS 458 (T&T Clark, 2012), 173–74.

6. On these criteria, see further Obermann, *Die christologische Erfüllung der Schrift*, 70–76; cf. Margaret Daly-Denton, "Going Beyond the Genially Open 'Cf.': Intertextual Reference to the Old Testament in the New," *Milltown Studies* 44 (1999): 48–60.

7. The combination of both criteria rules out passages which are introduced by a citation formula but have no identifiable reference(s) in the Scriptures (John 17:12; 19:28). On those passages which qualify as composite allusions or scriptural paraphrases rather than citations, and this despite the presence of a citation formula and some recognizable words/themes from scriptural sources (John 7:42; 8:17; 12:34), see Maarten J. J. Menken, *Old Testament Quotations in the Fourth Gospel: Studies in Textual Form*, CBET 15 (Kok Pharos, 1996), 16–17; Ruth Sheridan, *Retelling Scripture: "The Jews" and the Scriptural Citations in John 1:19–12:15*, BibInt 110 (Brill, 2012), 106.

formula (1:23; 2:17; 6:31, 45; 7:38; 10:34; 12:15, 38, 39, 40; 13:18; 15:25; 19:24, 36, 37).⁸ In addition, the quotation of Ps 118(117):25-26 in John 12:13 belongs to the category of direct quotation despite the absence of a citation formula; it bears striking resemblance to its psalm source, and its presentation in direct speech—as the content of the crowd's spontaneous acclamation—is dictated by the narrative setting.

As to what these fifteen quotations disclose about John's knowledge of Scripture, we first note that the Fourth Gospel, like many of its ancient Jewish and early Christian counterparts, draws above all from three scriptural sources that, albeit anachronistically, can be described as belonging to a "canon within the canon": eight of the citations are taken from the Psalms, though sometimes in combination with other scriptural sources, while four are drawn from the prophecies of Isaiah and two from Zechariah.⁹ Somewhat surprisingly, given the emphasis in the first half of the narrative on what Moses has written in "the scripture" or "the law," there are no marked quotations from Genesis in John, and explicit citations from elsewhere in the Pentateuch are limited to the description of Jesus's unbroken bones as scriptural fulfillment (John 19:36; cf. Exod 12:10, 46; Num 9:12 LXX).¹⁰ One important factor in this regard is that the retelling

---

8. In the case of John 19:37, the scriptural quotation is tied to the one that immediately precedes it (19:36) through the use of the words καὶ πάλιν.

9. Psalms: John 2:17 (Ps 69:9 [68:10]); 6:31 (Ps 78[77]:24); 7:38 (Ps 78[77]:16, 20); 10:34 (Ps 82[81]:6); 12:13 (Ps 118[117]:26); 13:18 (Ps 41:9 [40:10]); 15:25 (Ps 69:4 [68:5] and/or possibly Ps 35[34]:19); 19:24 (Ps 22:18 [21:19]). To these occurrences one may add Jesus's pronouncement, "I thirst," in John 19:28 (Ps 69:21 [68:22]). See Margaret Daly-Denton, *David in the Fourth Gospel: The Johannine Interpretation of the Psalms*, AGJU 47 (Brill, 2000), 115-242; Andrew C. Brunson, *Psalm 118 in the Gospel of John: An Intertextual Study on the New Exodus Pattern in the Theology of John*, WUNT 2/158 (Mohr Siebeck, 2003), 180-239. Isaiah: John 1:23 (Isa 40:3); 6:45 (Isa 54:13); 12:38 (Isa 53:1); 12:40 (Isa 6:10). See Catrin H. Williams, "Isaiah in John's Gospel," in *Isaiah in the New Testament*, ed. Steve Moyise and Maarten J. J. Menken (T&T Clark, 2005), 101-17; Daniel J. Brendsel, *"Isaiah Saw His Glory": The Use of Isaiah 52-53 in John 12*, BZNW 208 (de Gruyter, 2014). Zechariah: John 12:15 (Zech 9:9); 19:37 (Zech 12:10). See Adam Kubiš, *The Book of Zechariah in the Gospel of John* (Gabalda, 2012), 27-218; William Randolph Bynum, "Quotations of Zechariah in the Fourth Gospel," in *Abiding Words: The Use of Scripture in the Gospel of John*, ed. Alicia D. Myers and Bruce G. Schuchard, RBS 81 (SBL Press, 2015), 47-74.

10. Cf. Richard B. Hays, *Echoes of Scripture in the Gospels* (Baylor University Press, 2016), 287. On John 1:51 as an unmarked quotation from Gen 28:12 and on various Genesis allusions in John's Gospel, see Maarten J. J. Menken, "Genesis in

of the exodus events in the Psalms, rather than the originating narratives, often forms the basis of John's portrayal of Jesus' life-giving significance (e.g., John 6:31; 7:38).

Exact identification of the source(s) behind John's citations is no easy task. The fact that so many of them do not correspond precisely to known Hebrew (MT) or Greek (LXX) versions of the passages in question has led many scholars, particularly in earlier generations, to argue that John was citing texts imprecisely from memory or may even have been influenced by targumic traditions.[11] Having said that, in more recent decades scholars have been adopting a variety of new perspectives and applying a range of different methodological tools to come to terms with the challenges posed by the question of John's acquaintance with and use of Scripture. By focusing not only on the question of sources and textual form but also on *the function* of John's marked citations, Maarten Menken and others have painstakingly applied source- and redaction-critical methods to argue that the distinctive wording of the majority of these quotations is the result of Johannine redaction,[12] motivated by christological factors and legitimated on exegetical grounds because they remain within the boundaries of known Jewish interpretive techniques. As well as only retaining those elements of direct relevance to the surrounding Johannine context, redactional features identified in

---

John's Gospel and I John," in *Genesis in the New Testament*, ed. Maarten J. J. Menken and Steve Moyise, LNTS 466 (Bloomsbury, 2012), 84–95. An indirect quotation evoking Deut 17:6, 19:15 and Num 35:30 is widely detected in John 8:17. See especially Michael Labahn, "Deuteronomy in John's Gospel," in *Deuteronomy in the New Testament: The New Testament and the Scriptures of Israel*, ed. Steve Moyise and Maarten J. J. Menken, LNTS 358 (T&T Clark, 2007), 84–87; Ruth Sheridan, "The Testimony of Two Witnesses: John 8:17," in Myers and Schuchard, *Abiding Words*, 161–84.

11. For John citing texts imprecisely from memory, see, e.g., Charles Goodwin, "How Did John Treat His Sources?" *JBL* 73 (1954): 61–75. See also the third section of this essay on how the processes of memory/memorization as understood in ancient media studies can shed a different light on the likely citation practices of John and other New Testament writers. For the influence by targumic traditions, see, e.g., Edwin D. Freed, *Old Testament Quotations in the Gospel of John*, NovTSup 11 (Brill, 1965), 127–30.

12. In addition to Menken's *Old Testament Quotations*, see Bruce G. Schuchard, *Scripture within Scripture: The Interrelationship of Form and Function in the Explicit Old Testament Citations in the Gospel of John*, SBLDS 133 (Scholars Press, 1992), and, more recently, Michael A. Daise, *Quotations in John: Studies on Jewish Scripture in the Fourth Gospel*, LNTS 610 (Bloomsbury T&T Clark, 2020).

John's quotations—and analogous to widely attested Jewish exegetical devices—include the addition, omission, and substitution of words/phrases, the inclusion of composite expressions (see further below), and the changing of verbal tenses and line sequences.[13]

Some caution must, admittedly, be displayed when seeking to reconstruct the precise source-texts and modifications made to John's scriptural quotations.[14] Nevertheless, significant inroads have been made by Menken and others into understanding John's handling of quotations, insofar as they can be delineated from known versions of the underlying scriptural sources and also into what can be gleaned from such redactional activity about the profile of John's scriptural literacy. Most of John's quotations draw on Septuagintal versions of the passages in question, although some cases point to engagement with the Hebrew versions of those sources (cf. John 12:40; 13:18; 19:37).[15] Furthermore, and particularly important for exploring the possible depth of John's scriptural acquaintance, the exegetical techniques identifiable in the explicit quotations militate against a rigid form of prooftexting but rather lend support to the view that John frequently takes into account the wider context of those quotations. Contextual appropriation occasionally comes to light in an overt fashion, as in the explanatory comment in 12:41 that Isaiah spoke the words of 53:1 (John 12:38) and 6:10 (John 12:40) because "he saw his [Jesus'] glory," with reference to the glorious divine manifestation experienced by the prophet in his temple-vision (Isa 6:2 LXX: "and the house was full of his glory"

---

13. Some of these devices also resemble ancient rhetorical techniques of *paraphrasis,* such as those outlined by Theon (*Prog.* 62, 108). See further Myers, *Characterizing Jesus,* 72, 84.

14. For example, Sheridan, *Retelling Scripture,* 22–25, argues that the search for the original version of John's quotations is problematic given the pluriformity of ancient Hebrew and Greek text versions. See, however, Menken, *Old Testament Quotations,* 14; Daise, *Quotations in John,* 4–12, also 26: "a hypothesis which traces an anomaly [in John's quotations] to an extant source is to be preferred over one that traces it to a putative one; and … an anomaly which cannot be traced to any extant source is best ascribed to the style or exegetical methods (and thereby *Tendenz*) of the fourth evangelist (or redactor)."

15. Bauckham, *Gospel of Glory,* 132, 154–56, further proposes that reliance on the Hebrew text best accounts for some of the exegetical connections attested in John's indirect scriptural references, including the linking together of Exod 12:3 and Isa 53:7 in John 1:29, based on their shared use of the Hebrew term for lamb (שֶׂה).

[δόξα]), which is the setting for the second Isaianic quotation (6:10).[16] In response, moreover, to the scriptural quotation cited by the crowds in John 6:31, "He gave them bread from heaven to eat" (cf. Ps 78[77]:24; Exod 16:4, 15), Jesus evokes the broader exodus context by noting that the Israelites died after eating the manna (John 6:49; cf. Num 14:23), while the influence of Exod 16 is evident in the reference to the "murmuring" (γογγύζω) of "the Jews" (John 6:41, 43), like that of their ancestors in the desert (Exod 16:2, 8 LXX; cf. 15:24; 17:3).[17] Such examples, some overt and others more veiled, demonstrate how scriptural quotations operate integrally as part of John's narrative design,[18] also confirming their christological and rhetorical functions within the text.

Additional evidence of John's scriptural-contextual awareness is afforded by the exegetical maneuvers undergirding those citations in which "literary borrowing occurs in a manner that includes two or more passages (from the same or different authors) fused together and conveyed as though they are only one."[19] Over half of the fifteen quotations in John fit this definition, in that discrete words or phrases from other scriptural source texts are inserted into the (primary) text to form what amounts to a single *composite citation*.[20] In similar fashion to the Jewish exegetical

---

16. Cf. also the references to the Servant's glorification in Isa 52:13 LXX (δοξασθήσεται), which occur in the immediate vicinity of the words cited by John in 12:38. See further Catrin H. Williams, "'Seeing the Glory': The Reception of Isaiah's Call-Vision in John 12:41," in *Judaism, Jewish Identities and the Gospel Tradition: Festschrift for Professor Maurice Casey*, ed. James Crossley (Equinox Press, 2010), 245–72.

17. See Judith Lieu, "Narrative Analysis and Scripture in John," in *The Old Testament in the New Testament: Essays in Honour of J. L. North*, ed. Steve Moyise, JSNTSup 189 (Sheffield Academic, 2000), 148.

18. See now R. Alan Culpepper, "Quotation as Commentary: The Good News of a King on a Donkey (John 12:12–15)," in *The Gospel of John*, vol. 4 of *Biblical Interpretation in Early Christian Gospels*, ed. Thomas R. Hatina, LNTS 613 (T&T Clark, 2020), 139–54.

19. Sean A. Adams and Seth M. Ehorn, "What Is a Composite Citation? An Introduction," in *Jewish, Graeco-Roman, and Early Christian Uses*, vol. 1 of *Composite Citations in Antiquity*, ed. Sean A. Adams and Seth M. Ehorn, LNTS 525 (Bloomsbury T&T Clark, 2016), 4.

20. John 6:31; 7:38; 12:13; 12:15; 12:40; 13:18; 19:36; 19:37. For discussion of the composite features in these quotations, see Catrin H. Williams, "Composite Citations in the Gospel of John," in *New Testament Uses*, vol. 2 of *Composite Citations in Antiquity*, ed. Sean A. Adams and Seth M. Ehorn, LNTS 593 (Bloomsbury T&T Clark, 2018), 94–127. John's fondness for bringing together disparate scriptural sources in

device later described by the rabbis as *gezerah shawah* and already commonly attested in late Second Temple Jewish texts, redactional activity in John's explicit quotations includes the bringing together of two or more distant texts on the basis of the shared vocabulary (catchword links) and/or analogous themes to be found in the wider contexts of those texts.[21] Thus, even if some of John's explicit citations were already firmly anchored in early Christian tradition, prompting some scholars to propose that John had access to an existing collection of *testimonia*,[22] there is no evidence to indicate that the additional scriptural elements had already been built into John's composite citations and that those citations were in circulation during a pre-Johannine stage of composition. The composite material in these quotations is too closely aligned with John's distinctive portrayal of Jesus for this to have been the case. Similar to the ripple effect of the wider context of scriptural quotations that is visible in their new Johannine setting (in John 6, 12, and indeed several other chapters), the composite citations affirm the Evangelist's much broader, and deeper, familiarity with Israel's Scriptures and point to a profoundly literate scriptural exegete. John's meticulous reworking of certain quotations also implies much more

---

explicit quotations was already recognized by C. K. Barrett, "The Old Testament in the Fourth Gospel," *JTS* 48 (1947): 157.

21. For example, the crowd's appeal to the past provision of manna in John 6:31, "He gave them bread from heaven to eat" (ἄρτον ἐκ τοῦ οὐρανοῦ ἔδωκεν αὐτοῖς φαγεῖν), does not correspond exactly to any single source. Ps 77:24 LXX most closely resembles John 6:31, but with the exception of two features: it lacks ἐκ τοῦ (before οὐρανοῦ) and φαγεῖν. However, the exact phrase ἐκ τοῦ οὐρανοῦ—required to highlight Jesus's identity as the one who *descended from* heaven (John 6:32–33, 38) rather than simply as "heavenly bread" (ἄρτον οὐρανοῦ)—occurs in the analogously worded Exod 16:4 LXX, and the verbal form φαγεῖν is used specifically for eating bread in Exod 16:15 LXX. See further Williams, "Composite Citations," 97–100. For examples in the Dead Sea Scrolls, the writings of Philo, and various Septuagint translations, see Catrin H. Williams, "John, Judaism, and 'Searching the Scriptures,'" in *John and Judaism: A Contested Relationship in Context*, ed. R. Alan Culpepper and Paul N. Anderson, RBS 87 (SBL Press, 2017), 77–100.

22. Isa 40:3 (John 1:23; Mark 1:3 par.); Zech 9:9 (John 12:15; Matt 21:5; cf. Mark 11:1–10). Other explicit quotations in John are embedded as allusions within the narrative in the Synoptic Gospels: Isa 6:9–10 (John 12:40; cf. Mark 4:12); Ps 41:9 [40:10] (John 13:18; cf. Mark 14:18 par.); Ps 22:18 [21:19] (John 19:24; cf. Mark 15:24 par.). See Martin C. Albl, *"And Scripture Cannot Be Broken": The Form and Function of the Early Christian Testimonia Collections*, NovTSup 96 (Brill, 1999); Alessandro Falcetta, "The Testimony Research of James Rendel Harris," *NovT* 45 (2003): 280–99.

than a passing acquaintance with first-century Jewish exegetical principles and practices.[23]

Deciphering the interpretive mechanisms at work in John's composite quotations also serves as a valuable transition point from the relative comfort zone of direct—and largely identifiable—quotations to the exploration of other, more implicit, modes of scriptural reference. It cannot be denied, of course, that the particularly broad span of scriptural allusiveness in John's Gospel makes it difficult to tap into, delineate and explain the likely extent of its scriptural associations.[24] Some measure of what John knows, certainly beyond the content of its scriptural quotations, is indicated by the prominence of references to John's Gospel among the thirty-four pages of NA[28] dedicated to possible scriptural citations and allusions in the New Testament writings.[25] Even if not all of them are equally convincing and verifiable, the large number of scriptural references proposed for John suggests that the author is thoroughly immersed in Israel's Scriptures and that the gospel's narratives and discourses are deliberately designed to evoke a whole host of multilayered scriptural associations. On the high end of the scripture-spectrum, and inspiring strong levels of exegetical certainty, are John's unmissable references to key events and figures from Israel's past (e.g., John 1:51; 3:14; 4:5–6; 6:30–33; 12:41), as well as distinctive verbal parallels intended to act as interpretive keys with the capacity to unlock the meaning of their immediate (and wider) context (e.g., 1:1, 17; 6:41, 43; 10:16; 20:22). At the other end of the scale are those fleeting scriptural echoes that may (or may not) be intended for activation and consumption by John's

---

23. On John's familiarity with and indebtedness to ancient Jewish exegetical techniques and strategies, see, e.g., Peder Borgen, *Bread from Heaven: An Exegetical Study of the Concept of Manna in the Gospel of John and the Writings of Philo*, NovTSup 10 (Brill, 1965); Gary T. Manning, *Echoes of a Prophet: The Use of Ezekiel in the Gospel of John and in the Literature of the Second Temple Period*, JSNTSup 270 (T&T Clark, 2004); Jutta Leonhardt-Balzer, "The Johannine Literature and Contemporary Jewish Literature," in *The Oxford Handbook of Johannine Studies*, ed. Judith M. Lieu and Martinus C. de Boer (Oxford University Press, 2018), 155–70.

24. The interpretive challenges posed by John's frequently indirect use of Scripture are articulated by Lieu, "Narrative Analysis and Scripture in John," 144–45.

25. This extends to a 581-page list of John's likely scriptural parallels in Hans Hübner, *Evangelium secundum Iohannem*, vol. 1.2 of *Vetus Testamentum in Novo* (Vandenhoeck & Ruprecht, 2003).

audiences.[26] The possibility must also be entertained that one of John's characteristic rhetorical strategies is to engage in deliberate allusiveness, evoking scriptural themes, motifs and symbols in a consciously indirect, even paraphrastic, manner in order to encourage direct participation by the gospel's audiences in the task of "searching the Scriptures" (cf. John 5:39). This possibility will be examined more fully in the next section of this essay. Certainly, the recognition that the Evangelist works with a wide compass of scriptural evocations raises important questions not only about John's access to Israel's Scriptures but also how that accessed knowledge and its distinctive Johannine interpretation is intended to be passed on to readers and hearers.

How John Knows (and Communicates) Scripture

To examine these issues further, it is necessary to consider which medium or media would have been at John's disposal for the purpose of receiving and citing Israel's Scriptures and also for conveying the importance of Scripture for formulating the Johannine presentation of Jesus. Intertextuality in various guises has, to a great extent, functioned in recent decades as the overarching framework for the study of the use of the Old Testament in the New, including John's familiarity with and use of Scripture. The emphasis, then, falls on the literary relationship between texts as *written* compositions and on the reception of those writings by audiences in their capacity as *readers*. However, scholars increasingly acknowledge that first-century texts like John's Gospel emerged from a cultural (or ancient media) environment in which textuality and orality, and the interactive dynamics between them, were key factors in the composition, transmission and reception of texts.[27] This is not to deny that John betrays close familiarity with scriptural traditions that circulated in written form, and

---

26. For a helpful discussion of various categories of allusion (proper naming [including citation], definite description, paraphrase, self-echo, and literary conventions), see Susan E. Hylen, *Allusion and Meaning in John 6*, BZNW 137 (de Gruyter, 2005), 53–59, 152–56.

27. See further the essays in Anthony Le Donne and Tom Thatcher, eds., *The Fourth Gospel in First-Century Media Culture*, LNTS 426 (T&T Clark, 2011); and, with specific reference to the *use* of the Jewish Scriptures in New Testament writings, see Catrin H. Williams, "How Scripture 'Speaks': Insights from the Study of Ancient Media Culture," in *Methodology in the Use of the Old Testament in the New: Context and Criteria*, ed. David Allen and Steve Smith, LNTS 579 (T&T Clark, 2020), 53–69.

that—as we shall see—the evangelist repeatedly highlights the *writtenness* of Scripture. However, the likely impact of the contexts in which such scriptural texts were heard by a listening audience should also be taken into account, as well as how the transmission of those texts in new compositions were often filtered through the oral-textual matrix of Jewish exegetical traditions current in the first century CE.

It is undoubtedly true that John places great emphasis on the *written* testimony of Scripture, including repeated use of the formula "it is written" (ἐστιν γεγραμμένον) to introduce a number of scriptural quotations in the first half of the gospel (2:17; 6:31, 45; 10:34; 12:14). Similarly, attention is drawn by John to what Moses (1:45; 5:46) and the prophets (1:45; cf. 6:45) *wrote* about Jesus, while the writtenness of Scripture is of course also encapsulated in the word itself: ἡ γραφή, "the writing." It does not necessarily follow that the highlighting of scriptural textuality in John acts as a prompt or marker that the author has been able to consult written texts directly or that the texts can, or should, be accessed visually by the intended audiences. John's use of the expression "as it is written" serves primarily as a rhetorically motivated appeal to the undisputed authoritative status of Scripture—an authority that is "not limited to the actual words they contain."[28] Having said that, the actualization of *written Scripture* is also expressed through *verbal speech* in John's narrative, as when the spoken prophecy of Isaiah (John 1:23: "the prophet Isaiah said," quoting Isa 40:3) is presently enacted in the witnessing utterance of John the Baptist ("he said"). Scripture, as a result, is distinctively presented by John as both a written and speaking authority (ἡ γραφὴ εἶπεν; cf. 7:38, 42; 19:24, 37), whose true meaning as testimony to Jesus is activated through its divinely given "oral enactment" in the Johannine present.[29]

In light, moreover, of increasingly audience-oriented approaches to the interpretation of New Testament texts, the *dialogical* function of John's knowledge of Scripture demands closer scrutiny, particularly since

---

28. Rafael Rodríguez, *Structuring Early Christian Memory: Jesus in Tradition, Performance and Text*, LNTS 407 (T&T Clark, 2010), 165–66. See also Holly Hearon, "Mapping Written and Spoken Word in the Gospel of Mark," in *The Interface of Orality and Writing: Speaking, Seeing, Writing in the Shaping of New Genres*, ed. Annette Weissenrieder and Robert B. Coote, BPC 11 (Cascade, 2015), 382–83.

29. Michael Labahn, "Scripture *Talks* Because Jesus *Talks*: The Narrative Rhetoric of Persuading and Creativity in John's Use of Scripture," in Le Donne and Thatcher, *Fourth Gospel in First-Century Media Culture*, 133–54.

the author frequently intervenes to address anticipated audiences directly (e.g., 19:35; 20:31; 21:24). How do the frequent explicit, and implicit, references to Israel's Scriptures in John's Gospel relate to its communicative aims? Or, phrased differently, what are hearers and readers expected to know of, and about, Scripture, and how is that knowledge meant to deepen or evolve in and through interaction with John's story of Jesus?

As proposed earlier in this study, John can at times engage in intricate textual and exegetical maneuvers in the citation of Scripture, particularly in composite quotations formulated to serve the gospel's narrative and Christology. It is quite possible, of course, that what underpins those maneuvers compositionally was not intended to be identified and dissected, at least initially, by the gospel's audiences; the focus, rather, could be upon the rhetorical impact of the finished product of the explicitly signaled scriptural quotations. Nevertheless, the varying degrees of allusiveness in John's scriptural references does raise the question of how many echoes would need to be heard and recognized by audiences for them to be kept on the Johannine track. These are not unimportant issues if, as often proposed, the gospel's originally envisaged audiences were not limited to those of Jewish heritage but also included actual or potential believers from a gentile background. Multilayered engagement with the Jewish Scriptures in John, much like its polyvalent vocabulary, suggests that the text has been shaped to appeal of a wide spectrum of hearers/readers, ranging from those with high levels of scriptural literacy—visual and/or aural—to those with perhaps only limited acquaintance of Israel's principal stories.[30] Certainly, a variety of scenarios can be envisaged as to how John's audience(s) would have been able to acquire or retrieve scriptural knowledge; it could include multiple recitations of the gospel within communal settings, prompting scripturally competent believers to provide explanatory comments to others less well-versed in Jewish texts and traditions, that is, by offering reflections on the content of John's Gospel in combination with a searching of the Jewish Scriptures.

---

30. See especially Craig R. Koester, *Symbolism in the Fourth Gospel: Meaning, Mystery, Community*, 2nd ed. (Fortress, 2003), 18–24. See also Jörg Frey, "Heil und Geschichte im Johannesevangelium: Zum Problem der 'Heilsgeschichte' und zum fundamentalen Geschichtsbezug des Heilsgeschehens im vierten Evangelium," in *Heil und Geschichte: Die Geschichtsbezogenheit des Heils und das Problem der Heilsgeschichte in der biblischen Tradition und in der theologischen Deutung*, ed. Jörg Frey, Stefan Krauter, and Hermann Lichtenberger, WUNT 248 (Mohr Siebeck, 2009), 483–84.

Given that first-century texts were commonly delivered orally and received aurally by their audiences, a range of communicative strategies and techniques can be identified in John's text that have been built into the narrative to illuminate and enhance its appeals to scriptural testimony. The rhetorical impact of John's reading of the Jewish Scriptures should not be limited to its overt signaling of Scripture and its content, because it also encourages the evocation and elucidation of more veiled scriptural references through repetition, close-knit configuration and their gradual unfolding within the Johannine text. In line with the guidance provided by ancient rhetorical theorists like Quintilian,[31] John's Gospel can also use intentionally ambiguous arguments, metaphors, riddles, as well as *subtle allusions to other texts* to encourage readers and hearers to seek deeper levels of resonance and meaning;[32] John's audiences are invited to fill gaps and to make new links by drawing from their culturally, including scripturally, inherited (or more recently acquired) memory pool.[33] It is striking in this respect that John's allusive scriptural references often occur in discourses that disclose various facets of Jesus's identity. Thus, the identification of Jesus as bread (John 6:25–59), shepherd (10:1–21, 22–30), or vine (15:1–11) draw on multilayered metaphors that, at the same time, progressively and innovatively recall a rich reserve of scriptural resources.[34] It often appears unnecessary to pin down John's scriptural deposit to

---

31. Quintilian (*Inst.* 9.2.71) states, for example, that textual elusiveness and allusiveness challenge audiences to be "led to seek out the secret which they would not believe if they heard it openly stated, and to believe in that which they have found out for themselves."

32. Dale C. Allison, "The Old Testament in the New Testament," in *The New Cambridge History of the Bible: From the Beginnings to 600*, ed. James Carleton Paget and Joachim Schaper (Cambridge University Press, 2013), 487: the "regular effect" of scriptural allusions is "to move hearers to become more active."

33. On the role played by memory in the reception of the Jewish Scriptures in New Testament writings and in how they were heard by audiences, see, e.g., Tom Thatcher, "Cain and Abel in Early Christian Memory: A Case Study in 'The Use of the Old Testament in the New,'" *CBQ* 72 (2010): 732–51; Williams, "How Scripture 'Speaks,'" 63–69. For insights from contemporary social memory studies, see the next section of this essay.

34. For an attempt at investigating how John engages rhetorically with the notion of scriptural allusiveness for the purpose of audience participation, see Catrin H. Williams, "Persuasion through Allusion: Evocations of 'Shepherd(s)' and their Rhetorical Impact in John 10," in *Come and Read: Interpretive Approaches to the Gospel of John*, ed. Alicia D. Myers and Lindsey S. Jodrey (Fortress Academic, 2020), 111–24.

individual references and single meanings (or indeed to identifiable verses or discrete passages), since they can evoke not one but a network of associations drawn from Israel's Scriptures and also the broader interpretive frames associated with those texts and traditions. Audiences, as a result, are encouraged through such strategies to be drawn into a distinctively Johannine understanding of culturally resonant, and scripturally rooted, multifaceted images.

How John Shapes What John Knows

Some attention has already been paid in this essay to the ways in which John's diverse modes of scriptural reference—along the sliding scale of direct quotations to varyingly visible allusions—operate as part of John's narrative design. This relates specifically to the rhetorical function of Scripture in the Johannine portrayal of Jesus,[35] although the identification of other rhetorical techniques and related strategies within the gospel prompts one to delve deeper in relation to what John knows and to ask: what does the shaping of scriptural references within the narrative ("how") disclose about John's aims ("why") with regard to the meaning and significance attributed to the Jewish Scriptures in light of John's story of Jesus?

There is no doubt that John's Gospel seeks to maintain a fine balance between two key hermeneutical principles, namely, that Israel's Scriptures repeatedly provide the backdrop or screen for the telling of the gospel narrative, but also that Jesus is to be understood as the interpretive key to those Scriptures. The centrality of these two principles for John becomes evident from the outset of the narrative, both allusively, through the positioning of the story's origins "in the beginning" (John 1:1; cf. Gen 1:1 LXX), and overtly, in the programmatic statement attributed to Philip in one of the gospel's earliest scenes, "We have found him about whom Moses in the law and also the prophets wrote, Jesus son of Joseph from Nazareth" (1:45; cf. 5:39, 46–47). These hermeneutical keys set out clearly, for John's audiences, that the Jewish Scriptures in their entirety are deemed to be essential to the gospel's interpretive framework in that they point forward and bear witness to Jesus. As far as literary structures are concerned, the

---

35. On how John's appeals to the authority of Israel's Scriptures work to bolster the persuasive force of its message, see especially Myers, *Characterizing Jesus* (with the aid of classical Greek and Roman rhetorical categories) and Sheridan, *Retelling Scripture* (using contemporary rhetorical theory).

characteristically Johannine understanding of the witnessing role of Scripture is further signposted at decisive points elsewhere in the narrative, such as the *framing* of the beginning and end of Jesus's public ministry so that they are in alignment with what "Isaiah said" (John 1:23; 12:38–41) and also with the post-glorification elucidation of Jesus's words and deeds when they, in conjunction with what Scripture has written about him, are "remembered" (2:17, 22; 12:13–16).[36]

It could be argued that these structural markers or *inclusios* fulfill the hermeneutical function that should be accomplished by *individual* enactments of scriptural testimony to Jesus, though the latter are limited to a relatively small and diverse cluster of citations in the gospel narrative.[37] Once again, however, John's carefully conceived schema comes to light in the methodical distribution of citation formulas attached to these fifteen quotations. There is a conscious clustering of two distinct citation patterns, marked by a shift from what "is written" (ἐστιν γεγραμμένον) in the account of Jesus's public ministry (John 2:17; 6:31, 45; 10:34; 12:14), in the first main part of the gospel (1:19–12:36), to how Scripture is "fulfilled" (ἵνα ἡ γραφὴ πληρωθῇ) in the second part (12:38; 13:18; 15:25; 17:12; 19:24, 36), following the announcement of the arrival of Jesus's hour (12:23).[38] In the first half of the gospel, where the focus is on debate about Jesus's identity and authority, Scripture serves as a written (and speaking) witness to Jesus; in the second half, particular emphasis is placed on how Jesus's death and departure amount to the explicit *fulfillment* of Scripture. Furthermore, in the context of the scriptural allusion embedded in

---

36. On the ways in which John projects the christological significance of Israel's Scriptures through the use of *inclusio*, see, e.g., Alicia D. Myers, "A Voice in the Wilderness: Classical Rhetoric and the Testimony of John (the Baptist) in John 1:19–34," in Myers and Schuchard, *Abiding Words*, 131–38; Bynum, "Quotations of Zechariah in the Fourth Gospel," 47–49, 72–74; and, in particular, Daise, *Quotations in John*, 9–11, 124, 198–99.

37. For the view that the witnessing function of Scripture may be stated (e.g., John 1:45) but remains largely undemonstrated in John, see Lieu, "Narrative Analysis and Scripture in John," 160. She also makes the highly plausible suggestion that the fact that "so much scriptural imagery lies below the surface of the narrative perhaps reinforces the reader's awareness that this belongs not to the level of the events of Jesus' ministry but to that of a believing remembering" (162).

38. See Craig A. Evans, *Word and Glory: On the Exegetical and Theological Background of John's Prologue*, JSNTSup 89 (JSOT Press, 1993), 174–77; Obermann, *Die christologische Erfüllung der Schrift*, 78–89, 348–50.

Jesus's utterance, "I thirst," in John 19:28 (cf. Ps 69:21 [68:22]), Scripture is described as being brought to its ultimate *completion* (ἵνα τελειωθῇ ἡ γραφή) through Jesus's death,[39] echoing Jesus's earlier declarations that the purpose of his earthly mission is to complete his Father's work (4:34; 5:36; 17:4; cf. 19:30: τετέλεσται).

What does it mean, then, for John to claim, in 19:28, that Scripture is not only fulfilled (πληρόω) in and through Jesus but has now reached its goal (τελειόω)? Does it point to Israel's Scriptures as having reached their all-encompassing conclusion, albeit without necessarily devaluing Israel's past or claiming that scripture is now redundant (cf. John 10:35)? Or does the emphasis fall on Scripture as a written prophecy that remains empty until filled with Jesus's revelation?[40] There has been much debate in recent Johannine scholarship as to whether the emphasis in John's Christology on Jesus as the exclusive revealer of God (cf. 1:18) diminishes or even annuls the salvific-historical value of Israel's scriptures, that is, if they are interpreted solely as testimonies to Jesus.[41] A central hermeneutical challenge in this regard is determining the Johannine stance on the precise relationship between the past and present. It is a stance that does not articulate clearly, for example, why the prologue offers such a highly compressed understanding of how the past revelation of the Logos relates to salvation

---

39. Cf. Hans Hübner, *Hebräerbrief, Evangelien und Offenbarung*, vol. 3 of *Biblische Theologie des Neuen Testaments* (Vandenhoeck & Ruprecht, 1995), 199: "Mit Jesu Tod ist das τέλος des Offenbarungs- und Erlösungsgeschehens gegeben. Jesus selbst erkennt, daß nun alles zu seinem Ziel gekommen ist." See also Hengel, "Die Schriftauslegung des 4. Evangeliums," 278–79.

40. Maarten J. J. Menken, "Observations on the Significance of the Old Testament in the Fourth Gospel," *Neot* 33 (1999): 125–43.

41. Among those who argue that the salvific-revelatory significance of Israel's history as expressed in the Jewish Scriptures is significantly played down through John's handling of Scripture are: Kraus, "Johannes und das Alte Testament," 1–23; Michael Theobald, "Schriftzitate im 'Lebensbrot'-Dialog Jesu (Joh 6): Ein Paradigma für den Schriftgebrauch des vierten Evangelisten," in *The Scriptures in the Gospels*, ed. Christopher M. Tuckett, BETL 131 (Leuven University Press, 1997), 355–56, 361–65 (arguing that Scripture, for John, is a christological text separable from Israel's history); cf. also Christian Dietzfelbinger, "Aspekte des Alten Testaments im Johannesevangelium," in *Frühes Christentum*, vol. 3 of *Geschichte - Tradition - Reflexion: Festschrift für Martin Hengel zum 70. Geburtstag*, ed. Hermann Lichtenberger (Mohr Siebeck, 1996), 203–18. Others argue that John attaches importance to Israel's salvation history in the past; see especially Hengel, "Die Schriftauslegung des 4. Evangeliums," 260–71; Frey, "Heil und Geschichte im Johannesevangelium," 488–89.

history (1:1–5 [or 1:1–12?]), and whether figures like Abraham, Moses, and Isaiah are presented as paradigms for the witness of God's Word in Israel (e.g., 5:46; 8:56; 12:41; cf. 1:12)[42] or, alternatively, only as looking forward to the coming of Jesus as the Word incarnate?

Some light may possibly be shed on these questions if John's understanding of the past is examined through the lens of commemorative keying and framing. This approach, as applied in social memory theories, involves the pairing, even conflating, of events and figures from the remembering present with images or symbolically meaningful patterns from the remembered past,[43] which, in John's case, involves the memory of Israel's (scriptural) past. Keying does not, essentially, work with a hermeneutical model of foreshadowing, typology, or fulfillment; rather it interprets present realities in analogical terms by *enacting* elements tied to landmark figures and events from the past.[44] Hence, in the case of John's prologue, the Sinai theophany is evoked in the references to "glory" (cf. Exod 33:18, 22) and "grace and truth" (34:6) being manifested in Jesus (John 1:14–17). The exact force of the comparison is notoriously difficult to establish, since there is no explicit mention in the prologue of the actual revelation of God's glory in Israel's past, no indication that the Sinai revelation foreshadows or is a type of that which has come through the Logos, and no hint that Jesus fulfils what was originally promised to Moses. The Sinai event certainly functions as the theophanic model for articulating the significance of the revelation of the incarnate Word, but, with the aid of mnemonic keying, the two events are assimilated in such a way that the focus is not on whether these divine qualities were already manifested in the distant past, but on the fullness of the grace and truth embodied in Jesus. A related strategy can be identified when Jesus corrects the crowd's use of Scripture to support their request for bread to form a Moses-like sign, "He gave them bread from heaven to eat" (John 6:30–31). The con-

---

42. Hengel, "Die Schriftauslegung des 4. Evangeliums," 263–68.

43. See especially Barry Schwartz, *Abraham Lincoln and the Forge of National Memory* (University of Chicago Press, 2000), 18–20. See Thatcher, "Cain and Abel in Early Christian Memory," 732–51; and, with reference to John's Gospel, see Catrin H. Williams, "Patriarchs and Prophets Remembered: Framing Israel's Past in the Gospel of John," in Myers and Schuchard, *Abiding Words*, 187–212.

44. Myers, *Characterizing Jesus*, 182, discusses the function of the rhetorical technique of *synkrisis* in similar terms; John seeks to clarify Jesus's identity by "placing him alongside" scriptural events and figures, with Jesus held to be "greater than what is already acknowledged as great."

trast highlighted by Jesus between the two God-given events to accentuate the superiority of the present gift (6:32) again functions like a form of keying, because, in order for this scriptural correlation to be effective, God has to be recognized as the giver of "bread from heaven" in the past as well as the present. Thus, operating on the principle of integration, it is striking that in Jesus's response the crowds are projected as the recipients of bread in the past—"who gave you" (δέδωκεν ὑμῖν)—and the present—"who gives you" (δίδωσιν ὑμῖν). As in the case of the Moses-Jesus comparison in the prologue, interpreting the highly enigmatic declarations in John 6:30–32 in analogical terms need not negate the connection and degree of continuity between them, although it does, at the same time, involve acknowledging that John asserts the superiority of the salvific gift offered by Jesus.

The evidence surveyed in this brief study enables one, finally, to draw the following conclusion as far as John's shaping of Scripture is concerned: through its close and frequent interaction with the Jewish Scriptures, the Johannine text in fact sets itself up as belonging to the category of γραφή—new Scripture.[45] There are numerous textual indicators that this is the case, though not in the sense that John's Gospel becomes a replacement for Israel's Scriptures. To the contrary, the continued relevance of the Jewish Scriptures for the Johannine presentation of Jesus is maintained at key points in the narrative (1:45; 5:39; 20:9).

At one level, the relationship between the Scriptures and John's text is presented in symbiotic terms, as already indicated by the unmissable connection between the first words of the gospel (John 1:1) and the opening words of Scripture (Gen 1:1). Their close association is also intimated by the emphasis on the importance of post-Easter believing in and remembering of both Scripture and Jesus's word (John 2:22; cf. 2:17; 12:16; see also 15:20; 16:4), as well as on the fulfillment of one, like the other (18:9, 32). This connection is encapsulated, most strikingly, in the emphasis placed upon the gospel text, like Scripture, as bearing written

---

45. Cf. Francis J. Moloney, "The Gospel of John as Scripture," *CBQ* 67 (2005): 454–68; Klaus Scholtissek, "'Geschrieben in diesem Buch' (Joh 20,30): Beobachtungen zum kanonischen Anspruch des Johannesevangeliums," in *Israel und seine Heilstraditionen im Johannesevangelium: Festgabe für Johannes Beutler SJ zum 70. Geburtstag*, ed. Michael Labahn, Klaus Scholtissek, and Angelika Strotmann (Schöningh, 2004), 219–24; Susanne Luther, "The Authentication of the Narrative: The Function of Scripture Quotations in John 19," in Hatina, *Biblical Interpretation in Early Christian Gospels*, 4:155–66.

testimony to Jesus.[46] The distribution of references to their *writtenness* is no mere coincidence in this respect. Up until John 19 all occurrences of γράφω refer exclusively to the decisive testimony of Scripture, while its use to denote the inscription on the cross (19:19–22) again perpetuates, albeit inadvertently, the witnessing function of *writing*. Accordingly, the preponderance of references to γράφω in the descriptions of the gospel's aims (20:30–31; 21:24–25) highlights the authoritative quality of John's witness to Jesus[47]—from the assertion that "these things are written" (20:31: γέγραπται) to bring about or strengthen belief, to the confirmation that what has been written (ὁ γράψας) is tantamount to true testimony (μαρτυρία; 21:24).

John undoubtedly signals a close connection between Scripture and the gospel text, but they are not presented as identical nor is one wholly subsumed under the other. This may well have prompted John to describe the gospel text not as "writing/scripture" (γραφή) but rather as "book" (βιβλίον; 20:30–31; cf. 21:25), with a marked shift from one to the other: from signposting the enduring witness of the written Scriptures to Jesus (John 1:45–20:9) to highlighting what, for John, amounts to the incomparable, and life-giving,[48] testimony of the written gospel. What follows from this, and different from its Synoptic counterparts (especially Luke 1:1–4), is that the authority claimed for John's Gospel is stated at the end rather than the beginning of the book. Hand in hand, therefore, with the assertion that Scripture reaches its ultimate goal when Jesus completes his earthly mission (19:28), John presents "the words of God" recorded in Israel's Scriptures as finding their interpretive key and eschatological

---

46. See Johannes Beutler, "The Use of 'Scripture' in the Gospel of John," in *Exploring the Gospel of John: In Honor of D. Moody Smith*, ed. R. Alan Culpepper and C. Clifton Black (Westminster John Knox, 1996), 153–54. Cf. also Labahn, "Scripture *Talks* Because Jesus *Talks*," 135–40.

47. On John's "textual self-consciousness," with particular reference to 20:30–31 and 21:24–25, see Chris Keith, *The Gospel as Manuscript: An Early History of the Jesus Tradition as Material Artifact* (Oxford University Press, 2020), 134–36.

48. The Johannine emphasis on receiving the gift of life through believing in Jesus via the gospel's written testimony to him (20:30–31) contrasts with the position attributed to Jesus's opponents that life is available in the Scriptures, that is, in isolation from its witness to Jesus (5:39–40). See further Maarten J. J. Menken, "What Authority Does the Fourth Evangelist Claim for His Book?," in *Paul, John, and Apocalyptic Eschatology: Studies in Honour of Martinus C. de Boer*, ed. Jan Krans et al., NovTSup 149 (Brill, 2013), 194; cf. Keith, *Gospel as Manuscript*, 138–39.

fulfillment in the Word made flesh,[49] whose voice is said to be inscribed and definitively elucidated within the Johannine text itself.

---

49. Cf. Obermann, *Die christologische Erfüllung der Schrift*, 380–87. See also Deborah Forger, "Jesus as God's Word(s): Aurality, Epistemology and Embodiment in the Gospel of John," *JSNT* 42 (2020): 283.

8

Gospel

Wendy E. S. North

"Begin at the beginning," the king said gravely, "and go on till you come to the end: then stop." With these words the King of Hearts instructs the White Rabbit where to begin reading out some verses in *Alice's Adventures in Wonderland*, with a grasp of the obvious that does little to commend the proceedings in the eyes of a disproportionately sized Alice at the time. Even so, however, it is interesting to reflect in light of this that when it came to the much graver task of gospel-writing, two authors out of our canonical four, Mark and John, chose to begin precisely at the beginning in their accounts of the life of Jesus of Nazareth. In what follows, we shall examine and discuss how they began, how they ended, and with what measure of affinity they proceeded in between.

Similarities and Differences: A Survey

Mark opens with the words: "The beginning of the Gospel of Jesus Christ" (1:1). He then embarks on his narrative with a quotation he attributes to Isaiah (Isa 40:3; see also Mal 3:1) to introduce the figure of John the Baptist (1:2–6). John is then presented as one who heralds the arrival of another who is stronger, whose sandals he is unworthy to untie, and who will baptize with the Holy Spirit (1:7–8). This is followed by the scene of Jesus's baptism by John, in which the Spirit descends upon him and a voice from heaven identifies him as God's beloved Son (1:9–11). Thereafter, following a brief account of Jesus's temptations in the wilderness and of John's arrest (1:12–13), Mark tells of the beginning of Jesus's ministry in Galilee and the call of the first disciples (1:14–20). Mark's chapter then concludes with

Jesus healing many in Capernaum and beyond and with the rapid spread of his popularity in consequence (1:21-45).

John's Gospel also begins at the beginning, but in this case the beginning preexists everything; his "in the beginning" is a clear reminiscence of the first words of Genesis (Gen 1:1), as John reaches back to God and his Word before creation (John 1:1-2). The Genesis narrative is also instrumental in setting the agenda for the remainder of John's paragraph, in which creation, life, light, darkness, and humankind all figure (1:3-5). Even so, however, in John's hands the literal in the Genesis text soon shades into the metaphorical, as "the life" in the Word becomes "the light" of all people and we learn that it shines in the darkness that did not overwhelm it (1:4-5; cf. 12:35).

Thus, in what is perhaps the most remarkable of openings to a biography, John traces the beginning of his story of Jesus Christ to the beginning of all beginnings. Even so, these opening lines do not yet define the goal and purpose of his prologue. This first comes into view in the aside about the Baptist in verses 6-8, who is presented here as prime witness to the light. John then adds significantly to this in verses 9-13, where he focuses on the entry of the light into the created world and its reception, first negatively in terms of ignorance and rejection of the light, and then positively, in that those who believed thereby gained the right to become "children of God" (cf. also 11:52).

Finally, at 1:14, John arrives at his goal, crystallizing into a few memorable words the implication of the previous lines: "And the Word became flesh and lived among us." And with this the tone changes: now we are in history; now we hear of the witness of the believing "we"; now the Baptist appears in his familiar role, heralding the one who comes after him; and now also we hear of the law given through Moses and of the revelation of grace and truth through "Jesus Christ" (1:14-17).[1] Significantly also, from this point onwards, John will refer to Jesus in language appropriate to sonship. This is already implied in the prologue, where Jesus is twice referred to as "the only one" (*monogenēs*) in the context of God as Father (1:14, 18), and later confirmed by John himself in his references to Jesus as the "only Son" of God in the programmatic 3:16-21 (vv. 16, 18).[2]

---

1. On John 1:5, 9, 11 as pointers to the declaration in 1:14 and the change of tone thereafter, see Ruth B. Edwards, *Discovering John: Content, Interpretation, Reception*, 2nd ed. (SPCK, 2014), 101-2, 107-9.

2. There is strong manuscript evidence in favor of reading "God," not "Son," after

John embarks on his narrative proper in 1:19, beginning with the witness of the Baptist and also now coming recognizably into line with the Markan narrative. Accordingly, the Isaiah reference familiar from Mark 1:3 reappears, this time on the lips of the Baptist himself (John 1:23), as also does his announcement of one who is to follow whose sandals he is unworthy to untie (1:27). There are also some differences: first, in place of Mark's stronger one (1:7), John supplies a repetition of the Baptist's declaration in 1:15 that his successor ranks before him because he "was" before him (1:30); and, second, John does not record the actual baptism but instead has the Baptist recall the event. Even so, the terms are familiar enough, as we learn that Jesus is one who will baptize with the Holy Spirit, of the descent of the Spirit on Jesus, and of the witness that Jesus is the Son of God (1:32–34; Mark 1:8, 10–11). John's first chapter then concludes with the call of the first disciples (1:35–51). Thus, while it can scarcely be said that John has followed Mark slavishly, the two accounts are sufficiently in step, from "the beginning" and the formal title "Jesus Christ" to the witness of the Baptist, the description of the baptism and the call of the disciples, for the reader with a prior knowledge of Mark to recognize an affinity. Moreover, as John's narrative unfolds, there emerge further points where his witness coincides specifically with Mark's. Notable examples are as follows.

In the course of the public ministry, Jesus's instruction to the paralytic in 5:8, "Rise, take up your bed and walk," is exact to the wording in Mark 2:9. In this context, John's word for "bed" (*krabbatos*) creates a specific link with the Markan version (John 5:9, 11; Mark 2:11, 12) that is unmatched in the equivalent accounts in Matthew and Luke (Matt 9:2–8; Luke 5:17–26; note, however, Acts 5:15; 9:33). In the Galilean episode in chapter 6, John's wording in the opening miracle story proves to be exact to Mark's on three counts: first, the cost of the bread (John 6:7; Mark 6:37), which is common to John and Mark only; second, the number and gender of those fed (John 6:10; Mark 6:44); and, third, the amount of food left over (John 6:13; Mark 6:43). John also adheres to the Markan order of events by following the miracle story immediately with Jesus's walk on the sea (John 6:16–21; Mark 6:45–52) as, indeed, Matthew also does (14:22–27), but Luke does not (see

---

"only" in 1:18. See Bruce M. Metzger, *A Textual Commentary on the Greek New Testament*, 2nd ed. (Deutsche Bibelgesellschaft, 1994), 169–70. Nevertheless, the evidence in John 3:16, 18 must surely weigh here. Moreover, the same usage in the remarkably similar credal statement in 1 John 4:9 confirms this as Johannine house style.

9:10–17).³ Further evidence comes from John's account of the anointing in 12:1–8, where the description of the oil and its sale price are exact to Mark (John 12:3, 5; Mark 14:3, 5) and both are common to John and Mark only. Also, Jesus's declaration in John 12:7 that Mary may keep the ointment for his burial more nearly resembles Mark's description of the women arriving at the tomb (16:1) than it does John's later burial scene (19:38–42).

In the passion narrative, where events in John are in step with the Markan order once more, there are further verbal parallels. These begin at the scene of Jesus's arrest (John 18:10; Mark 14:47) and at his trial before the high priest John and Mark share references to the maidservant (18:17; Mark 14:66, 69), to Peter "warming himself" (18:18, 25; Mark 14:54, 67), Peter's denials (18:25, 27; Mark 14:68, 70, 71), and the casual violence meted out to Jesus (18:22; Mark 14:65). In particular, Jesus's defense in 18:20 strongly resembles his objection at his arrest in Mark 14:49, and both trial accounts intercalate scenes relating to Jesus and to Peter (John 18:13–27; Mark 14:53–72).⁴ Perhaps most striking of all, however, are the extensive verbal links in the trial before Pilate. These include Pilate's first question, "Are you the King of the Jews?" and Jesus's answer, "You say" (John 18:33, 37; Mark 15:2), Pilate's offer to release "the King of the Jews" (John 18:39; Mark 15:9); and the soldiers' mocking words (John 19:3; Mark 15:18) as well as details such as the early timing of the trial (John 18:28; Mark 15:1), the fact that "accusations" were brought (John 18:29; Mark 15:3), that Jesus was "handed over" to Pilate (John 18:30; Mark 15:1) and remained silent when questioned (John 19:9; Mark 15:5). Of these, the form of Pilate's offer is common to John and Mark only, as are references to Jesus as an evil-doer, the imperial purple of his robe (John 18:30, 19:2; Mark 15:17), and the information that Pilate "handed Jesus over" to be crucified (John 19:16; Mark 15:15). There is even a redundant "again" in John's narrative in 18:40 that may owe much to the influence of Pilate's second question in Mark 15:12.⁵

---

3. Further on John 6 as a whole in relation to Mark 6:32–8:30, see especially Andrew T. Lincoln, *The Gospel According to St John*, BNTC 4 (Hendrickson, 2005), 209–41.

4. See Lincoln, *Gospel according to Saint John*, 449.

5. See Lincoln, *Gospel according to Saint John*, 458–59 on links with Mark's text here. For the suggestion that John's "again" stems from Mark 15:13, see C. K. Barrett, *The Gospel according to St. John: An Introduction with Commentary and Notes on the Greek Text*, 2nd ed. (SPCK, 1978), 539; also Johannes Beutler, S.J., *A Commentary on the Gospel of John*, trans. Michael Tait (Eerdmans, 2017), 470.

This brings us to our present point: John begins at the beginning as does Mark; significantly also, John's final links with Mark are at its close (John 20:1-2; Mark 16:1-2);[6] and between the two there is a series of remarkable verbal and narrative correspondences.[7] All told, the evidence suggests that if what John knew included other gospels, the case for his knowledge and use of Mark is a compelling one and deserves serious consideration in our approach to his work.[8] Even so, to approach John with Mark in mind is at the same time to become aware that the evidence of affinity must be balanced by the recognition of other features of John's narrative that suggest profound and irreconcilable difference.

To begin with, those points of contact with Mark, however remarkable, tend to be occasional rather than consistent. Second, there are marked dissimilarities in the order, timing, and location of events in John. The reader with a knowledge of Mark, for example, having kept pace with John to the end of his first chapter, would scarcely expect to find an account of the temple incident in Jerusalem as early as the second (John 2:13-16; cp. Mark 11:15-17). Further differences include the general focus of Jesus's ministry in Judea against the backdrop of the feasts, twice including Passover (2:13; 5:1; 6:4; 7:2; 10:22; 12:1), and also the dating of Jesus's death to the day of preparation for Passover rather than Passover itself (John 18:28; 19:31; cp. Mark 14:12; 15:1). Third, there are marked absences in John of material in Mark, including Jesus's exorcisms, transfiguration, words of institution at the Last Supper, and detail of his Jewish trial. Fourth, John's reshaping of the narrative also involves the inclusion of additional material at key points, for example, the miracle of the water into wine at the beginning of Jesus's ministry (2:1-11), the raising of Lazarus as the pivotal point in the gospel plot (11:1-44) and Jesus's action in washing the

---

6. See further, Barrett, *Gospel according to St. John*, 562, who compares Mark 16:2 for the construction, "on the first day of the week" in John 20:1 (cf. also 20:19).

7. John and Mark also share a significant number of individual sayings. Compare for example, John 4:44 and Mark 6:4; John 12:25 and Mark 8:35; John 13:20 and Mark 9:37; John 13:21 and Mark 14:18; see further the discussion in Lincoln, *Gospel according to Saint John*, 35-37.

8. As D. Moody Smith points out, contacts between John and Mark "are not nearly so numerous or extensive as the agreements among the synoptics, but they nevertheless exist." See D. Moody Smith, *Johannine Christianity: Essays on Its Setting, Sources, and Theology* (University of South Carolina Press, 1984), 191. Further on the links between John and Mark, see the chapter by Paul N. Anderson on "Testimony" in the present volume.

disciples' feet at the Last Supper (13:3–11). Finally, there are the extended discourses that characterize his teaching in John but are unparalleled in the Mark-driven Synoptic tradition.[9]

In sum, if we are prepared to maintain that what John knew included Mark, then the question that arises from that is: Why does what John wrote differ so conspicuously from the Second Gospel? Put otherwise, how do we account for the distinctiveness of John when set against the background of Mark and, for that matter, against the background of the relative fidelity to Mark to be found in Matthew and Luke? We shall attempt to explore this in the following terms.

The Making of John's Gospel

At this point, we shall not begin at the beginning but rather at the end of John's Gospel, specifically his closing remarks in 20:30–31.[10] Here, he concludes Jesus's story with a direct address to his readers in which he makes the following points: first, that Jesus did many other signs that are not written in his book; second, that the things that are written are in order that they may believe and so have life. Finally, then, John provides us with a glimpse into his aims as a narrator, in which he indicates that there are two aspects to his work: first, that what he wrote does not encompass all he knew; second, that what he has chosen to include is not only a record of events but also an interpretation of their meaning to nurture his readers' faith.[11] What, then, precisely are the things that are written in John's book, viewed in the light of this closing address?

---

9. See especially the recent detailed discussion of gospel relationships, including both similarities and differences, in Harold W. Attridge, "John and the Other Gospels," in *The Oxford Handbook of Johannine Studies*, ed. Judith M. Lieu and Martinus C. de Boer (Oxford University Press, 2018), 44–62. C. K. Barrett and R. E. Brown also provide detailed evidence on similarities and differences, reaching radically differing conclusions. See Barrett, *Gospel according to St. John*, 42–54; Raymond E. Brown, *The Gospel according to John*, AB 29 (Doubleday, 1966), 1.XLIV–XLVII.

10. The gospel, of course, continues for another chapter, which focuses on the story of the Johannine disciples and is possibly a later addition. See further, Francis J. Moloney, "Closure," in *How John Works: Storytelling in the Fourth Gospel*, ed. Douglas Estes and Ruth Sheridan, RBS 86 (SBL Press, 2016), 238–39.

11. In agreement with Lincoln that John's reference to believing in 20:31 should have the force of continuing in faith; so Lincoln, *Gospel according to St. John*, 504 n. 1, 506.

As regards the first aspect of his work, broadly speaking the absence in John of material available in Mark is unsurprising in this context. Also relevant here are the references that John makes to events offstage.[12] Thus, for example, in 3:24, he refers to the imprisonment of the Baptist that he neither relates nor sees reason to explain. Similarly, he includes general remarks about Jesus's miracle-working activity (2:23; 3:2; 6:2) and refers in passing to the expectation of the end-time (5:28–29; 6:39, 40, 44, 54), Jesus's eucharistic words at the Last Supper (6:53–58), the appointment of "the Twelve" (6:70–71; cf. 20:24), and Jesus's agonized prayer in Gethsemane (12:27; 18:11). In addition, Mary Magdalene's "we" in 20:2 indicates that John is perfectly aware there was more than one woman at the empty tomb. In other words, the evidence in his gospel is consistent with the position that John knows more than he relates and, furthermore, that he expects his readers to have some prior knowledge of events. Thus, the indicators are that John's is by no means a first proclamation of the gospel story and that he has taken advantage of that by exercising a certain latitude in the telling. This brings us to the second aspect of his work.

Of itself, John's capacity for interpretation of Jesus's story does not single him out among gospel writers, but the extent of it does. This is a marked characteristic of his work that is also supported by key evidence in the gospel itself. In the context of the farewell discourses, Jesus informs the disciples of the coming of the Spirit-Paraclete, who will replace him after he has gone and will bring to the disciples' remembrance an understanding of the meaning of events that is unavailable to them at the time (14:15, 26; cf. 15:26; 16:7–15). In this prediction, we note what appears to be a consciousness on John's part of a process of interpretation of what was known that was undertaken at the behest of the Spirit-Paraclete, as he describes it.[13] In this self-percep-

---

12. See on this, D. Moody Smith, *John*, ANTC (Abingdon, 1999), 123, 134; Smith, *Johannine Christianity*, 143. See further, with specific reference to 20:30–31, Andrew T. Lincoln, *Truth on Trial: The Lawsuit Motif in the Fourth Gospel* (Hendrickson, 2000), 176.

13. As Jörg Frey comments, "the Evangelist demonstrates a hermeneutical awareness of the transformation processes behind his work" which he explains as "an effect of the Spirit." See Jörg Frey, "From the 'Kingdom of God' to 'Eternal Life': The Transformation of Theological Language in the Fourth Gospel," in *Glimpses of Jesus through the Johannine Lens*, vol. 3 of *John, Jesus and History*, ed. Paul N. Anderson, Felix Just, S.J., and Tom Thatcher, ECL 18 (SBL Press, 2016), 455.

tion, there surely resides the key to much that we find in his gospel; as the instrument of the Spirit, John has set about a profound and radical transformation of what he knew, and so has written its meaning for the faith of his readers. In terms of his use of Mark, this strongly implies that while John may have put pen to paper in the knowledge of the second gospel, what he finally produced was an interpretation of Markan material that was recognizably Johannine in style and perspective. Thus, in view of John's closing address together with evidence in his gospel, we may reasonably expect that if John has known and used Mark, he has not only chosen what material to take up but also in the process he has reconceived that material in his own terms. What, then, may we say of Mark's contribution to the making of John?

Markan Influence in the Making of John

As we have noted, John has reconfigured the order and timing of events so that Jesus's ministry is largely spent in Judea rather than in Galilee. This is to advantage as far as John's presentation of Jesus is concerned. Earlier, we recognized that the goal of his prologue is to present Jesus as the Word become flesh, the only Son of the Father who reveals God in the world (1:14, 16–18). We also noted that this section of John's prologue has links with the programmatic 3:16-21. Thus, for the theologically minded John, the credal statement in 3:16 that God gave his only Son for love of the world is not only the starting-point for all "love-talk" within the gospel[14] but is also the foundation for his presentation of Jesus's death as an act of self-giving love in which God's character is supremely revealed (10:11, 15, 17; 15:13; cf. 1:14, 18). In view of this focus, it makes Johannine sense to place the temple incident in Jerusalem at Passover toward the beginning of the ministry, thereby reconceiving Jesus's progress so that each Passover becomes a dress-rehearsal for the last and the whole takes place in the shadow of the cross.

To the point here is that this is a process in which Mark's account has retained its influence. Jesus's declaration in John 2:19, "Destroy this temple, and in three days I will raise it," which John is at pains to explain

---

14. So Jörg Frey, "Love-Relations in the Fourth Gospel: Establishing a Semantic Network," in *Repetitions and Variations in the Fourth Gospel: Style, Text, Interpretation*, ed. Gilbert Van Belle, Michael Labahn, and P. Maritz, BETL 223 (Peeters, 2009), 186.

as a reference to the resurrection (2:21–22), strongly resembles the false witness brought against Jesus at his Jewish trial and taunt at his crucifixion according to Mark (14:58; 15:29). Moreover, while John's version in 2:19 has the verb "to raise" rather than Mark's "to build," we note that the Markan verb reappears in the response of "the Jews" in John 2:20. Furthermore, John's rendering of the saying together with his explanation can be said to make explicit what is already implied in Mark's text, both in the phrase "in three days," which John also has, but especially in Mark's "not made with hands" in 14:58.

In chapter 5, John returns Jesus to Jerusalem for a feast and so provides a different setting from Mark for his account of the healing of the paralyzed man (5:1–7). Nevertheless, as we have noted, Jesus's instruction to the paralytic in 5:8, "Rise, take up your bed and walk," is exact to the wording in Mark 2:9. There are also further indicators in John's narrative to suggest the continuing influence of Mark's text. In 5:13, for example, John includes a late and unprecedented reference to a crowd, which is a key feature in the Markan setting for the cure (Mark 2:1–4). There is also Jesus's warning to the cured man in 5:14, suggesting a link between sin and disease that is consistent with Jesus's argument according to Mark (2:9–11), but out of keeping with the attitude John himself ascribes to Jesus at a later point (9:2–3). Finally, the accusation of blasphemy that the Jewish authorities bring against Jesus in John 5:18 (cf. 10:30) has already been aired in the minds of the scribes according to Mark 2:9. Another difference here is that John presents this as a Sabbath healing. Even so, we need not search far in the Markan context before the issue of Jesus's actions on the Sabbath comes to the fore (2:23–28) and is followed immediately by the Sabbath healing of the man with the withered hand (3:1–6).

On the occasion of John's second reference to Passover in 6:4, we find Jesus suddenly back in Galilee (6:1), where the miracle of the feeding of the five thousand takes place. Here, John brings aspects of Mark's two accounts of the miracle together with further material from the Markan context to inform his own account (John 6:1–15; Mark 6:30–44; 8:1–10, cf. vv. 11–21), an attentiveness that seems to extend even to supplying a reason for Jesus's sudden withdrawal after the miracle where Mark does not oblige (Mark 6:45; cf. John 6:15). John also includes references to the passion in the discourse that ensues, arguably influenced by Mark's description of the blessing of the loaves in 6:41 (cf. 14:22) to introduce Jesus's eucharistic language from the Last Supper at this earlier point

(John 6:52–58) and also to draw in Judas Iscariot, who ate Jesus's bread before betraying him on that occasion (6:70–71; 13:18, 21–30).[15]

This tendency in John toward explication in relation to Mark's text is also evident elsewhere in his narrative. In particular, there are points where John explicitly quotes from Scripture where Mark's narrative implies it. Compare, for example, John's quotation of Zech 9:9 at the triumphal entry in 12:15 and Mark 11:1–10 and, similarly, his quotation of Ps 41:9 at the Last Supper in 13:18 and Mark 14:18. Furthermore, in the crucifixion scene, John quotes Ps 22:19 (19:24) where Mark implies it (Mark 15:24) and also explicitly acknowledges Jesus's fulfilment of Scripture (Ps 69:21) by contrast with Mark (19:28–29; cf. Mark 15:36). In the same explicatory vein, John introduces the name Caiaphas for the high priest, which was probably common enough knowledge at the time that Mark chose not to include (11:49; 18:13–14, 24, 28; see also Matt 26:3, 57).[16]

A further aspect of Mark's contribution to the making of John brings us to John's passion narrative where, as we have noted, his account comes into line with the Markan order and where further verbal links with Mark are well in evidence. In his composition of the trial before Pilate, these are sufficiently remarkable to suggest that John's much longer version has been deliberately based on Mark's text, which he has amplified with further material, filling its gaps and adding new insights.[17] As we have noted, in 18:33 John repeats Pilate's first question, "Are you the King of the Jews?," in Mark 15:2. Then, between the question and Jesus's answer in the Markan verse, John has introduced further comment by Jesus that elaborates on the meaning of his kingship (John 18:36). Similarly, in 18:37, his version both extends and clarifies Jesus's meaning following Mark's terse "You say" in the same verse. These and other examples we have noted strongly suggest that John's Roman trial has been fashioned from a close reading of the Markan text.[18]

---

15. Further on John 6 as a whole in relation to Mark 6:32–8:30, see especially Lincoln, *Gospel according to Saint John*, 209–41.

16. See Helen K. Bond, "At the Court of the High Priest: History and Theology in John 18:13–24," in *Aspects of Historicity in the Fourth Gospel*, vol. 2 of *John, Jesus, and History*, ed. Paul N. Anderson, Felix Just, S.J., and Tom Thatcher, ECL 2 (Society of Biblical Literature, 2009), 322.

17. See especially Francis Watson, *Gospel Writing: A Canonical Perspective* (Eerdmans, 2013), 384–89 for an analysis of John's Roman trial as based on a Markan template supplemented by reference to Matthew and Luke.

18. See Barrett's comment on 18:33 that "John's narrative at this point follows Mark closely," adding that 18:34–37 may be regarded as an expansion of Mark's "You

Finally, we return to the beginning of the gospel story in both Mark and John and also to the ending as envisaged by both authors. As we have noted, while Mark announces the beginning of the gospel, John's beginning takes us back to prehistory before the narrative begins. Furthermore, while Mark's narrative is open-ended, leaving the news of the resurrection yet to be conveyed (16:1–8) and all three remaining gospels add an account of Jesus's appearances to the disciples (Matt 28:16–20; Luke 24:36–53; John 20:19–29), the ending John actually envisages extends once again beyond the time of the narrative. Thus, in 20:29, Jesus's final ringing words bless those who have not seen yet believe and open up the postresurrection future. In the course of his narrative, John has twice informed his readers that the disciples were in no position to understand the meaning of events at the time but would do so at a later point (2:22; 12:16). That later point is the advent of the Spirit-Paraclete, who ushers in an era that includes John himself as narrator of Jesus's story and those for whom he writes. Moreover, as we have seen, John's own interpretation of events and of the meaning and significance of Jesus is consciously articulated from this postresurrection Spirit-led perspective. It is important to add here that the one disciple who does understand in the course of John's narrative, who appears first in the Last Supper scene as "the disciple whom Jesus loved" (13:23; cf. 19:26; 20:2), is also the one disciple at the close who has not seen yet believes (20:8–9). By these means, John has sought to bridge the time between the remembered past of Jesus's story and his readers' present experience.[19]

Thus, it seems that John has not only built on the time-frame of the Markan narrative but has also significantly extended it. The result is a combination of this-worldly history and symbolic, meta-historical frame-

---

say." He also suggests that "John is probably expounding, and thereby attaching more precise meaning to, the obscure Markan words" (*Gospel according to St. John*, 536, 537). Further on John's links with Mark, see Lincoln, *Gospel according to Saint John*, 458–59; and Watson, *Gospel Writing*, 387, 392.

19. On the link between Jesus's final blessing directed to the reader and the experience of the disciple whom Jesus loved, see Moloney, "Closure," 234 with n. 28, 235; further on John's purposes for those living without Jesus, see Wendy E. S. North, *A Journey Round John: Tradition, Interpretation and Context in the Fourth Gospel*, LNTS 534 (Bloomsbury T&T Clark, 2015), 193–206. John also refers to space beyond the narrative to present Jesus as bridging the gap between the disciples in the world and the world beyond; see Susanne Luther, "Space," in Estes and Sheridan, *How John Works*, 70–71.

work that is arguably the most powerful factor in the making of his gospel to contribute to its distinctiveness and to mark it out as a radically transformed version of what he knew.[20] The effects of this are readily apparent in his presentation of Jesus. Thus, while indications of Jesus's other-worldly identity are by no means absent from Mark (see 1:24, 34; 3:11; 5:6–7; 8:29; 9:7; 15:39), it is quintessential of John's presentation of him that Jesus consistently declares his identity in terms that resonate beyond narrative boundaries. We have already noted his gift for crystallizing meaning into words in 1:14, and this is a part of the transformative process whereby whatever John narrates he renders in his own style, including Jesus's speech. Thus, declarations such as "I am the bread of life" (6:35, 48), "I am the light of the world" (8:12; 9:5), "I am the good shepherd" (10:11, 14), and "I am the resurrection and the life" (11:25) on Jesus's lips in John represent powerful and effective articulations of his meaning and significance. Particularly remarkable in this context is John's attribution to Jesus of the simple, theophanic "I am" and its appropriate consequences at his arrest (18:5–6), in which Jesus as the revelatory word speaks God's words and confirms his identity for faith (13:19; see also John 8:24, 58; Deut 32:39; Isa 41:4; 43:10, 13; 46:4; 48:12). Even here, however, it seems that the Markan text continues its influence as we note that the scene in John makes explicit the implications of Jesus' "I am" in Mark 14:62.[21]

Conclusion

We cannot know whether the author of Mark was the first to inscribe oral memories of Jesus in the story form he called a gospel. What seems certain, however, is that his work became sufficiently well-known to be formative for how Matthew and Luke would set about the task. Indeed, Luke's prologue already takes up and applies Mark's beginning to his own role as historian (Luke 1:2). For the same reason, it is likely that Mark was influential in the making of John. In this case, however, the evidence is less straightforward, suggesting a knowledge of Mark on the one hand and, on

---

20. On this aspect of John, see Susanne Luther, "From Bethlehem, according to the Promise—or Rather from Nazareth? Narrative and History in John's Gospel," *Early Christianity* 8 (2017): 29; see also Eve-Marie Becker, *The Birth of Christian History: Memory and Time from Mark to Luke-Acts*, AYBRL (Yale University Press, 2017), 19–20, 145–46.

21. See further, Lincoln, *Gospel according to Saint John*, 220, 446.

the other, a more complex interaction with the Second Gospel. Thus, as we have seen, from Mark's beginning to further remarkable verbal parallels with what follows, John's account exhibits an agreement with Mark that can scarcely be brushed aside. Equally, however, we also noted conspicuous differences in John with regard to the order, location and timing of events, significant absences of Markan material, and also the inclusion of non-Markan material at key narrative points. In attempting to account for this combination of similarity and difference, we began with John's closing address to his readers in 20:30–31 and viewed the content of his narrative from that perspective. This proved an apt context in which to approach narrative differences and also to note passing references to events in John. Similarly, this approach served to point us to key evidence in the gospel to indicate that what John wrote was a profoundly reconceived version of what he knew, attributed by him to a post-resurrection access of understanding conveyed by the Spirit-Paraclete. Taking John's approach into account, evidence of Markan influence in John suggests not only a fidelity to the Markan narrative and its context but also a freedom in the telling whereby Markan material has been expanded and developed in the service of a larger vision in which its implications are creatively set forth. In sum, John not only pursued the task of gospel-writing in the knowledge of Mark's text but also what he wrote reflects that knowledge and engages with its content in ways that interpret and transform it.

9
Testimony

Paul N. Anderson

The Gospel of John features centrally a number of testimonies designed to convince hearers and readers that Jesus is the Christ, the Son of God, and that believing, they might have life in his name (20:30–31). In navigating the living waters of the Gospel of John, it is helpful to remember that the threefold thrust of the Johannine signs, the fulfilled word, and the testifying witnesses are woven together as a braided cord, inviting Jewish and gentile audiences alike to come to faith in Jesus as the Christ.[1] While some of John's later material calls for abiding in Christ and his community of faith, the central aim of John's narrative is apologetic.

On one hand, the testimonial features of the narrative can be viewed as aspects of a court case in which evidence is presented to the audience-as-jury, inviting a verdict of belief in Jesus as a result of the evidence.[2] So do characterization and other rhetorical devices.[3] John is also very

---

1. For an overall treatment of how the Johannine narrative leads hearers and readers into transformative faith (John 20:30–31), see Paul N. Anderson, *Navigating the Living Waters of the Gospel of John: On Wading with Children and Swimming with Elephants*, Pendle Hill Pamphlet 352 (Pendle Hill Press, 2000); see also Anderson, "The Fulfilled Word in the Gospel of John: A Polyvalent Analysis," in *The Gospel of John*, vol. 4 of *Biblical Interpretation in Early Christian Gospels*, ed. Thomas R. Hatina, LNTS 613 (T&T Clark, 2020), 57–81.

2. Andrew T. Lincoln, *Truth on Trial: The Lawsuit Motif in the Fourth Gospel* (Hendrickson, 2000); Martin Asiedu-Peprah, *Johannine Sabbath Conflicts as Juridical Controversy*, WUNT 2/132 (Mohr Siebeck, 2001); George L. Parsenios, *Rhetoric and Drama in the Johannine Lawsuit Motif*, WUNT 258 (Mohr Siebeck, 2010).

3. See especially R. Alan Culpepper, *Anatomy of the Fourth Gospel: A Study in Literary Design* (Fortress, 1983); David W. Wead, *The Literary Devices in John's Gospel*, ed. Paul N. Anderson and R. Alan Culpepper, rev. and exp. ed., JMS 7 (Wipf & Stock,

different from the Synoptics, and its highly theological thrust might call into question its historical character for some.

This has led some scholars to argue that the evangelist had no firsthand knowledge of Jesus and his ministry, despite its own claims to eyewitness testimony and memory (19:34-35; 21:20-24). Rudolf Bultmann, for instance, claimed that John's story of Jesus was founded upon alien sources and distorted by an ecclesial redactor.[4] Alternatively, such scholars as C. K. Barrett and the Leuven School assumed John built upon the Synoptics, thus having no or little distinctive testimony of its own.[5] However, John's account is not simply an abstract narrative removed from its originative contexts. Despite John's perplexing riddles, its distinctive memory of Jesus deserves to be understood within an overall Johannine theory.[6] Thus, John's distinctive testimony about Jesus of Nazareth, as well as the Johannine witness motif, are best considered within an overall view of John's dialogical autonomy.[7]

The Dialogical Autonomy of the Fourth Gospel

By dialogical autonomy, I mean that, first, John's witness to Jesus and his ministry is not dependent on other traditions or folkloric myths. It represents an individuated account, likely familiar with other traditions but with its own memory and voice. Second, John's narrative reflects several levels of dialogue, which help us understand more clearly how its witness is conveyed.

2018); Steven A. Hunt, D. François Tolmie, and Ruben Zimmermann, eds., *Character Studies in the Fourth Gospel: Narrative Approaches to Seventy Figures in John*, WUNT 314 (Mohr Siebeck, 2013).

4. Rudolf Bultmann, *The Gospel of John: A Commentary*, trans. G. R. Beasley-Murray, JMS 1 (Wipf & Stock, 2014). See the dearth of evidence supporting his highly diachronic inferences of underlying sources and overlaying redactions in this extensive analysis of Bultmann's marshalled evidence: Paul N. Anderson, *The Christology of the Fourth Gospel: Its Unity and Disunity in the Light of John 6*, 3rd ed. (Cascade, 2010), 48-136.

5. Barrett, *Gospel according to St. John*, 45.

6. For a fuller treatment of the origin and character of three dozen key Johannine riddles—theological, historical, and literary—see Paul N. Anderson, *The Riddles of the Fourth Gospel: An Introduction to John* (Fortress, 2011).

7. Anderson, *Riddles of the Fourth Gospel*, 125-56.

John's Autonomy

Given that more than eighty-five percent of John's story of Jesus has no direct overlap with the Synoptic Gospels, we must consider John's tradition an autonomous tradition rather than a derivative one. Further, where John's tradition coincides with elements, say, of Mark, none of the contacts are verbatim or identical for more than a word or two. Thus, the overall judgment of P. Gardner-Smith, that Johannine independence is the most critically plausible inference, stands.[8] Additionally, C. H. Dodd's demonstration that the Johannine tradition reflects an independent Synoptic-like historical memory of Jesus is bolstered by considering distinctive parallels with the gospel's passion narratives and the attributed works and words of Jesus.[9] In these ways, John's accounts of elements in the ministry of Jesus, while different from those of the Synoptics, are also more like those narratives than like folkloric features of contemporary Hellenistic religions.

Then again, John's pervasive autonomy need not imply total independence or lack of knowledge of Mark, at least. And, John's relationships with each of the Synoptic traditions were not identical.[10] (1) From the earliest stages of the Johannine and the pre-Markan tradition (30–70 CE), some degree of interfluentiality is plausible. With Peter and John preaching throughout Samaria in Acts 8, some of the buzz words and graphic details shared between the Johannine and Markan traditions may be rooted in this kind of oral tradition cross-influence, whoever the preaching sources of these narratives might have been. (2) Assuming that written Mark was performed among the churches, it is likely that the Johannine evangelist may have become familiar with Mark's story of Jesus between 70 and 80

---

8. P. Gardner-Smith, *Saint John and the Synoptic Gospels* (Cambridge University Press, 1938). Whereas Gardner-Smith identified four striking differences between John 6 and Mark 6, a closer analysis shows forty-five similar-yet-different features when John 6 is compared with Mark 6 and 8: Anderson, *Christology of the Fourth Gospel*, 97–107.

9. C. H. Dodd, *Historical Tradition in the Fourth Gospel* (Cambridge University Press, 1963).

10. See an overall theory of John's relations to the Synoptic traditions, as well as several phases in the Johannine-Markan relationship: Paul N. Anderson, "Interfluential, Formative, and Dialectical: A Theory of John's Relation to the Synoptics," in *Für und Wider die Priorität des Johannesevangeliums*, ed. Peter Leander Hofrichter, TTS 9 (Olms, 2002), 19–58; Anderson, "Mark, John, and Answerability: Interfluentiality and Dialectic between the Second and Fourth Gospels," *Liber Annuus* 63 (2013): 197–245.

CE.[11] Thus, the first edition of John (assuming John 1:1–18 and chapters 6, 15–17, and 21 were added later) augments Mark with five distinctive signs and new material.[12] John also sets a few things straight, and its first edition displays an apologetic thrust (80–85 CE).[13] (3) Given that Luke departs from Mark in ways that coincide with John at least six dozen times, the most plausible inference is that the formative Johannine tradition served as one of Luke's sources.[14] Given the fact that the Q tradition includes Johannine features, we may also infer some sort of intertraditional contact (assuming the existence of Q and that Luke did not have access to Matthew).[15] (4) Later contacts between the formative Matthean and Johannine traditions reflect some form of dialectical engagement, bolstering each other's presentation of Jesus as the Jewish Messiah/Christ and reflecting some dialectical engagement regarding ecclesial structure and church order issues (85–100 CE).[16] (5) The evangelist continued to teach and write, and after the evangelist's death, the Johannine elder writes the Johannine Epistles, and he then adds the later material to the finalized

---

11. The most compelling treatment of John's familiarity with Mark is Ian D. Mackay, *John's Relationship with Mark: An Analysis of John 6 in Light of Mark 6–8*, WUNT 2/182 (Mohr Siebeck, 2004), who argues that the Johannine evangelist may have heard mark performed among the churches, accounting for general familiarity and autonomy without being dependent on a written text.

12. With Barnabas Lindars, *The Gospel of John*, NCBC (Eerdmans, 1982).

13. With both Carson and Brown on the purpose(s) of the Johannine Gospel, the first edition is apologetic and evangelistic—leading people into first-belief; the final edition calls for solidarity with Jesus and his community in a more pastoral way (Brown). See Donald A. Carson on the primary rhetorical thrust of John 20:31, "The Purpose of the Fourth Gospel: John 20:31 Reconsidered," *JBL* 106 (1987): 639–51; and Raymond E. Brown, *The Gospel According to John XIII–XXI*, AB 29A (Doubleday, 1970), 1060.

14. With F. Lamar Cribbs, "A Study of the Contacts that Exist between St. Luke and St. John," in *SBL 1973 Seminar Papers* (Society of Biblical Literature, 1973), 1–93; Cribbs, "St. Luke and the Johannine Tradition," *JBL* 90 (1971): 422–50; and Cribbs, "The Agreements that Exist between St. Luke and St. John," in *SBL 1979 Seminar Papers* (Scholars Press, 1979), 215–61. Paul N. Anderson, "Acts 4:19–20—An Overlooked First-Century Clue to Johannine Authorship and Luke's Dependence upon the Johannine Tradition," *The Bible and Interpretation*, September 2010, https://bibleinterp.arizona.edu/opeds/acts357920.

15. Anderson, "Interfluential, Formative, and Dialectical."

16. Paul N. Anderson, "'*You* Have the Words of Eternal Life!' Is Peter Presented as *Returning* the Keys of the Kingdom to Jesus in John 6:68?," *Neot* 41 (2008): 6–41; see also Anderson, *Christology of the Fourth Gospel*, 221–50.

gospel and circulates it as the testimony of the Beloved Disciple, whose testimony is true (ca. 100 CE). This later material harmonizes the Johannine narrative with the synoptic accounts and reflects a more pastoral interest.[17] (6) Finally, interestingly, some of the material in the second ending of Mark contains a few Johannine details.[18] Thus, John's story of Jesus represents an autonomous tradition developing alongside the other traditions, but not dependent on them, as a bi-optic complement to the Markan accounts.

Johannine Dialogism

Understanding John's dialogism is also essential for discerning its character, development, and meaning. As a great deal of theological tension accompanies virtually every theme in John, discerning the character and origin of its dialectical features is essential for understanding its meaning.

1. The evangelist was a dialectical thinker, who thought in both-and ways instead of either-or dichotomies.[19] This feature suggests a first-order level of thinking versus second-order reasoning—the sort of thing that an eyewitness might testify to, rather than the citing of second-hand material. Many details are left undeveloped in John, and the narrator conveys direct interest in the subject—Jesus—rather than tradition. For instance, the evangelist emphasizes abiding *in* Christ (John 15:1–8) whereas the Elder advocates abiding *in the teaching about* Christ (2 John 9).

2. The narrative also reflects intratraditional dialogue, including earlier impressions that are adjusted by later reflections.[20] For instance, the disciples only realize in postresurrection consciousness that Jesus is speaking of his body when he declared the destruction and three-day reconstruction of "this temple" (John 2:19–22).[21] While signs are embellished and

---

17. Paul N. Anderson, "On 'Seamless Robes' and 'Leftover Fragments': A Theory of Johannine Composition," in *The Origins of John's Gospel*, ed. Stanley E. Porter and Hughson T. Ong, JS 2 (Brill, 2015), 169–218.

18. Anderson, "Mark, John, and Answerability."

19. With C. K. Barrett, *New Testament Essays* (SPCK, 1972), 49–69; Paul N. Anderson, "The Cognitive Origins of John's Christological Unity and Disunity," *HBT* 17 (1995): 1–24.

20. Anderson, *Christology of the Fourth Gospel*, 167–251.

21. See especially Richard B. Hays, "Reading Scripture in the Light of the Resurrection," in *The Art of Reading Scripture*, ed. Ellen F. Davis and Richard B. Hays (Eerdmans, 2003), 216–38.

featured centrally in John's narrative, blessed are those who have not seen these signs and yet believe (John 20:29).[22]

3. Likewise, John's story of Jesus develops in intertraditional dialogue with other traditions, at times reinforcing Synoptic accounts, and at other times engaging them correctively. For instance, John appears to follow Mark's general pattern of beginning with the ministries of John the Baptist and Jesus (John 1:6-8, 15, 19-42), including distinctive signs and sayings, concluding with the last days of Jesus in Jerusalem and appearance narratives. However, in contrast to Mark, John presents the temple incident as an inaugural sign, shows Jesus as traveling to and from Jerusalem several times, and places the last supper on the day before the Passover as a fellowship meal. God's love must be expressed in community, and Jesus never promised to return before all the disciples had passed away; Peter (and others) got it wrong from day one.[23]

4. The central purpose of the Fourth Gospel centers on the human-divine dialogue, whereby the Revealer conveys God's love and truth to the world and invites a response of faith such that all who believe become children of God and are welcomed into the divine family. The gospel conveys this motif by means of the prophet-like-Moses agency schema that is rooted in Deut 18:18-22. Thus, because the Son says and does nothing other than what the Father instructs, any responses to the Son are the same as responding to the Father.[24]

5. John's story of Jesus occurs within a highly dialectical situation with six additional societal crises (in addition to Johannine-Synoptic dialectics) over seven decades. Dialectical engagements included those between religious leaders in Judea and followers of John the Baptist (30-70 CE); Pharisaic leaders in the Asia Minor synagogue and representatives of the Roman imperial cult (70-85 CE); and docetizing traveling ministers and proto-Ignatian hierarchical leaders such as Diotrephes (85-100 CE).[25]

---

22. Anderson, *Christology of the Fourth Gospel*, 137-65.

23. Paul N. Anderson, "Mark and John: The Bi-Optic Gospels," in *Jesus in Johannine Tradition*, ed. Robert T. Fortna and Tom Thatcher (Westminster John Knox, 2001), 175-88; see also Anderson, *Christology of the Fourth Gospel*, 87-88, 153-60, 170-93; and Anderson, "Mark, John, and Answerability."

24. Peder Borgen, "God's Agent in the Fourth Gospel," in *The Interpretation of John*, ed. John Ashton, 2nd ed. (T&T Clark, 1997), 83-96; Paul N. Anderson, "The Having-Sent-Me Father: Aspects of Agency, Encounter, and Irony in the Johannine Father-Son Relationship," *Semeia* 85 (1999): 33-57.

25. Paul N. Anderson, "Bakhtin's Dialogism and the Corrective Rhetoric of the

6. In addressing its evolving audiences, John's story of Jesus is crafted rhetorically so as to engage hearers and readers in an imaginary dialogue with Jesus even as it tells its story. Hence, miscomprehension is always rhetorical. When discussants in the narrative get it right, such is a positive example for others to follow; when discussants get it wrong, such reflects a negative example to be avoided.[26]

Narrative Testimonies within the Emerging Johannine Tradition

As the Johannine tradition develops alongside other traditions, the testimonies of its witnesses are operative in a number of distinctive ways.[27]

First, characters in the narrative witness to Jesus being the Messiah in the early narrative, with the implication that later audiences will continue to be witnesses in the world. Second, what Jesus had testified in Mark 6:4 is set straight in John 4:44: Despite Jesus's rejection in Nazareth, not everyone in the north did the same, as the Samaritans and the Galileans receive Jesus warmly. Third, the Father bears witness to the Son during his ministry, but the Spirit continues to bear witness to followers of Jesus—reminding them of and leading them into truth—especially in the later stages of the Johannine tradition. Fourth, the words and works of Jesus in the narrative testify to his authentic agency as the Son of the Father—fulfilling the prediction of Moses in Deut 18:15–22. Jesus's continuing words of assurance provide consolation for later followers as they face challenges within the Johannine situation. Fifth, the testimonies in the narrative further its revelational motif and invite emerging audiences to respond in faith to the divine initiative. When characters misunderstand their testimony and Jesus's testimony, we see a rhetorical feature meant to challenge and correct inadequate understandings of the truth.[28] Sixth, the confessional

---

Johannine Misunderstanding Dialogue: Exposing Seven Crises in the Johannine Situation," in *Bakhtin and Genre Theory in Biblical Studies*, ed. Roland Boer, SemeiaSt 63 (Society of Biblical Literature, 2007), 133–59; see also Anderson, "Mark, John, and Answerability."

26. Anderson, *Christology of the Fourth Gospel*, 221–51.
27. Anderson, "On 'Seamless Robes.'"
28. On revelation and rhetoric—two dialogical modes in John 6, see Paul N. Anderson, "The *Sitz im Leben* of the Johannine Bread of Life Discourse and its Evolving Context," in *Critical Readings of John 6*, ed. R. Alan Culpepper, BibInt 22 (Brill, 1997), 1–59; on John 9, see Paul N. Anderson, "Revelation and Rhetoric in John 9:1–10:21: Two Dialogical Modes Operative within the Johannine Narrative," in *Modern and*

focus of the Johannine prologue attests to transformative experiences of faith among Johannine believers, and it invites later audiences to receive the message of the story and thereby be welcomed into the divine family where they can encounter fully God's love. Emerging first as a response to the narration (as did 1 John 1:1–3; note the similarities with John 1:1–5, 9–14, 16–18), the Johannine Logos hymn is added to the front of the narrative as an experientially engaging introduction to what follows.[29]

Characters as Witnesses

The primary testimony in the narrative is carried forth by the characters themselves.[30] Especially when characters believe or when they point audiences to the right way to think or act, these characters become guides to later audiences and show the way forward. Of course, when actants in the narrative miscomprehend Jesus's words, they serve as negative examples, as miscomprehension in narrative is always rhetorical and corrective.[31]

John the Baptist, the Prime Witness

In John's story of Jesus, John the Baptist serves as the prime witness from the beginning. In that sense, the Johannine narrative augments the beginning of Mark's narrative by adding scenarios before the events reported in Mark 1. Contra Mark 1:14, Jesus's ministry began *before* John was thrown into prison (John 3:24). In addition to the first and second miracles of Jesus filling out his early ministry (John 2:1–11; 4:46–54), we see him ministering

---

Ancient Literary Criticism of the Gospels: Continuing the Debate on Gospel Genre(s), ed. Robert Matthew Calhoun, David P. Moessner, and Tobias Nicklas, WUNT 451 (Mohr Siebeck, 2020), 441–70.

29. Paul N. Anderson, "On Guessing Points and Naming Stars: The Epistemological Origins of John's Christological Tensions," in *The Gospel of John and Christian Theology*, ed. Richard Bauckham and Carl Mosser (Eerdmans, 2007), 311–45; Anderson, "The Johannine *Logos*-Hymn: A Cross-Cultural Celebration of God's Creative-Redemptive Work," in *Creation Stories in Dialogue: The Bible, Science, and Folk Traditions; Radboud Prestige Lecture Series by R. Alan Culpepper*, ed. R. Alan Culpepper and Jan G. van der Watt, BibInt 139 (Brill 2015), 219–42.

30. James Montgomery Boice, *Witness and Revelation in the Gospel of John* (Zondervan, 1970).

31. Bakhtin references this as "stupidity" in narrative; cf. Anderson, "Bakhtin's Dialogism."

alongside John the Baptist in complementary ways. Thus, as an augmentation and modest correction of Mark, John the Baptist is featured at the beginning of Jesus's ministry as the prime witness in a number of ways.

First, the narrator clarifies that while John came from God, he was not the light that enlightens humanity; rather, John came saying that Jesus was before him in terms of precedence, even though he came after him in terms of timing (1:6–8, 15). As a means of evangelizing some Baptist adherents believing him to have been the Messiah, John testifies that he is not the Christ, but that he is merely a friend of the bridegroom. To console fellow Baptist adherents who might be discouraged that Jesus was garnering more followers than John, the Baptist affirms that Jesus must increase, while he must decrease. The ascendency of Jesus's ministry fulfills his joy, and John's elevation of Jesus above his own ministry points contemporary and future Baptist-adherents to Jesus as the one they should follow (3:22–30).

Second, as John had testified that Jesus is "the Lamb of God, who takes away the sin of the world" (1:29, 36), the narrator presents some of his followers as breaking away and becoming disciples of Jesus (vv. 37–51). Andrew goes and finds his brother, Peter, and Philip finds Nathanael. Having witnessed John's testimony regarding the Spirit descending upon Jesus as he came up out of the water (v. 32), some of John's disciples become the first followers of Jesus. This informal calling narrative thus provides a helpful backdrop for understanding more fully how Jesus is remembered as calling several others to follow him (Mark 1:16–20; 2:13–17), contextualizing and making more believable the more programmatic calling of the Twelve in Mark 3:13–19.[32]

A third feature seems rather odd, but it prepares the way for the theological presentation of Jesus as fulfilling the typologies of Elijah and Moses in the Fourth Gospel. When the Jerusalem authorities come to John asking if he were Elijah or the prophet (Moses—as depicted in Mark 6:15; 9:12–13), John declares that he is not. Rather, he came as a voice crying in the wilderness, making straight the pathway for the Lord (John 1:19–28). The appearance of Moses and Elijah had also been featured in the Markan transfiguration scenario (Mark 9:2–8), but this and most of

---

32. Andreas J. Köstenberger, "Who Were the First Disciples of Jesus? An Assessment of the Historicity of the Johannine Call Narrative (John 1:35–51)," in *Glimpses of Jesus through the Johannine Lens*, vol. 3 of *John, Jesus, and History*, ed. Paul N. Anderson, Felix Just, S.J., and Tom Thatcher, ECL 18 (SBL Press, 2016), 189–200.

Mark's material are omitted by the first Johannine edition—likely as an interest in nonduplication. Whatever the case, the Fourth Gospel presents Jesus as fulfilling the miraculous ministries of Elijah and Moses by the feeding of the multitudes with barley loaves (*artous krithinous*), raising Lazarus from the dead, and performing signs that John did not.[33] In that sense, the Baptist's testimony that he is neither Elijah nor the eschatological prophet clears the ground for these typologies to be fulfilled by Jesus, the prototypical Jewish Messiah.

Disciples and Actants as Witnesses

In addition to John, disciples of Jesus in the narrative also serve as witnesses to Jesus as the Messiah/Christ. Andrew and Philip bring Peter and Nathanael to Jesus, inviting them with the same invitational words: "Come and see" (John 1:39, 46).[34] Philip becomes a bridge between Jesus and the Greek seekers at the Jerusalem festival, suggesting his cross-cultural association, providing a link to missions among the Samaritans and beyond (Acts 8:4–40; 21:20–22). Because the disciples believe, they implicitly testify to Jesus and his mission throughout the narrative (John 2:2–22; 12:16; 20:10, 25; although Peter and others get it wrong sometimes). More explicitly, the eyewitness testifies that water and blood poured forth from the pierced side of Jesus (19:34–35); Thomas confesses upon touching the flesh wounds of Jesus: "My Lord, and my God!" (20:28; challenging the rise of emperor worship under Domitian [81–96 CE]); and the Beloved Disciple points out the Lord to Peter (21:7). In addition to testifying that Jesus is the Messiah/Christ, these presentations also address pointedly divisive issues within the Johannine situation as reflected in the Johannine Epistles.[35]

---

33. Jesus indeed fulfills the Moses and Elijah typologies in the Gospel of John, showing Jesus to be Israel's true Eschatological Prophet: Paul N. Anderson, "Jesus, the Eschatological Prophet in the Fourth Gospel: A Case Study in Dialectical Tensions," in *Reading the Gospel of John's Christology as Jewish Messianism: Royal, Prophetic, and Divine Messiahs*, ed. Benjamin E. Reynolds and Gabriele Boccaccini, AGJU 106 (Brill, 2018), 271–99.

34. Paul N. Anderson, "'Come and See!' Philip as a Connective Figure in the Fourth Gospel in Polyvalent Perspective," in Hunt, Tolmie, and Zimmermann, *Character Studies in the Fourth Gospel*, 162–82.

35. See especially Anderson, "*Sitz im Leben*," 1–59; see also Anderson, "Bakhtin's Dialogism."

In somewhat subtle ways, those for whom Jesus performs his signs also become witnesses within the narrative. Thus, the steward of the wedding celebration becomes an unwitting testifier to the climactic ministry of Jesus as one who saves the best for last (John 2:9–10; referencing the raising of Lazarus, the glorification of Jesus, or both); the servants of the royal official testify to the very hour that his son was healed (4:49–53); some Jews in Jerusalem believe on account of the healing of the lame man and his witness (5:1–15; 7:21–31); the formerly blind man testifies that whereas once he was blind, "now I see" (9:25); and climactically, following the raising of Lazarus, many believe on account of his testimony (11:27, 45; 12:9–11).

While testimony and witness language are not used as pervasively in John 15–17, Jesus prays that the Father will preserve his disciples who are in the world but not of the world. By their love and unity they will be a witness to the world, that the world might believe; and despite believers encountering tribulation in the world, Jesus has overcome the world (17:6–21). In that sense, the agency which Jesus received from the Father continues in the agency of the Spirit, who proceeds from the Father and is sent by the Son (14:16, 26; 15:26; 16:7). The Spirit's role is to instruct and remind believers of the teachings of Jesus, and the Spirit commissions believers as testifying witnesses in the world. In particular, it is by their love demonstrated that followers of Jesus will be known by others (13:34–35).

Women as Witnesses

Perhaps most striking within the Johannine witness motif is the fact that women are portrayed as pivotal apostolic witnesses. In particular, the woman at the well becomes an apostle to the Samaritans (4:4–43), and Mary Magdalene becomes an apostle to the apostles (20:11–18).[36] When Jesus demonstrates knowledge of the Samaritan woman and her marital situation, the woman declares that this knowledge shows him to be the Messiah, and it testifies to her spiritual recognition. Likewise, Mary witnesses the empty tomb and later encounters the risen Lord, and she witnesses to Peter and the disciples that she saw the Lord and that he is alive. For a brief period, Mary is the first believer in the resurrected Lord.

---

36. Paul N. Anderson, *The Fourth Gospel and the Quest for Jesus: Modern Foundations Reconsidered*, LNTS 321 (T&T Clark, 2006), 164–66.

While male disciples (other than the Beloved Disciple) are nowhere to be found at the crucifixion scene, two Marys and the mother of Jesus are present at the cross. The entrustment of the mother of Jesus to the Beloved Disciple then symbolizes the transfer of continuity from Jesus to Johannine Christianity—a further testimony as to its apostolic legacy within the Jesus movement.

The Father and the Spirit as Witnesses

In addition to human testimonies, the Father and the Spirit witness to Jesus in the Gospel of John. These testimonies are intrinsically linked to Jesus's testimony about his relationship to the Father and the Spirit, as the relationship of the Son with the Father and the Spirit is one of agency, moving in multiple directions.[37]

The Testimony of the Father

The Father's testimony about the Son, emerging from the debates over his healing the lame man on the Sabbath, affirms the Son's representative agency. This healing angers the religious leaders in Jerusalem, who charge Jesus with breaking the Sabbath. Jesus claims to do the work of his Father, which carries forth the work of his commissioned agency, as predicted by Moses in Deut 18:15-18. He also appeals to the authority of two witnesses, which includes the testimony of the Father, as well as his own (Deut 19:15; John 5:1-38). Jesus continues the claim that the Father testifies on his behalf in John 8:17, and yet, knowledge of the Father's testimony hinges upon the religious leaders knowing the Father intimately, which Jesus questions.

Following his final entry into Jerusalem, Jesus is troubled about his impending hour. He prays that the Father would glorify his own name, and a voice sounds from heaven, declaring: "I have glorified it, and I will glorify it again" (John 12:28). Some present thought it was thunder; others thought it was an angel. Jesus declares, however, that this was given for the sake of others—not for himself. The narrator then interprets the message as an indication of the means of death by which Jesus would die—a prefig-

---

37. On the Johannine Mosaic agency schema, see Anderson, "Having-Sent-Me Father."

uring of the events in John 18–19 (vv. 29–33). These are some of the ways the Father's testimony witnesses to the authentic agency of the Son and the means by which he would glorify God.

The Testimony of the Spirit

In contrast to the Father's testimony during the ministry of Jesus, the testimony of the Spirit—the Advocate—is promised after the departure of Jesus. The Holy Spirit will abide with the disciples and in them (John 14:17); will teach them everything and remind them of what Jesus has said (14:26); will testify on behalf of Jesus regarding the truth (15:26); will convict the world of sin and of righteousness (16:8); and will guide disciples into all truth, declaring what has been heard from Jesus and glorifying him by conveying his truth faithfully (16:13–15). If chapters 15–17 represent later material delivered in the Johannine tradition, these references to the Spirit likely reflect the community's sense of guidance received as memories of Jesus's teachings find connections in the later Johannine situation. They also reflect the reception of the Spirit by followers of Jesus, promised in the upper room, where he breathed on his followers and invited them to receive the Holy Spirit (20:21–23). In that sense, the words of Jesus at the Feast of Tabernacles had been fulfilled (7:37–38): "Let anyone who is thirsty come to me, and let the one who believes in me drink. As the scripture has said, 'Out of the believer's heart shall flow rivers of living water.'"

Jesus: The Testimony of His Works and Words

The debates with Jerusalem's religious leaders regarding the Father's authorization and the Spirit's manifestation, however, hinged upon controversies regarding the authority of Jesus and his legitimation in light of his challenges to the codes and standards of the Pharisees and the priests. While the Synoptics present a single visit to Jerusalem at the end of his ministry, organizing all the intense debates with religious leaders as a climactic set of scenarios leading to the trials and crucifixion of Jesus, John's presentation is more realistic. Jesus travels to and from Jerusalem at least four times over a multiyear ministry, as any observant Jewish leader would have done. Thus, rather than seeing the temple incident as the last straw within a series of challenges, John's narrative presents that event as a prophetic demonstration at the beginning of his ministry—continuing the challenges to religious purity laws and righteousness codes that John the Baptist had issued during his provocative ministry.

In contrast to Mark's rendering, John presents the temple incident as an inaugural prophetic demonstration, challenging the cultic purity laws of the priests that had supplanted a place of worship with a marketplace. His double-meaning declaration regarding the destruction of the temple and its being rebuilt in three days added an additional offense and puzzlement. On one hand, it seems to reference the destruction of the Jerusalem temple, which would elicit knowing nods from later audiences following its destruction by the Romans in 70 CE. On the other hand, early hearers and readers would see it as a veiled reference to the resurrection of Jesus's body—the new temple, not made with human hands—wherein believers across the bounds of time, space, culture, and ethnicity would find unity in the new age of access to God by faith (John 2:13–21; Acts 7:48; 17:24; Heb 9:24). After all, those who aspire to worship in spirit and in truth are those whom the Father seeks actively to draw into worship (John 4:21–24).

Jesus likewise challenged Jewish Sabbath codes, healing the lame man and the blind man in Jerusalem on the Sabbath (John 5:1–9; 9:1–14)—actions that brought swift challenges from the Pharisees. The temple incident and Sabbath healings by Jesus in John and the Synoptics cohere enough in terms of corroborative impression to suggest that these reports likely reflect intentional deeds of Jesus which led to controversial engagement with religious authorities.[38]

The Son's Testimony to the World

In the Fourth Gospel, the Son testifies to truth in the world, and yet, his testimony is received unevenly. Some believe, and others do not. In Johannine perspective, this reception is rooted in what Bultmann describes as a dualism of decision: forcing persons to receive the revelation and thus the Revealer or to reject the Father's saving-revealing initiative with life- and death-producing outcomes (John 6:27). Again, the precipitating offenses of Jesus are related to the temple incident and his Sabbath healings, but the

---

38. Jesus heals people on the Sabbath in Galilee (Mark 1:21–33 and 3:1–6), and his disciples are accused of breaking the Sabbath by eating morsels of grain as they passed through the fields (2:23–28). This leads to challenges of his authority by religious leaders, and his contested reception in Jerusalem in John 5–10 offers a corroborative impression of this being a remembered controversy related to his ministry.

offenses escalate as Jesus claims to be operating on behalf of the Father's agency and challenges the faithless bases for religious leaders rejecting his works and words. This leads to charges of his being a sinner, committing blasphemy, and speaking presumptuously about himself.

In John's perspective, those who believe in the Son receive eternal life as children of God, born not of human schemes or initiative but born of divine initiative (1:10–13). Those who believe Moses and the Scriptures believe in Jesus because Moses wrote of him, and the Scriptures testify to his authentic agency from the Father (1:45; 5:39, 46). Those who know the Father know the Son, and those who know the Son also know the Father (14:7). Jesus is the light of the world, and those who walk in the light will not stumble in darkness (8:12; 9:5; 11:9; 12:35, 46). He is the way, the truth, and the life (14:6), and those who believe in him receive life in his name (3:15–18, 36; 5:24; 6:40, 47; 11:25–26; 20:31). His kingdom is one of truth, and all who belong to the truth attend his voice (18:36–37). They shall know the truth, and the truth shall set them free, guided by the Spirit and sanctified in the truth (8:32; 14:17; 15:26; 16:13; 17:17).

However, the gospel explains the problem of unbelief is a result of those who love the darkness rather than light (3:19–21; 12:45–46), who love the glory of humans rather than the glory of God (5:44; 7:18 12:43), who neither hear the Father's voice nor see his form, nor have his word abide in them (5:37–38). Those who do not believe find Jesus's sayings hard to accept (6:60, 66); they know where Jesus is from (geographically, 7:27) but do not know where Jesus really comes from (spiritually, 8:14; 9:28); they know neither Jesus nor the Father who sent him (7:29; 8:19, 47, 55; 15:21; 17:25); they do not embrace the truth (8:45–46; 18:38); they see Jesus as a sinner (9:24); they claim "we see" (9:41) yet are not members of his flock (10:26); and they worry that the whole world might believe in Jesus (which threatens a Roman crackdown, 11:48).

This set of binary responses to Jesus as the Revealer explains why Jesus emphasizes to Nicodemus that seeing the kingdom of God requires being born "from above" (*anōthen*, 3:3–5). Water purification will not suffice; one must also be born of the Spirit in order to glimpse and enter the kingdom of God. That which is born of the flesh remains such, but that which is born of the Spirit is spirit. That's the sort of thing that a teacher of Israel ought to know, and yet, ironically, the spiritual character of the religious quest is overlooked among religious leaders who ought to know better (3:6–11).

That being the case, it is inaccurate to see the Johannine critique of the unbelieving religious world as anti-Semitic, or even anti-Jewish. If Jesus is heralding the spirituality at the heart of historic Judaism, including the revelatory and transformative work of the Holy Spirit, these are radically prophetic Jewish concerns, not the supplanting of one religion by another.[39] That the Galilean prophetic figure—who speaks experientially about the revelatory work of the Spirit and is motivated by the loving concern at the heart of temple and synagogue worship—is not received by the Judean religious leaders is explained in conventional terms. With an allusion to Plato's Allegory of the Cave, those who abide in the dark refuse to come to the light, lest it expose their platforms and schemes which are rooted in human origin rather than the divine initiative (3:18–21).[40] Thus, the Son "testifies to what he has seen and heard, yet no one accepts his testimony" (3:32); and yet, whoever accepts "his testimony has certified, this, that God is true" (3:33). Religious and societal leaders are understandably threatened by the Revealer, because he testifies against the world, that its works are evil (7:7).

Things start to come to a head when Jesus performs healings in Jerusalem on the Sabbath in John 5 and 9. Upon his healing the lame man, the religious leaders challenge Jesus for working on the Sabbath. Jesus responds that the Father works on the Sabbath, and that he is doing the work of the Father in performing such healings (5:16–17). Since these religious leaders perform circumcisions on the Sabbath, Jesus accuses them of hypocrisy in that they judge by appearances rather than substance (7:19–24). On this score, the Father-Son relationship takes center stage. The religious leaders now interpret the reference of Jesus to God as his Father as making himself "equal to God," despite his clarification that such was not his point (5:18). Jesus clarifies that he can do nothing on his own, but that he does only what he sees the Father doing (5:19).[41] This leads,

---

39. The religious anthropological work of John K. Riches regarding Jesus and authentic Judaism also applies to John's presentation of Jesus: *Jesus and the Transformation of Judaism* (Darton, Longman, & Todd, 1980). The northern prophet thus challenges the centralized religion of Judea, not Judaism proper: Paul N. Anderson, "Anti-Semitism and Religious Violence as Flawed Interpretations of the Gospel of John," in *John and Judaism: A Contested Relationship in Context*, ed. R. Alan Culpepper and Paul N. Anderson, RBS 87 (SBL Press, 2017), 265–311.

40. Anderson, *Christology of the Fourth Gospel*, 197.

41. Thus, the tension between the subordinate and egalitarian Father-Son relationship in the Fourth Gospel is not a factor of different literary sources or contradictory

then, into the main emphasis within the Father-Son relationship in John: the prophet-like-Moses agency schema, rooted in Deut 18:15–22.

> [15] The LORD your God will raise up for you a prophet like me from among your own people; you shall heed such a prophet.... [17] Then the LORD replied to me: "They are right in what they have said. [18] I will raise up for them a prophet like you from among their own people; I will put my words in the mouth of the prophet, who shall speak to them everything that I command. [19] Anyone who does not heed the words that the prophet shall speak in my name, I myself will hold accountable. [20] But any prophet who speaks in the name of other gods, or who presumes to speak in my name a word that I have not commanded the prophet to speak—that prophet shall die." [21] You may say to yourself, "How can we recognize a word that the LORD has not spoken?" [22] If a prophet speaks in the name of the LORD but the thing does not take place or prove true, it is a word that the LORD has not spoken. The prophet has spoken it presumptuously; do not be frightened by it.

What we have here is a battle over Mosaic (and thus biblical) authority between the religious leaders of Judea and an unauthorized prophet from Galilee. Instead of the temple being a mercantile industry, excluding those who could not afford the officially approved sacrificial animals (sold in Jewish coin instead of Roman currency), zeal for the Father's house requires its being an open place of worship for all. Instead of forbidding Sabbath healing work in keeping the third commandment, Jesus provokes cognitive dissonance as a means of heightening awareness of the loving purpose of the Mosaic law by performing healings on the Sabbath.[42] This leads to his authority being challenged by the Jerusalem leader, whereupon Jesus claims to be acting within the prophet-like-Moses Agency schema, even claiming that the Scriptures testify on his behalf, if they would only read them rightly (5:37–39). Therefore, rather than transgressing the law of Moses by his prophetic and healing ministries, Jesus is fulfilling the prophecy of Moses with his testifying works and his words.

Christologies; it reflects flip-sides of the same coin, the Jewish Mosaic agency-schema, rooted in Deut 18:15–22. See Anderson, *Christology of the Fourth Gospel*, 173–81, 221–24, 260–62, 266–68.

42. On the application of Leon Festinger's cognitive dissonance theory to the provocative words and works of Jesus, see Paul N. Anderson, "Jesus and Transformation," in *Psychology and the Bible: A New Way to Read the Scriptures*, ed. J. Harold Ellens and Wayne G. Rollins, PRS (Praeger, 2004), 4:305–28.

The Testifying Works of Jesus

In John 5:36, Jesus claims to have a testimony greater than John's: the works that the Father has given him to complete. These works testify that Jesus was sent from the Father. Despite the religious leaders' asking John whether he was the prophet or Elijah, they did not believe his testimony about Jesus fulfilling those roles (5:33–35; cf. 1:19–36).[43] However, when Jesus returns to the site of John's earlier ministry across the Jordan, people believe in him there because of the signs he performed (in contrast to the ministry of John, 10:40–42). Thus, when the leaders tried to arrest Jesus, no one laid a hand on him because many in the crowd connected his performance of signs with messianic activity (7:30–31; 11:47). Then again, the gospel also seems to disparage signs-faith; for example, Jesus challenges people not to seek signs instead of the person that they point to (4:46; 6:26, 30); and the evangelist assures later audiences that those who believe without seeing are especially blessed (20:29). Nonetheless, if people cannot believe in the authenticity of Jesus and his mission, they can at least embark upon the path of faith by believing in his signs as embryonic openness to glimpsing the workings of God (10:25; 14:11).

The Testifying Words of Jesus

While the Johannine Jesus expands upon a number of images and themes within his revelatory discourses, he delivers his testimonial emphases within his heated engagements with religious authorities in John 5–10. Here Jesus's central argument appeals to his calling to carry forth the work of the Father; he does not carry out his own work, but he carries out the work of the one who sent him (3:30; 5:30; 6:38, 57; 8:16, 29, 42; 9:4) and furthers the Father's teaching (7:16; 8:26, 28). This is the nourishment of Jesus (4:30)—to believe in the Son is to believe in the Father who sent him (5:24; 6:29; 12:44), and this is the Father's will (6:39–40). Likewise, to receive the Son is to receive the Father, but to dishonor the Son is to dishonor the one who sent him (5:23, 38). Judgment results from the ways people respond to the Revealer and the truth he reveals (3:19; 9:39; 12:48). While the Son judges no one, the Father has entrusted judgment to the

---

43. Anderson, "Jesus, the Eschatological Prophet."

Son (5:21–30; 8:15–16; 12:27). Thus, the evangelist outlines the Mosaic agency schema here within these debates:[44]

The Testimony of Jesus as the Mosaic Prophet

- God will raise up a prophet like Moses, whom the people of God should heed (Deut 18:15); the Scriptures and Moses testify to Jesus and his prophetic agency (John 1:45; 3:35; 5:20, 37–39, 45–46; 6:31–32)
- This prophet will say nothing of his own, but only what God instructs him to say (Deut 18:18); the Son does and says nothing except what the Father instructs (John 5:19; 7:28; 8:28, 38; 10:18, 32; 12:49–50)
- Those who do not heed the words the prophet speaks in God's name will be held accountable by God (Deut 18:19); to reject the Son is to reject the Father and to be held accountable by God (John 1:45; 5:23; 8:16)
- A prophet who speaks presumptuously should be put to death (Deut 18:20); Jesus is accused of speaking about himself and of blasphemy, thus deserving of death (John 5:18; 7:1, 19–25; 8:13, 37; 12:9), but he does not testify on his own (John 5:30–47; 8:14–18; 10:25; 15:26–27)
- The authentic prophet's word always comes true (Deut 18:21–22); predictions of Jesus come true (John 2:22; 4:53; 5:21; 11:14; 13:11; 16:16–33; 21:19), and Jesus says things ahead of time so that when they come true, the authenticity of his mission will be confirmed (John 7:39; 12:33; 13:19; 14:29; 18:32)

As the above parallels show, the testimonies of John the Baptist, the Father, the Spirit, and the works and words of Jesus are a rooted in confirming his agency from the Father, fulfilling the Mosaic prophet typology rooted in Deut 18:15–22. Even the challenges to his authorization claim that he is speaking presumptuously about himself (Deut 18:19–20) and that this is why he should be put to death. Jesus, however, asserts that he is not speaking his own will but that of the Father; he is

---

44. For a fuller treatment of twenty-four parallels between the prophet-like-Moses agency schema of Deut 18:15–22 and the Father-Son relationship in the Gospel of John, see Anderson, "Having-Sent-Me Father."

not the only witness to himself, but there are a multiplicity of witnesses who confirm the authenticity of his mission. Ironically, those who accuse Jesus of blasphemy (John 8:59; 10:33) themselves commit blasphemy at the trial of Jesus by claiming to have no king but Caesar (19:15). In both his challenges to temple and synagogue practices in the name of God's love, however, Jesus testifies to liberating truth, which is what he has ultimately come to do (8:32; 18:37).

John's Christological Thrust: That to Which the Witnesses Testify

While christological titles abound in the Gospel of John, the evangelist declares its central christological thrust in two pivotal paragraphs: John 3:31–36 and 12:44–50.[45] In these two summaries of Jesus's mission, the one who comes from above (1) testifies to what he has seen and heard as a light in the darkness; (2) testifies that God is true, speaks the words of God, and gives the Spirit without measure; (3) testifies that whoever believes him believes in the one who sent him and receives eternal life (as the Father gives life);[46] and, (4) testifies that whoever rejects the Son or his word incurs God's wrath and judgment by that word on the last day, as Jesus speaks only what the Father has instructed). The evangelist designed the testimonies within this central christological structure to convince emerging audiences that Jesus is authentically sent from the Father, represents the Father faithfully, delivers his words, and accomplishes his work.

It has been said that Gospel of John features a Revealer without a revelation, but such a quip misses the central thrust of its testimony. In challenging the world and that which is rooted in creaturely schemes and human initiative, Jesus in John invites receptivity and responsiveness to spiritual realities and the divine initiative. Revelation thus challenges religious and political hegemony, calling forth trust in a God who loves, acts, and speaks, which is what Jesus as the Christ reveals. That his word comes true attests to his divine commission, and that his words and works affirm

---

45. William R. G. Loader, "The Central Christological Structure of the Fourth Gospel," *NTS* 30 (1984): 23–35; and Anderson, *Christology of the Fourth Gospel*, 1–31. This content is affirmed in the prologue (John 1:1–18), restated in the climactic prayer of Jesus (17:1–26), and exhorted in the narrative's purpose statement (20:30–31).

46. With Marianne Meye Thompson, *The God of the Gospel of John* (Eerdmans, 2001).

the truth holds open the promise of liberation and the gift of eternal life. Indeed, that abundant life begins not only in the then and there but also in the here and now for those who believe (10:10).

10
Memory

Christopher A. Porter

Before we can consider how John uses memory within the narrative of the Fourth Gospel, we must first consider what we mean by *memory*. Memory is not a foreign concept to us. We all have some concept of remembering and what it means to remember. Most of these instinctive understandings of memory will likely rely on a framework of memory as a database or storehouse in which distinct memories are stored. In the *Theaetetus* dialogue, Plato gives the analogy of memory as a wax tablet. Memories, then, are like stamps or imprints on the wax tablet and are thus remembered and known (*Theaet.* 191d–e). Conversely, what cannot be imprinted on the wax tablet is obliterated or forgotten. The wax tablet is an exact representation of the perception accessible in memory.

Augustine extends Plato's analogy through the imagery of a storehouse, describing the mind as having "fields and roomy chambers of memory, where are the treasures of countless images" (*Conf.* 10.8.12 [*NPNF* 1:145]). The beautiful imagery of a "memory palace" or storehouse gives rise to an idea of being able to wander through the memories of one's life, accessing them at will and with ease. One might explore a room that contains childhood memories or another alcove where romantic memories are kept. Indeed, Augustine reflects that memories are "caught up, with a marvelous quickness, and laid up, as it were, in most wonderful garners" all "laid up ready to hand" (*Conf.* 10.9.16, 10.11.18 [*NPNF* 1:146, 147]). Our modern ideas of memory as a hard drive or storage device owe much to Plato and Augustine's early concepts.

However, we probably instinctively sit with unease at this type of memory representation. Many of us are all too aware of the fallibility of memory at critical times. From the trivial matter of being unable to find our keys, struggling to remember an acquaintance's name, forgetting key anniversary dates, being unable to recall information in an exam, or misremembering a past flame's number as 867-5309. Similarly, what we remember is often quite selective, and our memories can be shrouded by the fog of time. Just try remembering in detail what you ate for lunch yesterday, a week ago, a month ago, or last year. Overall, we tend to forget or minimize the less important routine information in favor of certain events. Augustine himself recognizes this, as he compares his changeable memory with the unchangeable nature of God (*Conf.* 10.25.36 [*NPNF* 1:152]).

How, too, does this more complex framework of memory work within narratives, specifically the narrative of the Fourth Gospel? Before we start diving into how John uses memory, we will first explore some frameworks for understanding memory and then apply these to questions of narrative epistemology.

Theories of Memory

If we should treat the metaphor of a memory storehouse with caution, then how should we think about memory? In the past century, philosophers and psychologists have come to a rough consensus on an approach that sees different types of memory. At the highest level, we can construct a rough distinction between *declarative* and *procedural* memory. Declarative memory is dedicated to information and events, while procedural memory focuses on skills and acts. We may think of declarative memory as understanding how a bike works, while procedural memory stores how we actually ride a bike. For our purposes in this study of the Fourth Gospel, we will focus on declarative memory, although we will return to the overlap between declarative and procedural memory later. Declarative memory may be further distinguished into memories that are semantic and those that are episodic. *Semantic memory* is the remembering of propositions and raw information, while *episodic memory* is the memory of an event or episode. Psychologist Henry Roediger suggested that these two categories of memory are the sole mechanisms of accessing the past and proposed that these could be discerned through a remember-know paradigm of human memory.[1] Episodic memories tend to be recalled and "remembered," while specific semantics are viewed as "known."

---

1. Henry L. Roediger III, "Why Retrieval Is the Key Process in Understanding

However, these categories of memories cannot be considered fixed or static, as there is significant overlap between memorial engagement. For example, when one is learning to ride a bicycle, the procedural memory of riding the bicycle is embedded within the episodic memory of actually learning to ride. Or when recalling a past colleague this remembering invokes the semantic memory of their phone number. Furthermore, memories also cannot be considered to be immutable, as if they are checked-in to the storehouse of the mind and remain there unchanging. Rather, memories appear to be—at least in part—changeable and varying over time. You may not remember the colleague's phone number correctly.

Before memory is dismissed as cognitively unreliable, useless for epistemological and narratological concerns, many studies have been conducted into the reliability of human memory. Robert McIver has helpfully collected many of these studies in his investigation *Memory, Jesus, and the Synoptic Gospels*. McIver's research concludes that, while it "may not be possible to give an a priori guarantee for the exact accuracy … of such memories," there is an overall reliability that approaches a "first-order faithfulness."[2] Overall, he agrees with psychologists of memory James Michael Lampinen and Timothy N. Odegard, who see memory as broadly "constructing a more or less accurate rendition of the gist of past events."[3]

Moreover, several studies have shown that there are a variety of methods for increasing reliability of memory access. Presenting individuals with an associated stimulus that primes—increases the speed of retrieval—certain memories serves as an effective mechanism for improving remembering of episodic and semantic memories, as one would expect.[4] These memory primes can take on a variety of different forms, from a simple associative label displayed before testing, to longer patterns of locative imagining similar to Aristotle's structure of arranging the mind (*Mem. rem.* 451b). Smells, tastes, physical locations, and even emotions can function as strong memory primes to improve recall of events and

---

Human Memory," in *Memory, Consciousness, and the Brain: The Tallinn Conference*, ed. Endel Tulving (Psychology Press, 1999), 60–66.

2. Robert K. McIver, *Memory, Jesus, and the Synoptic Gospels*, RBS 59 (Society of Biblical Literature, 2011), 80.

3. James Michael Lampinen and Timothy N. Odegard, "Memory Editing Mechanisms," *Memory* 14.6 (2006): 649.

4. David E. Huber et al., "Effects of Repetition Priming on Recognition Memory: Testing a Perceptual Fluency-Disfluency Model," *JEP: LMC* 34.6 (2008): 1321.

details. The waft of a certain spice may bring back powerful memories of childhood or a loved one. Seeing a location, or the ruins of a location, may recall a flood of memories associated with that place.

Social Memory Theory

Memory is not restricted to the personal interior of the subject's mind and cannot be considered just the purview of individuals. But rather memories are shared and communicated with others and placed in relationship to other's memories of the same events. As Tom Thatcher argues, "personal memories are 'social,' ultimately public in nature."[5] This socialization of memory was pioneered by the French sociologist Maurice Halbwachs, who coined the framework of "collective memory" as a means of investigating how personal memories are interacted with as a social phenomenon.[6] In this framework, diverse memories are collated and organized into social frameworks in order to inform the structure of the social groups which contain various members. Within this conceptualization, no memory is purely an individual's but incorporates the memories of others in the social groups that they are embedded within. As Daniel Pioske reflects: "Our parents' memories, our grandparents' memories, the memories passed down through the generations, become our memories by virtue of being raised within a particular community and reared among the past stories recalled within it."[7] These corporate memories not only assist in the recall of events, but also in the integration of those events into the identity of the individual within the group and the group with each other. Additionally, as the memorialized events are shared amongst a community, they become a communal resource for building a shared narrative world.[8] Within this shared narrative world, they may be then deployed to reinforce group cohesion, build group identity, or even as a resource for

---

5. Tom Thatcher, *Why John Wrote a Gospel: Jesus—Memory—History* (Westminster John Knox, 2006), 56.

6. Alan Kirk, "Social and Cultural Memory," in *Memory, Tradition, and Text: Uses of the Past in Early Christianity*, ed. Alan Kirk and Tom Thatcher, SemeiaSt 52 (Society of Biblical Literature, 2005), 2.

7. Daniel D. Pioske, *Memory in a Time of Prose: Studies in Epistemology, Hebrew Scribalism, and the Biblical Past* (Oxford University Press, 2018), 71.

8. Martha Augoustinos, "History as a Rhetorical Source: Using Historical Narratives to Argue and Explain," in *How to Analyse Talk in Institutional Settings: A Casebook of Methods*, ed. Alec McHoul and Mark Rapley (Continuum, 2001), 140.

deploying intragroup or intergroup arguments. Shared social narratives form a strong basis for memory within narratives.

Narrative Memory Hypothesis

Further, memory does not appear to be merely an aggregate of discrete procedures, semantics, and episodes. Rather, there are strong indications that memories are organized and collated together to create internally coherent narratives. Psychologist Jerome Bruner has argued that "we organize our experience and our memory of human happenings mainly in the form of narrative," and further cognitive studies have supported this "narrative hypothesis" of memory.[9] Narratives therefore form a type of cognitive object and assemble memorial components in order to give coherence to a discourse by the process of narrative inference.[10] In order to build a coherent narrative, this process may involve the incorporation of memorial components from other experiences or even social memory components into the new cognitive memory schema for storage and later use. Carlos León has further hypothesized that these cognitive processes are not only in effect for episodic memory structures, but also incorporate semantic and procedural memories within their scope.

In addition, as narratives are also forms of social communication, Bruner further reasoned that they can form a type of social contract to engage in the sharing of memories via narrative discourse.[11] León's research has extended this proposal to highlight cognitive models of sharing narrative memories in a publicly narrated form.[12] These public narrations involve the recall and highlighting of salient events and details of various cognitive memorial components and their construal in a structured narrative form with the appropriate social narrative meta-information to aid in communication. This publicly shared structured narrative model of a

---

9. Jerome Bruner, "The Narrative Construction of Reality," *Critical Inquiry* 18.1 (1991): 4. See also: Nicolas Szilas, "Towards Narrative-Based Knowledge Representation in Cognitive Systems," in *Sixth Workshop on Computational Models of Narrative (CMN 2015)*, ed. Mark A. Finlayson et al., OASIcs 45 (Schloss Dagstuhl, 2015), 133; and Roger C. Schank and Robert P. Abelson, *Scripts, Plans, Goals, and Understanding: An Inquiry Into Human Knowledge Structures* (Psychology Press, 1997).

10. Carlos León, "An Architecture of Narrative Memory," *BICA* 16 (2016): 22.

11. Bruner, "Narrative Construction of Reality," 5.

12. León, "Architecture," 28.

personal or social memory is then consumed by the recipient and a corresponding process of internal cognitive construction takes place to build an internally coherent narrative for the audience.

Integrating Memory and Narrative

This process of memory transmission bears striking similarity to the pattern of semiotic narrativity outlined by Umberto Eco in *The Role of the Reader*.[13] Eco describes a distinction between the consumption of discourse and the consumption of narrative. In this perspective, Eco's "Model Reader" fills in the blanks of a discourse with a series of inferences that are drawn from the broader narrative and the social conventions of the text. In short, the narrative communicates memories to the reader, who then proceeds to assemble these into new memories of their own, by incorporating them with their own existing memory structures in a process of cognitive construction. From an epistemological perspective, narratives are not merely stories about events, but a means of communicating memories and processing knowledge about the world. Coherent internal memory narratives are critical for the external communication of memory events to any possible audience.

How John Uses Memory

Turning to the gospel, the evangelist draws upon memory throughout the narrative composition process. In some places, he draws upon the palace of memories and embeds them into the gospel narrative, while in others he taps into the available wells of social memory to illustrate and illuminate the memory theater he creates. As a narrative, the gospel presents itself as a form of recorded memory—albeit somewhat simplistically—to be communicated to the audience; however, the mode of memorialization varies in different parts of the narrative.

Memory as Accuracy Attestations

Although we may debate if every event recorded in the gospel is a memory of some form, some parts of the narrative claim to be exactly that: remem-

---

13. Umberto Eco, *The Role of the Reader: Explorations in the Semiotics of Texts* (Indiana University Press, 1979).

bered semantics. For example, while the specificity of the 153 fish caught in in the postresurrection catch (21:11) has spawned a plethora of interpretations—from gematria and triangular numbers to tables of nations and zoological symbolism—at the very least it serves in the narrative as a mundane remembering of the exact number of fish caught.[14] Indeed as Timothy Wiarda highlights, the narrative "offers the reader no hint concerning any symbolism in the miraculous catch of fish."[15] Rather, the specificity of details in the narrative serves to draw the audience into the story and cognitively provides a form of internal authentication of remembering to the communicated memorialization. This inclusion of small ancillary details in the narrative is found not only here with the 153 fish but also with the details of the stone jars at Cana (2:6), the length of the invalid's illness (5:5), and the feeding of five thousand with five loaves and two fish.[16] Further examples come with what Douglas Estes terms "definite articles of familiarity," a process of pointing to specific items that are evidently familiar to the author, even if opaque to the audience.[17] These arise throughout the Fourth Gospel, including "the fig tree" (1:48) and "the boat" (21:3) alongside culturally familiar items such as "the temple."[18] All of these brief details serve to illuminate the narrative and concretize the details surrounding events.

Memory as Eyewitness Testimony

These ancillary details have given cause for some to propose that the primary form of gospel memorialization is that of eyewitness testimony.

---

14. Edward W. Klink III, *John*, ZECNT (Zondervan, 2016), 901. While there may well be significant further detail contained within the presentation of the 153 fish, this does not negate the cognitive effect of the specificity within the narrative. For more on the 153 fish see the extensive summary of perspectives collected in R. Alan Culpepper, "Designs for the Church in the Imagery of John 21:1–14," in *Imagery in the Gospel of John: Terms, Forms, Themes, and Theology of Johannine Figurative Language*, ed. Jörg Frey, Jan G. van der Watt, and Ruben Zimmermann, WUNT 200 (Mohr Siebeck, 2006), 383–94.

15. Timothy Wiarda, "John 21:1–23: Narrative Unity and Its Implications," *JSNT* 14.46 (1992): 60.

16. Craig R. Koester, *Symbolism in the Fourth Gospel: Meaning, Mystery, Community* (Fortress, 1995), 269.

17. Douglas Estes, *The Temporal Mechanics of the Fourth Gospel: A Theory of Hermeneutical Relativity in the Gospel of John*, BibInt 92 (Leiden: Brill, 2008), 244.

18. Estes, *Temporal Mechanics of the Fourth Gospel*, 247–48.

Richard Bauckham has been most prolific in this area, proposing that the gospels should be trusted as a form of eyewitness account and observing that the Beloved Disciple serves functionally to authenticate the narrative within the Fourth Gospel.[19] This coheres well with the narrated notations observing that the Beloved Disciple functions as a "witness"—or has "testified"—to the events of the gospel (19:35, 21:24). This witness motif is illustrated in the crucifixion scene, where the gospel records an unusual choice being made to pierce Jesus's side with a spear, rather than breaking his legs. Here it is noted that the Beloved Disciple "who saw [ἑωρακὼς] this has witnessed [μεμαρτύρηκεν], and his witness is true" (19:35), and the narrative links this testimony with the objective of belief throughout the Fourth Gospel (20:31) and the "fulfillment" (πληρωθῇ) of Exod 12:46 and Zech 12:10. However, these memorial notations are not merely an indication of the presence of a memory within the narrative, but rather serve to highlight the veracity of the narrative and serve a larger goal. One key aspect is the authentication of the narrated memory, especially in relation to the intertextual referent that is incorporated into the narrative "that scripture would be fulfilled."[20]

While the crucifixion memory is a relatively constrained application of memorialization within the narrative of the Fourth Gospel, the second explicit "testify" (μαρτυρέω) reference broadens the scope to the events of the whole gospel. This raises a question for the astute reader of the Fourth Gospel: what is the scope of memory that John 21:24 is testifying to? Is this merely the context of the Petrine reinstatement or something greater? Bauckham recognizes that the classification of witness in the gospel conveys more than merely cognitive remembrance.[21] At this broader level, Andrew Lincoln argues that the overarching motif of the Fourth Gospel is that of a cosmic trial where the gospel itself forms part of an eyewitness testimony.[22] On this view, the memories embedded within the narrative serve not just as points of knowledge, but as testimony woven throughout the story. This is the form of eyewitness testimony that is internally attributed within the narrative, with extradiegetic—outside of the narra-

---

19. Richard Bauckham, *Jesus and the Eyewitnesses: The Gospels as Eyewitness Testimony*, 2nd ed. (Eerdmans, 2017), 386.

20. Andrew T. Lincoln, "The Beloved Disciple as Eyewitness and the Fourth Gospel as Witness," *JSNT* 24.3 (2002): 13.

21. Bauckham, *Jesus and the Eyewitnesses*, 386.

22. Lincoln, "Beloved Disciple," 11.

tive—interjection from the narrator of 21:24 that "this is the disciple who testifies to these things and who wrote them down. We know that his testimony is true" serving as the culmination of the memorialization of the gospel. This form of forensic memorialization "is linked to a reference to what could be seen with one's eyes, and this sort of seeing also features in the later episode of the Beloved Disciple seeing and believing at the empty tomb (20.8)."[23] Therefore, while the category of witness may entail much more than basic memory, it does not entail any less than the narrative communication of the author's cognitive memory structures. As Lincoln observes, "testimony is ... the mode or function of this Gospel's narrative, the illocutionary act that the narrative itself makes explicit."[24]

Shared Social Memory

While these memorializations highlight aspects of memory as accurate within the gospel, it also raises a larger question as to whose memories are on display within the gospel. Certainly, some markers identify the Beloved Disciple as observing, testifying, and writing down the events on display (21:24). But simultaneously the authentication statement of 21:24 also introduces a degree of ambiguity within the narrative. Here the extradiegetic interruption identifies a secondary group who is further authenticating the written memorialization of the Beloved Disciple. While some consider this to be simply an oddity of composition, others have raised that this is likely an indicator of a community standing behind the writings of the Fourth Gospel.[25]

Indeed, there are many indications throughout the gospel that point toward specific markers as being used for memorial purposes, or as a type of memory prime, in order to prompt further recollection and engagement with the narrative. Thatcher has suggested that many narrative features of the gospel may be used as memory primes in a form of ancient "memory theater" to aid in the telling of a consistent and coherent narrative. He writes that "following this model [of a memory theater] would narrate Jesus' signs and sayings by visualizing a place and occasion, locating images of Jesus and other actors against this backdrop, and then

---

23. Lincoln, "Beloved Disciple," 14.
24. Lincoln, "Beloved Disciple," 20.
25. Craig S. Keener, *The Gospel of John: A Commentary* (Baker Academic, 2003), 2:1240.

describing the interactions that he imagined between them."²⁶ Within this context the high levels of detail within the signs narrative and the complexity of interactions in various discourses take on a new light. Memories can be incorporated within a narrative structure, and semantic features are integrated into broader episodic interactions and relayed in narrative form for audience engagement. This integration of memory and narrative engages the audience and incorporates them into the memory world of the story, effectively allowing for the memories of the gospel to become the memories of the audience. Memories are communicated to the reader and integrated into their own mental schema.

However, broader than the communal memory theater that appears in the narrative engagement of the gospel, other features seem to indicate that some aspects of the gospel rely on a degree of background knowledge that is communally understood by the author(s) and audience of the narrative. While many of the narratives do not rest on accessing these shared social memories, for a model audience many of the narratives take on further richness in their narrative exposition. Throughout the gospel, the narrative regularly provides chronological and locative features that not only structure the broader narrative but also serve as memory primes to elucidate details for the audience. Thatcher has argued—extending Fernando Segovia's work—that John orients his gospel around the narrative settings of the story, and many of these settings serve to highlight the memory context for the discourse that follows.²⁷ In just the opening few chapters, we see a series of locative markers that centers Jesus's ministry around Galilee (e.g., 1:43, 2:1, 4:43, 4:46), on the way to Galilee (4:3), or in the temple (2:12, 5:14).

Additionally, some of the descriptive memory primes and locative markers carry a stronger level of detail. The healing of the paralytic John 5 does not merely occur in Jerusalem but takes place at the time of a Jewish festival (5:1), at a pool near the Sheep Gate (5:2) that is also noted to be called Bethesda in Aramaic, and the pool is surrounded by five colonnades, where many disabled people used to lie (5:3), and the healing happens to

---

26. Tom Thatcher, "John's Memory Theatre: A Study of Composition in Performance," in *The Fourth Gospel in First-Century Media Culture*, ed. Anthony Le Donne and Tom Thatcher, LNTS 426 (T&T Clark, 2013), 87.

27. Tom Thatcher, "The Shape of John's Story: Memory-Mapping the Fourth Gospel," in *Memory and Identity in Ancient Judaism and Early Christianity: A Conversation with Barry Schwartz*, ed. Tom Thatcher, SemeiaSt 78 (SBL Press, 2014), 218.

occur on the Sabbath (5:9). The audience almost does not need any knowledge of the location, as John's memories of the setting and surrounds are provided for them. If they remember the location, then these act as further memory primes and concretely locate the action of the narrative in space and time. As Thatcher notes "the level of incidental detail evident in the first Cana miracle and the Bethesda story are entirely typical of John's presentation of all of Jesus' signs."[28] John does not merely have memories of these locations, or has discovered details about them, but wants to communicate the richness of these memories to his audience. These memory primes have a communicative quality to them.

Within the gospel, the locative markers and ancillary details assist the audience in constructing a richer narrative world by using their own memories of these locations as an integrative mechanism for the action happening within the narrative. By integrating the world of the text with the world outside of the text, the audience is driven to integrate the narrative with their own thought world. The audience is asked to place themselves within the narrative as it is occurring and by implication determine how they would react to the events of the gospel. John's memories become the audience's memories.[29]

John brings this narrative embedding to a particular poignancy as many of the key interactions and conflicts are located within the context of the Jerusalem temple. For John's audience, the salience of the temple as a key location within their social world would only serve to heighten the memory interactions for those scenes.[30] This would only be further emphasized if, as is consensus, John was writing after the cataclysmic events of 70 CE that left the temple as a layer of rubble. Far from reducing the salience of the location, the presence of the ruins of Jerusalem and the *Judaea Capta* coinage would be an ever-present reminder of the temple and its destruction.[31] Through the narrative, these physical memory

---

28. Thatcher, "John's Memory Theatre," 88.

29. Halbwachs highlights this function of shared memorialization in his investigation of shared social history and collective memory; see Maurice Halbwachs, *La mémoire collective* (Presses Universitaires de France, 1950), 66.

30. Christopher A. Porter, *Johannine Social Identity Formation after the Fall of the Jerusalem Temple: Negotiating Identity in Crisis*, BibInt 194 (Brill, 2021), 101.

31. D. Bernard Hoenig, "The Other Side of the Coin: Israel Answers Ancient Rome's Judea Capta Series with Liberata Medals," *BAR* 7.2 (1981): 44. Daniel Pioske also observes this same effect with relation to the history of Gath, despite its ruined state; see Pioske, *Memory in a Time of Prose*, 133.

primes also become associated with the narrative and subsequently serve to prime the overarching narrative of the gospel.

Cultural Memory Primes

John does not restrict the narrative to physical primes for social memory engagement, as he engages with memorialized figures such as the patriarchs throughout the narrative. Jacob appears in relationship to the well near Sychar (John 4), and Moses is repeatedly remembered throughout various encounters (1:45, 3:14, 5:45, 6:32, 7:19). But this may best be seen with the lengthy engagement in John 8 over the figure of Abraham. This encounter starts with the interlocutors confronting to Jesus about being "descendants of Abraham" (σπέρμα Ἀβραάμ; 8:33) and immediately recalls the framework of the patriarchal narrative. As Catrin Williams observes of this appellation, this is a "self-description for which the text's original audience would require no further explanation, due to its well-established role as a designation for the children of Israel, and which, in all likelihood, many of the Gospel's first hearers would, at one time, have used to describe themselves."[32] This invocation of the memory of Abraham as their ancestor par excellence serves to reinforce an ascribed identity construction along with secondary memories of the entire history of Israel that is associated with this memory structure. However, this memory structure involves a degree of selective memory reconstruction, as the interlocutors add to the memorial invocation "we have never been slaves to anyone" (οὐδενὶ δεδουλεύκαμεν πώποτε; 8:33). The selective nature of this reconstruction would be just as stark for the audience as it is within the narrative, as this confrontation comes during a festival celebrating Israel's freedom from slavery in Egypt and their subsequent wilderness period.[33] As Keener notes, "a claim that the Israelites had never been subjugated politically, however, would be absurd. Plainly, Israelites endured slavery in Egypt."[34]

Subsequently, the dissonance between the reconstructed Abrahamic memory and the cultural memory of the time is used to fuel the narrative. While Abraham's foregrounded figure gives way to a longer discussion of sin and slavery, the broader context of Israel and slavery

---

32. Catrin H. Williams, "Abraham as a Figure of Memory in John 8.31–59," in Le Donne and Thatcher, *Fourth Gospel in First-Century Media Culture*, 213.
33. Keener, *Gospel of John*, 1:747.
34. Keener, *Gospel of John*, 1:747.

assists in illuminating the discourse at hand. While slavery is at the forefront, the context of Abraham gives rise to the correlation between being "children of Abraham" and the need to imitate Abraham in order to confirm their heritage.[35] This background engagement eventually culminates in the later challenge to the memorial reconstruction of the "believing Jews" (πρὸς τοὺς πεπιστευκότας αὐτῷ Ἰουδαίους; 8:31). If they are not acting in line with the behavior of Abraham, then their claim to be in the lineage of Abraham is called into question. Actions hold precedence over lineage: "If you were Abraham's children, you would be doing what Abraham did" (8:39). Here John inverts the reconstruction of Abraham that is presented in 8:33. Rather than current circumstances changing the memory, the invoked memory informs the current circumstance. This line of reasoning comes to a crescendo with the accusation that the true lineage that Jesus's interlocutors should claim is that of the Devil (8:44). Furthermore, this new indication of lineage inherently functions within the text as a memory prime recalling a series of attributes from the shared cultural memory, including being "a murderer from the beginning" (8:44).[36] It is this new set of memorialized attributes that the narrative applies to Jesus's interlocutors and is brought to the logical conclusion of picking up stones to throw at Jesus (8:59).

Thus, John deploys the memorial landscape of social memory as the battlefield for the thrusts and ripostes that form the narrative engagement within the scene. Each movement rests upon and utilizes the shared memories at hand to build and deploy their social arguments. Without a rich shared social memory to draw upon, these narrative skirmishes would be significantly diminished and forced to rely on a different set of narrative arguments.[37]

Extradiegetic Memorializations

The final category of memory in John's Gospel is perhaps the most explicit, but only appears twice within the narrative. In John 2:22 and 12:16, the nar-

---

35. Williams, "Abraham as a Figure of Memory," 214.
36. Such as the later recorded targumic tradition of the devil being the true father of Cain. See too the parallel reasoning in 1 John 3:12; Keener, *Gospel of John*, 1:761.
37. See the discussion on categorization and particularization in Michael Billig, *Arguing and Thinking: A Rhetorical Approach to Social Psychology*, 2nd ed. (Cambridge University Press, 1996), 130–55.

rator steps into the story with an extradiegetic notation that only after the resurrection experience did the disciples "remember" (ἐμνήσθησαν; 2:22, 12:16) what had occurred and the significance of the events. Here the narrator steps into the story at two critical junctures to briefly reveal a broader understanding behind the events of the gospel, a peek into the mind of the evangelist and, indeed, the other disciples.[38] These extradiegetic interjections collapse the memorial timeline of the narrative, bringing the far horizon of the future beyond the narrative to bear upon the present action within the story.[39]

In John 2, the brief incursion causes the memory of the temple clearing to function at several levels. In the first level, the narrative remembers the events of the temple clearing: the whip braiding, the sheep, the cattle, and the moneychangers. This is the setting of the action within the narrative and forms the structure around which the story is related. At a second level, the story engages with a series of social memory engagements, centered around the ambiguous intertextuality inherent in the saying on Jesus's lips: "Stop turning my Father's house into a market!" (2:16).[40] In addition, there is a third level of memorial engagement within the world of the text, as it is the disciples who remember (μιμνῄσκομαι; 2:18) inside the narrative and link this incident to Ps 69:9 and the zeal of the Psalmist there.

If this was the extent of the memorialization, it would already present a complex web of memory primes for the audience to activate. However, the extradiegetic interjection of 2:21–22 presents a new layer of memorialization as the narrator interrupts the cognitive processing of the narrative to provide new information. Here we find an interpretive note that narrows the scope of the web of memorial connections down to the context of the "temple of his body" (2:21) and the resurrection narrative (2:22). This narrowing of scope accomplishes two simultaneous ends. First, it trims the web of connections from Jesus's saying and the explicit Ps 69:9 referent to focus the memorialization upon those that link to the body-as-temple

---

38. George L. Parsenios engages with this further in chapter 6.

39. Michael Labahn, "Scripture *Talks* Because Jesus *Talks*: The Narrative Rhetoric of Persuading and Creativity in John's Use of Scripture," in Le Donne and Thatcher, *Fourth Gospel in First-Century Media Culture*, 151.

40. Unlike Mark this saying is not a clear citation of Isaiah and Jeremiah, but rather invokes a host of themes that are linked to the shared social memory; Keener, *Gospel of John*, 1:527–28.

context. Second, it drives the narrative engagement deeper within that well of knowledge and subsequently provides an ideal categorical response. The narrator reflects that "the disciples recalled what he had said, and they believed the scripture and the words that Jesus had spoken" (2:22). This may be viewed as a form of "story" and "discourse" as described by Seymour Chatman, in his structural engagement of the same elements.[41] Chatman distinguishes between a "reading" of a story—the narrative at hand here—and the "reading out" of a discourse—the extradiegetic interjection—which drives a reader's engagement with the "deep narrative structures" of the text.[42]

This model of extradiegetic interjection is paralleled in John 12, where we find a similar pattern of engagement with various levels of memory. Again, the first level involves the memory of the entry into Jerusalem, waving palm branches and serenading Jesus's procession. The second level invokes a host of simple and composite citations and intertextual memorialization.[43] These memory engagements build a broad web of connections for the audience and drives their cognitive interaction with the narrative. Into this mix the narrator interjects once more and provides further details for the audience. After the pattern of John 2, here too the disciples do not understand the events that are presented before them, or the intertextual references. Instead, the narrator notes that only after Jesus was glorified that "they remembered that these things had been written about him and had been done to him" (12:16). Similar to the extradiegetic interjection of 2:22 this supplies a prototypical response for the audience, that they too would remember these events.

Paraclete Prompted Recall

John's form of remembering in the Fourth Gospel is not only about what John knows but also about what is supplied to John for the narrative. In John 14, we find a commitment within the text that the prototypical remembering of the Fourth Gospel is not just a function of contextual reframing after the resurrection, but through the assistance of the Paraclete. This passage begins with the observation that the words of Jesus

---

41. Seymour Chatman, *Story and Discourse: Narrative Structure in Fiction and Film* (Cornell University Press, 1980), 41–42.

42. Chatman, *Story and Discourse*, 42.

43. Keener, *Gospel of John*, 2:868–69.

(14:24) are given in person and therefore should be remembered in this context (14:25). However, the following verse introduces a new form of recall for the disciples: the Paraclete (14:26). This counsellor is given to "remind you of all that I have said to you," a continual personal mnemonic prime. Here we see a progression from personal experience and interaction to a pattern of assisted and prompted recall through the Paraclete.[44] Thatcher suggests that "for John, then, the Spirit is the archive of the community's Jesus tradition, preserving both the content of his memory and the correct interpretation of that data."[45]

John as a Memory Tradent

Throughout John's Gospel, the evangelist has sought to recall and integrate various memory sources—including the Beloved Disciple and the other disciples—along with shared social memories and even other gospel sources in building a robust and communicative narrative. In this way, John acts not just as an ancient or impassionate historian, recording the facts of history as he sees it, but as a memory tradent, passing on memories for other's consumption and engagement.

But John is not alone in this task. In the narrative, there is not only John's memory at work, nor just the memory of the disciples; rather, John ascribes at least part of the recalling function of memory to the operation of the Paraclete. In the, admittedly flawed, metaphor of memory as the library of the mind, the Paraclete functions as a particularly helpful research librarian, directing the patron to the memories and assisting in their interpretation. However, in the narrative the Paraclete does not just act as an archivist but also serves as a co-tradent with John in passing on the gospel narrative to the audience.

Memory and Narrative Identity Formation

However, there is another aspect to human memory and how John functions as a memory tradent for his audience: the power of identity formation

---

44. As Schnackenburg cogently observes: "The Paraclete, then, simply continues Jesus' revelation, not by providing new teachings, but only by taking what Jesus himself 'taught' to a deeper level." See Rudolf Schnackenburg, *The Gospel according to St. John*, trans. David Smith and G. A. Kon (Crossroad, 1990), 3:83.

45. Thatcher, *Why John Wrote a Gospel*, 32.

through memorialized narrative. As we have seen, the notion of memory as merely a storehouse has been proven a rather limiting framework. But the effect of memory as narrative extends further, in relationship with mechanisms of individual and social identity formation. This is most famously seen in the curious case of Phineas Gage (1823–1860), who survived having a four-foot tamping iron blown through his head in a construction accident. After the injury, Gage could entirely remember his past life but continually denied that identity and instead construed a new life for himself.[46] The base memories of his life were not sufficient for the constitution of identity. Paul Ricoeur philosophically mused on the question of the constitution of identity in his 1991 interaction with Derek Parfit's channeling of Locke and Hume. He supposed that "the question of identity is deliberately posed as the outcome of narration. According to my thesis, the narrative constructs the durable character of an individual, which one can call his or her narrative identity."[47] Along with Ricœur, we can see that one of the functions of memories organized as narrative is to function as the basis for personal identity formation. Indeed, this observation has been further informed by psychological research focusing on how individual autobiographical narratives are often used to construct and reinforce personal identity. This narrative identity theory is presented as an ongoing extrapolation of autobiographical narratives throughout an individual's lifespan as a continually cognitively affective process.[48] Dan McAdams, one of the pioneers of the approach, describes narrative identity as follows:

> Over developmental time, selves create stories, which in turn create selves (McLean et al., 2007). Through repeated interactions with others, stories about personal experiences are processed, edited, reinterpreted, retold, and subjected to a range of social and discursive influences, as the storyteller gradually develops a broader and more integrative narrative identity.[49]

---

46. Christopher Watkin, "If My Brain is Damaged, Do I Become a Different Person? Catherine Malabou and Neuro-Identity," in *Reconstructing Identity: A Transdisciplinary Approach*, ed. Nicholas Monk et al. (Palgrave Macmillan, 2017), 24–30.
47. Paul Ricoeur, "Narrative Identity," *PT* 35.1 (1991): 77.
48. Jefferson A. Singer, "Narrative Identity and Meaning Making Across the Adult Lifespan: An Introduction," *JPers* 72.3 (2004): 443.
49. Dan P. McAdams and Kate C. McLean, "Narrative Identity," *CDPS* 22.3 (2013): 235.

But this mechanism of identity formation is not limited to individual constructions, but rather—as Martha Augoustinos from the University of Adelaide argues—also impacts upon corporate identity.[50] Indeed, we may see this in the British identity generated through Winston Churchill's narrativization of the Dunkirk evacuation. Churchill's "We Shall Fight on the Beaches" oration to Parliament in 1940 was not only a memorable piece of oration, but also a stirring construal of national identity in a time of crisis. As Haslam, Reicher and Platow write of the speech:

> These are words we still remember. We can see their craft in reconstruing events so as to engender a sense of national achievement, to entrench Churchill's own position, and to mobilize the population for the gathering storm.[51]

This inversion of the national disaster in retreat at Dunkirk was deployed as a form of triumph and has cemented itself in the British national identity and Churchill's own identity. Through this narratively driven construction of paired personal and corporate identity, we see how the same mechanisms of narrative identity construction are often at work in corporate identity construal.

How does this help us with the place of memory in the narration of John's Gospel? Does the encoding of memories within the Johannine narrative serve a greater function than the merely communicative? I would suggest that the purpose statement of John 20:30–31 would indicate that a greater direction is at hand than merely historical recollection and communication but drives toward a mechanism for identity formation. As the narrator notes here, there are many memories—of signs—that were not recorded within the volume, but that they have recorded these specific memories within the narrative for the purpose that the reader "may believe that Jesus is the Messiah" (20:31). Here the purpose statement highlights the reason for the narrativized memorialization throughout the gospel and presents the requisite response. The memories embedded

---

50. Mark Rapley and Martha Augoustinos, "'National Identity' as a Rhetorical Resource," in *Language, Interaction and National Identity: Studies in the Social Organisation of National Identity in Talk-in-Interaction*, ed. Stephen Hester and William Housley, CPQR (Ashgate, 2002), 204.

51. S. Alexander Haslam, Stephen D. Reicher, and Michael J. Platow, *The New Psychology of Leadership: Identity, Influence and Power* (Psychology Press, 2011), 214.

within the narrative are not just the memories of the author, or of any generative community, but they invite the reader into the narrative, to take on these narrativized memories as their own. To allow the memories of the gospel to shape their own belief.

Memories in the Fourth Gospel are not only what John knows, but what he wants his audience to know. For the ideal reader of the gospel narrative the memories embedded within are to become their own memories. The restoration of sight to the once-blind-man, their own restoration of sight. The supper in the upper room, their supper. The narrator's memories are to become their memories. So that, along with the disciples, they can "remember what he had said … and believe the Scripture and the words that Jesus had spoken" (2:22). For John, memory is not just a means of historical record or a communication of ideas, but an opportunity for the audience to enter into the memorialized narrative, taking on the story and integrating themselves into it.

11
Community

Stan Harstine

The question of what John knows opens several avenues for investigation before any answer can be offered. These inquiries vary from "What do I think John knows?" and "What have I been told about John?" to include "How does John's information relate to other similar accounts?" and, finally, "Where do I think John got his information?" One's assumptions, spoken or unspoken, about these questions influence one's response to the primary question. Each of these questions can be pursued from a variety of angles, and several are indeed addressed in other chapters of this book. For the purposes of discussing what John knows in relationship to community, the final question invites focused attention.

"Where does John get his shared knowledge?" This line of inquiry introduces the issue of sources, source material, oral traditions, and the process by which the Gospel of John was ultimately composed, copied, and distributed in the first century. Every investigation into these issues includes a series of assumptions, whether conscious or subconscious. For the purpose of this discussion, I choose to categorize these assumptions as (1) traditional, (2) mystical, and (3) logical. A reader of John may hold aspects of one, two, or even all three categories in her or his mind when approaching the text as it stands today. Various stories in the Gospel of John may elevate one assumption over the others so that it becomes nearly conscious in the mind of the reader. Once a reader becomes aware of these assumptions, they form a model that shapes her or his reading. Acknowledging one's assumptions is crucial since they are the starting point for any reading of the Fourth Gospel. They represent the foundation stone for interpretation and provide fuel for disagreements between different readers. Understanding them becomes critical for understanding this question.

The series of assumptions I refer to as traditional are shared with biblical interpreters from the precritical era—from the time of the apostolic writings until the middle of the eighteenth century.[1] Current readers may hold this perspective fully or in part, depending on their own background. The traditional model shares a relatively common view of inspiration—that is, in the way they view the phrase "God-breathed." Many classical artistic renderings of a gospel writer reflect this perspective. The author sits either at a desk or on a rock with a writing utensil in hand while a symbolic reference to the Holy Spirit infuses him with the words to write.[2] One version of this Holy Spirit–inspired model views the gospel as fully divine with zero input from the gospel writer. In a case like this, the question, What did John know?, becomes irrelevant because John contributed nothing at all.

The second model, the mystical model, is an adaptation of the first model and developed around the turn of the twentieth century. One of the best known figures who proposed this model for the origin of John's Gospel is Evelyn Underhill.[3] She describes John as a "mystic seer" and the content of this writing as "the vivid first-hand knowledge, the immovable certitude of the mystic 'in union' with the Object of his adoration," which contains "not the historical, but the eternal 'Gospel,' seen in vision by a great spiritual genius who had realized in its deepest completest sense—as the Synoptics had not—the meaning of Christianity."[4] In the mystical model, the Gospel according to Saint John is not according to Saint John at all. It derives from a mystical vision, similar to what Revelation records. This second assumption also makes our answer to the question, What did John know?, largely irrelevant.

The third model, the logical model, is an outflow of the early modern period of critical thinking. During this period, questions regarding the source(s) of this material, the reason(s) for the differences seen in John's

---

1. David S. Dockery, "The History of Pre-critical Biblical Interpretation," *Faith and Mission* 10 (1992): 3–33.

2. For an example, see Lorenza Costa, *Saint John the Evangelist*, 1505, the High Altar Piece from San Pietro in Vincoli, Faenza, The National Gallery, London, https://tinyurl.com/SBLPress03119a1.

3. Evelyn Underhill, *The Mystic Way: A Psychological Study in Christian Origins* (Dent & Sons, 1913).

4. Underhill, *Mystic Way*, 219, 229. For more information on the mystical viewpoint see Jey J. Kanagaraj, *"Mysticism" in the Gospel of John: An Inquiry into the Background*, JSNTSup 158 (Sheffield Academic, 1998).

Gospel, and the role of the individual author on the final product found in our Bibles today took center stage. This model places an individual, that is, John, at the center of the investigation and asks a series of questions about the gospel from various perspectives. Initial inquiries focused on whether the author was indeed the apostle John. Later, studies investigated what could be known or proven according to contemporary standards of historical reality. During the 1960s and 1970s, several scholars began asking about the community to which John belonged. This question was not far afield, since, sociologically speaking, during the Roman era persons belonged to, and were identified with, a community. Other concerns also dominate this discussion, concerns such as uncovering the identity of the Beloved Disciple, identifying various strata developed within the community, even perhaps proposing early written versions of this information. It was during the 1980s and following that scholars of the Fourth Gospel, failing to identify a singular answer to these various questions due primarily to the varied assumptions each scholar brought to his or her investigation, turned to literary models of scholarship. This model sought to limit its investigation to universally accessible evidence, the text of the gospel, which required no speculative decisions or individually concocted scenarios. These efforts placed greater emphasis on the human component in the creation of the text. What John knows becomes a logical part of the investigation for which there is evidence through which one can now sift.

As one can see, the assumptions brought to any discussion are as important to the outcome as the discussion itself. What follows emphasizes the logical approach to the Gospel of John in order to suggest a few areas where something might be said specifically about what John knows as a result of community. Community does not necessarily indicate an official school of philosophy and will not be defined based on a proposed ethnic basis, nor on a geographical location.[5] In this instance, community refers to those individuals with whom the author has spoken or interacted

---

5. For the proposal of an official school of philosophy, see R. Alan Culpepper, *The Johannine School: An Evaluation of the Johannine-School Hypothesis Based on an Investigation of the Nature of Ancient Schools*, SBLDS 26 (Scholars Press, 1975), and Troels Engberg-Pedersen, *John and Philosophy: A New Reading of the Fourth Gospel* (Oxford University Press, 2017). For a detailed discussion of the probable makeup of the community, see Craig S. Keener, *The Gospel of John: A Commentary* (Hendrickson, 2003), 1:140–232. Ephesus, for example, has been proposed as a geographic location. See Keener, *Gospel of John*, 1:142–49.

with directly. The following two parts of this chapter describe areas within the gospel where John has gleaned information in some way other than personal knowledge or experience. Two specific areas of knowledge will be considered: inherited traditions and inherited teachings. The first section will examine traditions with regard to John the Baptist, Moses, and the Messiah. The second section will examine specific ideas within John which demonstrate a shared teaching component with other early Christian communities.

Traditions Inherited by John

Whenever we are reading through the gospel accounts, somewhere in the back of our mind lies an image of the author.[6] Occasionally this image is visual, as in a classical painting of one or more of the evangelists.[7] At other times, this image is rather vague or simplistic. The image for the author that guides this discussion is called the implied author, the author we visualize from the text itself. This writer is unnamed, is described as the one whom Jesus loved, is sometimes titled the Beloved Disciple, and appears as one of the first two followers of Jesus (1:37–39). We refer to this person as John because Christians nearly two thousand years before us assigned that name to the writer of this particular gospel account.

Why is the implied author's identity important in discussing what John knows? Quite simply, the identity assigned places parameters on the discussion. The Beloved Disciple is not officially introduced into the narrative timeline until John 13:23. If we identify the implied author as the Beloved Disciple, then the accounts found in John 1–12 are not necessarily experienced by the Beloved Disciple and have somehow been passed down to him or her. When I identify this implied author as one of the first two followers of Jesus, Andrew being the other, then this disciple serves as a witness to most of the activities in John 1–12 as well. Other authors may identify the author or implied author in various ways, yet the image of the implied author we form when hearing or reading the text affects the decisions we make concerning the Fourth Gospel.[8]

---

6. Wayne C. Booth, *The Rhetoric of Fiction*, 2nd ed. (University of Chicago Press, 1983), 71.

7. See Lorenza Costa, *Saint John the Evangelist*, mentioned above.

8. James L. Resseguie, "Point of View," in *How John Works: Storytelling in the Fourth Gospel*, ed. Douglas Estes and Ruth Sheridan, RBS 86 (SBL Press, 2016), 79–96.

So, then, what traditions were inherited by the author of the Fourth Gospel? What can we deduce from the story in front of us concerning what was, and was not, first-hand knowledge by the implied author? This discussion identifies three primary ideas: John the Baptist, Moses, and the Messiah. Several other traditions could be investigated to varying degrees as well if space permitted, topics such as the relationship between Jews and Samaritans, the inter-Jewish conflict between groups like the Pharisees, priests and Levites, or the various festivals. What does John know concerning these three traditions? What does John inherit from someone else?

John the Baptizer

The Gospels of Luke and John provide the most information regarding this one named John who came baptizing in the wilderness around the Jordan River. Yet just as Luke provides unique material concerning John the Baptist's birth, John provides unique material concerning John the Baptist's activities. Where does our implied author gain such information?

When we consider John the Baptist's first appearance in John 1:19–36, two individuals are with him who will later follow Jesus: Andrew and an unnamed disciple. It is entirely probable that these two have first-hand knowledge of these encounters with priests, Levites, and those sent by the Pharisees. The Baptizer's statement of his call using the words of Isaiah is included in the three other canonical gospels. But the questioning by religious leaders and the identification of Jesus by the Baptizer stand as unique information provided by the implied author.

During the second appearance of the Baptizer in John 3:25–36, neither of these two disciples is identified as present since they now follow Jesus rather than John. Where does the implied author, identified as one of these two gain this information? Following our suppositions discussed in part 1, this implied author would collect such information from the broader community. Where and when this happened is unknown and would be mere speculation. However, some observations provide helpful parameters.

See also R. Alan Culpepper, *Anatomy of the Fourth Gospel: A Study in Literary Design* (Fortress, 1983), 13–50; and Jeffrey Lloyd Staley, *The Print's First Kiss: A Rhetorical Investigation of the Implied Reader in the Fourth Gospel*, SBLDS 82 (Scholars Press, 1988), 27–37.

As a reader of the Bible living in a country and time quite distant from the original setting, minimizing the scope and scenery comes naturally. To that end, we focus on Jesus who walks through the countryside constantly in a spotlight from heaven. Anything or anyone outside the spotlight's illumination is mentally ignored because we simply cannot fill in these shaded spaces. However, since Andrew and "John" were disciples of John, they would have various connections with individuals and the families of other disciples of the Baptizer. In other words, it is entirely possible that they engaged in conversation with people outside the immediate circle of Jesus and his disciples. Thus, this information might have come to their attention quite quickly after these words were spoken:

> A person does not receive a single thing unless it is given to him out of heaven. You remind me that I said, "I am not the Messiah," as well as "I was sent ahead of *the Messiah*." The bridegroom has the bride; the groom's friend who stands alongside and listens to the groom rejoices completely because of the groom's voice. My rejoicing is fully complete. *The Messiah* must gain more attention, and I must receive less attention. (3:27–30, my translation)

The possibility also exists that a group of individuals who had followed the Baptizer lived in the area of Ephesus (Acts 19:2–7). As one location given for the composition of the Fourth Gospel, our author might have encountered this information in that area of the world. In either case, this traditional material would have been inherited from a second party rather than directly by our implied author.

Moses Traditions

A second area where John's shared knowledge was received from his community can be found in his inclusion of Moses. Unlike the Synoptic Gospels, which focus on Moses as a synonym for the torah, the Fourth Gospel portrays Moses as a character in the story.[9] Since John did not encounter Moses directly, his information regarding Moses's actions and roles was inherited from a community. Even though Moses appears on the literary scene in John 1:17 and 3:14–15, his appearances in John 5–7 will maintain our focus.

---

9. Stan Harstine, *Moses as a Character in the Fourth Gospel: A Study in Ancient Reading Techniques*, JSNTSup 229 (Sheffield Academic, 2002).

The Fourth Gospel reports a conversation between Jesus and the temple officials following a man's healing from his own long-term, physical infirmity. In this volley of words, primarily from Jesus, the Scriptures are called as one witness, and Moses is called as a second, different witness. Moses is presented as having written about Jesus—the phrase Philip uses to invite Nathanael to follow Jesus in 1:45—and also as playing the role of accuser. In between these two descriptions lies a third: Jesus is speaking to a people who have placed their hope in Moses. Here we encounter insider information our author would have understood and known to be true from his community, either before following Jesus, during his time with Jesus, or in the years between Jesus's resurrection and the writing of these words.

Moses next appears within a conflict-loaded conversation in John 6. When those whom he fed the previous day reach Jesus, the implied author once more introduces Moses into the discussion, this time to clarify the crowd's misunderstanding of the historical feeding of their ancestors. The traditions surrounding Moses's life are on center stage. What did Moses do during the exodus? What miracles did Moses perform? The Fourth Gospel appears to correct misinformation that directly associated the manna with Moses. Moses worked no signs; rather, God performed the miracle in order to provide for the people.[10] The people want a(nother) sign like Moses performed to demonstrate Jesus compared to Moses. This gospel story will not go there. Instead, it addresses this misinformation by clarifying the reality of the situation. John would have been aware of both sides of this scenario because of the community(ies) that shaped his living.

Several layers of contemporary understanding of Moses are present within John 7, centered around Moses and the law. In a fashion similar to John 5, Moses is called as a witness to validate Jesus's testimony concerning himself. The commandment concerning circumcision and its association with Moses is corrected and related back to the patriarchs. The concern for Sabbath keeping and traditions surrounding the Sabbath are received traditions through many generations. The author relates them to the reader with clarity and conciseness. The conversation among the people turns to whether Jesus is the Christ and whether the leaders already know this but are not yet announcing it to them. These conversations also represent material inherited by John.

---

10. See Exod 16:4–30 for the bread from heaven comparison.

We can see in these three chapters that material related to Moses is part of the tradition John inherits. These teachings on Moses, his signs, Scripture, and the law are not unique to this one element of Judaism. Instead, the communities within Judaism continued to propagate and transfer this information from one to another and from one generation to the next.[11]

Messianic Expectations and Titles

Among the unique characteristics of the gospel, the titles assigned to Jesus by those he encounters ranks at the top. The first chapter introduces us to seven: Lamb of God (1:29), Spirit Baptizer (1:33), Son of God (1:34, 49), rabbi/teacher (1:38), Messiah/Christ (1:41), One written about in the Law and Prophets (1:45), and king of Israel (1:49). Many of these are used elsewhere by additional characters in the gospel, as with rabbi (3:2 and 26, 4:31, 6:25, 9:2, and 11:8), Son of God (10:35, 11:27, 19:7, and 20:30), and Messiah (4:28, 7:26–31, 11:27, and 20:30). The remainder of this section will focus on what John knew concerning the Messiah.

John is the only New Testament writer to include the Hebrew/Aramaic word, Messiah, as a title for Jesus. The Greek word, Christ, is far more frequently utilized, which explains the narrator's additional information on the two occasions this word is used, John 1:41 and 4:25. This term, which means "an anointed person," has taken on considerable meaning in Christian interpretations of historical writings like the biblical canon, as well as in other noncanonical writings of the period. Many Christian readers of the gospel identify with this tendency and find messianic individuals and messianic descriptions throughout the earlier biblical literature when they read it. Other readers assume that messianic expectations dominate the cultural milieu of the period. The challenge lies not in identifying what ancient texts say, but rather in sifting through what we think we know as fact, which has no basis in the historical situation.[12]

---

11. "It is quite obvious that the figure of Moses was of considerable importance throughout the entire intertestamental period, both in Palestine and Egypt, and is given frequent mention in a number of diverse sources." D. S. Russell, *The Old Testament Pseudepigrapha: Patriarchs and Prophets in Early Judaism* (SCM Press, 1987), 95. For examples see Harstine, *Moses as a Character*, 99–118.

12. See Marinus de Jonge, "Messiah," *ABD* 4:777–88. See his parallel article on "Christ," *ABD* 1:914–21 as well for further clarification.

What does John know concerning messianic expectations? The situations where the gospel utilizes this term will help clarify this response. When Andrew tells his brother Simon about Jesus, he describes him as the Messiah. What does Andrew know about Jesus from this Gospel's perspective? Quite simply, at a minimum he knows what the Gospel of John records John the Baptist stating. The Baptizer tells the Jewish authorities that this individual is far superior to himself (1:27). Furthermore, he announces to those within hearing, which would include Andrew, that this individual takes away sin, existed prior to the Baptizer, has the Spirit abiding upon him, will baptize with the Spirit, and is the Son of God (1:29–34). The next time John identifies Jesus, Andrew leaves John and addresses Jesus as rabbi, a term that likely carried the connotation of "most knowledgeable teacher." Yet Andrew tells Simon that Jesus is the Messiah, not merely a rabbi. When Simon comes to meet Jesus, Jesus uses his authority to rename Simon, giving him the Aramaic name, Cephas (1:37–42). We are more familiar with the Greek form of his name, Peter. So, in the account of Andrew and Simon, John includes Aramaic names twice.

In the second account, a woman of Samaria speaks about the Messiah who is coming.[13] Her encounter with Jesus transitions through several titles: disrespected Jewish guy, respectful sir, and prophet (4:7–24). Her final words are a statement that the Messiah will come and "announce everything to us." She heads for her city when Jesus's disciples arrive at the well. She tells her own people about Jesus and asks whether he might be the Christ (since the Messiah/Christ relationship was already discussed, 4:29). After listening to Jesus for several days, the townsfolk assign another title to Jesus, Savior of the World. Not only is John aware of certain Jewish expectations as described by the Baptizer, but the religious expectations of the Samaritans are also known to him. More information is associated with this coming Messiah than merely an anointing. This Messiah will be greater than John the Baptist, will possess the Spirit of God, and will be able to announce everything to those he encounters. These characteristics are described elsewhere in the Fourth Gospel without utilizing the term Messiah.[14]

---

13. Although much has been written about the Samaritan expectation of a coming figure, this is not our main journey. See most recently, Matthew V. Novenson, "Jesus the Messiah: Conservatism and Radicalism in Johannine Christology," in *Portraits of Jesus in the Gospel of John*, ed. Craig R. Koester, LNTS 589 (T&T Clark, 2019), 109–23.

14. See, for instance, John 7:37–39 on the Spirit and John 18:4 and 19:28 on knowing all things.

John presents us with a tremendous quantity of information not available within the other three canonical gospels. Some of this knowledge is gleaned, if my assumption concerning the author is correct, from firsthand experience with Jesus and his discussions. However, the information concerning the Samaritan woman's discussion with Jesus had to be gleaned in the several days Jesus spent in that town or in future interactions with these Samaritan followers of Jesus the Messiah. Further information into Samaritan expectations of a coming Messiah would also need to come from those he associated with—his community. These traditions are one element of what John knows. We turn now to the teachings John inherited from his community.

Teachings Inherited by John

When one asks the question, What does John know?, the normal response leans in the direction of basic information, specifically, what original words of Jesus does John report. While this path has been followed by others,[15] another roadway will be taken here. By using the word *inherit*, I make no claims as to the authorship of the Fourth Gospel. Rather, I am introducing what one would call a *shared inheritance*. When one enters that stage of life where one's parents' generation has passed away, then the activities of that generation consist of memories by those surviving. When cousins gather at reunions or on vacations, stories surface about what one uncle did or about an event several cousins experienced. These stories create a shared inheritance where no single individual holds all the information—or can remember all the information. The community shares the stories of others, with the eldest ones often having the most to share.[16]

These teachings inherited by John can include not only those the author remembers, but also teachings others recall for the author. This body of material can include information the author does not have an eyewitness—or earwitness—account of but rather has gleaned from others along life's pathway. Three teachings rise to the surface from the Fourth Gospel: the Spirit and birth, testimony language, and Pauline expressions. These seem to be gleaned from or perhaps reflected by the community John engages with during his own life experience. As with the traditions

---

15. See especially the work by the Jesus Seminar.
16. See Barbara A. Misztal, *Theories of Social Remembering* (Open University Press, 2003), 83–91.

previously discussed, other teachings could be examined including those on light, life, the signs emphasis, Father-Son descriptions, and even the "I am" sayings.

The Spirit and Birth

Alan Culpepper proposes that the phrase "he gave them the right to become children of God" in John 1:12 is the "prologue's climactic affirmation."[17] Not only is the idea of birth, especially by the Spirit, central to the prologue it also rests as central to the Fourth Gospel.[18] Birth by the Spirit is accentuated in Jesus's discussion with Nicodemus in John 3. However, John 20 provides the key element when Jesus commands his disciples to "receive the Holy Spirit." This moment represents the actual birth in John's Gospel and not merely a Johannine Pentecost scene.[19] Since John 3 and John 20:22 form an *inclusio*, what teachings regarding birth and spirit does John share with his community?

Teachings on the Spirit occur in John 3, 4, 7, and then in John 14 and 16. The Beloved Disciple is reportedly present at the last two instances and the unnamed disciple would likely be present at the John 3 and 7 instances as well. Only in John 4 does Jesus have anything to say concerning the Spirit apart from his disciples. Within Jesus's discussion with the woman from Samaria, her statement turns the dialogue toward the topic of worship. After identifying Jesus as a prophet, she declares the status quo, worship by some at Jerusalem and by her own people at Samaria. Jesus builds upon her assumption and clarifies its error on both parts:

> But the hour is coming, in fact it is already here, when the true worshippers will worship the Father in both spirit and truth; for the Father is seeking this kind of people to worship him. God is spirit, the people who worship him must worship him in both spirit and truth. (4:23–24)

---

17. R. Alan Culpepper, "The Pivot of John's Prologue," *NTS* 27 (1980): 31.

18. Stan Harstine, "The Children of God and the Son of God in the Johannine Gospel and Epistles," in *Anatomies of the Gospels and Beyond: Essays in Honor of R. Alan Culpepper*, ed. Mikeal C. Parsons, Elizabeth Struthers Malbon, and Paul N. Anderson, BibInt 164 (Brill, 2018), 369–85.

19. Urban C. von Wahlde, *Commentary on the Gospel of John*, vol. 2 of *The Gospel and Letters of John* (Eerdmans, 2010), 858–62. For a broader perspective, see Cornelis Bennema, "The Giving of the Spirit in John's Gospel: A New Proposal?" *EvQ* 74.3 (2002): 195–213.

No longer will worship occur at limited geographical locations; it is now defined by its essence. Not only must God be known—which Jesus notes occurs through the Jews—but must be approached by the Spirit. This teaching, spoken to the woman and likely repeated by her, serves as one element preserved through the community.

Testimony Language

The language of testimony, sometimes spoken of as witness, is a prominent theme throughout the Fourth Gospel. John the Baptist serves as the first witness (1:6, 15, and 19–32). Jesus then calls many witnesses to his defense in John 5. Once again, this discussion must distinguish between what John knew and what he learned from the community.

The starting point for the Gospel of John is always the section, 1:1–18, frequently identified as the prologue; John's words before the narrative begins. While it serves as an introduction, it likewise serves as an overture to the larger production. Much debate abounds on the parameters and limits as well as the origin and sources of the information contained within.[20] However, building on the paradigm provided at the beginning of this chapter concerning the author, I propose the section we call the prologue did not originate in an author's mind after sitting down to write. Instead, it grew, one could even say evolved, over time as it was stated and shared within the faith community where the author lived, breathed, and worked. Through repetition and combination, it came to be a united construct for starting the narrative of this gospel. The emphasis on testimony and witness plays a major role within its structure.

The Fourth Gospel serves as a witness for the life of the Logos incarnate. John the Baptist comes to witness (1:7), he gives testimony that he is not the Messiah, Elijah, or the Prophet (1:19–23), and he shares the testimony he was given concerning this coming individual (1:32–34). The emergence of followers of Jesus occurs through testimony as well. Andrew shares his witness with Simon, Philip with Nathanael, and then Jesus provides a witness to those gathered concerning his true identity (1:37–51). The signs, in Greek *sēmeion*, which can also be translated as a proof, form

---

20. Jan A. du Rand, "Repetitions and Variations: Experiencing the Power of the Gospel of John as Literary Symphony," *Neot* 30 (1996): 59–70. See earlier, Clayton R. Bowen, "The Fourth Gospel as Dramatic Material," *JBL* 49 (1930): 292–305. For the recent debate see P. J. Williams, "Not the Prologue of John," *JSNT* 33 (2011): 375–86.

a structure for John 1–12 and the testimony by Jesus about his origin, purpose, and authority. One would be remiss not to ask where this emphasis derives from.

Adopting the common dating range given to the Fourth Gospel, 90–95 CE, places the final composition of this gospel six decades following the resurrection of Jesus. What happened during those sixty years? Did John remain silent? Were the people who heard the Gospel of John read for the first time unaware of any of its contents? Although such questions may seem overly simplistic, they form the basis for many individuals' assumptions when reading this gospel. Of course, one would say, people talked. People told stories. People repeated the best stories. People provided a witness to what Jesus had done, what Jesus had said, and which of his activities had the greatest impact and importance. This gospel becomes, in this scenario, the written testimony concerning Jesus, the Messiah and the Son of God:

> Now, to be sure, Jesus did many different signs in the presence of his followers which have not been written in this account, but these signs have been written so that you can trust that Jesus is the Messiah, God's Son and so that those who trust in his name may experience life. (20:30–31)

This gospel states its entire purpose as providing a testimony of the testimonies given by those surrounding John.

When we examine the Fourth Gospel and its focus on testimony, the entire writing must also be viewed as a testimony of testimonies for a later group of individuals by those who had been telling the story. The last few verses of the gospel inform us that this is so:

> This one is the disciple who provides testimony concerning these events and who has written them; we know that his testimony is true. Now Jesus did many other signs as well, if they were to be written accordingly, I think that the world itself would not be able to contain the result. (21:20–21)

The testimonies of the community of individuals who observed Jesus, of those who heard these witnesses, and of those who have been talking about him ever since exceed the ability for humanity to record. Testimony is one tradition that depends on a community sharing their own perspective.

Pauline Expressions

The discussion around what John knows frequently focuses on its relationship with the three Synoptic Gospels, particularly Mark. Periodically, the focus will turn to what John and Paul share in common.[21] In this instance, the most common parallel comes with the pairing of faith-believe, one a noun and the other a verb, both from the same Greek cognate *pistis-pisteuō*. Faith, the noun, is present within the Synoptic Gospels and Paul yet absent in John. Believe, the verb, is present in all three but occurs most frequently in John.[22] Paul's emphasis on faith bears many similarities to John's emphasis on believing. Since others have addressed this broad topic, this segment will focus on more specific similarities found in John 8 and 12.[23]

In Jesus's discussion with the crowd over the idea of being free, he uses the distinction between a slave and a son to make his point clear. A key element of Paul's message of the good news incorporates the same imagery. Responding to a second, posed question concerning his message Paul utilizes slavery as the imagery for not continuing in sin, namely that a slave obeys the master (Rom 6:15–23). Later as he describes the outcome of those who experience the righteousness of God through faith, Paul introduces the imagery of a son. No longer is a person enslaved and forced to comply with the sin dominated realm of the flesh. In Jesus, specifically by the Spirit, these individuals have the status of sons (read today as both sons and daughters) in relationship to God. The benefit is the joint inheritance shared with Jesus (Rom 8:12–17).

This imagery existed across a broad spectrum of Christianity within the first century. Even the Letter to the Ephesians, received by a Christian community in or near the same location as the traditional originating region of John's Gospel, includes the encouragement to act and behave as children of God (Eph 5:1, 6–8, 15).[24] Any discussion of the relationship

---

21. See Engberg-Pedersen, *John and Philosophy*, 310–44.

22. Without adjusting for shared passages within the Synoptics, *pistis* appears 24 times in Matthew-Luke and 142 times in Romans–Philemon. On the other hand, *pisteuō* appears 34 times in Matthew-Luke, 54 times in Romans–Philemon, and 98 times in John. Accordance 12.3.1, Oaktree Software, NA[28] text.

23. For a detailed discussion on faith in the New Testament, see Dieter Lührmann, "Faith: New Testament," *ABD* 2:749–58.

24. On relating the Fourth Gospel to events in Ephesus, see R. Alan Culpepper, "Temple Violation: Reading John 2:13–22 at the Temple of Artemis in Ephesus," in *The Opening of John's Narrative (John 1:19–2:22): Historical, Literary, and Theological*

between ideas found in Paul and John quickly becomes a chicken and the egg scenario, when one observes that Paul wrote Romans nearly thirty years prior to the date assigned to John's Gospel. These commonly held ideas suggest a shared inheritance. Another indicator of a shared inheritance with other middle and late first century writings can be seen in their use of similar citations from Scripture and methods of rhetorical presentation. Within Judaism, Pharisees demonstrated a common method of discussion often referred to as *midrash* demonstrated in later rabbinic writings in the Mishnah and Talmud. This method is readily apparent in Paul's writing to the Romans as well as in some of his other letters (Rom 10:5–13). As individuals interact within their own communities and engage with outside communities, the conversations typically coalesce around similar themes, and in this case Scriptural passages.

After the voice from heaven sounds forth in John 12, Jesus disappears from the narrative and the evangelist expresses his point of view. As John explains the failure to believe by those who had seen Jesus's signs, he relies on the prophet Isaiah (12:37–43). The appeal to Isa 53 concerning this people's refusal to believe is identical with one Paul uses in Rom 10:

> But none have obeyed the proclamation. Isaiah says, "Lord, who has believed our message?" Therefore, faith is from a message and this message comes through the words of the Messiah. (Rom 10:16–17)

This shared argument on the topic of belief, or lack thereof, demonstrates a common practice among various early Christian communities.

Yet the evangelist does not stop with a single scriptural passage to demonstrate the failure of those who saw Jesus's signs. He incorporates a second, this time a rendition of Isa 6:10. This practice of using double proofs is a common practice by Paul as well. In Rom 9, Paul argues God's word has not failed. He then provides a quotation in 9:7, explains it, and then provides another quotation in 9:9. Shortly after, while discussing the promise continuing through Rebekah's children, he provides a quotation in 9:12 and another in 9:13.

Not only do we find the evangelist appealing to a common passage from Isaiah to clarify the absence of belief, the evangelist also utilizes a common technique to identify the serious nature of this claim. These

---

Readings from the Colloquium Ioanneum 2015 in Ephesus, ed. R. Alan Culpepper and Jörg Frey, WUNT 385 (Mohr Siebeck, 2017), 289–313.

actions are indicators of a shared community. Such can be true even when individuals do not personally interact. When a professor teaches at a university for a lengthy time, many groups of students will pass through her classes and never share time on campus. However, they will share common anecdotes uttered by the professor. They will also learn a common way of thinking about the topic they studied in her courses.

Conclusion

One could develop an opinion on the origin of John's Gospel that eliminates any human involvement. Such a presumption would encourage, if not espouse, a docetic view of Christ, ironic given John's influence on the doctrine of the Incarnation. However, when one views the origin of John from within human followers of Jesus as Messiah, then one acknowledges that these followers formed a community of like-minded individuals. We do not currently possess sufficient evidence to break these communities down by their region or city. However, we have abundant evidence that travel did occur to some degree between regions and cities.[25] This movement by people would facilitate the exchange of ideas.

The Fourth Gospel provides internal evidence that the evangelist shared common traditions and teachings with a broader community of Christ followers in the first century. Common traditions surrounding the figures of Moses, John the Baptist, and the coming Messiah place it within a community familiar with first-century Judean Judaism. Teachings on the Holy Spirit, a new birth, and giving witness to Jesus demonstrate similarities with other early-Christian writings. Specifically, the rhetoric and language shared with certain Pauline writings should give pause to efforts that draw sharp contrasts between these two writers. As with many other human experiences, a greater understanding of the broader shared milieu that contributes to what John knows enhances the experience for readers of the Gospel of John.

---

25. For instance, see the text of Acts on Paul's travels and the evidence of letter carriers in Paul's writings as well as the historical data on trade and travel within the Roman Empire. See also Glen L. Thompson and Mark Wilson, "The Route of Paul's Second Journey in Asia Minor: In the Steps of Robert Jewett and Beyond," *TynBul* 67 (2016): 217–46, or Pausanias, who records his travels throughout the Peloponnesian Isthmus in *Description of Greece*.

12

Identity

Andrew J. Byers

Textual material has a tendency of resisting the confines of its pages. Questions are raised for readers that cannot be addressed without recourse to the extratextual, that is, to the potential realities that lie outside the codex binding or beyond the scroll's length. In the study of John's Gospel, readers who wish to take recourse to extratextual material that is historical in nature find much empty space at the end of the tantalizing threads that beckon beyond the page. The only consolation comes in the form of scholars' hypothetical reconstructions of the setting from which the gospel emerged and for which it was a rhetorical address. Though the excesses of new criticism that promoted readings that were concerned only with the intratextual are less influential today, narrative-critical studies nonetheless tend to restrain the inquisitive impulses of John's readers not by silencing the questions but by redirecting them back to the narrative confined to the gospel text.[1]

The intratextual questions this chapter addresses are more general than those of previous chapters. Rather than focusing on one particular angle within John ("community," "imagination," "ethics," for example), this chapter asks about the persona that gives voice to Johannine ideas about each of those topics. The interest here is not so much in the actual identity of the real author(s) and possible redactor(s) behind the gospel text. Such

---

1. See the discussion on new criticism by James L. Resseguie, *Narrative Criticism and the New Testament: An Introduction* (Baker Academic, 2005), 21–30. For a recently published account of narrative criticism and John's Gospel, see Jo-Ann Brant, "The Fourth Gospel as Narrative and Drama," in *The Oxford Handbook of Johannine Studies*, ed. Judith M. Lieu and Martinus C. De Boer (Oxford University Press, 2018), 186–202.

a historically oriented venture is of imminent importance yet rests beyond the scope of the narrative-critical reading offered here.[2] The questions at hand, rather, are internal to the narrative and centered on the identity of the Fourth Gospel's implied author and his epistemology: Who is he (as a literary projection from the text)? What does he know? And how does he know it?[3]

Drawing on an image from Thomas Mann, R. Alan Culpepper refers to the narrator of the Fourth Gospel as the "whispering wizard."[4] In John, this wizard and the implied author share the same voice. Since this voice primarily whispers (a style of narration that is subtle and unobtrusive), the identity of the implied author can only be discerned through inference.[5] There are a few moments, however, when the voice is more intrusive, making the enterprise of inference an ostensibly more straightforward task and leaving us with the impression that the gospel writer is none other than that disciple "whom Jesus loved."[6] Though it may well be the case that the Beloved Disciple and the evangelist and real author are one and the same, the remit of this chapter is to offer what may be understood as "inferential exegesis" for the purpose of understanding the personage whom the evangelist projects into being *within* the narrative by the work of *producing* a narrative, that of the implied author in the figure below.[7]

---

2. For the historical identity of the Beloved Disciple, see Dean Furlong, *The Identity of John the Evangelist: Revision and Reinterpretation in Early Christian Sources* (Lexington/Fortress Academic, 2020) and Richard Bauckham, *Jesus and the Eyewitnesses: The Gospels as Eyewitness Testimony*, 2nd ed. (Eerdmans, 2017), 550–87. An excellent overview of the Beloved Disciple's literary functions and prospective historical contingencies is offered by Tom Thatcher, "The Beloved Disciple, the Fourth Evangelist, and the Authorship of the Fourth Gospel," in *The Oxford Handbook of Johannine Studies*, ed. Judith M. Lieu and Martinus C. De Boer (Oxford University Press, 2018), 83–101.

3. For the idea of the implied author, see Wayne C. Booth, *The Rhetoric of Fiction*, 2nd ed. (University of Chicago Press, 1961), 70–71; R. Alan Culpepper provides a detailed discussion on the implied author in John in *Anatomy of the Fourth Gospel: A Study in Literary Design* (Fortress, 1983), 15–49.

4. Culpepper, *Anatomy of the Fourth Gospel*, 15.

5. Culpepper, *Anatomy of the Fourth Gospel*, 16.

6. See, e.g., John 19:35 and 21:24–25; cf. 13:23.

7. On the point of view of the Beloved Disciple as narrator, see James L. Resseguie, "The Beloved Disciple: The Ideal Point of View," in *Character Studies in the Fourth Gospel: Narrative Approaches to Seventy Figures in John*, ed. Steven A. Hunt, D. Francois Tolmie, and Ruben Zimmerman, WUNT 314 (Mohr Siebeck, 2013), 537–49;

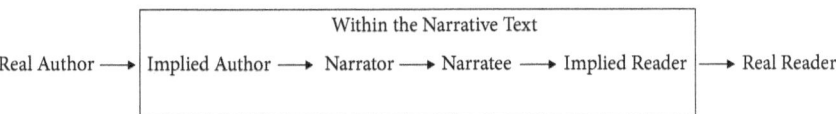

First Impressions: Meeting the Implied Author in the Prologue

First impressions are important, so in light of my own constraints of the page the focus will be on the gospel's prologue. In recognition of the foundational significance of narrative openings, John 1:1–18 is regularly mined for insights into the ensuing story.[8] But the question of what might be learned from this text about the identity of the Fourth Gospel's implied author does not tend to arise in prologue studies, probably due to longstanding assumptions that John's opening was a later appendage derived from an early Logos hymn or a polemically reconfigured paean to John the Baptist.[9] Yet whatever the prologue's possible prehistory, the Fourth Gospel does not come to us without it. Someone wrote and put the finishing touches on John 1:1–18,

---

and Resseguie, "Point of View," in *How John Works: Storytelling in the Fourth Gospel*, ed. Douglas Estes and Ruth Sheridan, RBS 86 (SBL Press, 2016), 79–96. Regularly employed by New Testament scholars, the figure below is drawn from Seymour Chatman, *Story and Discourse: Narrative Structure in Fiction and Film* (Cornell University Press, 1978), 151. Though I am content to view the Beloved Disciple as the evangelist and perhaps also John the Elder in 1–3 John, on a literary reading of John we only have access to an intratextual implied author who is "reconstructed by the reader from the narrative"; see Chatman, *Story and Discourse*, 148.

8. Bruce J. Malina and Richard L. Rohrbaugh, *Social Science Commentary on the Gospel of John* (Fortress, 1998), 5; Morna D. Hooker, "Beginnings and Endings," in *The Written Gospel*, ed. Markus Bockmuehl and Donald A. Hagner (Cambridge University Press, 2005); Warren Carter, "The Prologue and John's Gospel: Function, Symbol and the Definitive Word," *JSNT* 39 (1990): 35–58; Elizabeth Harris, *Prologue and Gospel: The Theology of the Fourth Evangelist*, JSNTSup 107 (Sheffield Academic, 1994); Adele Reinhartz, *The Word in the World: The Cosmological Tale in the Fourth Gospel*, SBLMS 45 (Scholars Press, 1992), 16–28; John F. O'Grady, "The Prologue and Chapter 17 of the Gospel of John," in *What We Have Heard From the Beginning: The Past, Present, and Future of Johannine Studies*, ed. Tom Thatcher (Baylor University Press, 2007), 215–28.

9. For an early Logos hymn, see Adolf von Harnack's influential article "Über das Verhältniß des Prologs des vierten Evangeliums zum ganzen Werk," *ZTK* 2 (1892): 189–231. For a paean to John the Baptist, see Rudolf Bultmann, "The History of Religions Background of the Prologue to the Gospel of John," in *The Interpretation of John*, ed. John Ashton, IRT 9 (SPCK, 1986), 18–35.

and its implied author makes direct contact with his audience, including himself within the first-person plural pronoun as a participant within the overarching plotlines that are about to unfold.

The Johannine prologue can therefore be understood in part as an introduction of the implied author to his readers.[10] What does he want his audience to know about himself in his initial self-introduction as the author of a text, and what does he want us to know about what he knows? David Beck has pointed out that there is only one identity with which the gospel is concerned—the "only One whose name is significant and whose identity maters" is Jesus.[11] Though I affirm that claim, it is nonetheless true that the identity of Jesus in the Fourth Gospel is mediated and that mediation occurs textually through, as we are led to believe, one whom Jesus loved. The identity of the implied author is therefore significant even if only because, like the script he writes for John the Baptist, he points to Jesus who must ever increase as others decrease.

So who is he, this implied author who points us beyond himself to the Word made flesh? Taking up threads first stitched into the prologue and following them throughout the gospel, his identity will be presented below as an exegete, a theologian, a historian, and as a member of a witness-bearing community.

The Implied Author as Exegete: In the beginning ...

The evangelist establishes himself first and foremost in the prologue as an *exegete*.[12] To begin with, the evocative "in the beginning" is to suggest scribal authority to write scripturally, perhaps even to write Scripture.[13]

---

10. Chatman, *Story and Discourse*, 147: "The narrator's presence derives from the audience's sense of some demonstrable communication. If it feels it is being told something, it presumes a teller."

11. David R. Beck, "'Whom Jesus Loved': Anonymity and Identity, Belief and Witness in the Fourth Gospel," in *Characters and Characterization in the Gospel of John*, ed. Christopher W. Skinner, LNTS 461 (Bloomsbury T&T Clark, 2013), 223.

12. *Pace* Ismo Dunderberg, who, in his insightful study, regards the Beloved Disciple as entrusted more with the *transmission* (of Jesus' understanding of the Father) than with *interpretation*. See his *The Beloved Disciple in Conflict? Revisiting the Gospels of John and Thomas* (Oxford University Press, 2006), 143–44.

13. For an argument that John envisions his gospel as Scripture, see Rekha M. Chennattu, "Scripture," in Estes and Sheridan, *How John Works*, 171–86 (esp. 185). Chris Keith also argues that "John" envisions himself as writing Scripture in *The Gospel*

Such a radical rereading (rewriting?) of the opening of Israel's sacred testimony to its God could only be offered by someone who understands himself as an enlightened interpreter of preeminent hermeneutical competence.[14] Scriptural allusions and echoes permeate the prologue: the Word "tabernacles" among us, recalling the presence of YHWH amid the wilderness camp of Israel; the (non)seeing of the divine in verse 18 recalls Moses's partial glimpsing of God from the crevice on Sinai; the language of grace and truth likely rearticulates the divine attributes of steadfast love and faithfulness paired throughout the Bible.[15] Through such allusions and echoes Scripture flows like blood throughout the entire gospel text, coloring every discourse and underpinning every sign.

Our first impression of the implied author, therefore, is that he is an exegete par excellence. His self-introduction as one with a story to tell makes clear that his knowing is grounded in an *exegetical epistemology*. Put differently, scriptural interpretation is established in the prologue as a significant epistemological mode for the implied author in his narration of all that follows. To understand the identity of "John" and to discern what he knows and how he knows it, we must attend to this exegetical epistemology. What are the core convictions underlying Johannine exegesis that inform what and how the implied author knows?

The Convictions of Johannine Exegesis (1): Jesus is the Supreme Exegete

By the prologue's end, its most foundational conviction of Johannine exegesis is clear, that Jesus is the supreme epistemological source for understanding Israel's God: "no one has seen God at any time; the only God [Jesus], the one in the bosom of the Father—that one has exegeted [ἐξηγήσατο] him" (1:18; cf. 5:37).[16] Though Moses is celebrated in this gospel, he is clearly portrayed as hermeneutically subordinate to Jesus ("no one has ever seen

---

as Manuscript: An Early History of the Jesus Tradition as Material Artifact (Oxford University Press, 2020), 138.

14. For a helpful overview of the Johannine scholarship on Scripture in the Fourth Gospel, see Alicia D. Myers, "Abiding Words: An Introduction to Perspectives on John's Use of Scripture," in *Abiding Words: The Use of Scripture in the Gospel of John*, ed. Alicia D. Myers and Bruce G. Schuchard, RBS 81 (SBL Press, 2015), 1–20.

15. See Marianne Meye Thompson, *John: A Commentary*, NTL (Westminster John Knox, 2015), 34.

16. My translation. Unless otherwise noted, all other translations are from the NRSV.

God"—1:18); the great prophet's epistemological vocation as Israel's chief revealer of the divine is relegated to the christological sidelines. Like John the Baptist, Moses is a faithful witness to Jesus (made clear in 5:39–47), but Jesus brings a more comprehensive knowledge of who God is.[17] Moses wrote Scripture, yet Jesus reports that in so doing he "wrote about me" (5:46). As a divine figure embedded within the sacred writings, it is no wonder that Jesus's words in the gospel narrative are weighted equally with the Scripture that he is uniquely equipped to interpret (see e.g., John 2:22). If the implied author is an exegete par excellence, he is so in a derivative sense, reliant on the epistemological supremacy of Jesus.

Yet their exegetical epistemological is strikingly coaligned. In John 1:18, Jesus's position in the bosom of the Father (εἰς τὸν κόλπον τοῦ πατρὸς) is established as an *epistemological location*, a vantage point for superior exegesis: no one (not even Moses) possesses such epistemological sight as the one within the Father's embrace. With this locus established in the prologue, the implied author narrates himself within such a position around the midpoint of his gospel: "one of his disciples—one whom Jesus loved—was reclining next to him" (13:23). That latter phrase in the Greek is, more literally, "in the bosom of Jesus [ἐν τῷ κόλπῳ τοῦ Ἰησοῦ]." Just as Jesus's exegetical and epistemological authority lies in his position in the bosom of his Father, so the evangelist's derivative yet nonetheless authoritative hermeneutical license lies in his parallel position in the bosom of Jesus. If Jesus is the supreme exegete of God because he is within the Father's bosom, the implied author is the supreme exegete of Jesus since he is within the bosom of the Father's one and only Son.

It is important to observe here the connection between love and this exegetical epistemology. To depict someone in the bosom of another is to depict a scene of intimacy and affection.[18] The image is paternal in John 1:18, and in 13:23 there is the first description of the implied author as "one whom Jesus loved." Superior exegesis arises from these positions of intimacy. Had the question that drives this book, What does John know?, been posed directly to "John," his initial response may well have been, "I

---

17. On John's portrayal and appropriation of Moses, see Catrin H. Williams, "Patriarchs and Prophets Remembered: Framing Israel's Past in the Gospel of John," in Myers and Schuchard, *Abiding Words*, 187–212.

18. In the Septuagint, the connotations can be maternal (Num 11:2; Ruth 4:16; 1 Kgs 3:20; 17:19; Sir 9:1; Lam 2:12), romantic/sexual (Gen 16:5; Deut 13:7; 28:54, 56; 2 Sam 12:8), paternal (Isa 49:22), or pastoral (2 Sam 12:3).

know that I am *loved*." And being loved is revelatory. This revelatory function of love is foundational for the epistemology of Jesus—"the Father loves the Son and shows him all that he himself is doing" (5:20). The same is true for the "one whom Jesus loved" in Jesus's bosom and also for all Jesus's disciples: "those who love me will be loved by my Father, and I will love them and *reveal myself* to them" (14:21b, emphasis added). There is a sense in which the implied author's position in Jesus's bosom is unique: only he could occupy this physical space at the table in the Farewell Discourse.[19] But his epistemology is to some degree shareable and inclusive since he is not the only one Jesus loves within the narrative (e.g., 11:5, 13:1) and certainly not the only one Jesus will love beyond the narrative, as sayings such as those in 14:21 and 17:26 make clear (not to mention the repeated corporate address of "beloved" in 1 John).[20] He writes from an epistemological station that parallel's Jesus own, yet implicitly invites his audience into that epistemological space (3:16; 20:30–31).

Within the narrative, however, the interpretative faculties of the "one whom Jesus loved" are not epistemologically complete. In response to the author-as-character's inquiry as to the identity of the betrayer, Jesus offered an unequivocal signal: "the one to whom I give this piece of bread." Once the bread has been unmistakably given to Judas Iscariot, it is evident from 13:28 that something is hermeneutically deficient since "no one at the table," thus surely inclusive of the implied author, understood what just happened. This exegetical incompetence, in spite of the epistemological position in the bosom of Jesus who loves him, may be explained by a second core conviction of Johannine exegesis.

The Convictions of Johannine Exegesis (2): Easter Is an Epistemological Act

An important shift in the implied author's "expositional mode" in 2:22 reveals this second conviction: Johannine exegesis hinges on Easter.[21]

---

19. Richard Bauckham, *The Testimony of the Beloved Disciple: Narrative, History, and Theology in the Gospel of John* (Baker Academic, 2007), 83.
20. Susan E. Hylen, *Imperfect Believers: Ambiguous Characters in the Gospel of John* (Westminster John Knox, 2009), 95; and Craig S. Keener, *The Gospel of John: A Commentary* (Hendrickson, 2003), 2:918.
21. Culpepper relies on Meir Sternberg's language of "exposition" to describe John's narrative mode of communicating what he knows to his audience; see Culpep-

Jesus's mysterious correlation of the temple and his body in 2:19 is only perceivable in light of a resurrection hermeneutic: "After he was raised from the dead, his disciples remembered that he had said this; and they believed the scripture and the word that Jesus has spoken" (2:22). Scripture, placed on par with the word of the Word, cannot be epistemologically opened (at least not completely) apart from the opening of Christ's tomb. By supplying the explanatory comment in 2:22, the implied author also intimates that this "hermeneutic of resurrection" is operative throughout his act of narration, even while presenting himself within the narrative as one lacking Easter's epistemological insights.[22]

The implied author therefore initiates his narratorial relationship with his audience by establishing himself as an exegete and in so doing establishes exegetical knowing as foundational for Johannine epistemology. This scriptural knowing is premised on the convictions that Jesus is the ultimate exegete who speaks scripturally (as the evangelist *writes* scripturally) and knows through being loved by his Father. The implied author shares a similar epistemological position that qualifies him as an exegete and as an interpreter of Jesus. Yet his exegetical competence within the narrative as a character is inferior to the postresurrection hermeneutic through which he tells his story. In summary: love underwrites the exegetical epistemology of Jesus and the evangelist, and Easter is an epistemological act.

The Implied Author as Theologian: ... and the Word Was God

As the above discussion already suggests, this exegete is also a *theologian*. It would be anachronistic, of course, to dress John in the clothing of today's vocational lecturers and professors of theology and religious studies, but his retrospective reading of Gen 1 in which the divine figure of the Logos was already and ever present protologically requires sustained reflection and sophisticated theological acumen, evident even in the first lines. By opening with the prepositional phrase "in the beginning," the author creates the expectation (amid Jewish readers/auditors) that the next word to follow is "God." He supplies instead "the Word," suggesting that λόγος and

---

per, *Anatomy of the Fourth Gospel*, 18–20; and Sternberg, *Expositional Modes and Temporal Ordering in Fiction* (Johns Hopkins University Press, 1978), 1.

22. The phrase *hermeneutic of resurrection* is taken from Richard B. Hays, "Reading Scripture in Light of the Resurrection," in *The Art of Reading Scripture*, ed. Ellen F. Davis and Richard B. Hays (Eerdmans, 2003), 216–38.

θεός are to be equated. Yet the following phrase suggests that two distinct divine beings are in view since "the Word was with God" (1:1b). The first line advances the idea of unity, while the second conveys plurality. The next two lines reinforce this patterned and paralleled set of convictions—unity: "the Word was God" (1:1c); plurality: "this one was in the beginning with God" (1:2a).[23] The author works within the frame of Israel's Scriptures, yet he pushes the limned theological boundaries into the peripheral shades and then shines a bright christological light into the penumbra.

With astonishing literary skill, the implied author crafts a sophisticated balance of both theological precision and imprecision throughout the prologue. The imprecision of conceptually freighted words such as "light," "life," "darkness," "world," and, of course, also "word" and "god," has the potential to draw the interests of a wide range of readers. Yet precision emerges as the semantic range for these terms narrows over the sequence of the prologue. By the end of an ingenious program of disambiguation, "God" and the "Logos-Light-Life" are presented in more specific and filial terms as the "Father" and the one and only son (ὁ μονογενής) "Jesus Christ."[24]

Who is this implied author? He does not *tell* us he is a theologian, but his work in the prologue *shows* us that a theologian he most certainly is, and one of extraordinary skill and ability (and not without the specter of controversy). Contrary to contemporary—and often unfair—caricatures of the professional theologian, however, John is not content to discourse merely in the lofty and the abstract, nor is he content to remain objectively aloof from his audience. He is quick to identify himself within the "we all" of the testifying community of God's children and he seeks to engage his audience pastorally, carefully selecting his material for a pastoral purpose: that those engaging with his text might believe and continue on in their belief (20:30–31).

Though the prologue is regarded as one of the most exemplary theological compositions of early Christianity, the implied author-theologian behind it refuses to end with the preexistent Christ in the Father's bosom. His theological propositions grow plotlines and interweave characters (among whom he finds himself) placed on Jewish and Samaritan soil,

---

23. Andrew J. Byers, *Ecclesiology and Theosis in the Gospel of John*, SNTSMS 166 (Cambridge University Press, 2017), 30–37.

24. Byers, *Ecclesiology*, 49–59. See also the discussion in Peter M. Philips, *The Prologue of the Fourth Gospel: A Sequential Reading*, LNTS 294 (Bloomsbury T&T Clark, 2006), 168–69, 197.

on Jerusalem pavements, and at a Galilean wedding. He is a *narrative* theologian, one whose story generates Christology and whose Christology generates story. This implied author has been profoundly moved by his inexhaustible subject matter, propelled into creative and painstaking reflection over the identity of Jesus as the faithful embodiment of Israel's God, and compelled to craft his highly developed thinking into literary form. Narrative epistemology is not simply a feature of John's Gospel; the gospel is itself a work arising from a narrative epistemology of a certain kind: the personal narrative of someone who has over time wrought his knowledge from a post-Easter theological interpretation of Jesus.[25] Though it may be a historically unsatisfying response to the question of the evangelist's actual identity, the ancient epitaph "John the Theologian" is nonetheless apt for the implied author.[26]

The Implied Author as Historian: … There Was a Man …

Without any trace of modernity's sense of theology's awkward incompatibility with history, the implied author is also self-consciously a *historian* providing details of events both earthly and divine within the earthly sphere: "there was a man sent from God, whose name was John" (1:6). History, theology, and Scripture are interlaced, marshalled, and subsumed into the implied author's epistemological authority. Though interpreters have understood John 1:6–8 and 1:15 as awkward intrusions of Baptist material into the otherwise magisterial poetry of John 1:1–5, 1:9–14, and 1:16–18, the final (and only extant) version of the prologue betrays no self-conscious unease in this interweaving of John the Baptist's introduction into the introductions of God and the Logos. Exegete, theologian, and historian are not separate vocations for the implied author. Each mode

---

25. I am not suggesting here that early Christology was *low* and late Christology, after cumulative theological development, was *high*. I appreciate, however the helpful clarification offered by Jörg Frey that "there was at least a *linguistic* development with an increasing willingness to attribute a divine status to Jesus, and such a willingness is most distinctively visible in John"—from *Theology and History in the Fourth Gospel: Tradition and Narration* (Baylor University Press, 2018), 18.

26. See D. Moody Smith, *The Theology of the Gospel of John*, NTT (Cambridge University Press, 1995), 1; C. K. Barrett, *The Gospel according to St John: An Introduction with Commentary and Notes on the Greek Text*, 2nd ed. (SPCK, 1978), 103; and Frey, *Theology*, 13–14 (who credits Origen with the first application of ὁ θεόλογος to John).

is dovetailed and constitutive of the broader vocation of gospel writing. Grounded in his exegetical epistemology, the implied author is a historical theologian because underpinning his theology is a God who became embedded within the spheres of time and place; he is a theological historian because history has to do with the God who creates it *with* the Word and enters it *as* the Word. It is his duty as a historian that obliges him to transcend the bounds of our own historiographical conventions. He attests to protological realities and eschatological certainties to offer a faithful account of what he knows to be true about the one who is "the Truth" (14:6).[27]

The implied author's presentation of history is dually anchored in a personal claim and in a theological conviction. The claim is that he has been an eyewitness to certain events in Jesus's earthly ministry.[28] He is uniquely equipped to chronicle the historical scenes appearing in his gospel because, at least for some of those scenes, he was on-site at the time. In each of his intradiegetic appearances, he is presented in epistemologically significant narrative positions: *at the Jordan* (probably) when Jesus's public ministry began (1:35–39); *in the bosom of Jesus* at the final supper (13:23–28); *in the courtyard* (possibly) of the high priest during Jesus's interrogation (18:15–16);[29] *at the cross* (19:25–27; 35–37); *at the tomb* (20:2–10); and *in the boat* with other disciples for the final appearance of Jesus in the gospel (21:2–8). The implied author can address his audience at the gospel's end with such epistemological confidence in the truthfulness of Jesus's historical reality because of his presence at these narrative locations (19:35; 20:30–31; 21:21–25).

---

27. Andrew Lincoln situates John's historically grounded witness-bearing within a theologically grounded lawsuit motif, drawn from Scripture and driving the narrative action; see Andrew T. Lincoln, *Truth on Trial: The Lawsuit Motif in the Fourth Gospel* (Hendrickson, 2000).

28. See Bauckham, *Jesus and the Eyewitnesses*, 384–411. Bauckham has made the case that the Beloved Disciple is the unnamed disciple of John the Baptist who, along with Andrew, first follows Jesus in the gospel. He finds this claim affirmed in Jesus's statement in John 15:27 in which he addresses those present for his Farewell Discourse, which includes the Beloved Disciple, as those who have been with him "from the beginning." See his *Jesus and the Eyewitnesses*, 390–93, 397, 402, and also *Testimony of the Beloved Disciple*, 85–86.

29. A classic treatment of this potential appearance of the author is Frans Neirynck, "The 'Other Disciple' in Jn 18:15–16," *ETL* 51.1 (1975): 113–41.

Yet as discussed above, just being present as an eyewitness is not sufficient to the Johannine task of history writing.[30] His other anchor point as a historian is the conviction that retroactive revelation is required and has indeed been granted. Extradiegetic hindsight outweighs intradiegetic insight. As an eyewitness he saw the blood and water flow from Jesus's side (19:35); as the beneficiary of a later revelatory act he understood its fulfillment of Scripture (19:36). Seeing the empty tomb, and even believing at the time in its significance, are functions of his eyewitness testimony as a character within the story (20:5, 8); understanding its meaning (20:9) is a function of retrospective divine revelation through a resurrection hermeneutic (and guided by the Spirit-Paraclete, discussed presently). For the implied author, offering a historical chronicle without inspired interpretive insights is bad—at least *deficient*—history. It is clear from the prologue that the narratorial voice arises from someone rigorously committed to presenting history, but history of a certain kind: "the author shows that he is not attempting to record 'history' without interpreting it, for to do so would mean that the reader might miss its significance."[31] Johannine history is history that can accommodate cosmic reality and the intrusion of the divine.

The Implied Author as a (Divine) Community Member: We Have Seen ...

Though we will not conclude this chapter having mined John 1:1–18 of all that it might reveal to us about the identity of the implied author and what he knows and how he knows it, it is important to end the discussion pointing out that he is an exegete, a theologian, and a historian *within a community*. The communal nature of discipleship is so important for the

---

30. As Gail O'Day put it, "the Gospel is crafted to foreground the inseparability of event and interpretation, story and theology," in "The Word Become Flesh: Story and Theology in the Gospel of John," in *Literary and Social Readings of the Fourth Gospel*, vol. 2 of *What Is John?*, ed. Fernando F. Segovia, SymS 7 (Scholars Press, 1988), 67. Arguing that eyewitness testimony is already emphasized in the prologue (through the "we" in 1:14), Richard Bauckham writes that "empirical observation and theological perception are inextricable" in Johannine thought (*Jesus and the Eyewitnesses*, 404). In fact, for Bauckham, John's "highly reflective interpretation" of his recorded gospel events makes his composition even more recognizable within the conventions of Greco-Roman historiography (*Jesus and the Eyewitnesses*, 410–11).

31. Culpepper, *Anatomy of the Fourth Gospel*, 28.

implied author that he self-identifies with the "we" of the wider social context of his audience. This use of the first-person plural forms an *inclusio* opening and closing the gospel:

> And the Word became flesh and lived among us [ἐν ἡμῖν], and we have seen [ἐθεασάμεθα] his glory... from his fullness we all [ἡμεῖς πάντες] received, grace upon grace. (1:14, 16)

> This is the disciple who is testifying to these things and has written them, and we know [οἴδαμεν] that his testimony is true. (21:24)

He may speak of himself in the third-person singular, as in 21:24a above and also in 19:35. But in the first-person, he will never speak as "I," only as "we," except in the gospel's final line: "I suppose [οἶμαι] the world itself could not contain the books that would be written" (21:25).

This gospel's curious chorus of voices in 21:24–25 (third-person singular, first-person plural, first-person singular) has invited interpreters to propose a range of complex possibilities to explain the elusive figure(s) behind the text. Perhaps the "I" in 21:25 is the narrator, previously having used a narratorial "we," as distinct from the Beloved Disciple (the "author" in that he authorizes the gospel), peeking out from behind the storytelling curtain as his composition draws to its close.[32] Perhaps the "we" in 21:24 (and possibly in 1:14, 16) signifies the Johannine school or editorial board that may or may not include the Beloved Disciple.[33] In the narrative-critical analysis offered in this book, however, there is no need to distinguish between a redactor or group of redactors, a narrator, and the real author. Within the sphere of the gospel text, the implied author presents himself

---

32. See, e.g., Andrew T. Lincoln, *The Gospel according to St John*, BNTC 4 (Continuum, 2005), 522–23.

33. The Beloved Disciple is eliminated as a participant within this plural voice if it is assumed that John 21 was a later edition. See, e.g., Raymond E. Brown, *The Gospel according to John XIII–XXI*, AB 29A (Doubleday, 1970), 1125. Another proposal is that the "we" is an authorial "we" that is, in fact, the voice of a single author who presents himself (within the conventions of ancient compositional practices) in the plural to strengthen credibility; see, e.g., D. A. Carson, *The Gospel according to John*, PNTC (Eerdmans, 1991), 684. Most helpful, in my view, is the suggestion that the "we" of 1:14 and 21:24 is that of "authoritative testimony," as argued by Richard Bauckham (in his reading, the "we all" of 1:16 has a different and wider referent that extends beyond the "we" of eyewitnesses to the Incarnate Christ) in his *Jesus and the Eyewitnesses*, 370–83.

as an "I" within a "we," writing self-consciously from within a social context. What does this indicate about his identity?

The Implied Author and the Divinized Community

For one, the implied author refuses to situate himself outside the relational import of his gospel's message (thus demonstrating no interest in attaining something akin to modernity's treasured epistemological vantage point of supposed objectivity). He is grounded, rather, within the subjective and experiential realm of a specific group culture that is generated and formed by his subject matter. Within Johannine understanding, subjective and experiential would not have been envisaged as epistemological liabilities. Interpersonal relationships and participation within a corporate identity are assets because, no matter how grand the theological vision and how high the Christology, in the Johannine literature, cosmic truth and propositional theology bear social ramifications. As briefly mentioned above, the expansive and recondite terms of the prologue's inaugural statements gradually disambiguate. Coordinated alongside this sequential progression of "God" and "Logos" toward the greater particularity and specificity is the gradual disambiguation of terms referring to humanity: "all," "humankind," "world," "his own" (neuter), and "his own" (masculine) are brought into sharpened focus with the filial language of the "children of God" (1:13). The interlinking of God, the Logos, and humanity in this literary disambiguation shows that, for the author, there is no theology or Christology apart from ecclesiology. The entry of the Logos into the domain of creation effects a division within human beings between those who receive him and those who do not. The former become a new humanity generated through faith in Jesus out of the divine realm, "out of God" (ἐκ θεοῦ).[34]

By including himself within the confession "we have seen his glory" (1:14), the implied author self-identifies with this new humanity of the children of God. As the gospel unfurls its scrolled account of Jesus, the divine origin of this new humanity is affirmed and further clarified. There can be no doubt that the community within which the author places himself is a *divine* community, regenerated out of God (ἐκ θεοῦ—1:13) and from above (ἄνωθεν—3:3, 7), entrusted with divine functions (20:22–23),

---

34. Byers, *Ecclesiology*, 49–59.

allowed to utter divine speech (9:9), and invited to participate with the heavenly glory Jesus shares with the Father (17:5, 22). As the citation of Ps 82 in John 10:34 intimates, those to whom the Logos of God came (i.e., those who received the Logos in 1:12 and become divine children in 1:13) can be rightly recognized as "gods."[35] It is to this social group that the implied author belongs. His epistemology qua author is that of a divinized mortal incorporated within a new, glorified humanity. He stands among those who have seen the incarnate Logos and have thus become transformed.

The Epistemological Practices of the Implied Author's "We"

Though the implied author appears within the gospel narrative in unique epistemological positions (see above), the epistemology he presents of the divine community certainly enriches what we can know about what he knows and how he knows it. The social vision cast throughout the narrative is that of a people, a flock, who know because they are known (10:14–15). Since he has situated himself within this group epistemology, the knowledge of the Johannine communal "we" ("we speak of what we know," 3:11) and its modes of knowing, understanding, and receiving revelation are important in discerning the implied author's identity. In an attempt to provide a concise analysis of this epistemology of Johannine community-life, we will consider briefly five epistemological practices, all of which are integrated and socially configured.

The first is that of *believing*. For John's Gospel, belief unlocks knowledge, an act often portrayed metaphorically as sight.[36] A second epistemological practice of Johannine community is *obeying the Father*. When "the Jews" at the Feast of Booths in Jerusalem marveled at Jesus's knowledge, it was largely because they had no idea to what it should be attributed: "How does this man have such learning, when he has never been taught?" (7:15). In Jesus's response to their bewilderment, he directly links epistemology with a condition of one's motives and values, that of obedient submission to God's will. The one who is willing to obey the Father and exalt his glory above any other (5:41–44; 7:18; 12:37–43) will be epistemologically

---

35. Byers, *Ecclesiology*, 186–99.
36. See John 9 where blindness/sight is correlated with what "the Jews" know with what the man born blind knows (or is beginning to know). For other passages in which believing and knowing are connected, see John 4:41–42; 6:69.

enabled to discern truth (7:17). In addition to believing and obeying is the practice of *loving one another*. The implied author who knows that he is loved by Jesus assigns epistemological power to the communal practice of loving others: "By this everyone will know that you are my disciples, if you have love for one another" (13:35). Treated already by Christopher A. Porter in chapter 10, *collective remembering* is also intimated as an extradiegetic and post-Easter epistemological communal discipline:

> After he was raised from the dead, his disciples remembered that he had said this; and they believed the scripture and the word that Jesus had spoken. (2:22; cf. 2:17)

> His disciples did not understand these things at first; but when Jesus was glorified, then they remembered that these things had been written of him and had been done to him. (12:16)

This social act of remembering is unlocked by the opening of Jesus's tomb. It is also divinely guided beyond his ascension (14:2). A fifth practice of Johannine communal life to note here is therefore the discipline of *following the guidance of the Spirit-Paraclete*. Though the Spirit is present within the narrative as a character, his primary role lies beyond the narrative.[37] That role is explicitly epistemological. In addition to prompting a collective recall of the words of Jesus during his earthly ministry, this divine agent "guides into all the truth" (16:13) and "will teach you everything" (14:26). Johannine knowing is retrospective because of Jesus's resurrection, but also ongoing because of the Spirit's presence.

The implied author's narratival investment in highlighting these epistemological practices of an envisaged community life surely indicates that they have shaped his own knowledge and modes of knowing. From the moment he writes "we have seen" and "we all" have received unbounded grace in the prologue, readers and hearers of the Fourth Gospel are alerted to the significance of the implied author's social framework and its values and disciplines. He believes, obeys the divine will, loves others, remembers within a community frame, and writes under the guidance of the Spirit-Paraclete who guides him to and teaches him the truth. In Johannine idiom, all these practices might be placed under the rubric of abiding. The implied author, therefore, is one who abides in the vine of Jesus.

---

37. Byers, *Ecclesiology*, 226–28.

Conclusion

Who is the wizard who whispers his narratorial voice then tears through the curtain of the page to speak directly to his readers? With the prologue as the hermeneutical entry point for tracking multiple strands throughout the Fourth Gospel, I have argued that the implied author is an exegete, a theologian, a historian, and a member of a divine community. He writes from within the symbolic epistemological vantage point of Jesus's embrace and knows what he knows through retrospective revelation unlocked by the empty tomb and through ongoing revelation guided by the Paraclete. He is presented as one who knows the truth, which has set him free, and also will free all those who follow his invitation to abide in his epistemological domain.

Bibliography

Adams, Sean A., and Seth M. Ehorn. "What Is a Composite Citation? An Introduction." Pages 1–16 in *Jewish, Graeco-Roman, and Early Christian Uses*. Vol. 1 of *Composite Citations in Antiquity*. Edited by Sean A. Adams and Seth M. Ehorn. LNTS 525. Bloomsbury T&T Clark, 2016.

Albl, Martin C. *"And Scripture Cannot Be Broken": The Form and Function of the Early Christian Testimonia Collections*. NovTSup 96. Brill, 1999.

Allison, Dale C., Jr. *Constructing Jesus: Memory, Imagination, and History*. Baker, 2010.

———. "The Old Testament in the New Testament." Pages 479–502 in *The New Cambridge History of the Bible: From the Beginnings to 600*. Edited by James Carleton Paget and Joachim Schaper. Cambridge University Press, 2013.

Altes, Liesbeth Korthals. *Ethos and Narrative Interpretation: The Negotiation of Values in Fiction*. University of Nebraska Press, 2014.

Anderson, Paul N. "Acts 4:19–20—An Overlooked First-Century Clue to Johannine Authorship and Luke's Dependence upon the Johannine Tradition." *The Bible and Interpretation*. September 2010. https://bibleinterp.arizona.edu/opeds/acts357920.

———. "Anti-Semitism and Religious Violence as Flawed Interpretations of the Gospel of John." Pages 265–311 in *John and Judaism: A Contested Relationship in Context*. Edited by R. Alan Culpepper and Paul N. Anderson. RBS 87. SBL Press, 2017.

———. "Bakhtin's Dialogism and the Corrective Rhetoric of the Johannine Misunderstanding Dialogue: Exposing Seven Crises in the Johannine Situation." Pages 133–59 in *Bakhtin and Genre Theory in Biblical Studies*. Edited by Roland Boer. SemeiaSt 63. Society of Biblical Literature, 2007.

———. *The Christology of the Fourth Gospel: Its Unity and Disunity in the Light of John 6*. 3rd ed. Cascade, 2010.

———. "The Cognitive Origins of John's Christological Unity and Disunity." *HBT* 17 (1995): 1–24.

———. "'Come and See!' Philip as a Connective Figure in the Fourth Gospel in Polyvalent Perspective." Pages 162–82 in *Character Studies in the Fourth Gospel: Narrative Approaches to Seventy Figures in John*. Edited by Steven A. Hunt, D. François Tolmie, and Ruben Zimmermann. WUNT 1/314. Mohr Siebeck, 2013.

———. "The Fulfilled Word in the Gospel of John: A Polyvalent Analysis." Pages 57–81 in *The Gospel of John*. Vol. 4 of *Biblical Interpretation in Early Christian Gospels*. Edited by Thomas R. Hatina. LNTS 613. T&T Clark, 2020.

———. "The Having-Sent-Me Father: Aspects of Agency, Encounter, and Irony in the Johannine Father-Son Relationship." *Semeia* 85 (1999): 33–57.

———. "Interfluential, Formative, and Dialectical: A Theory of John's Relation to the Synoptics." Pages 19–58 in *Für und Wider die Priorität des Johannesevangeliums*. Edited by Peter Leander Hofrichter. TTS 9. Olms, 2002.

———. "Jesus and Transformation." Pages 305–28 in *Psychology and the Bible: A New Way to Read the Scriptures*. Edited by J. Harold Ellens and Wayne G. Rollins. Vol 4. PRS. Westport: Praeger, 2004.

———. "Jesus, the Eschatological Prophet in the Fourth Gospel: A Case Study in Dialectical Tensions." Pages 271–99 in *Reading the Gospel of John's Christology as Jewish Messianism: Royal, Prophetic, and Divine Messiahs*. Edited by Benjamin E. Reynolds and Gabriele Boccaccini. AGJU 106. Brill, 2018.

———. "The Johannine *Logos*-Hymn: A Cross-Cultural Celebration of God's Creative-Redemptive Work." Pages 219–42 in *Creation Stories in Dialogue: The Bible, Science, and Folk Traditions; Radboud Prestige Lecture Series by R. Alan Culpepper*. Edited by R. Alan Culpepper, and Jan G. van der Watt. BibInt 139. Brill 2015.

———. "Mark and John: The Bi-Optic Gospels." Pages 175–88 in *Jesus in Johannine Tradition*. Edited by Robert T. Fortna and Tom Thatcher. Westminster John Knox, 2001.

———. "Mark, John, and Answerability: Interfluentiality and Dialectic between the Second and Fourth Gospels." *Liber Annuus* 63 (2013): 197–245.

---. *Navigating the Living Waters of the Gospel of John: On Wading with Children and Swimming with Elephants*. Pendle Hill Pamphlet 352. Pendle Hill Press, 2000.

---. "On Guessing Points and Naming Stars: The Epistemological Origins of John's Christological Tensions." Pages 311–45 in *The Gospel of John and Christian Theology*. Edited by Richard Bauckham and Carl Mosser. Eerdmans, 2007.

---. "On 'Seamless Robes' and 'Leftover Fragments': A Theory of Johannine Composition." Pages 169–218 in *The Origins of John's Gospel*. Edited by Stanley E. Porter and Hughson T. Ong. JS 2. Brill, 2015.

---. "Prologue: Critical Views of John, Jesus, and History." Pages 1–6 in *Critical Appraisals of Critical Views*. Vol. 1 of *John, Jesus, and History*. Edited by Paul N. Anderson, Felix Just, S.J., and Tom Thatcher. SymS 44. Society of Biblical Literature, 2007.

---. *The Fourth Gospel and the Quest for Jesus: Modern Foundations Reconsidered*. LNTS 321. T&T Clark, 2006.

---. "Revelation and Rhetoric in John 9:1–10:21: Two Dialogical Modes Operative within the Johannine Narrative." Pages 441–70 in *Modern and Ancient Literary Criticism of the Gospels: Continuing the Debate on Gospel Genre(s)*. Edited by Robert Matthew Calhoun, David P. Moessner, and Tobias Nicklas. WUNT 451. Mohr Siebeck, 2020.

---. *The Riddles of the Fourth Gospel: An Introduction to John*. Fortress, 2011.

---. "The *Sitz im Leben* of the Johannine Bread of Life Discourse and Its Evolving Context." Pages 1–59 in *Critical Readings of John 6*. Edited by R. Alan Culpepper. BibInt 22. Brill, 1997.

---. "'You Have the Words of Eternal Life!' Is Peter Presented as *Returning* the Keys of the Kingdom to Jesus in John 6:68?" *Neot* 41 (2008): 6–41.

Anderson, Tory S. "From Episodic Memory to Narrative in a Cognitive Architecture." Pages 2–11 in *Sixth Workshop on Computational Models of Narrative (CMN 2015)*. Edited by Mark A. Finlayson, Ben Miller, Antonio Lieto, and Remi Ronfard. OASIcs 45. Schloss Dagstuhl, 2015.

Antovic, Mihailo, and Cristóbal Pagán Cánovas. *Oral Poetics and Cognitive Science*. Linguae & Litterae 56. de Gruyter, 2016.

Aquinas, Thomas. *Commentary on the Gospel of John: Chapters 1–5*. Translated by Fabian Larcher and James A. Weisheipl. Catholic University of America Press, 2010.

Ashton, John. *Understanding the Fourth Gospel*. Oxford University Press, 1991.

Asiedu-Peprah, Martin. *Johannine Sabbath Conflicts as Juridical Controversy*. WUNT 2/132. Mohr Siebeck, 2001.

Asma, Stephen T. *The Evolution of Imagination*. University of Chicago Press, 2017.

Attridge, Harold W. "The Cubist Principle in Johannine Imagery: John and the Reading of Images in Contemporary Platonism." Pages 47–60 in *Imagery in the Gospel of John: Terms, Forms, Themes, and Theology of Johannine Figurative Language*. Edited by Jörg Frey, Jan G. van der Watt, and Ruben Zimmermann. WUNT 200. Mohr Siebeck, 2006.

———. "John and the Other Gospels." Pages 44–62 in *The Oxford Handbook of Johannine Studies*. Edited by Judith M. Lieu and Martinus C. de Boer. Oxford University Press, 2018.

Audi, Robert. *Epistemology: A Contemporary Introduction to the Theory of Knowledge*. 2nd ed. Routledge, 2003.

Augoustinos, Martha. "History as a Rhetorical Source: Using Historical Narratives to Argue and Explain." Pages 135–45 in *How to Analyse Talk in Institutional Settings: A Casebook of Methods*. Edited by Alec McHoul and Mark Rapley. Continuum, 2001.

Aune, David E. *The New Testament in Its Literary Environment*. Westminster, 1987.

Bailey, Kenneth. *Jacob and the Prodigal Son: How Jesus Retold Israel's Story*. InterVarsity Press, 2003.

Barrett, C. K. *The Gospel according to St John: An Introduction with Commentary and Notes on the Greek Text*. 2nd ed. Westminster, 1978.

———. *New Testament Essays*. SPCK, 1972.

———. "The Old Testament in the Fourth Gospel." *JTS* 48 (1947): 155–69.

Bauckham, Richard. "The Beloved Disciple as Ideal Author." *JSNT* 49 (1993): 21–44.

———. *Gospel of Glory: Major Themes in Johannine Theology*. Baker, 2015.

———. "Historiographical Characteristics of the Gospel of John." *NTS* 53 (2007): 17–36.

———. *Jesus and the Eyewitnesses: The Gospels as Eyewitness Testimony*. 2nd ed. Eerdmans, 2017.

———. "John for Readers of Mark." Pages 147–71 in *The Gospels for All Christians: Rethinking the Gospel Audiences*. Edited by Richard Bauckham. Eerdmans; T&T Clark, 1997.

———. *The Testimony of the Beloved Disciple: Narrative, History, and Theology in the Gospel of John*. Baker Academic, 2007.

Beck, David R. "'Whom Jesus Loved': Anonymity and Identity, Belief and Witness in the Fourth Gospel." Pages 221–39 in *Characters and Characterization in the Gospel of John*. Edited by Christopher W. Skinner. LNTS 461. Bloomsbury T&T Clark, 2013.

Becker, Eve-Marie. *The Birth of Christian History: Memory and Time from Mark to Luke-Acts*. AYBRL. Yale University Press, 2017.

Becker, Michael. "Spirit in Relationship–Pneumatology in the Gospel of John." Pages 331–42 in *The Holy Spirit, Inspiration, and the Cultures of Antiquity: Multidisciplinary Perspectives*. Edited by Jörg Frey and John Levison. de Gruyter, 2014.

Bekken, Per Jarle. *The Lawsuit Motif in John's Gospel from New Perspectives: Jesus Christ, Crucified Criminal and Emperor of the World*. NovTSup 158. Brill, 2015.

Bennema, Cornelis. "Christ, the Spirit and the Knowledge of God: A Study in Johannine Epistemology." Pages 107–33 in *The Bible and Epistemology: Biblical Soundings on the Knowledge of God*. Edited by Mary Healy and Robin Parry. Paternoster, 2007.

———. *Encountering Jesus: Character Studies in the Gospel of John*. 2nd ed. Fortress, 2014.

———. "The Giving of the Spirit in John's Gospel: A New Proposal?" *EvQ* 74.3 (2002): 195–213.

———. *The Power of Saving Wisdom: An Investigation of Spirit and Wisdom in Relation to the Soteriology of the Fourth Gospel*. WUNT 2/148. Mohr Siebeck, 2002.

Berlin, Adele. *Poetics and Interpretation of Biblical Narrative*. BLS. Almond, 1983.

Bernecker, Sven. *Reading Epistemology: Selected Texts with Interactive Commentary*. Blackwell, 2006.

Beutler, Johannes, S.J. *A Commentary on the Gospel of John*. Translated by Michael Tait. Eerdmans, 2017.

———. "The Use of 'Scripture' in the Gospel of John." Pages 147–62 in *Exploring the Gospel of John: In Honor of D. Moody Smith*. Edited by R. Alan Culpepper and C. Clifton Black. Westminster John Knox, 1996.

Billig, Michael. *Arguing and Thinking: A Rhetorical Approach to Social Psychology*. 2nd ed. Cambridge University Press, 1996.

Boice, James Montgomery. *Witness and Revelation in the Gospel of John*. Zondervan, 1970.

Bond, Helen K. "At the Court of the High Priest: History and Theology in John 18:13–24." Pages 313–24 in *Aspects of Historicity in the Fourth Gospel*. Vol. 2 of *John, Jesus, and History*. Edited by Paul N. Anderson, Felix Just, S.J., and Tom Thatcher. ECL 2. Society of Biblical Literature, 2009.

Booth, Wayne C. *The Rhetoric of Fiction*. 2nd ed. University of Chicago Press, 1983.

———. "Where Is the Authorial Audience in Biblical Narrative—and in Other 'Authoritative' Texts?" *Narrative* 4 (1996): 235–53.

Borgen, Peder. *Bread from Heaven: An Exegetical Study of the Concept of Manna in the Gospel of John and the Writings of Philo*. NovTSup 10. Brill, 1965.

———. "God's Agent in the Fourth Gospel." Pages 83–96 in *The Interpretation of John*. Edited by John Ashton. 2nd ed. T&T Clark, 1997.

Bowen, Clayton R. "The Fourth Gospel as Dramatic Material." *JBL* 49 (1930): 292–305.

Boyarin, Daniel. "The Gospel of the *Memra*: Jewish Binitarianism and the Prologue to John." *HTR* 94 (2001): 243–84.

———. "*Logos*, A Jewish Word: John's Prologue as Midrash." Pages 546–49 in *The Jewish Annotated New Testament*. Edited by Amy-Jill Levine and Marc Zvi Brettler. Oxford University Press, 2011.

Brant, Jo-Ann. "The Fourth Gospel as Narrative and Drama." Pages 186–202 in *The Oxford Handbook of Johannine Studies*. Edited by Judith M. Lieu and Martinus C. de Boer. Oxford University Press, 2018.

Brendsel, Daniel J. *"Isaiah Saw His Glory": The Use of Isaiah 52–53 in John 12*. BZNW 208. de Gruyter, 2014.

Brodie, Thomas L. *The Crucial Bridge: The Elisha-Elisha Narrative as an Interpretive Synthesis of Genesis-Kings and a Literary Model for the Gospels*. Liturgical, 2000.

———. *The Gospel according to John: A Literary and Theological Commentary*. Oxford University Press, 1997.

———. "Luke the Literary Interpreter: Luke-Acts as a Systematic Rewriting and Updating of the Elijah-Elisha Narrative." PhD diss., University of St. Thomas, 1981.

Brooke, George J. "Biblical Interpretation in the Qumran Scrolls and in the New Testament." Pages 60–73 in *The Dead Sea Scrolls: Fifty Years after Their Discovery*. Edited by Lawrence H. Schiffman, Emanuel Tov, and James C. VanderKam. Israel Exploration Society, 2000.

———. "Miqdash Adam, Eden, and the Qumran Community." Pages 285–301 in *Gemeinde ohne Tempel/Community without Temple: Zur Substituierung und Transformation des Jerusalemer Tempels und seines Kults im Alten Testament, antiken Judentum und frühen Christentum*. Edited by Beate Ego, Armin Lange, and Peter Pilhofer. WUNT 118. Mohr Siebeck, 1999.

———. "The Ten Temples in the Dead Sea Scrolls." Pages 417–34 in *Temple and Worship in Biblical Israel: Proceedings of the Oxford Old Testament Seminar*. Edited by John Day. LHBOTS 422. T&T Clark, 2007.

Brown, Raymond E. *The Gospel according to John I–XII*. AB 29. Doubleday, 1966.

———. *The Gospel according to John XIII–XXI*. AB 29A. Doubleday, 1970.

Brown, Tricia Gates. *Spirit in the Writings of John: Johannine Pneumatology in Social-Scientific Perspective*. JSNTSup 253. T&T Clark, 2003.

Bruner, Jerome. "The Narrative Construction of Reality." *Critical Inquiry* 18.1 (1991): 1–21.

Brunson, Andrew C. *Psalm 118 in the Gospel of John: An Intertextual Study on the New Exodus Pattern in the Theology of John*. WUNT 2/158. Mohr Siebeck, 2003.

Buch-Hansen, Gitte. *"It Is the Spirit That Gives Life": A Stoic Understanding of Pneuma in John's Gospel*. BZNW 173. de Gruyter, 2010.

Bühner, Jan-Adolph. "σκηνόω." *EDNT*, 3:252.

Bulloch, Anthony W. "The Future of a Hellenistic Illusion." Pages 209–30 in *Greek Literature in the Hellenistic Period*. Vol. 7 of *Greek Literature*. Edited by Gregory Nagy. Routledge, 2001.

Bultmann, Rudolf. *The Gospel of John: A Commentary*. Translated by G. R. Beasley-Murray et al. Westminster, 1971.

———. "The History of Religions Background of the Prologue to the Gospel of John." Pages 18–35 in *The Interpretation of John*. Edited by John Ashton. IRT 9. SPCK, 1986.

Burge, Gary M. *The Anointed Community: The Holy Spirit in the Johannine Tradition*. Eerdmans, 1987.

Burridge, Richard A. *Imitating Jesus: An Inclusive Approach to New Testament Ethics*. Eerdmans, 2007.

Bunzl, Martin. "How to Change the Unchanging Past." *Clio* 25 (1996): 181–93.

Byers, Andrew J. *Ecclesiology and Theosis in the Gospel of John*. SNTSMS 166. Cambridge University Press, 2017.

Bynum, William Randolph. "Quotations of Zechariah in the Fourth Gospel." Pages 47–74 in *Abiding Words: The Use of Scripture in the Gospel of John*. Edited by Alicia D. Myers and Bruce G. Schuchard. RBS 81. SBL Press, 2015.

Carignan, Michael I. "Fiction as History or History as Fiction? George Eliot, Hayden White, and Nineteenth-Century Historicism." *Clio* 29 (2000): 395–415.

Carson, D.A. *The Gospel according to John*. PNTC. Eerdmans, 1991.

———. "The Purpose of the Fourth Gospel: John 20:31 Reconsidered." *JBL* 106 (1987): 639–51.

Carter, Warren. "The Prologue and John's Gospel: Function, Symbol and the Definitive Word." *JSNT* 39 (1990): 30–58.

Casey, Maurice. *Is John's Gospel True?* Routledge, 1996.

Charteris-Black, Jonathan. *Politicians and Rhetoric: The Persuasive Power of Metaphor*. 2nd ed. Palgrave Macmillan, 2011.

Chatman, Seymour. *Story and Discourse: Narrative Structure in Fiction and Film*. Cornell University Press, 1980.

Chennattu, Rekha M. "Scripture." Pages 171–86 in *How John Works: Storytelling in the Fourth Gospel*. Edited by Douglas Estes and Ruth Sheridan. RBS 86. SBL Press, 2016.

Chester, Andrew. "Citing the Old Testament." Pages 141–69 in *It Is Written: Scripture Citing Scripture: Essays in Honor of Barnabas Lindars*. Edited by D. A. Carson and H. G. M. Williamson. Cambridge University Press, 1988.

Clay, Diskin. *Platonic Questions: Dialogues with the Silent Philosopher*. Pennsylvania State University Press, 2000.

Collins, John J. *The Apocalyptic Imagination: An Introduction to Jewish Apocalyptic Literature*. 2nd ed. Eerdmans, 1998.

Comer, Christopher, and Ashley Taggart. *Brain, Mind, and the Narrative Imagination*. Bloomsbury Academic, 2021.

Condit, Celeste M. "The Functions of Epideictic: The Boston Massacre Orations as Exemplar." *Communication Quarterly* 33.4 (1985): 284–98.

Connerton, Paul. *How Societies Remember*. Themes in the Social Sciences. Cambridge University Press, 1989.

Connick, C. Milo. "The Dramatic Character of the Fourth Gospel." *JBL* 67 (1948): 159–69.

Corrigan, Kevin. *A Less Familiar Plato: From Phaedo to Philebus*. CSRP. Cambridge University Press, 2023.

Coste, Didier. *Narrative as Communication*. THL 64. University of Minnesota Press, 1989.
Crawford, Sidnie W. *Rewriting Scripture in Second Temple Times*. Eerdmans, 2008.
Cribbs, F. Lamar. "The Agreements that Exist between St. Luke and St. John." Pages 215–61 in *SBL 1979 Seminar Papers*. Scholars Press, 1979.
———. "St. Luke and the Johannine Tradition." *JBL* 90 (1971): 422–50.
———. "A Study of the Contacts that Exist between St. Luke and St. John." Pages 1–93 in *SBL 1973 Seminar Papers*. Society of Biblical Literature, 1973.
Culpepper, R. Alan. *Anatomy of the Fourth Gospel: A Study in Literary Design*. Fortress, 1983.
———. "Designs for the Church in the Imagery of John 21:1–14." Pages 383–94 in *Imagery in the Gospel of John: Terms, Forms, Themes, and Theology of Johannine Figurative Language*. Edited by Jörg Frey, Jan G. van der Watt, and Ruben Zimmermann. WUNT 200. Mohr Siebeck, 2006.
———. *The Johannine School: An Evaluation of the Johannine-School Hypothesis Based on an Investigation of the Nature of Ancient Schools*. SBLDS 26. Scholars Press, 1975.
———. "The Pivot of John's Prologue." *NTS* 27 (1980): 1–31.
———. "Quotation as Commentary: The Good News of a King on a Donkey (John 12:12–15)." Pages 139–54 in *The Gospel of John*. Vol. 4 of *Biblical Interpretation in Early Christian Gospels*. Edited by Thomas R. Hatina. LNTS 613. T&T Clark, 2020.
———. "Temple Violation: Reading John 2:13–22 at the Temple of Artemis in Ephesus." Pages 289–313 in *The Opening of John's Narrative (John 1:19–2:22): Historical, Literary, and Theological Readings from the Colloquium Ioanneum 2015 in Ephesus*. Edited by R. Alan Culpepper and Jörg Frey. WUNT 385. Mohr Siebeck, 2017.
Daise, Michael A. *Quotations in John: Studies on Jewish Scripture in the Fourth Gospel*. LNTS 610. Bloomsbury T&T Clark, 2020.
Daly-Denton, Margaret. *David in the Fourth Gospel: The Johannine Interpretation of the Psalms*. AGJU 47. Brill, 2000.
———. "Going Beyond the Genially Open 'Cf.': Intertextual Reference to the Old Testament in the New." *Milltown Studies* 44 (1999): 48–60.
Danto, Arthur C. *Narration and Knowledge*. Columbia University Press, 1985.

De Brigard, Felipe. *Memory and Remembering*. CE. Cambridge University Press, 2023.

Diogenes Laertius. 1925. *Lives of Eminent Philosophers, Volume I: Books 1–5*. Translated by R. D. Hicks. LCL 184. Harvard University Press.

Dionysius of Halicarnassus. *Ancient Orators. Lysias. Isocrates. Isaeus. Demosthenes. Thucydides*. Vol. 1 of *Critical Essays*. Translated by Stephen Usher. LCL 465. Harvard University Press, 1974.

Dietzfelbinger, Christian. "Aspekte des Alten Testaments im Johannesevangelium." Pages 203–18 in *Frühes Christentum*. Vol. 3 of *Geschichte – Tradition – Reflexion: Festschrift für Martin Hengel zum 70. Geburtstag*. Edited by Hermann Lichtenberger. Mohr Siebeck, 1996.

Dockery, David S. "The History of Pre-critical Biblical Interpretation." *Faith and Mission* 10 (1992): 3–33.

Dodd, C. H. *Historical Tradition in the Fourth Gospel*. Cambridge University Press, 1963.

———. *The Interpretation of the Fourth Gospel*. Cambridge University Press, 1953.

Dorter, Kenneth. "The Significance of the Speeches in Plato's *Symposium*." *Philosophy and Rhetoric* 2 (1969): 215–34.

Dray, William H. *History as Re-enactment: R.G. Collingwood's Idea of History*. Clarendon, 1995.

Duke, Paul D. *Irony in the Fourth Gospel*. John Knox, 1985.

Dunderberg, Ismo. *The Beloved Disciple in Conflict? Revisiting the Gospels of John and Thomas*. Oxford University Press, 2006.

Eco, Umberto. *The Role of the Reader: Explorations in the Semiotics of Texts*. Indiana University Press, 1979.

Edwards, Ruth B. *Discovering John: Content, Interpretation, Reception*. 2nd ed. SPCK, 2014.

Engberg-Pedersen, Troels. *John and Philosophy: A New Reading of the Fourth Gospel*. Oxford University Press, 2017.

Engmann, Joyce. "Imagination and Truth in Aristotle." *JHP* 14 (1976): 259–65.

Estes, Douglas. "Dualism or Paradox? A New 'Light' on the Gospel of John." *JTS* 71 (2020): 90–118.

———. "Isaiah's Glory in John's Gospel: Isaiah versus Caesar for John's Text-Immanent Reader." Pages 285–302 in *The Function of the Reader in the Formation and the Reception of the Book of Isaiah*. Edited by Sehoon Jang and Archibald L. H. M. van Wieringen. SCCB 11. Brill Schöningh, 2024.

———. "Rhetorical *Peristaseis* (Circumstances) in the Prologue of John." Pages 191–207 in *The Gospel of John as Genre Mosaic*. Edited by Kasper Bro Larsen. SANt 3. Vandenhoeck & Ruprecht, 2015.

———. *The Questions of Jesus in John: Logic, Rhetoric, and Persuasive Discourse*. BibInt 115. Brill, 2012.

———. *The Temporal Mechanics of the Fourth Gospel: A Theory of Hermeneutical Relativity in the Gospel of John*. BibInt 92. Brill, 2008.

———. "Time." Pages 41–57 in *How John Works: Storytelling in the Fourth Gospel*. Edited by Douglas Estes and Ruth Sheridan. RBS 86. SBL Press, 2016.

———. "The Tree of Life in the Apocalypse of John." Pages 183–216 in *The Tree of Life*. Edited by Douglas Estes. TBN 27. Brill, 2020.

———. "Unasked Questions in the Gospel of John: Narrative, Rhetoric, and Hypothetical Discourse." Pages 229–45 in *Asking Questions in Biblical Texts*. Edited by Archibald L. H. M. van Wieringen and Bart J. Koet. CBET 114. Peeters, 2022.

Estes, Douglas, and Ruth Sheridan, eds. *How John Works: Storytelling in the Fourth Gospel*. RBS 86. SBL Press, 2016.

Evans, Craig A. *Word and Glory: On the Exegetical and Theological Background of John's Prologue*. JSNTSup 89. JSOT Press, 1993.

Falcetta, Alessandro. "The Testimony Research of James Rendel Harris." *NovT* 45 (2003): 280–99.

Flower, Linda. *The Construction of Negotiated Meaning: A Social Cognitive Theory of Writing*. Southern Illinois University Press, 1994.

Foley, John Miles. "Analogues: Modern Oral Epics." Pages 196–212 in *A Companion to Ancient Epic*. Edited by John Miles Foley. BCAW. Blackwell, 2005.

———. *Immanent Art: From Structure to Meaning in Traditional Oral Epic*. Indiana University Press, 1991.

———. *Oral Tradition and the Internet: Pathways of the Mind*. University of Illinois Press, 2012.

———. *The Singer of Tales in Performance*. Voices in Performance and Text. Indiana University Press, 1995.

———. *Traditional Oral Epic: The Odyssey, Beowulf, and the Serbo-Croatian Return Song*. University of California Press, 1990.

———. "Words in Tradition, Words in Text: A Response." *Semeia* 65 (1994): 169–80.

Forger, Deborah. "Jesus as God's Word(s): Aurality, Epistemology and Embodiment in the Gospel of John." *JSNT* 42 (2020): 274–302.

Fornara, Charles William. *The Nature of History in Ancient Greece and Rome*. University of California Press, 1983.
Freed, Edwin D. *Old Testament Quotations in the Gospel of John*. NovTSup 11. Brill, 1965.
Frey, Jörg. *Das johanneische Zeitverständnis*. Vol. 2 of *Die johanneische Eschatologie,*. WUNT 110. Mohr Siebeck, 1998.
———. "From the 'Kingdom of God' to 'Eternal Life': The Transformation of Theological Language in the Fourth Gospel." Pages 439–58 in *Glimpses of Jesus through the Johannine Lens*. Vol. 3 of *John, Jesus and History*. Edited by Paul N. Anderson, Felix Just, S.J., and Tom Thatcher. ECL 18. SBL Press, 2016.
———. "The Gospel of John as a Narrative Memory of Jesus." Pages 261–84 in *Memory and Memories in Early Christianity: Proceedings of the International Conference Held at the Universities of Geneva and Lausanne*. Edited by Simon Butticaz and Enrico Norelli. WUNT 398. Mohr Siebeck, 2018.
———. "Heil und Geschichte im Johannesevangelium: Zum Problem der 'Heilsgeschichte' und zum fundamentalen Geschichtsbezug des Heilsgeschehens im vierten Evangelium." Pages 459–510 in *Heil und Geschichte: Die Geschichtsbezogenheit des Heils und das Problem der Heilsgeschichte in der biblischen Tradition und in der theologischen Deutung*. Edited by Jörg Frey, Stefan Krauter, and Hermann Lichtenberger. WUNT 248. Mohr Siebeck, 2009.
———. "Love-Relations in the Fourth Gospel: Establishing a Semantic Network." Pages 171–98 in *Repetitions and Variations in the Fourth Gospel: Style, Text, Interpretation*. Edited by Gilbert Van Belle, Michael Labahn, and P. Maritz. BETL 223. Peeters, 2009.
———. *Theology and History in the Fourth Gospel: Tradition and Narration*. Baylor University Press, 2018.
Fumerton, Richard. *Epistemology*. First Books in Philosophy. Blackwell, 2006.
Furlong, Dean. *The Identity of John the Evangelist: Revision and Reinterpretation in Early Christian Sources*. Lexington/Fortress Academic, 2020.
Gardner-Smith, P. *Saint John and the Synoptic Gospels*. Cambridge University Press, 1938.
Genette, Gérard. *Narrative Discourse: An Essay in Method*. Translated by Jane E. Lewin. Cornell University Press, 1980.

Gerber, Edward H. *The Scriptural Tale in the Fourth Gospel: With Particular Reference to the Prologue and a Syncretic (Oral and Written) Poetics.* BibInt 147. Brill, 2016.
Gese, Hartmut. *Zur biblischen Theologie: Alttestamentliche Vorträge.* BEvT 78. Kaiser, 1977.
Goldstein, Leon J. *Historical Knowing.* University of Texas Press, 1976.
Goodwin, Charles. "How Did John Treat His Sources?" *JBL* 73 (1954): 61–75.
Grethlein, Jonas. "Social Minds and Narrative Time: Collective Experience in Thucydides and Heliodorus." *Narrative* 23 (2015): 123–39.
Halbwachs, Maurice. *La mémoire collective.* Presses Universitaires de France, 1950.
Halperin, David M. "Plato and the Erotics of Narrativity." Pages 93–129 in *Oxford Studies in Ancient Philosophy: Supplementary Volume 1992, Methods of Interpreting Plato and His Dialogues.* Edited by James C. Klagge and Nicholas D. Smith. Oxford University, 1992.
Hankinson, R. J., and Marguerite Deslauriers. "Aristotle on Imagination and Action: Introduction." *Dialogue* 29 (1990): 3–4.
Harnack, Adolf von. "Über das Verhältniß des Prologs des vierten Evangeliums zum ganzen Werk." *ZTK* 2 (1892): 189–231.
Harris, Elizabeth. *Prologue and Gospel: The Theology of the Fourth Evangelist.* JSNTSup 107. Sheffield Academic, 1994.
Harris, William V. *Ancient Literacy.* Harvard University Press, 1989.
Harstine, Stan. "The Children of God and the Son of God in the Johannine Gospel and Epistles." Pages 369–85 in *Anatomies of the Gospels and Beyond: Essays in Honor of R. Alan Culpepper.* Edited by Mikeal C. Parsons, Elizabeth Struthers Malbon, and Paul N. Anderson. BibInt 164. Brill, 2018.
———. *Moses as a Character in the Fourth Gospel: A Study in Ancient Reading Techniques.* JSNTSup 229. Sheffield Academic, 2002.
Haslam, S. Alexander, Stephen D. Reicher, and Michael J. Platow. *The New Psychology of Leadership: Identity, Influence and Power.* Psychology Press, 2011.
Hays, Richard B. *Echoes of Scripture in the Gospels.* Baylor University Press, 2016.
———. "Reading Scripture in the Light of the Resurrection." Pages 216–38 in *The Art of Reading Scripture.* Edited by Ellen F. Davis and Richard B. Hays. Eerdmans, 2003.

Hearon, Holly. "Mapping Written and Spoken Word in the Gospel of Mark." Pages 379–92 in *The Interface of Orality and Writing: Speaking, Seeing, Writing in the Shaping of New Genres*. Edited by Annette Weissenrieder and Robert B. Coote. BPC 11. Cascade, 2015.

Hengel, Martin. "The Prologue of the Gospel of John as the Gateway to Christological Truth." Pages 265–94 in *The Gospel of John and Christian Theology*. Edited by Richard Bauckham and Carl Mosser. Eerdmans, 2008.

———. "Die Schriftauslegung des 4. Evangeliums auf dem Hintergrund der urchristlichen Exegese." *JBT* 4 (1989): 249–88.

Hezser, Catherine. *Jewish Literacy in Roman Palestine*. TSAJ 81. Mohr Siebeck, 2001.

Hirsch-Luipold, Rainer. *Gott wahrnehmen: Die Sinne im Johannesevangelium (Ratio Religionis Studien IV)*. WUNT 374. Mohr Siebeck, 2017.

———. "Klartext in Bildern: ἀληθινός κτλ., παροιμία – παρρησία, σημεῖον als Signalwörter für eine bildhafte Darstellungsform im Johannesevangelium." Pages 61–102 in *Imagery in the Gospel of John: Terms, Forms, Themes, and Theology of Johannine Figurative Language*. Edited by Jörg Frey, Jan G. van der Watt, and Ruben Zimmermann. WUNT 200. Mohr Siebeck, 2006.

Hoenig, D. Bernard. "The Other Side of the Coin: Israel Answers Ancient Rome's Judea Capta Series with Liberata Medals." *BAR* 7.2 (1981): 44–46.

Hogan, Patrick Colm. *Cognitive Science, Literature, and the Arts: A Guide for Humanists*. Routledge, 2003.

Hood, Jason B. "Matthew 1:1–17 as a Summary of Israel's Story: The Messiah, His Brothers, and the Nations." PhD diss., University of Aberdeen, 2009.

Hooker, Morna D. "Beginnings and Endings." Pages 184–202 in *The Written Gospel*. Edited by Markus Bockmuehl and Donald A. Hagner. Cambridge University Press, 2005.

———. *Beginnings: Keys that Open the Gospels*. Trinity Press International, 1997.

Hornblower, Simon. *A Commentary on Thucydides*. 3 vols. Oxford University Press, 2008.

Horsley, Richard A. *Bandits, Prophets, and Messiahs: Popular Movements at the Time of Jesus*. Harper San Francisco, 1985.

———. "Oral and Written Aspects of the Emergence of the Gospel of Mark as Scripture." *Oral Tradition* 25 (2010): 93–114.

———. "A Prophet Like Moses and Elijah: Popular Memory and Cultural Patterns in Mark." Pages 166–90 in *Performing the Gospel: Orality, Memory, and Mark: Essays Dedicated to Werner Kelber*. Edited by Richard A. Horsley, Jonathan A. Draper, and John Miles Foley. Fortress, 2006.

Hoskyns, Edwyn Clement. *The Fourth Gospel*. Rev. ed. Faber & Faber, 1950.

Huber, David E., Tedra F. Clark, Tim Curran, and Piotr Winkielman. "Effects of Repetition Priming on Recognition Memory: Testing a Perceptual Fluency-Disfluency Model." *JEP: LMC* 34.6 (2008): 1321.

Hübner, Hans. *Hebräerbrief, Evangelien und Offenbarung*. Vol. 3 of *Biblische Theologie des Neuen Testaments*. Vandenhoeck & Ruprecht, 1995.

———. *Evangelium secundum Iohannem*. Vol. 1.2 of *Vetus Testamentum in Novo*. Vandenhoeck & Ruprecht, 2003.

Huizinga, Leroy A. "The Matthean Jesus and Isaac." Pages 63–81 in *Reading the Bible Intertextually*. Edited by Richard B. Hays, Stefan Alkier, and Leroy A. Huizenga. Baylor University Press, 2009.

———. *The New Isaac: Tradition and Intertextuality in the Gospel of Matthew*. NovTSup 131. Brill, 2009.

Hunt, Steven A., D. François Tolmie, and Ruben Zimmermann, eds. *Character Studies in the Fourth Gospel: Narrative Approaches to Seventy Figures in John*. WUNT 314. Mohr Siebeck, 2013.

Hylen, Susan E. *Allusion and Meaning in John 6*. BZNW 137. de Gruyter, 2005.

———. *Imperfect Believers: Ambiguous Characters in the Gospel of John*. Westminster John Knox, 2009.

Hymes, Dell. "Ethnopoetics, Oral-Formulaic Theory, and Editing Texts." *Oral Tradition* 9 (1994): 330–70.

Jackson, Howard M. "Ancient Self-Referential Conventions and Their Implications for the Authorship and Integrity of the Gospel of John." *JTS* 50 (1999): 1–34.

Johnston, George. *The Spirit-Paraclete in the Gospel of John*. SNTSMS 12. Cambridge University Press, 1970.

Jonge, Marinus de. "Christ." *ABD* 1:914–21.

———. "Messiah." *ABD* 4:777–88.

Juhasz, Joseph B. "Greek Theories of Imagination." *Journal of the History of the Behavioral Sciences* 7 (1971): 39–58.

Kahn, Charles H. *Plato and the Socratic Dialogue: The Philosophical Use of a Literary Form*. Cambridge University Press, 1996.

Kanagaraj, Jey J. *"Mysticism" in the Gospel of John: An Inquiry into the Background*. JSNTSup 158. Sheffield Academic, 1998.

Kee, Howard Clark. "Knowing the Truth: Epistemology and Community in the Fourth Gospel." Pages 254–80 in *Neotestamentica et Philonica: Studies in Honor of Peder Borgen*. Edited by David E. Aune, Torrey Seland, and Jarl Henning Ulrichsen. NovTSup 106. Brill, 2003.

Keener, Craig S. *Christobiography: Memory, History, and the Reliability of the Gospels*. Eerdmans, 2019.

———. *The Gospel of John: A Commentary*. 2 vols. Baker Academic, 2003.

Keith, Chris. *The Gospel as Manuscript: An Early History of the Jesus Tradition as Material Artifact*. Oxford University Press, 2020.

Kelber, Werner. *The Oral and the Written Gospel: The Hermeneutics of Speaking and Writing in the Synoptic Tradition, Mark, Paul, and Q*. Indiana University Press, 1997.

Kennedy, Joel. *The Recapitulation of Israel: Use of Israel's History in Matthew 1:1–4:11*. WUNT 257. Mohr Siebeck, 2008.

Kinkade, M. Dale. "Native Oral Literature of the Northwest Coast and Plateau." Pages 33–45 in *Dictionary of Native American Literature*. Edited by Andrew Wiget. GRLH. Garland, 1994.

Kirk, Alan. "Social and Cultural Memory." Pages 1–24 in *Memory, Tradition, and Text: Uses of the Past in Early Christianity*. Edited by Alan Kirk and Tom Thatcher. SemeiaSt 52. Society of Biblical Literature, 2005.

Kirk, Alan, and Tom Thatcher. "Jesus Tradition as Social Memory." Pages 25–42 in *Memory, Tradition, and Text: Uses of the Past in Early Christianity*. Edited by Alan Kirk and Tom Thatcher. SemeiaSt 52. Society of Biblical Literature, 2005.

Klink III, Edward W. *John*. ZECNT. Zondervan, 2016.

Koester, Craig R. *Symbolism in the Fourth Gospel: Meaning, Mystery, Community*. Fortress, 1995.

———. *Symbolism in the Fourth Gospel: Meaning, Mystery, Community*. 2nd ed. Fortress, 2003.

Köstenberger, Andreas J. "'I Suppose' (οἶμαι): The Conclusion of John's Gospel in Its Literary and Historical Context." Pages 72–88 in *The New Testament in Its First Century Setting: Essays on Context and Background in Honour of B. W. Winter on His Sixty-Fifth Birthday*.

Edited by P. J. Williams, Andrew D. Clarke, Peter M. Head, and David Instone-Brewer. Eerdmans, 2004.

———. "Who Were the First Disciples of Jesus? An Assessment of the Historicity of the Johannine Call Narrative (John 1:35–51)." Pages 189–200 in *Glimpses of Jesus through the Johannine Lens*. Vol. 3 of *John, Jesus, and History*. Edited by Paul N. Anderson, Felix Just, S.J., and Tom Thatcher. ECL 18. SBL Press, 2016.

Kraus, Wolfgang. "Johannes und das Alte Testament: Überlegungen zum Umgang mit der Schrift im Johannesevangelium im Horizont Biblischer Theologie." *ZNW* 88 (1997): 1–23.

Kubiś, Adam. *The Book of Zechariah in the Gospel of John*. Gabalda, 2012.

Kysar, Robert. *John: The Maverick Gospel*. John Knox, 1993.

Labahn, Michael. "Deuteronomy in John's Gospel." Pages 82–98 in *Deuteronomy in the New Testament: The New Testament and the Scriptures of Israel*. Edited by Steve Moyise and Maarten J. J. Menken. LNTS 358. T&T Clark, 2007.

———. "Scripture *Talks* Because Jesus *Talks:* The Narrative Rhetoric of Persuading and Creativity in John's Use of Scripture." Pages 133–54 in *The Fourth Gospel in First-Century Media Culture*. Edited by Anthony Le Donne and Tom Thatcher. LNTS 426. T&T Clark, 2011.

Lampinen, James Michael, and Timothy N. Odegard. "Memory Editing Mechanisms." *Memory* 14.6 (2006): 649–54.

Larsen, Brian. *Archetypes and the Fourth Gospel: Literature and Theology in Conversation*. T&T Clark, 2018.

Larsen, Kasper Bro. *Recognizing the Stranger: Recognition Scenes in the Gospel of John*. BibInt 93. Brill, 2008.

Le Donne, Anthony, and Tom Thatcher, eds. *The Fourth Gospel in First-Century Media Culture*. LNTS 426. T&T Clark, 2011.

Lee, Dorothy. *Flesh and Glory: Symbol, Gender, and Theology in the Gospel of John*. Herder & Herder, 2002.

León, Carlos. "An Architecture of Narrative Memory." *BICA* 16 (2016): 19–33.

Leonhardt-Balzer, Jutta. "The Johannine Literature and Contemporary Jewish Literature." Pages 155–70 in *The Oxford Handbook of Johannine Studies*. Edited by Judith M. Lieu and Martinus C. de Boer. Oxford University Press, 2018.

Lieu, Judith. "Narrative Analysis and Scripture in John." Pages 144–63 in *The Old Testament in the New Testament: Essays in Honour of J. L.*

North. Edited by Steve Moyise. JSNTSup 189. Sheffield Academic, 2000.

Lincoln, Andrew T. "The Beloved Disciple as Eyewitness and the Fourth Gospel as Witness." *JSNT* 24.3 (2002): 3–26.

———. *The Gospel according to St John*. BNTC 4. Hendrickson, 2005.

———. *Truth on Trial: The Lawsuit Motif in the Fourth Gospel*. Hendrickson, 2000.

Lindars, Barnabas. "The Fourth Gospel an Act of Contemplation." Pages 23–35 in *Studies in the Fourth Gospel*. Edited by F. L. Cross. Mowbray, 1957.

———. *The Gospel of John*. NCBC. Eerdmans, 1982.

Lindemann, Mary, ed. *Ways of Knowing: Ten Interdisciplinary Essays*. Studies in Central European Histories 31. Brill, 2004.

Loader, William R. G. "The Central Christological Structure of the Fourth Gospel." *NTS* 30 (1984): 23–35.

Longinus. *On the Sublime*. In Aristotle's *Poetics*. Translated by W. Hamilton Fyfe. Revised by Donald A. Russell. LCL 199. Harvard University Press, 1995.

Lord, Albert B. *The Singer of Tales*. Harvard University Press, 1960.

Lührmann, Dieter. "Faith: New Testament." *ABD* 2:749–58.

Luther, Susanne. "The Authentication of the Narrative: The Function of Scripture Quotations in John 19." Pages 155–66 in *Biblical Interpretation in Early Christian Gospels, Volume 4: The Gospel of John*. Edited by Thomas R. Hatina. LNTS 613. T&T Clark, 2020.

———. "The Authentication of the Past: Narrative Representation of History in the Gospel of John." *JSNT* 43 (2020): 67–84.

———. "From Bethlehem, according to the Promise—or Rather from Nazareth? Narrative and History in John's Gospel." *Early Christianity* 8 (2017): 9–29.

———. "Space." Pages 59–77 in *How John Works: Storytelling in the Fourth Gospel*. Edited by Douglas Estes and Ruth Sheridan. RBS 86. SBL Press, 2016.

Lyman, Mary Redington Ely. *Knowledge of God in Johannine Thought*. Macmillan, 1925.

Mackay, Ian D. *John's Relationship with Mark: An Analysis of John 6 in Light of Mark 6–8*. WUNT 2/182. Mohr Siebeck, 2004.

MacRae, G. W. "Theology and Irony in the Fourth Gospel." Pages 103–13 in *The Gospel of John as Literature: An Anthology of Twentieth-Century Perspectives*. Edited by Mark W. G. Stibbe. NTTS 17. Brill, 1993.

Malina, Bruce J., and Richard L. Rohrbaugh. *Social Science Commentary on the Gospel of John*. Fortress, 1998.

Manning, Gary T. *Echoes of a Prophet: The Use of Ezekiel in the Gospel of John and in the Literature of the Second Temple Period*. JSNTSup 270. T&T Clark, 2004.

Mauser, Ulrich W. "God in Human Form." *Ex Auditu* 16 (2000): 81–99.

McAdams, Dan P., and Kate C. McLean. "Narrative Identity." *CDPS* 22.3 (2013): 233–38.

McIver, Robert K. *Memory, Jesus, and the Synoptic Gospels*. RBS 59. Society of Biblical Literature, 2011.

Meeks, Wayne. *The Prophet-King: Moses Traditions and the Johannine Christology*. NovTSup 14. Brill, 1967.

Menken, Maarten J. J. "Genesis in John's Gospel and I John." Pages 83–98 in *Genesis in the New Testament*. Edited by Maarten J.J. Menken and Steve Moyise. LNTS 466. Bloomsbury, 2012.

———. "Observations on the Significance of the Old Testament in the Fourth Gospel." *Neot* 33 (1999): 125–43.

———. *Old Testament Quotations in the Fourth Gospel: Studies in Textual Form*. CBET 15. Kampen: Kok Pharos, 1996.

———. "What Authority Does the Fourth Evangelist Claim for His Book?" Pages 186–202 in *Paul, John, and Apocalyptic Eschatology: Studies in Honour of Martinus C. de Boer*. Edited by Jan Krans, Bert Jan Lietaert Peerbolte, Peter-Ben Smit, and Arie Zwiep. NovTSup 149. Brill, 2013.

Metzger, Bruce M. *A Textual Commentary on the Greek New Testament*. 2nd ed. Deutsche Bibelgesellschaft, 1994.

Meyer, Michel. *Meaning and Reading: A Philosophical Essay on Language and Literature*. P&B 4.3. Benjamins, 1983.

Misztal, Barbara A. *Theories of Social Remembering*. Open University Press, 2003.

Mlakuzhyil, George. *The Christocentric Literary Structure of the Fourth Gospel*. AnBib 117. Editrice Pontificio Istituto Biblico, 1987.

Modrak, Deborah K. W. "Aristotle on *Phantasia*." Pages 15–26 in *The Routledge Handbook of Philosophy of Imagination*. Edited by Amy Kind. Routledge, 2016.

Moloney, Francis J. "Closure." Pages 225–39 in *How John Works: Storytelling in the Fourth Gospel*. Edited by Douglas Estes and Ruth Sheridan. RBS 86. SBL Press, 2016.

———. "The Gospel of John as Scripture." *CBQ* 67 (2005): 454–68.

Mooij, J. J. A. *Fictional Realities: The Uses of Literary Imagination.* UPGCL 30. Benjamins, 1993.

Morley, Neville. *Writing Ancient History.* Duckworth, 1999.

Munslow, Alun. *Deconstructing History.* 2nd ed. Routledge, 2006.

Myers, Alicia D. "Abiding Words: An Introduction to Perspectives on John's Use of Scripture." Pages 1–20 in *Abiding Words: The Use of Scripture in the Gospel of John.* Edited by Alicia D. Myers and Bruce G. Schuchard. RBS 81. SBL Press, 2015.

———. *Characterizing Jesus: A Rhetorical Analysis of the Fourth Gospel's Use of Scripture in Its Presentation of Jesus.* LNTS 458. T&T Clark, 2012.

———. "A Voice in the Wilderness: Classical Rhetoric and the Testimony of John (the Baptist) in John 1:19–34." Pages 119–40 in *Abiding Words: The Use of Scripture in the Gospel of John.* Edited by Alicia D. Myers and Bruce G. Schuchard. RBS 81. SBL Press, 2015.

Neirynck, Frans. "The 'Other Disciple' in Jn 18:15–16." *ETL* 51.1 (1975): 113–41.

Newbigin, Lesslie. *The Light Has Come: An Exposition of the Fourth Gospel.* Eerdmans, 1982.

Neyrey, Jerome H., S.J. *The Gospel of John.* NCBC. Cambridge University Press, 2006.

———. *The Gospel of John in Cultural and Rhetorical Perspective.* Eerdmans, 2009.

———. "John III: A Debate over Johannine Epistemology and Christology." *NovT* 23 (1981): 115–27.

North, Wendy E. S. *A Journey Round John: Tradition, Interpretation and Context in the Fourth Gospel.* LNTS 534. Bloomsbury T&T Clark, 2015.

Novenson, Matthew V. "Jesus the Messiah: Conservatism and Radicalism in Johannine Christology." Pages 109–23 in *Portraits of Jesus in the Gospel of John.* Edited by Craig R. Koester. LNTS 589. T&T Clark, 2019.

Obermann, Andreas. *Die christologische Erfüllung der Schrift im Johannesevangelium: Eine Untersuchung zur johanneischen Hermeneutik anhand der Schriftzitate.* WUNT 2/83. Mohr Siebeck, 1996.

O'Day, Gail. "The Word Become Flesh: Story and Theology in the Gospel of John." Pages 67–76 in *Literary and Social Readings of the Fourth Gospel.* Vol. 2 of *What Is John?* Edited by Fernando F. Segovia. SymS 7. Scholars Press, 1988.

O'Grady, John F. "The Prologue and Chapter 17 of the Gospel of John." Pages 215–28 in *What We Have Heard From the Beginning: The Past, Present, and Future of Johannine Studies*. Edited by Tom Thatcher. Baylor University Press, 2007.

Oliver, Mary Beth, Arienne Ferchaud, Chun Yang, Yan Huang, and Erica Bailey. "Absorption and Meaningfulness: Examining the Relationship Between Eudaimonic Media Use and Engagement." Pages 253–69 in *Narrative Absorption*. Edited by Frank Hakemulder, Moniek M. Kuijpers, Ed S. Tan, Katalin Bálint, and Miruna M. Doicaru. Linguistic Approaches to Literature 27. Benjamins, 2017.

Painter, John. "The Idea of Knowledge in the Johannine Gospel and Epistles." PhD diss., University of Durham, 1968.

Palmén, Ritva. *Richard of St. Victor's Theory of Imagination*. IMP 8. Brill, 2014.

Parsenios, George L. "Anamnesis and the Silent Narrator in Plato and John." *Religions* 8.47 (2017): 1–11.

———. *Departure and Consolation: The Johannine Farewell Discourses in Light of Greco-Roman Literature*. NovTSup 117. Brill, 2005.

———. "'No Longer in the World' (John 17:11): The Transformation of the Tragic in the Fourth Gospel." *HTR* 98 (2005): 1–21.

———. *Rhetoric and Drama in the Johannine Lawsuit Motif*. WUNT 258. Mohr Siebeck, 2010.

———. "The Silent Spaces between Narrative and Drama." Pages 85–98 in *The Gospel of John as Genre Mosaic*. Edited by Kasper Bro Larsen. SANt 3. Vandenhoeck & Ruprecht, 2015.

———. "The Testimony of John's Narrative and the Silence of the Johannine Narrator." Pages 1–18 in *The Opening of John's Narrative (John 1:19–2:22): Historical, Literary, and Theological Readings from the Colloquium Ioanneum 2015 in Ephesus*. Edited by R. Alan Culpepper and Jörg Frey. WUNT 385. Mohr Siebeck, 2017.

Pascal, Blaise. *Pensées*. Dutton, 1958.

Pastorelli, David. *Le Paraclet dans le corpus johannique*. BZNW 142. de Gruyter, 2006.

Pausanias. *Description of Greece*. Translated by William Henry Samuel Jones. 5 vols. LCL. Harvard University Press, 1933.

Penwill, J. L. "Men in Love: Aspects of Plato's *Symposium*." *Ramus* 7 (1978): 143–75.

Pettersson, Bo. *How Literary Worlds Are Shaped: A Comparative Poetics of Literary Imagination*. Narratologia 54. de Gruyter, 2016.

Philips, Peter M. *The Prologue of the Fourth Gospel: A Sequential Reading*. LNTS 294. Bloomsbury T&T Clark, 2006.

Phillips, G.L. "Faith and Vision in the Fourth Gospel." Pages 83–96 in *Studies in the Fourth Gospel*. Edited by F. L. Cross. Mowbray, 1957.

Pioske, Daniel D. *Memory in a Time of Prose: Studies in Epistemology, Hebrew Scribalism, and the Biblical Past*. Oxford University Press, 2018.

Plato. *Euthyphro, Apology, Crito, Meno, Gorgias, Menexenus*. Vol. 1 of *The Dialogues of Plato*. Translated by R. E. Allen. Yale University Press, 1989.

———. *Plato's Phaedrus: Translated with an Introduction and Commentary*. Translated by R. Hackforth. Cambridge University Press, 1952.

———. *The Republic of Plato*. Translated by Allan Bloom. 2nd ed. Basic Books, 1991.

———. *Republic*. Edited and translated by Christopher Emlyn-Jones and William Preddy. 2 vols. LCL 237, 276. Harvard University Press, 2013.

———. *Theaetetus. Sophist*. Translated by Harold North Fowler. LCL 123. Harvard University Press, 1921.

Porter, Christopher A. *Johannine Social Identity Formation after the Fall of the Jerusalem Temple: Negotiating Identity in Crisis*. BibInt 194. Brill, 2021.

Potterie, Ignace de la. "Οἶδα et γινώσκω: Les deux modes de la connaissance dans le quatrième evangile." *Biblica* 40 (1959): 709–25.

Pratt, Jonathan. "The Epideictic *Agōn* and Aristotle's Elusive Third Genre." *AJP* 133.2 (2012): 177–208.

Quick, Catherine. "The Metonym: Rhetoric and Oral Tradition at the Crossroads." *Oral Tradition* 26 (2011): 597–600.

Rabinoff, Eve. *Perception in Aristotle's Ethics*. Northwestern University Press, 2018.

Rand, Jan A. du. "Repetitions and Variations: Experiencing the Power of the Gospel of John as Literary Symphony." *Neot* 30 (1996): 59–70.

Ranke, Leopold von. *Geschichte der romanischen und germanischen Völker von 1494 bis 1535*. Reimer, 1824.

Rapley, Mark, and Martha Augoustinos. "'National Identity' as a Rhetorical Resource." Pages 194–210 in *Language, Interaction and National Identity: Studies in the Social Organisation of National Identity in Talk-in-Interaction*. Edited by Stephen Hester and William Housley, CPQR. Ashgate, 2002.

Reinhartz, Adele. *Cast Out of the Covenant: Jews and Anti-Judaism in the Gospel of John.* Lexington/Fortress Academic, 2018.

———. *The Word in the World: The Cosmological Tale in the Fourth Gospel.* SBLMS 45. Scholars Press, 1992.

Reinsdorf, Walter. "How Is the Gospel True?" *SJT* 56 (2003): 328–44.

Resseguie, James L. "The Beloved Disciple: The Ideal Point of View." Pages 537–49 in *Character Studies in the Fourth Gospel: Narrative Approaches to Seventy Figures in John.* Edited by Steven A. Hunt, D. Francois Tolmie, and Ruben Zimmerman. WUNT 314. Mohr Siebeck, 2013.

———. *Narrative Criticism and the New Testament: An Introduction.* Baker Academic, 2005.

———. "Point of View." Pages 79–96 in *How John Works: Storytelling in the Fourth Gospel.* Edited by Douglas Estes and Ruth Sheridan. RBS 86. SBL Press, 2016.

Richards, I. A. *Principles of Literary Criticism.* Harcourt, Brace, 1928.

Riches, John K. *Jesus and the Transformation of Judaism.* Darton, Longman, & Todd, 1980.

Ricoeur, Paul. *Memory, History, Forgetting.* Translated by Kathleen Blamey and David Pellauer. University of Chicago Press, 2004.

———. "Narrative Identity." *PT* 35.1 (1991): 73–81.

Ritivoi, Andreea Deciu. *Paul Ricoeur: Tradition and Innovation in Rhetorical Theory.* State University of New York Press, 2006.

Roark, Tony. *Aristotle on Time: A Study of the Physics.* Cambridge University Press, 2011.

Robbins, Vernon K. "Progymnastic Rhetorical Composition and Pre-Gospel Traditions: A New Approach." Pages 111–48 in *The Synoptic Gospels: Source Criticism and the New Literary Criticism.* Edited by Camille Focant. BETL 110. Leuven University Press, 1993.

Robinson, Alan. *Narrating the Past: Historiography, Memory and the Contemporary Novel.* Palgrave Macmillan, 2011.

Rodríguez, Rafael. *Structuring Early Christian Memory: Jesus in Tradition, Performance and Text.* LNTS 407. T&T Clark, 2010.

Roediger, Henry L., III. "Why Retrieval Is the Key Process in Understanding Human Memory." Pages 52–75 in *Memory, Consciousness, and the Brain: The Tallinn Conference.* Edited by Endel Tulving. Psychology Press, 1999.

Russell, D. S. *The Old Testament Pseudepigrapha: Patriarchs and Prophets in Early Judaism.* SCM, 1987.

Ryan, Marie-Laure. *A New Anatomy of Storyworlds: What Is, What If, As If.* TIN. Ohio State University Press, 2022.

Schandorf, Michael. "A Gesture Theory of Communication." PhD diss., University of Illinois at Chicago, 2015.

Schank, Roger C., and Robert P. Abelson. *Scripts, Plans, Goals, and Understanding: An Inquiry Into Human Knowledge Structures.* Psychology Press, 1997.

Schinkel, Anders. "Imagination as a Category of History: An Essay Concerning Koselleck's Concepts of *Erfahrungsraum* and *Erwartungshorizont.*" HT 44 (2005): 42–54.

Schnackenburg, Rudolf. *The Gospel according to John.* Vol 1. Translated by Kevin Smyth. Herder & Herder, 1968.

———. *The Gospel according to John.* Vol 3. Translated by David Smith and G. A. Kon. Crossroad, 1990.

Scholtissek, Klaus. "'Geschrieben in diesem Buch' (Joh 20,30): Beobachtungen zum kanonischen Anspruch des Johannesevangeliums." Pages 207–26 in *Israel und seine Heilstraditionen im Johannesevangelium: Festgabe für Johannes Beutler SJ zum 70. Geburtstag.* Edited by Michael Labahn, Klaus Scholtissek, and Angelika Strotmann. Schöningh, 2004.

Schuchard, Bruce G. *Scripture within Scripture: The Interrelationship of Form and Function in the Explicit Old Testament Citations in the Gospel of John.* SBLDS 133. Scholars Press, 1992.

Schulz, Siegfried. *Das Evangelism nach Johannes.* NTD 4. Vandenhoeck & Ruprecht, 1987.

Schwartz, Barry. *Abraham Lincoln and the Forge of National Memory.* University of Chicago Press, 2000.

Sheridan, Ruth. *Retelling Scripture: "The Jews" and the Scriptural Citations in John 1:19–12:15.* BibInt 110. Brill, 2012.

———. "The Testimony of Two Witnesses: John 8:17." Pages 161–84 in *Abiding Words: The Use of Scripture in the Gospel of John.* Edited by Alicia D. Myers and Bruce G. Schuchard. RBS 81. SBL Press, 2015.

Shively, Elizabeth E. *Apocalyptic Imagination in the Gospel of Mark: The Literary and Theological Role of Mark 3:22–30.* BZNW 189. de Gruyter, 2012.

Sipiora, Phillip, and James S. Baumlin, eds. *Rhetoric and Kairos: Essays in History, Theory, and Praxis.* State University of New York Press, 2002.

Singer, Jefferson A. "Narrative Identity and Meaning Making Across the Adult Lifespan: An Introduction." *JPers* 72.3 (2004): 437–59.

Skinner, Christopher W., and Sherri Brown, eds. *Johannine Ethics: The Moral World of the Gospel and Epistles of John*. Fortress, 2017.

Smith, D. Moody. *Johannine Christianity: Essays on Its Setting, Sources, and Theology*. University of South Carolina Press, 1984.

———. *John*. ANTC. Abingdon, 1999.

———. *The Theology of the Gospel of John*. NTT. Cambridge University Press, 1995.

Smith, Ole Langwitz, ed. *Scholia Graeca in Aeschylum quae exstant Omnia*. 2 vols. Teubner, 1976.

Smith, Tyler. *The Fourth Gospel and the Manufacture of Minds in Ancient Historiography, Biography, Romance, and Drama*. BibInt 173. Brill, 2019.

Sosa Siliezar, Carlos R. *Creation Imagery in the Gospel of John*. LNTS 546. Bloomsbury T&T Clark, 2015.

Staley, Jeffrey Lloyd. *The Print's First Kiss: A Rhetorical Investigation of the Implied Reader in the Fourth Gospel*. SBLDS 82. Scholars Press, 1988.

Sternberg, Meir. *Expositional Modes and Temporal Ordering in Fiction*. Johns Hopkins University Press, 1978.

Stibbe, Mark W. G. *John as Storyteller: Narrative Criticism and the Fourth Gospel*. SNTSMS 73. Cambridge University Press, 1992.

Szilas, Nicolas. "Towards Narrative-Based Knowledge Representation in Cognitive Systems." Pages 133–41 in *Sixth Workshop on Computational Models of Narrative (CMN 2015)*. Edited by Mark A. Finlayson, Ben Miller, Antonio Lieto, and Remi Ronfard. OASIcs 45. Schloss Dagstuhl, 2015.

Thatcher, Tom. "The Beloved Disciple, the Fourth Evangelist, and the Authorship of the Fourth Gospel." Pages 83–101 in *The Oxford Handbook of Johannine Studies*. Edited by Judith M. Lieu and Martinus C. De Boer. Oxford University Press, 2018.

———. "Cain and Abel in Early Christian Memory: A Case Study in 'The Use of the Old Testament in the New.'" *CBQ* 72 (2010): 732–51.

———. "John's Memory Theatre: A Study of Composition in Performance." Pages 73–91 in *The Fourth Gospel in First-Century Media Culture*. Edited by Anthony Le Donne and Tom Thatcher. LNTS 426. T&T Clark, 2013.

———. "The Shape of John's Story: Memory-Mapping the Fourth Gospel." Pages 209–39 in *Memory and Identity in Ancient Judaism and Early Christianity: A Conversation with Barry Schwartz*. Edited by Tom Thatcher. SemeiaSt 78. SBL Press, 2014.

———. *Why John Wrote a Gospel: Jesus—Memory—History*. Westminster John Knox, 2006.

———. "Why John Wrote a Gospel: Memory and History in an Early Christian Community." Pages 79–97 in *Memory, Tradition, and Text: Uses of the Past in Early Christianity*. Edited by Alan Kirk and Tom Thatcher. SemeiaSt 52. Society of Biblical Literature, 2005.

Theissen, Gerd, and Annette Merz. *The Historical Jesus: A Comprehensive Guide*. Fortress, 1998.

Theobald, Michael. *Das Evangelium nach Johannes: Kapitel 1–12*. Regensburg: Pustet, 2009.

———. "Schriftzitate im 'Lebensbrot'-Dialog Jesu (Joh 6): Ein Paradigma für den Schriftgebrauch des vierten Evangelisten." Pages 327–66 in *The Scriptures in the Gospels*. Edited by Christopher M. Tuckett. BETL 131. Leuven University Press, 1997.

Tholuck, Augustus. *Commentary on the Gospel of John*. Translated by Charles P. Krauth. Smith, English, 1859.

Thompson, Glen L., and Mark Wilson. "The Route of Paul's Second Journey in Asia Minor: In the Steps of Robert Jewett and Beyond." *TynBul* 67 (2016): 217–46.

Thompson, Marianne Meye. *The God of the Gospel of John*. Eerdmans, 2001.

———. *The Humanity of Jesus in the Fourth Gospel*. Fortress, 1988.

———. *John: A Commentary*. NTL. Westminster John Knox, 2015.

Tieleman, Teun. "The Spirit of Stoicism." Pages 39–62 in *The Holy Spirit, Inspiration, and the Cultures of Antiquity: Multidisciplinary Perspectives*. Edited by Jörg Frey and John Levison. Ekstasis 5. de Gruyter, 2014.

Tilborg, Sjef van. *Imaginative Love in John*. BibInt 2. Brill, 1993.

Underhill, Evelyn. *The Mystic Way: A Psychological Study in Christian Origins*. Dent & Sons, 1913.

Vansina, Jan. *Oral Tradition as History*. University of Wisconsin Press, 1985.

Veyne, Paul. *Did the Greeks Believe in Their Myths? An Essay on the Constitutive Imagination*. Translated by Paula Wissing. University of Chicago Press, 1988.

Waetjen, Herman C. *The Gospel of the Beloved Disciple: A Work in Two Editions*. T&T Clark, 2005.

Wahlde, Urban C. von. *Commentary on the Gospel of John*. Vol. 2 of *The Gospel and Letters of John*. Eerdmans, 2010.

Walker, Jeffrey. *Rhetoric and Poetics in Antiquity*. Oxford University Press, 2000.
Waltke, Bruce K. *An Old Testament Theology: An Exegetical, Canonical, and Thematic Approach*. Zondervan, 2007.
Wang, Sunny Kuan-Hui. *Sense Perception and Testimony in the Gospel According to John*. WUNT 435. Mohr Siebeck, 2017.
Watkin, Christopher. "If My Brain Is Damaged, Do I Become a Different Person? Catherine Malabou and Neuro-Identity." Pages 21–40 in *Reconstructing Identity: A Transdisciplinary Approach*. Edited by Nicholas Monk, Mia Lindgren, Sarah McDonald, and Sarah Pasfield-Neofitou. Palgrave Macmillan, 2017.
Watson, Francis. *Gospel Writing: A Canonical Perspective*. Eerdmans, 2013.
Watson, Gerard. "Discovering the Imagination: Platonists and Stoics on *phantasia*." Pages 208–33 in *The Question of "Eclecticism": Studies in Later Greek Philosophy*. Edited by John M. Dillon and A. A. Long. University of California Press, 1988.
———. "Imagination: The Greek Background." *ITQ* 52 (1986): 54–65.
Watts, Rikki E. *Isaiah's New Exodus in Mark*. BSL. Baker Academic, 1997.
Wead, David W. *The Literary Devices in John's Gospel*. Edited by Paul N. Anderson and R. Alan Culpepper. Rev. and exp. ed. JMS 7. Wipf & Stock, 2018.
Webb, Ruth. "Sight and Insight: Theorizing Vision, Emotion and Imagination in Ancient Rhetoric." Pages 205–19 in *Sight and the Ancient Senses*. Edited by Michael Squire. The Senses in Antiquity. Routledge, 2016.
White, Hayden. *The Content of the Form: Narrative Discourse and Historical Representation*. Johns Hopkins University Press, 1987.
———. "The Historical Text as Literary Artifact." Pages 221–36 in *The History and Narrative Reader*. Edited by Geoffrey Roberts. Routledge, 2001.
———. *Metahistory: The Historical Imagination in Nineteenth-Century Europe*. Johns Hopkins University Press, 1973.
Wiarda, Timothy. "John 21:1–23: Narrative Unity and Its Implications." *JSNT* 14.46 (1992): 53–71.
Wise, Jennifer. *Dionysus Writes: The Invention of Theatre in Ancient Greece*. Cornell University Press, 2000.
Williams, Catrin H. "Abraham as a Figure of Memory in John 8.31–59." Pages 205–22 in *The Fourth Gospel in First-Century Media Culture*. Edited by Anthony Le Donne and Tom Thatcher. LNTS 426. T&T Clark, 2011.

———. "Composite Citations in the Gospel of John." Pages 94–127 in *New Testament Uses*. Vol. 2 of *Composite Citations in Antiquity*. Edited by Sean A. Adams and Seth M. Ehorn. LNTS 593. Bloomsbury T&T Clark, 2018.

———. "How Scripture 'Speaks': Insights from the Study of Ancient Media Culture." Pages 53–69 in *Methodology in the Use of the Old Testament in the New: Context and Criteria*. Edited by David Allen and Steve Smith. LNTS 579. T&T Clark, 2020.

———. "Isaiah in John's Gospel." Pages 101–17 in *Isaiah in the New Testament*. Edited by Steve Moyise and Maarten J. J. Menken. T&T Clark, 2005.

———. "John, Judaism, and 'Searching the Scriptures.'" Pages 77–100 in *John and Judaism: A Contested Relationship in Context*. Edited by R. Alan Culpepper and Paul N. Anderson. RBS 87. SBL Press, 2017.

———. "Patriarchs and Prophets Remembered: Framing Israel's Past in the Gospel of John." Pages 187–212 in *Abiding Words: The Use of Scripture in the Gospel of John*. Edited by Alicia D. Myers and Bruce G. Schuchard. RBS 81. SBL Press, 2015.

———. "Persuasion through Allusion: Evocations of 'Shepherd(s)' and their Rhetorical Impact in John 10." Pages 111–24 in *Come and Read: Interpretive Approaches to the Gospel of John*. Edited by Alicia D. Myers and Lindsey S. Jodrey. Fortress Academic, 2020.

———. "'Seeing the Glory': The Reception of Isaiah's Call-Vision in John 12:41." Pages 245–72 in *Judaism, Jewish Identities and the Gospel Tradition: Festschrift for Professor Maurice Casey*. Edited by James Crossley. Equinox, 2010.

Williams, P. J. "Not the Prologue of John." *JSNT* 33 (2011): 375–86.

Wolz, Henry G. "Philosophy as Drama: An Approach to Plato's *Symposium*." *PPR* 30 (1970): 323–53.

Yates, Frances A. *The Art of Memory*. Routledge & Kegan Paul, 1966.

Zimmermann, Ruben. "Figurenanalyse im Johannesevangelium: Ein Beitrag zu Sinn und Wahrheit narratologischer Exegese." *ZNW* 105 (2014): 20–53.

Zumstein, Jean. *Das Johannesevangelium*. KEK 2. Vandenhoeck & Ruprecht, 2016.

Zunshine, Lisa. *Why We Read Fiction: A Theory of Mind and the Novel*. Ohio State University Press, 2006.

Contributors

Paul N. Anderson (PhD, University of Glasgow) is Professor of Biblical and Quaker Studies at George Fox University in Newberg, Oregon, and an Extraordinary Professor of Religion at the North-West University of Potchefstroom, South Africa. Author or editor of some thirty books and over 400 essays, his Johannine books include *The Christology of the Fourth Gospel* (1996, 1997, 2010), *The Fourth Gospel and the Quest for Jesus* (2006, 2007), and *The Riddles of the Fourth Gospel* (2011). His contextual introduction to the New Testament is *From Crisis to Christ* (2014), and his book on Christian discipleship is *Following Jesus* (2013). A founding member of the John, Jesus, and History Project, he has edited or coedited six of its books and is editing four more, for an eventual total of thirteen. He edits three book series: Biblical Interpretation (Brill), the Johannine Monograph Series (Wipf & Stock), and the Quakers and the Disciplines Series (FAHE).

Richard Bauckham (PhD, University of Cambridge) is Emeritus Professor of New Testament Studies at the University of Saint Andrews, Scotland. He has published widely in the fields of New Testament, early Jewish studies and Christian theology. His many books include *Jesus and the Eyewitnesses* (2017), *Bible and Ecology* (2010), *The Theology of the Book of Revelation* (1993), *The Blurred Cross* (2024), and two books on the Gospel of John: *The Testimony of the Beloved Disciple* (2007) and *Gospel of Glory* (2015). He also writes poetry.

Jo-Ann A. Brant (PhD, McMaster University) is Professor Emeritus at Goshen College, IN. She is the author of *Dialogue and Drama: Elements of Greek Tragedy in the Fourth Gospel* (2004), and *John: New Testament Paideia Commentary Series* (2011). Brant also coedited two volumes, *Ancient Fiction: The Matrix of Early Christian and Jewish Narrative* (2005) and *The Ties that Bind: Negotiating Relationships in Early Jewish and Christian Texts, Contexts, and Reception History* (2023), in honor of Adele Reinhartz.

Andrew J. Byers (PhD, Durham) serves as Lecturer in New Testament at Ridley Hall Cambridge and is an Affiliated Lecturer in the Faculty of Divinity at the University of Cambridge. He is the author of four books, including two monographs on the Johannine Literature: *Ecclesiology and Theosis in the Gospel of John* (2017) and *John and the Others* (2021). He has also coedited three books on early Christianity and theology and culture: *Gospel Reading and Reception in Early Christianity* (2022), *One God, One People* (2023), and *Religion, Theology, and Stranger Things* (2024).

Douglas Estes (PhD, University of Nottingham) is Associate Professor of Religion at New College of Florida. Douglas has written or edited fourteen books, including *The Tree of Life* (2020), and published more than fifty essays and articles in journals such as *Journal of Theological Studies* and *Catholic Biblical Quarterly*. His Johannine works include *The Temporal Mechanics of the Fourth Gospel* (2018), *The Questions of Jesus in John* (2012), and *How John Works* (with Ruth Sheridan, 2016). He most recently edited *Theology and Tolkien: Practical Theology* (2023).

Edward H. Gerber (PhD, University of Wales, Trinity Saint David) is University Chaplain and Director of Campus Ministries at Trinity Western University in Langley, British Columbia. He is author of *The Scriptural Tale in the Fourth Gospel: With Particular Reference to the Prologue and a Syncretic (Oral and Written) Poetics* (2016), along with a number of articles for *The Bulletin of Ecclesial Theology*.

Stan Harstine (PhD, Baylor University) is Professor of Religion at Friends University in Wichita, Kansas. He is the author of three books, *Reading John Through Johannine Lenses* (2022), *A History of the Two-Hundred-Year Scholarly Debate about the Purpose of the Prologue to the Gospel of John* (2015), and *Moses as a Character in the Fourth Gospel* (2002). Harstine serves as the Johannine literature editor for *Religious Studies Review* and just finished as the area editor for Christian origins for short reviews.

Wendy E. S. North (PhD, University of Bangor) is an Honorary Research Fellow of the Department of Theology and Religion at the University of Durham, UK. She is the author of three books. Recent publications include "Revelation in Johannine Perspective: On Seeing the Glory in John 1:14" in *The Scriptures in the Book of Revelation and Apocalyptic Literature: Essays in Honour of Steve Moyise*, ed. Susan Docherty and Steve Smith (2023).

George L. Parsenios (PhD, Yale University) is Archbishop Iakovos Professor of Theology at the Holy Cross Greek Orthodox School of Theology, where he has also served as Academic Dean. Prior to coming to Holy Cross, he was Professor of New Testament at Princeton Theological Seminary for twenty years. His research focuses on the interaction of early Christianity with the classical world, and he is the author of three books on the Gospel and Letters of John and several essays on New Testament themes. Parsenios is currently translating John Chrysostom's twelve *Catechetical Homilies* into English. He is a priest in the Greek Orthodox Metropolis of Boston.

Christopher A. Porter (PhD, Ridley College [ACT]) is working on the Fourth Gospel with a particular emphasis in the intersection of theology and psychology. Previously, he has worked in personal and social identity and memory research and in computational linguistics. Trained in Psychology at ANU, he naturally brings a Social Identity (Tajfel and Turner et al.) framework to the consideration of the biblical text and theology. His book, *Johannine Social Identity Formation after the Fall of the Jerusalem Temple: Negotiating Identity in Crisis* (2022), applied a historically embedded social identity analysis to a reading of the Fourth Gospel. Currently, he is working on an introduction to social identity theory; theological approaches to social identity formation in the Fourth Gospel; a reception history of the Christology of the Fourth Gospel; and narrative identity construction and Christian formation.

Tyler Smith (PhD, Yale University) has worked as a postdoctoral scholar at the University of Ottawa and the University of Salzburg. He is the author of *The Fourth Gospel and the Manufacture of Minds in Ancient Historiography, Biography, Romance, and Drama* (2019) and several articles on cognitive themes in ancient Jewish literature in such journals as the *Journal for the Study of the New Testament*, the *Journal of Religion and Culture*, the *Journal for the Study of the Pseudepigrapha*, the *Journal of Ancient Judaism*, and *Vetus Testamentum*.

Catrin H. Williams (PhD, University of Cambridge) is Professor of New Testament at the University of Wales Trinity Saint David, Lampeter, UK, and Research Fellow at the Department of Old and New Testament of the University of the Free State, Bloemfontein, South Africa. She has written and edited several books on the Gospel of John and is the coeditor of the forthcoming *T&T Clark Handbook of Johannine Studies*. Williams is also the current general editor of the SNTS Monograph Series (Cambridge University Press).

Ancient Sources Index

Hebrew Bible/Old Testament		12:3	114
		12:10 (LXX)	112
Genesis	72	12:13	73
1	54, 208	12:46 (LXX)	112, 172
1:1	126, 130	13:12	74
1:1 (LXX)	110, 122	14:4	66
1:1–5	53	14:18	66
2:7 (LXX)	110	14:19–20	74
2:27	31	15:1–18	67
16:5 (LXX)	206	15:8–10	73
27:35 (LXX)	72	15:24	115
28:10–21	72	16	115
28:12	112	16:2 (LXX)	115
33:22–30	72	16:4	115
		16:4 (LXX)	116
Exodus		16:4–30	191
3:12	73	16:8 (LXX)	115
3:13–15	73	16:12	66
4:8–9	73	16:15	115
4:13	73	16:15 (LXX)	116
6:7	66	17:3	115
4:17	73	17:4	73
4:28	73	20:12	19
4:30	73	31:13	73
5:22	73	33:18	125
7:3	73	33:22	125
7:3–5	73	34:6	125
7:5	66		
7:9	73	Leviticus	
7:17	66	26:4–13	67
7:27	66		
8:18	73	Numbers	
10:1–2	73	9:12 (LXX)	112
10:2	66	11:2 (LXX)	206
11:9–10	73	14:10	73

-251-

Numbers (*continued*)		Ruth	
14:11	73	4:16	206
14:22	73		
14:23	115	1 Samuel	
16:28	73	12:7–15	67
35:30	113	12:8	73
Deuteronomy		2 Samuel	
4:34	73	7:23	73
5:16	19	12:3 (LXX)	206
6:22	73	12:8 (LXX)	206
7:19	73		
11:3	73	1 Kings	
13:6–11	100	3:20 (LXX)	206
13:7 (LXX)	206	8	67
17:6	113	17:17–24 (LXX)	31
18:15	161	17:19 (LXX)	206
18:15–18	154	17:21 (LXX)	110
18:15–22	149, 159, 161	20:13	66
18:18	161	20:28	66
18:18–22	128		
18:19	161	1 Chronicles	
18:19–20	161	1–9	67
18:20	161	16:8–36	67
18:21–22	161		
19:15	113, 154	Ezra	
26:5a–10a	67	5:11–17	67
26:8	73		
28:46	73	Nehemiah	
29	67	9	67
29:2	73	9:10	73
32	67	9:11–12	74
32:6	73		
32:18b	73	Psalms	
28:54 (LXX)	206	21:19 (LXX)	112, 116
28:56 (LXX)	206	22:18	112, 116
29:6	66	22:19	138
32:39	140	34:19 (LXX)	112
34:11	73	35:19	112
		40:10 (LXX)	112, 116
Joshua		41:9	112, 116, 138
23:2–4	67	68:5 (LXX)	112
24	67	68:10 (LXX)	112
24:5	73	68:22 (LXX)	112, 124
24:7	74	69:4	112

69:9	112, 178	16	67
69:21	112, 124, 138	16:1–9	74
73:9	73	16:62	66
77:16 (LXX)	112	20	67
77:24 (LXX)	112, 115–16	20:5–9	73
77:43	73	20:20	66
78	67	20:26	66
78:13–14	74	20:38	66
78:16	112	20:42	66
78:24	112, 115	20:44	66
78:43–51	73	22:16	66
81:6 (LXX)	112	23	67
82	215	24:27	66
82:6	112	25:5	66
104	67	25:7	66
104:27	73	25:11	66
105	67, 74	25:17	66
105:26	73	26:6	66
117:25–26 (LXX)	112	28:22–23	66
117:26 (LXX)	112	28:26	66
118	112	29:6	66
118:25–26	112	29:9	66
118:26	112	29:21	66
134:9	73	30:8	66
135	67	30:19	66
136	67	30:25–26	66
		32:15	66
Lamentations		33:29	66
2:12 (LXX)	206	34:27	66
		35:4	66
Ezekiel		35:9	66
6:7	66	35:15	66
6:10	66	36:11	66
6:13–14	66	36:23	66
7:4	66	36:38	66
7:27	66	37:6	66
11:10	66	37:9 (LXX)	110
11:12	66	37:9–10	31
12:15–16	66	37:13	66
12:20	66	38:23	66
13:14	66	39:6	66
13:21	66	39:22	66
13:23	66	39:28	66
14:8	66		
15:7	66		

ANCIENT SOURCES INDEX

Isaiah
1:2	74
5:1–7	66
6:1	53
6:2 (LXX)	114
6:9–10	116
6:10	112, 114–15, 199
11:2	30
40	54
40–66	69
40:3	112, 116, 119, 129
41:4	140
42:1	31
43:10	140
43:13	140
45:3	66
45:4–12	74
46:4	140
48:12	140
49:22 (LXX)	206
49:23	66
52–53	112
52:13 (LXX)	115
53	199
53:1	112, 114
53:7	114
54:13	112
61:1	31
63:12	73
63:12–17	73

Jeremiah
2:2–9	67
2:26–27	74
39:20	73

Daniel
9:1–27	67

Hosea
2:2–3	74

Micah
6:4	73
7:15	73

Habakuk
3:1–16	67

Zechariah
9:9	112, 116, 138
12:10	112, 172

Malachi
3:1	129

Deuterocanonical Books

Judith
5	67

Wisdom of Solomon
10–19	67
10:16	73
10:17–18	74
11–19	73

Sirach
9:1	206
36:5	73
44–50	67
45:3	73

Baruch
2:11	73

1 Maccabees
2:50–61 [2:49–68]	67

1 Esdras
1:14	74

3 Maccabees
2:1–20	67
6:1–15	67

4 Maccabees
16:18–23	67
18:11–19	67

ANCIENT SOURCES INDEX

Pseudepigrapha

Apocalypse of Abraham
23–31 67

Apocalypse of Adam
1.5 69
1.12 69

Artapanus
3.27 73

Ascension of Isaiah
3.13–4.18 67

Assumption of Moses
1–10 67

2 Baruch
53–74 67

1 Enoch
85–90 .... 67, 69
98.24–27 74

2 Enoch
30.14 69

Ezekiel the Tragedian
1.224–6 73

4 Ezra
2.1–2 74
3–6 67
7.106–11 67

Joseph and Aseneth 69

Jannes and Jambres
3.8 73

Liber antiquitatum biblicarum
9.10b 73
9.16b 73
10.1 73

10.5 74
10.7 73
32.1–17 67

Testament of Moses
1–10 67

Testament of Levi
14–18 67
18.10 69
19.1 69

Testament of Solomon
25.4 73

Dead Sea Scrolls

1QS
I, 21–II, 6 67
III, 13–24 69

4Q422
III, 5–13 73

4Q504
1–2 67
IV, 5–14 67

CD
"The Exhortation" 67

Ancient Jewish Writers

Josephus, *Bellum judaicum*
5.8.4 67
5.9.4 .... 67, 73
6.2.1 67

Philo, *De praemiis et poenis*
11–56 67

Philo, *De virtutibus*
199–227 67
217 39

Philo, *Hypothetica*
 8.5.11–6.8 67

Philo, *Legum allegoriae*
 3.1 69
 3.54 69

New Testament

Matthew
 1:1–17 67
 3:13–17 30
 9:2–8 131
 14:22–27 . . . . 43, 131
 21:5 116
 21:33–46 67
 26:3 138
 26:57 138
 28:16–20 139

Mark
 1 150
 1:1 129
 1:2–6 129
 1:3 . . . . 116, 131
 1:7 131
 1:7–8 129
 1:8 131
 1:9–11 . . . . 30, 129
 1:10–11 131
 1:12–13 129
 1:14 150
 1:14–20 129
 1:16–20 151
 1:19–36 . . . . 160, 189
 1:21–33 156
 1:21–45 130
 1:24 140
 1:34 140
 2:1–4 137
 2:9 . . . . 131, 37
 2:9–11 137
 2:11 . . . . 73, 131
 2:12 131
 2:13–17 151
 2:23–28 . . . . 137, 156
 3:1–6 . . . . 137, 156
 3:11 140
 3:13–19 151
 4:12 116
 5:6–7 140
 6 145
 6:4 . . . . 133, 149
 6:15 151
 6:30–44 137
 6:32–8:30 . . . . 132, 38
 6:37 131
 6:41 137
 6:43 131
 6:44 131
 6:45 137
 6:45–52 . . . . 43, 131
 8 145
 8:1–10 137
 8:11–21 137
 8:29 140
 8:35 133
 9:2–8 151
 9:7 140
 9:12–13 151
 9:37 133
 11:1–10 . . . . 116, 138
 11:4 73
 11:15–17 133
 11:40 73
 12:1–12 67
 12:41 73
 14:3 132
 14:5 132
 14:12 133
 14:17–20 18
 14:18 . . . . 116, 133, 138
 14:22 137
 14:36 104
 14:40 19
 14:47 132
 14:49 132
 14:53–72 . . . . 18, 132
 14:54 . . . . 18, 132
 14:54–72 18

ANCIENT SOURCES INDEX

14:58	137	1:1–4	127
14:62	140	1:1–5	52, 125, 210
14:65	132	1:1–12	125
14:66	132	1:1–18	68–70, 203–17, 146, 196
14:67	132	1:2	209
14:68	132	1:3–5	130
14:69	132	1:4–5	130
14:70	18, 132	1:5	33, 130
14:71	132	1:6	196, 210
15:1	132, 133	1:6–8	17, 130, 148, 151, 210
15:2	132, 138	1:6–18	52
15:3	132	1:7	196
15:5	132	1:9	130
15:9	132	1:9–13	130
15:12	132	1:9–14	150, 210
15:13	132	1:10–13	157
15:15	132	1:11	98, 130
15:17	132	1:12	58, 106, 125, 215, 195
15:18	132	1:13	214–15
15:24	116, 138	1:14	9–10, 13, 17, 41, 53, 107, 130, 136, 140, 212–14
15:29	137		
15:33	20	1:14–17	125, 130
15:36	138	1:15	17, 56, 131, 148, 151, 210, 196
15:37	20	1:16	10, 107, 213
15:39	140	1:16–18	136, 150, 210
16:1	132	1:17	41, 110, 117
16:1–2	133	1:18	28, 53–54, 124, 130, 131, 136, 205–6
16:1–8	139		
		1:19	131
Luke		1:19–22	79–80
1:2	23, 140	1:19–23	196
3:21–22	30	1:19–28	151
5:1–10	21	1:19–32	196
5:17–26	131	1:19–34	123
9:10–17	132	1:19–36	189
20:9–18	67	1:19–42	148
23:2	102	1:19–12:15	111
23:49	19	1:19–12:36	123
24:36–53	139	1:23	110, 112, 116, 119, 123, 131
		1:27	131, 193
John		1:29	20, 21, 114, 151, 192
1	39, 72	1:29–34	193
1–9	110	1:30	131
1:1	53, 110, 117, 122, 126, 209	1:32	32, 151
1:1–2	130	1:32–33	30

ANCIENT SOURCES INDEX

John (*continued*)
1:32–34	131, 196
1:33	72, 192
1:34	192
1:35	20–22
1:35–39	211
1:35–40	13, 15–17
1:35–51	131, 151
1:36	17, 151
1:37–42	193
1:37–51	151, 196
1:38	15, 41, 192
1:39	16, 152
1:41	192
1:43	174
1:45	110, 119, 122, 126, 157, 161, 176, 191, 193
1:45–51	23
1:45–20:9	127
1:46	152
1:47	72
1:48	171
1:49	192
1:51	72, 112, 117
2:1	23, 174
2:1–11	133, 150
2:1–3:36	73
2:1–11:57	73
2:2–22	152
2:6	171
2:9–10	153
2:11	10, 73
2:12	174
2:13	133
2:13–16	133
2:17	50, 112, 119, 123, 126, 216
2:18	73
2:18–20	100
2:19	101, 136–37, 208
2:19–22	147
2:20	25, 102, 137
2:20–22	88
2:21–22	137, 178
2:22	66, 109, 123, 126, 139, 161, 177–79, 183, 206–8, 216
2:23	73, 135
3	28, 34
3:1–21	56
3:2	26, 33, 73, 100, 135, 192
3:3	25, 214
3:3–5	157
3:4	25
3:5–8	33
3:6–11	157
3:7	35, 100, 214
3:8	25, 29
3:9	33, 100
3:10	34, 98, 100
3:10–13	12
3:11	215
3:13	25
3:14	101, 110, 117, 176
3:15–18	157
3:16	26, 130–31, 136, 207
3:16–17	106
3:16–21	130, 136
3:17	25
3:18	130–31
3:18–21	158
3:19	160
3:19–21	157
3:22–30	151
3:24	135, 150
3:25–26	189
3:26	192
3:27–30	190
3:30	160
3:31–36	83–84, 162
3:32	158
3:33	158
3:34	29, 31, 32, 36, 73, 161
3:35	161
3:36	157
4	195
4:3	174
4:4–43	153
4:5–6	117
4:5–26	56
4:7–24	193
4:8	57

4:9	35, 50	5:16–17	158
4:11	25	5:16–18	100
4:12	26	5:18	137, 158, 161
4:19	96–97	5:19	158, 161
4:21	97	5:19–24	105
4:22	103	5:20	207, 151
4:22–24	34	5:21	161
4:23	36, 97	5:21–39	161
4:23–24	195	5:23	160, 161
4:25	34, 192	5:23–24	73
4:28	192	5:24	157, 160
4:28–29	34	5:28–29	135
4:29	193	5:30	73, 160
4:30	160	5:30–47	161
4:31	192	5:33–35	160
4:34	73, 124	5:34	106
4:39–42	34	5:36	124, 160
4:41–42	215	5:36–38	73, 157
4:42	35	5:37	205
4:43	174	5:37–39	159, 161
4:44	133, 149	5:38	160
4:46	23, 160, 174	5:39	66, 109, 118, 122, 126, 157
4:46–54	150	5:39–40	127
4:48	73	5:39–47	206
4:49–53	105, 153	5:41–44	215
4:50–53	56	5:44	157
4:53	161	5:45	110, 176
4:54	73	5:45–46	161
5	191, 196	5:46	110, 119, 125, 157, 206
5–10	156, 160	5:46–47	122
5:1	133, 174	5:47	109
5:1–7	137	6	116, 138, 145, 146, 149, 191
5:1–15	153	6:1	137
5:1–38	154	6:1–15	137
5:2	174	6:1–21	22
5:3	174	6:2	73, 135
5:5	171	6:4	133, 37
5:6	48	6:7	131
5:7	48	6:9–12	44
5:8	131, 37	6:10	131
5:9	131, 175	6:13	131
5:11	106, 131	6:14	73, 97
5:13	137	6:15	42, 109, 137
5:14	137, 174	6:15–21	43
5:16	73	6:16–17	42

John (*continued*)
6:16–21	131
6:16–24	50
6:18–19	42
6:19	55
6:21	43
6:25	192
6:25–59	121
6:26	25, 73, 160
6:27	156
6:29	73, 160
6:30	73, 160
6:30–31	125
6:30–32	126
6:30–33	117
6:31	112–13, 115–16, 119, 123
6:31–32	161
6:32	110, 126, 176
6:32–33	116
6:35	140
6:36	91
6:38	116, 160
6:38–39	73
6:39	135
6:39–40	160
6:40	91, 135, 157
6:41	115, 117
6:42	26, 96, 102
6:43	115, 117
6:44	73, 135
6:45	110, 112, 119, 123
6:47	157
6:48	140
6:49	115
6:52–58	138
6:53–58	135
6:54	135
6:57	73, 160
6:60	157
6:63	29, 32, 33, 36
6:66	157
6:68	146
6:69	215
6:70–71	135, 38
7	28, 191
7:1	73, 161
7:2	133
7:3–10	105
7:7	158, 216
7:8	25
7:13	100
7:15	96, 98, 109, 215
7:16	73, 160
7:18	73, 157, 215
7:19	110, 176
7:19–25	161
7:21–31	153
7:22	110
7:23	73, 110
7:26–31	192
7:27	102, 157
7:28	161
7:28–29	26, 73
7:29	157
7:30	73
7:30–31	160
7:31	73
7:33	73
7:35	26
7:37–39	29, 39, 193
7:38	21, 66, 109, 112–13, 115, 119
7:39	41, 161, 88
7:40	97
7:42	66, 102, 109, 111, 119
7:44	73
7:45–52	56
7:47–49	100
7:49	110
7:51	100–101, 110
8	28, 198, 176
8:12	140, 157
8:13	98, 161
8:14	157
8:14–18	161
8:15–16	161
8:16	73, 160, 161
8:17	110–11, 113, 154
8:18	73
8:19	157
8:20	73

8:22	26	9:39–41	99
8:24	140	9:40	26
8:26	73, 160	9:41	157
8:28	101, 160–61	10	121
8:29	73, 160	10:1–21	121
8:31	177	10:10	163
8:32	157, 162	10:11	136, 140
8:33	25, 96, 176	10:12	99
8:37	161	10:12–13	99
8:38	161	10:14	140
8:39	177	10:14–15	215
8:39–40	98	10:15	28, 136
8:40	73	10:16	117
8:42	73, 160	10:17	107, 136
8:44	177	10:17–19	105
8:45–46	157	10:18	161
8:47	157	10:22	133
8:53	96	10:22–30	121
8:55	157	10:25	150, 161
8:56	125	10:25–30	98
8:58	140	10:26	157
8:59	73, 105, 162, 177	10:30	137
9	32, 215	10:31	73
9:2	192	10:31–39	100
9:2–3	137	10:32	161
9:3	97, 98	10:33	162
9:4	73, 160	10:34	110, 112, 119, 123, 215
9:5	140, 157	10:35	109, 124, 192
9:7	105	10:36	73
9:8–12	56	10:39	73
9:9	98, 215	10:40	73
9:13–34	56, 98	10:41	73
9:16	73	11	36
9:17	97	11:1–44	133
9:18	98	11:5	207
9:22	98, 100	11:6	105
9:24	26, 98, 157	11:8	192
9:25	98, 153	11:9	157
9:27	98	11:11–12	25
9:28	110, 157	11:14	161
9:29	110	11:24	25
9:31–34	98	11:25	140
9:34	98	11:25–26	157
9:36	98	11:27	192, 153
9:39	160	11:28–31	56

John (*continued*)

11:33	29, 32
11:40	10
11:42	73, 105
11:43	105
11:45	10, 153
11:47	73, 101, 160
11:47–53	56
11:48	157
11:48–50	26
11:49	101, 138
11:52	130
11:53	73
11:54	73
12	116, 179
12:1	133
12:1–8	132
12:3	132
12:5	132
12:7	132
12:9	161
12:9–11	153
12:10	73
12:12–15	115
12:13	112, 115
12:13–16	123
12:14	119, 123
12:15	112, 115–16, 138
12:16	88, 126, 139, 152, 178–79, 216
12:18	73
12:19	26, 177
12:23	123
12:24	97
12:25	133
12:27	29, 104, 135, 161
12:28	154
12:32	101
12:33	161
12:34	96, 110–11
12:35	130, 157
12:37	73
12:37–43	199, 215
12:38	112, 114–15, 123
12:38–41	110, 123
12:39	112
12:40	112, 114–16
12:41	114–15, 117, 125
12:43	98, 157
12:44	160
12:44–45	73
12:44–50	162
12:45–46	157
12:46	157
12:47	106
12:48	160
12:49	73
12:49–50	161
13	36
13:1	25, 207
13:3–11	134
13:11	161
13:18	109, 112, 114–16, 123, 138
13:18–19	21
13:19	140, 161
13:20	73, 133
13:21	29, 32, 133
13:21–26	18
13:21–30	138
13:23	13–15, 22, 41, 104, 139, 206
13:23–26	13–15, 17, 19, 21
13:23–28	211
13:25	14
13:25–29	21
13:28	207
13:31	105
13:34–35	153
13:35	216
13:38	21
14–16	37
14:1	29
14:2	216
14:5–8	25
14:6	211, 157
14:7	157
14:11	160
14:15	135
14:16	153
14:16–17	37–38
14:17	155, 157
14:24	73

14:24–26	180	18:5–6	140
14:25–26	38	18:9	126
14:26	29, 135, 153, 155, 216	18:10	18, 132
14:27	29	18:11	104, 135
14:30–31	82–83	18:13–14	138
15–17	146, 153	18:13–27	132
15:1–8	147	18:15	15, 16, 18
15:1–11	121	18:15–16	13, 15–16, 18, 22, 211
15:10	105	18:15–18	104
15:13	107, 136	18:15–27	18
15:20	86–87, 126	18:15–28	18–19
15:21	25, 73, 157, 207	18:17–18	18
15:25	110, 112, 123	18:18	18, 20, 132
15:26	38, 135, 153, 155, 157	18:19–23	18
15:26–27	87, 161	18:20	53, 132
15:27	11, 15, 17, 22–23	18:22	132
16:2	98	18:24	18, 138
16:4	87, 126	18:25	132
16:5	73	18:25–27	18, 21
16:7	101, 153	18:26	18
16:7–8	38	18:27	132
16:7–15	135	18:28	18, 132–33, 138
16:8	155	18:29	132
16:13	157, 216	18:30	101, 132
16:13–14	38	18:31	110
16:16–33	161	18:32	126, 161
16:33	101	18:33	132, 138
17:3	73	18:33–38	56
17:4	105, 124	18:34–37	138
17:5	215	18:34–40	100
17:6–21	153	18:36	138
17:8	73, 105	18:36–37	157
17:12	66, 109, 111, 123	18:37	132, 138, 162
17:14	105	18:38	157
17:17	157	18:38–19:16	98
17:18	73	18:39	132
17:21	73	18:40	132
17:22	215	19	126–27
17:23	73	19:2	132
17:24	105	19:3	26, 132
17:25	28, 73, 157	19:7	100, 101, 110, 192
17:26	207	19:9	132
18	36	19:14	26
18–19	155	19:15	102, 162
18:4	193	19:16	132

John (*continued*)
- 19:19–22 — 127
- 19:21 — 11, 101
- 19:22 — 26
- 19:24 — 66, 109, 112, 116, 119, 123, 138
- 19:25 — 20
- 19:25–26 — 13
- 19:25–27 — 211
- 19:26 — 14–15, 139
- 19:26–27 — 14–16, 18, 20–22, 104
- 19:28 — 19–21, 66, 109, 111–12, 124, 127, 193
- 19:28–29 — 138
- 19:29 — 20
- 19:30 — 20, 25, 31, 32, 72, 124
- 19:31 — 133
- 19:32–36 — 21
- 19:34 — 20, 21
- 19:34–35 — 144, 152
- 19:35 — 2, 13, 16–17, 20–22, 41, 50, 55, 84, 120, 172, 211–12
- 19:35–37 — 21, 211
- 19:36 — 109, 112, 115, 123, 212
- 19:36–37 — 20–21, 66
- 19:37 — 109, 112, 114–15, 119
- 19:38 — 100
- 19:38–42 — 56, 132
- 20 — 32, 36, 70, 90, 195
- 20:1–2 — 133
- 20:2 — 14–16, 135, 139
- 20:2–10 — 13–14, 20, 211
- 20:3 — 14
- 20:4 — 14
- 20:5 — 212
- 20:6 — 16
- 20:6–7 — 21
- 20:8 — 10, 14, 20–21, 173, 212
- 20:8–9 — 139
- 20:9 — 21, 36, 66, 109, 126, 212
- 20:10 — 152
- 20:11–18 — 56, 153
- 20:17 — 19
- 20:18 — 10
- 20:19 — 43, 100
- 20:19–29 — 139
- 20:21 — 73
- 20:21–22 — 31–32
- 20:21–23 — 155
- 20:22 — 31, 32, 39, 72, 110, 117, 195
- 20:22–23 — 214
- 20:24 — 135
- 20:25 — 10, 152
- 20:26 — 43
- 20:28 — 152
- 20:29 — 10, 20, 91, 139, 148, 160
- 20:30 — 11, 59, 126, 192
- 20:30–31 — 10, 90, 93, 106, 127, 134–35, 141, 143, 207, 209, 197
- 20:31 — 16, 36, 48, 120, 127, 134, 146, 157, 182
- 21 — 10, 36, 54, 146
- 21:1–23 — 10
- 21:2 — 13–14, 23
- 21:2–8 — 210
- 21:3 — 171
- 21:3–6 — 21
- 21:5–6 — 21
- 21:7 — 13–14, 21, 152
- 21:11 — 171
- 21:18–23 — 54
- 21:19 — 161
- 21:20 — 14–15
- 21:20–23 — 15–16
- 21:20–24 — 13, 144
- 21:21–23 — 12
- 21:21–25 — 211
- 21:22 — 16
- 21:22–23 — 11
- 21:24 — 1–2, 10–13, 15–17, 22, 37, 120, 127, 172–73, 213
- 21:24–25 — 10, 12, 127, 213
- 21:25 — 12, 50, 59, 127, 213

Acts
- 1:21–22 — 23
- 5:15 — 131
- 7 — 67
- 7:35 — 73
- 7:36 — 73
- 8:4–40 — 152

8:39	44	Greco-Roman Literature	
9:33	131		
13:16–41	67	Aelius Theon, *Progymnasmata*	
19:2–7	190	62	114
21:20–22	152	108	114

Romans
- 6:15–23   198
- 8:12–17   198
- 9   199
- 9–11   67
- 10:5–13   199
- 10:16–17   199

Ephesians
- 5:1   198
- 5:6–8   198
- 5:15   198

Hebrews
- 6:45   106
- 11:1–12:2   67
- 11:29   74

1 John
- 1:1–3   150
- 1:1–5   12, 150
- 2:3–5   30
- 4:9   131
- 4:11–16   12

2 John
- 9   147

3 John
- 9–12   12

Revelation
- 4:1–2   53
- 12:1–12   67
- 21:18   42

Rabbinic Works

Song of Songs Targum   67

Aeschylus, *Choephoroi*
- 168–178   82

Aeschylus, *Eumenides*
- 29   83

Aristotle, *De anima*
- 424b22–435b25   45
- 428a   45
- 428a16–18   41

Aristotle, *Ethica Eudemia*
- 1241a5–10   106

Aristotle, *Ethica Nicomachea*
- 1096a23   105
- 1102b38   104
- 1104a8–9   105
- 1104a14   105
- 1144a29–30   105
- 1147   100
- 1147a8   101
- 1166b5–29   102
- 1378a6   106

Aristotle, *De memoria et reminiscentia*
- 451b   167

Aristotle, *Rhetorica*
- 1358b   98
- 1378a112   103

Cicero, *De inventione rhetorica*
- 1.19   5

Diogenes Laertius, *Vitae philosophorum*
- 3.50   85

Longinus, *On the Sublime*
  15 — 46

Menander, *Rhetor*
  1.361.17–25 — 105

Pausanias, *Description of Greece* — 200

Philostratus, *Vita Apollonii*
  6.19 — 54

Plato, *Gorgias*
  486a–b — 89

Plato, *Meno*
  94d — 89
  95a — 89

Plato, *Phaedo*
  72e–78b — 86

Plato, *Phaedrus*
  261d–262d — 103
  271c — 103

Plato, *Respublica*
  392d — 79
  394b–c — 79
  517a — 88–89

Plato, *Sophista*
  264a — 45
  266d–267e — 51

Plato, *Symposium*
  172–74 — 90

Plato, *Theatetus*
  143a–c — 78, 85–88
  163d — 86–88
  191d–e — 165
  210d — 89

Quintilian, *Institutio oratoria*
  2.4.5 — 106
  2.5.18 — 106
  6.2.26–31 — 56
  6.2.29–30 — 45
  9.2.71 — 121

Rhetorica ad Herennium
  4.39.51 — 46

Thucydides, *History of the Peloponnesian War*
  3.113 — 80–81
  5.85–113 — 80–81

Early Christian Writings

Augustine, *Confessionum libri XIII*
  10.8 — 51
  10.8.12 — 165
  10.9.16 — 165
  10.11.18 — 165
  10.25.36 — 166

Modern Authors Index

Abelson, Robert P. 169
Adams, Sean A. 115
Albl, Martin C. 116
Alkier, Stefan 67
Allen, David 118
Allison, Dale C., Jr 44, 121
Altes, Liesbath Korthals 100
Anderson, Paul N. 2, 48, 116, 133, 143–63
Anderson, Tory S. 51
Antovic, Mihailo 61
Ashton, John 87, 148
Asiedu-Paprah, Martin 143
Asma, Stephen T. 49
Attridge, Harold W. 77, 134
Audi, Robert 3
Augoustinos, Martha 168
Aune, David 84
Bailey, Kenneth 67
Bakhtin, Mikhail 150
Barrett, C.K. 43, 89, 116, 210, 132–34, 138, 144, 147,
Bauckham, Richard 2, 9–12, 16–17, 19, 70, 84, 111, 114, 172, 202, 207, 211–13
Beck, David R. 204
Becker, Eve-Marie 140
Becker, Michael 38
Bekken, Per Jarle 94
Bennema, Cornelis 19, 27, 28, 195
Berlin, Adele 61
Bernecker, Sven 3
Beutler, Johannes 126–27, 132
Billig, Michael 177
Black, C. Clifton 127
Boccaccini, Gabriele 152
Boer, Roland 48
Boice, James Montgomery 150
Bond, Helen K. 138
Booth, Wayne C. 54, 56, 94, 188, 202
Borgen, Peder 117, 148
Bowen, Clayton R. 196
Boyarin, Daniel 69
Brant, Jo-Ann 201
Brendsel, Daniel J. 112
Brettler, Marc Zvi 69
Brodie, Thomas L. 60, 67
Brooke, George J. 66, 69
Brown, Raymond E. 55, 83, 134, 146, 213
Brown, Sherri 26
Brown, Tricia Gates 27
Bruner, Jerome 47, 169
Brunson, Andrew C. 112
Buch-Hansen, Gitte 27, 28
Bühner, Jan-Adolf 70
Bulloch, Anthony W. 46
Bultmann, Rudolf 43, 144, 156, 203
Bunzl, Martin 5
Burge, Gary M. 27
Burridge, Richard A. 26
Butticaz, Simon 52
Byers, Andrew J. 209, 215
Bynum, William Randolph 112, 123
Calhoun, Robert Matthew 150
Cánovas, Cristóbal 61
Carignan, Michael I. 5
Carleton Paget, James 121
Carson, D.A. 66, 146, 213
Carter, Warren 203
Casey, Maurice 5, 115

Charlesworth, James 52
Charteris-Black, Jonathan 99
Chatman, Seymour 179, 203, 204
Chennatu, Rekha M. 204
Chester, Andrew 66
Clarke, Andrew D. 13
Clay, Diskin 84–89
Collins, John J. 41
Condit, Celeste M. 102
Connerton, Paul 65
Connick, C. Milo 25
Comer, Christopher 47, 51
Coote, Robert B. 119
Corrigan, Kevin 41
Coste, Didier 51
Crawford, Sidnie W. 66
Cribbs, F. Lamar 146
Cross, F.L. 49
Crossley, James 115
Culpepper, R. Alan 5, 115–16, 127, 143, 149, 150, 171, 187, 189, 195, 198, 202, 207, 212
Daise, Michael A. 113–14, 123
Daly-Denton, Margaret 111–12
Danto, Arthur C. 5, 51
Davis, Ellen F. 147
Day, John 69
DeBoer, Martin C. 117, 127
De Brigard, Felipe 51
Deslauriers, Marguerite 45
Dietzfelbinger, Christian 124
Dillon, John M. 46
Dockery, David S. 186
Dodd, C.H. 69, 77, 145
Dorter, Kenneth 85
Draper, Jonathan A. 67
Dray, William H. 57
Duke, Paul 26
Dunderberg, Ismo 204
Eco, Umberto 170
Edwards, Ruth B. 130
Ego, Beate 69
Ehorn, Seth M. 115
Ellens, J. Harold 159
Engbert-Pedersen 77, 187, 198

Engmann, Joyce 45
Estes, Douglas 1, 6, 45, 46, 48, 50, 52, 53, 81, 171
Evans, Craig A. 123
Falcetta, Alessandro 116
Festinger, Leon 159
Finlayson, Mark A. 51
Flower, Linda 103
Foley, John Miles 59–65
Forger, Deborah 128
Fornara, Charles 84
Fortna, Robert T. 148
Freed, Edwin D. 113
Frey, Jörg 52, 77, 88, 120, 124, 135–36, 210
Fumerton, Richard 2, 3
Furlong, Dean 202
Gardner-Smith, Percival 145
Genette, Gérard 50
Gerber, Edward H. 60, 69, 71–72, 74
Gese, Hartmut 70
Goldstein, Leon J. 2
Goodwin, Charles 113
Grethlein, Jonas 4
Halbwachs, Maurice 175
Halperin, David 89–90
Hankinson, R.J. 45
Harnack, Adolf von 203
Harris, Elizabeth 68, 203
Harris, William V. 61
Harstine, Stan 190, 195
Hatina, Thomas R. 115, 126, 143
Haslam, S. Alexander 182
Hays, Richard B. 67, 112, 147, 208
Head, Peter M. 13
Hearon, Holly 119
Hengel, Martin 69, 110, 124–25
Hezser, Catherine 61
Hirsch-Luipold, Rainer 49, 77
Hoenig, D. Bernard 175
Hogan, Patrick Colm 63
Hood, Jason B. 67
Hooker, Morna D. 68, 203
Hornblower, Simon 81
Horsley, Richard 62, 67

MODERN AUTHORS INDEX

Hoskyns, Edwyn Clement	68	Lindemann, Mary	4
Huber, David E.	167	Loader, William R. G.	162
Hübner, Hans	117, 124	Long, A.A.	46
Huizinga, Leroy A.	67–68	Lord, Albert B.	62–64
Hunt, Steven A.	144	Lührmann, Dieter	198
Hylen, Susan E.	35, 118, 207	Luther, Susanne	48, 126, 139–40
Hymes, Dell	71	Lyman, Mary Redington Ely	28
Instone-Brewer, David	13	Kee, Howard Clark	28
Jackson, Howard M.	12	Keener, Craig	23
Jang, Sehoon	53	Kind, Amy	45
Jodrey, Lindsey S.	121	Koet, Bart J.	49
Johnston, George	27	MacKay, Ian D.	146
Jonge, Marinus de	192	MacRae, G.W.	26
Juhasz, Joseph B.	45	Malina, Bruce J.	203
Kahn, Charles	85	Manning, Gary T.	117
Keener, Craig S.	173, 175, 178, 187, 207	Mauser, Ulrich W.	73
Keith, Chris	127, 204	McAdams, Dan P.	181
Kelber, Werner	61	McLean, Kate C.	181
Kellog, Robert	64	McIver, Robert K.	167
Kennedy, Joel	67	Meeks, Wayne	97
Kincade, M. Dale	71	Menken, Maarten J.J.	111–14, 124, 127
Kirk, Alan	52, 65, 168	Merz, Annette	2
Klink, Edward W., III	171	Metzger, Bruce M.	131
Köstenberger, Andreas J.	12, 151	Meyer, Michel	95
Koester, Craig R.	120, 171	Misztal, Barbara A.	194
Krans, Jan	127	Mlakuzyil, George	60, 71
Kraus, Wolfgang	109, 124	Modrak, Deborah K.W.	45
Krauter, Stefan	120	Moessner, David P.	150
Kubiš, Adam	112	Moloney. Francis J.	126, 134, 139
Kysar, Robert	49, 68	Mooij, J.J.A.	58
Labahn, Michael	113, 119, 126–27, 178	Morley, Neville	52, 57
Lampinen, James Michael	167	Mosser, Carl	70
Lang, Armin	69	Moyise, Steve	112–13, 115
Larsen, Brian	58	Munslow, Alan	1, 5
Larsen, Kasper Bro	30, 52	Myers, Alicia D.	111–14, 121–23, 125, 205
Le Donne, Anthony	118–19		
León, Carlos	169	Nagy, Gregory	46
Lee, Dorothy	48	Neirynck, Frans	211
Leonhardt-Balzer, Jutta	117	Newbigin, Lesslie	68
Levine, Amy-Jill	69	Neyrey, Jerone H.	28, 94, 97, 103, 104, 105
Lichtenberger, Hermann	120, 124	Nicklas, Tobias	150
Lieu, Judith M.	115, 117, 123	Norelli, Enrico	52
Lincoln, Andrew T.	37, 39, 94, 132–35, 143, 172–73, 211, 213	North, James L.	115
		North, Wendy E.S.	139
Lindars, Barnabas	53, 146	Novenson, Matthew V.	193

… MODERN AUTHORS INDEX

Obermann, Andreas 109, 111, 123, 128
O'Day, Gail R. 212
Odegard, Timothy N. 167
O'Grady, John F. 203
Oliver, Mary Beth 95
Ong, Hughson T. 147
Palmén, Ritva 42
Painter, John 28
Parry, Milman 62
Pascal, Blaise 75
Parsenios, George L. 39, 78, 83, 86, 94, 143
Pastorelli, David 27
Penwill, J. L. 84
Pettersson, Bo 51, 57
Phillips, G.L. 49
Philips, Peter M. 209
Pilhofer, Peter 69
Pioske, Daniel D. 168, 175
Platow, Michael J. 182
Porter, Christopher A. 175
Porter, Stanley E. 147
Potterie, Ignace de la 28
Pratt, Jonathan 94
Quick, Catherine 66
Rabinoff, Eva 104, 105
Rand, Jan A. du 196
Ranke, Leopold von 4
Rapley, Mark 182
Reicher, Stephen D. 182
Reinhartz, Adele 35, 42, 52, 103, 106, 203
Reinsdorf, Walter 48
Resseguie, James L. 188, 201, 202
Reynolds, Benjamin 152
Richards, I.A. 44
Riches, John K. 158
Ricoeur, Paul 51, 181
Ritivoi, Andreea Deciu 102
Roark, Tony 45
Robbins, Vernon K. 60
Robinson, Alan 55
Roberts, Geoffrey 65
Rodríguez, Rafael 119
Roediger III, Henry L. 166
Rohrbaugh, Richard L. 203
Russell, D.S. 192
Ryan, Marie-Laure 54
Schandorf, Michael 102
Schank, Roger C. 169
Schaper, Joachim 121
Schiffman, Lawrence H. 66
Schinkel, Anders 51
Schnackenburg, Rudolf 68, 72, 180
Scholtissek, Klaus 126
Schuchard, Bruce G. 112–13, 123, 125
Schulz, Siegfried 43
Schwartz, Barry 125
Sheridan, Ruth 1, 6, 50, 111, 113–14, 122
Shively, Elizabeth E. 54, 58
Skinner, Christopher W. 26
Singer, Jefferson A. 181
Sipiora, Phillip 105
Smith, D. Moody 127, 133, 135, 210
Smith, Ole 83
Smith, Steve 118
Smith, Tyler 26
Sosa Siliezar, Carlos R. 110
Staley, Jeffrey Lloyd 189
Steinberg, Meir 207
Stibbe, Mark W.G. 26, 51, 52, 58
Strotmann, Angelika 126
Squire, Michael 46
Szilas, Nicolas 169
Taggart, Ashley 47, 51
Thatcher, Tom 48, 52, 65, 118–19, 121, 125, 148, 151, 168, 174–75, 180, 202
Theissen, Gerd 2
Theobald, Michael 80, 124
Tholuck, Augustus 44
Thompson, Glen L. 200
Thompson, Marianne Meye 28, 88, 162, 205
Tieleman, Teun 28
Tilborg, Sjef van 19
Tolmie, D. Francois 144, 152
Tov, Emanuel 66
Tuckett, Christopher M. 124
Underhill, Evelyn 186

VanderKam, James C.	66
Vansina, Jan	71
Veyne, Paul	52, 58
Wahlde, Urban C. von	195
Waetjen, Herman C.	70
Walker, Jeffrey	94
Waltke, Bruce K.	71
Wang, Sunny Kuan-Hui	49
Watkin, Christopher	181
Watson, Francis	138–39
Watson, Gerard	44, 45, 46, 54
Watt, Jan G. van der	77, 150
Watts, Rikki E.	67
Wead, David W.	143
Webb, Ruth	45, 56, 57, 58
White, Hayden	5, 52, 65
Weissenrieder, Annette	119
Wiarda, Timothy	171
Wieringen, Archibald L. H. M. van	49, 53
Wiget, Andrew	71
Williams, Catrin H.	112, 115–16, 118, 121, 125, 175–76, 206
Williams, P.J.	13, 196
Williamson, H. G. M.	66
Wilson, Mark	200
Wise, Jennifer	82
Yates, Frances A.	51
Zimmermann, Ruben	57, 144
Zumstein, Jean	43
Zunshine, Lisa	100

Subject Index

abide, abiding, 143, 147, 155, 157–58
Abraham, 72, 125
actants, 150, 152
Acts, 131, 140, 145–46, 152, 156
Adam and Eve, 68–70
agency, 148–49, 153–55, 157, 159, 161
akrasia, 100–102
alien, 47
ambiguity, 25, 30–31, 32, 35, 39–40, 118, 120–21
anagnorisis, 30, 33, 34–35
ancient media, 113, 118
Andrew, disciple of Jesus, 17, 23, 151–52, 188–90, 193, 196
angel, 47
annal, 1, 4, 6
appendix, Johannine, 10, 146
apocalypse, 41–42, 58
Apollonius of Tyana, 54
aposynagōgos, 98, 103
Aquinas, Thomas, 53
Aristotle, 45, 94, 102–5, 167
atomism, 3
audience, 25, 30, 36, 40, 52, 93–97, 106–7, 111, 118–22, 143, 149–50, 156, 160
author, 11–12, 14–15 146. *See also* John, implied author
  eyewitness, 9, 15, 21, 23, 146–47, 152
  ideal, 19
  mind of, 6
  we (authorial), 12
baptism, 30, 35
belief, believing, 126–27, 143, 146, 148, 150–53, 155, 157–58, 160, 162–63, 208–9, 212, 215–16

believers, 19, 150, 153, 156–57, 160, 162–63
Beloved Disciple, 9, 11–21, 36, 40, 50–51, 53–57, 104, 147, 152, 154, 172–73, 188, 195, 202–4, 211, 213
Bethel 72
blasphemy, 102, 105, 157, 161–62
blind man, 36, 98, 153, 156
bones
  dry, 110
  unbroken, 112
bread, heavenly, 115–16, 121, 125–26, 149
Caiaphas, 18, 101
Callimachus, 46
Cana, of Galilee, 22–23
canon, 112
Capernaum, 42
character, 12–15, 48, 57, 144, 147, 149–50, 152
characterization, 143
chief priests, 56, 56, 100–102
Christ, 143, 146, 151–52, 162, 192
Christianity, Johannine, 154
Christology, 113, 120, 144–50, 152, 156, 159, 162
chronicle, 1, 4, 6
Churchill, Winston, 182
commandments, 110, 159
continuum, 3
courtroom motif. *See* legal motif
creation, 53–55, 110
Dead Sea Scrolls, 116
desert, 115
dialogical autonomy, John's, 144–49

SUBJECT INDEX

dialogism, 147–48
dialogue, 25, 48, 56, 144, 147–50
   intertraditional, 146, 148
   intratraditional, 147
Dickens, Charles, 97
diegesis, 50
disciples, 11, 21–23, 29, 31–32, 36, 38, 39, 50, 53–55, 57, 98, 99, 110, 129, 131, 134–35, 139, 147–48, 151–56
   anonymous, 13–19
   female, 21, 153–54
   ideal, 19
   witnesses, as, 21, 32, 105, 106
divine presence, 10
divinization, 214–15
double entendre, 12, 35
dream, 45
earwitness, 56–57
ēgapa, 14
ekphrasis, 46
Elder/Presbyter, the Johannine, 146–47
Elijah, 31, 110, 151–52, 160
enargeia, 46
encomium, 103–4
empiricism, 4
ephilei, 14
epilogue. *See* appendix
epistemology, 1–4, 6, 150
   authority, 99, 100–102, 110, 119, 122, 127, 154–56, 159
   belief, 3, 29, 35, 37, 93, 98, 143, 146, 148, 150–53, 155, 157–58, 160, 162–63. *See also* trust
   certainty, 93, 99
   convictions, 94–95
   confusion, 35, 102
   convention, 102
exegetical, 204–8
experience, 3, 44–45, 47
   knowledge of God, 28
   limited, 55
   memory, 3
   misunderstanding, 25, 33
   narrative, 2, 25–26, 28, 143–53, 155, 162

experience (*continued*)
   opinion, 3
   propositional, 2
   reason, 3
   social, 93, 99, 107
   visual, 45–48, 51
ethics, 26
eunoia, 103, 106–7
Evangelist, Fourth. *See* John
event, 6, 21–23, 47–49, 55–58. *See also* scene
exegetical techniques, Jewish, 113–14, 116–17, 119
experience, virtual, 57
expulsion theory. *See aposynagōgos*
eyewitness, 9–24, 56–57, 144, 147, 152
Exodus, book of, 172
exodus, the, 113
Ezekiel, 31, 110
faith, 143, 148–50, 156, 198
Farewell Discourse, 207, 211
fast travel, 43
Father (God) 148–49, 153–62
fear, 43, 98, 100, 101, 103
fiction. *See* story
figurative language, 25, 53
folkloric features, 144–45
frank speech. *See parrhesia*
fulfilled word, 143, 149, 155
future, the, 54
Galilee, 22–23, 154, 159
Genesis, book of, 112
genre, 41
   micro-genre, 55
gezerah shawah, 116
glorification, 115, 123
glory, glorify, 10, 53–54, 97, 114, 125, 153–55, 157
   in creation and fall, 69–70
God, 53, 105, 130, 135–36, 140, 143, 148, 150–52, 155–62
golden house, 42, 47
gospel. *See also* Mark, Gospel of
   compiler/editor/redactor, 4, 144
   source, 4, 6, 144–46, 158

gospel (*continued*)
  writer, 3–4, 6
grace and truth, 125
group, 42, 50, 57
hearing, 35
hearers, 143, 149, 156
Hebrew, 113–14
Hegel, Georg, 51
historical, 144–45, 151
historical present, 55–56
historiography, 12, 24, 44, 49–52
history, 5, 42
  neutral, 4–5, 49
  objective, 5
  product of imagination, as, 58
  raw, 6
  storytelling, and, 24
humility, 30
hyperbole, 50, 96
ideal orator, 56–57
identity
  narrative identity, 180–82
  personal, 181–82
  social, 181
image
  digital, 43
  meaningful, 47–49
  productions of, 46
imagination, 41–58, 99, 149
  ability to see God, 53, 54
  author-derived, 47–49, 54, 57
  creative, 45–47
  expressive, 45–47
  fantasy, as, 44–45, 47
impossibility, as, 43–44, 47, 48
  memory, versus, 51
  negative perception of, 41, 44
  reader-focused, 47–49
  types of, 44
  visualization, as, 42–47, 49–51, 53, 57–58
imagining, 49, 104
imitation. *See* mimesis
implied author, 36–37, 43, 47–49, 57–58, 188, 202–17

inclusio, 13–15, 17, 123
interfluentiality, 145–46
intertextuality, 118
invalid, 48
irony, 26, 34
Isaac, 72
Isaiah, 110, 112, 114, 119, 123, 125
Israel, 69–70, 117, 124–25, 152, 157
Israelites, 115
  murmuring, 115
Jacob, 72
Jerusalem, 22, 148, 151–56, 158–59
Jesus, 42–43, 48, 50, 53–55, 57, 109–11, 120–26, 129–40, 143–62
  authority, 102, 104, 107
  image of, 43
  messianic identity, 31, 34, 37, 93, 102
  metaphoric identity, 96, 99, 104, 106
  prophetic attribution, 96–97
  risen, 21
  Son of God, 95, 104, 129–31, 136, 143
Jews, the, 28, 35–36, 100, 215
Johannine community, 10
John, the evangelist, 6, 56, 144–47, 160–62
John, Gospel of, 129–41, 144–63
John the Baptist, 12, 17, 30, 39, 40 56, 119, 129–30, 148–52, 156, 161, 188–90, 193, 196, 203–4, 206, 210, 211
  testimony of, 20, 148–52
Joseph of Nazareth, 122
Joseph of Arimathea, 56
Josephus, Flavius, 12
Judaism, 101, 158
  appropriation, 103
  dissociation from, 98–99
  parting of the ways, 93, 103
Judea, 148, 158–59
knowing. *See* epistemology
lamb, 114
  of God, 21
  of Passover, 20
law, the, 110, 112
Lazarus, 23, 152–53
Lee, Harper, 97

legal motif, 37–39
life, eternal, 29, 110, 113, 127, 148, 157, 162–63
literacy, 60–61
logical fallacy, 100–101
Logos, 69–70, 150. *See also* Word
Longinus, 46
love, 136, 139, 150, 152–53, 157, 162, 206–7
Luke, Gospel of, 131–32, 134, 138–40, 146, 148
manna, 115–16
Mark, Gospel of, 54, 17–20, 22, 129–34, 136–41, 145–52, 156
Martha of Bethany, 23, 36, 56
Mary of Bethany, 23, 36, 56, 132
Mary Magdalene, 20, 56, 135, 153–54
Mary, mother of Jesus, 19, 154
Masoretic Text, 113
Matthew, Gospel of, 131, 134, 138–40, 146
media, 59–60
memory/memories, 3, 24, 51, 57, 113, 121, 144–45, 155
 keying and framing, 125–26
memory, social, 121, 125, 168–69
memory, narrative 169–70
 remembering, as, 123, 151, 156
memory theater, 173–74
 theories of, 166–68
Messiah, 146, 149, 151–53, 161, 188–89, 192–93
metalepsis, 50
metaphors, 121
midrash, 199
mimesis, 26, 51, 54, 55, 57
mind's eye, 48, 53
miracle. *See also* signs
 nature, 42–43, 47, 50, 55. *See also* walk on water
 unimaginable, 43, 44, 47
Moses, 73, 110, 112, 122, 125–26, 148, 176, 188–92, 205–6
 signs, 73–74
Muratorian Canon, 13

myth, 2, 52–55
narrative, 1, 9, 143–53, 155, 162. *See also* diegesis, story
 apologetic, 143
 credibility, 93
 detail, 21
 inversions, 97
 memory, 169–70
 pastoral, 146–47
 rhetorical devices, 143
 rhetoricalization, 95–96, 143, 146, 148–50
 turn, 58
narrator, 20, 26, 48–50, 54–57, 93, 95, 104, 106, 147, 151, 154, 173, 202–4, 213
 interjection, 173, 178–79
 memory, 144–45, 155, 183
 omniscient, 55–56
Nathanael, disciple of Jesus, 22–23, 151–52
Nicodemus, 23, 28, 33–36, 37, 56, 100, 157
orality, 60–61, 118–19, 121
oral-traditional form, 62–68
Paraclete, the, 37–39, 135–36, 139, 141, 179–80, 212, 216, 217
paradox, 50, 99
parody, 101, 104
parousia, 12
parrhesia, 98, 105
Passion narrative, 145
Pauline expressions, 194, 198–99
past, the, 1–2, 4
Pentateuch, 109, 112
peristaseis, 52
Peter, 14–16, 18, 20–21, 36, 43, 54–55, 104, 145–46, 148, 151–53
phantasia, 45, 46, 56
phantasm, 43, 45
Pharisees, 35–36, 56, 97–100, 107, 148, 155–56
 tradition, 100–101
Philip, 23, 122, 151–52
Philo, 116

Philostratus, 46
phronesis, 102, 104–5
Pilate, 98, 101, 132, 138
Plato, 45, 46, 103, 165
pneuma. *See* spirit
pneumatology, 27
poetics, 60–62, 71
   metonymic referencing, 65
   oral-traditional form, 62–68
   pars pro toto speech, 65
   tension of essences, 63
polysemy, 25, 33, 35
popular movements, 66–67
positivism, 4
prayer, Jesus', 153–54, 162
priming
   divine, 26
   memory, 167, 174–78
prologue, 9–10, 52, 54, 96, 98, 104, 106, 110, 130, 136, 140, 150, 162, 196, 203–17
prop, 57
prophetic books, 110
prophet like Moses, 148, 159–62
Prophets, the, 109, 119
Psalms, the, 112–13
pseudepigrapha, 11
purpose, the evangelist's, 146, 148, 162
Q tradition, 146
questions, 52, 95–96
Quintilian, Marcus Fabius, 45, 56–57, 106, 121
Ranke, Leopold von, 4
reader, 2, 25, 47–49, 49, 93–94, 107, 143, 149, 156
recognition. *See anagnorisis*
relic, 55
resurrection, 137, 139–40, 147, 153, 156, 208, 212
revealer, 148, 156–58, 160, 162
Revelation, 42. *See also* apocalypse
revelation, divine, 3, 26, 29, 33, 39, 124, 149, 156, 162, 207, 212, 215, 217
rhetoric, 46, 48, 50, 52, 56, 58, 93–107, 115, 118–19, 121–22, 143, 146, 148–50

rhetoric (*continued*)
   cognitive, 103
   corrective, 148–50
   deliberative, 94
   epideictic, 94, 102
   forensic, 94
Richard of Saint Victor, 42–43
Richards, I.A., 44, 47–48
riddles, 121, 144
Roman law, 101
romanticism, 5
royal official, 56
royal we, 12
Samaritan woman. *See* woman at the well, Samaritan
Samaritans, 35, 37, 149, 152–53, 193–95
sarcasm, 98, 100
Sarepta, widow of, 110
scenario 150–51, 155
scene, 55–57, 154. *See also* event
scriptural allusions, 109, 117–18, 121–23
scriptural fulfilment, 112, 123, 125
scriptural quotations, 109–15, 117, 119–20, 122–23
Scripture, 109–28, 138, 155, 157, 159, 161, 204–6, 208, 210–12, 216
   citation formula, 111–12, 119, 123
   composite allusions, 111, 114
   composite quotations, 109, 114–17, 120
   fulfillment of, 21
semeia, 10, 30
sending motif, 31–32, 38
senses, the, 33
Septuagint, 113–14, 116
Servant, Isaianic, 115
setting, 57
shepherd, 121
signs, 143, 146–48, 152–53, 160, 162
skepticism, 4
sight, 10
signs. *See semeia*
Sinai, 110, 125
slavery, 198
Son of Man, 96, 97, 98

SUBJECT INDEX   277

Spirit, 25–40, 110, 149, 151–58, 161–62
Spirit and birth, 157, 194–95
Spirit-Paraclete. *See* Paraclete
Stoics, 27
story, 1, 5, 6, 47, 51, 94, 144–45, 147–51, 203, 205, 208, 210, 212–13
  factual, 1–2, 41–42
  fictional, 1–2, 41–42, 44, 47, 51
  miracle, 55
storyteller, 1–4, 6, 24, 42
summaries of Israel's story, 66–67
source, 6, 144–46, 158
structure, 59–75
  biblical literature, in, 66–68
  Fourth Gospel, in the, 68–75
  oral-traditional contexts, in, 60–66
symbol(ize), 48, 154
synkrisis, 125
Synoptic Gospels, 144–45, 147–48, 155–56
tabernacle, 70
targumic traditions, 113
teleportation, 43–45
temple, 147–48, 156, 158–59, 162
  vision, 114
temporal distance, 50
temporality, 49, 54
  epic world, 50–51, 54–55
  witness world, 50–51, 54–56
testimonia, 116
testimony, 3, 10, 12–13, 20, 22, 37–39, 41, 55–56, 109–10, 119, 121–25, 127, 143–44, 147, 149–56, 158, 160–62, 171–73, 194, 196–97, 212–13
tetelestai, 19
textuality, 118
theological, 144, 147, 150–51
Thespesion, gymnosophist, 54
Thomas, disciple of Jesus, 20, 23, 152
time. *See* temporality
tradition, 144, 146–50, 155
trial motif. *See* legal motif
trust, 98, 103, 106
truth, 20, 38, 41, 48, 53–54, 56, 58, 130, 148–49, 155–57, 160, 162

two-stage conclusion, 10–11
typology, 125
Van Tilborg, Sjef, 19
vine, 121
virtues, 99, 102–7
visualization, 45–47, 55. *See also* imagination
  abstract, 42, 53–54
walk on water. *See* miracle
warrior, divine, 54
wisdom, 28, 31
witness, 12, 16, 19–21, 143–44, 147, 149–55, 162
woman/women, 153–54
woman at the well, Samaritan, 34–36, 39, 40, 56–57, 96–97, 153, 193–95
women. *See* disciples
Word (*logos*), the, 37, 53–54, 58, 104, 124–25, 128, 130, 136, 150, 203–5, 208–11, 213–15. *See also* fulfilled word
words, of Jesus, 145–46, 149–50, 152, 155, 157, 159–62
world, 130, 136, 140, 148–49, 151, 153, 155–58, 162, 209, 213–14
world, narrative, 50–51, 54–55, 93. *See also* temporality
work, 124, 145, 149–50, 154–55, 157–62
worship, 34–36, 152, 156, 158–59
writer, ancient, 6, 44, 46, 49
Writings, the, 109
Zechariah, book of 112, 172

www.ingramcontent.com/pod-product-compliance
Lightning Source LLC
Chambersburg PA
CBHW051212300426
44116CB00006B/534